Feminism
and American
Literary History

Withdrawn

Feminism and American Literary History
Essays

Nina Baym

Rutgers University Press
New Brunswick, New Jersey

Library of Congress Cataloging-in-Publication Data
Baym, Nina.
Feminism and American literary history : essays / by Nina Baym.
p.   cm.
ISBN 0-8135-1854-7 (cloth)—ISBN 0-8135-1855-5 (pbk.)
1. American literature—History and criticism.   2. Feminism and literature—
United States.   3. Women and literature—United States.   4. Authorship—Sex
differences.   5. Sex role in literature.
I. Title.
PS152.B39   1992
810.9′00082—dc20   92-2854
CIP
British Cataloging-in-Publication information available

for Nancy and Geoffrey

Contents

Part 3. Feminist Writing, Feminist Teaching: Two Polemics

Preface

The poem is the cry of its occasion, a poet wrote. So too the critical essay. I emerged from graduate school believing that "literature" was a fixed set of beautifully written works expressing universal truths; that literary value was self-evident; that good criticism correctly analyzed the internal dynamics of literary works and paraphrased their themes.

Having been trained in logic and common sense as well as literature, however (and being as well an irremediable pragmatist), I soon came to see yawning gaps between these beliefs and the actualities of professional literary study. Of course, these discrepancies were becoming visible to many of us at the same time—"us" being the wave of untraditional academics who entered the suddenly enlarged profession in the early and mid-1960s. The expanded need for college teachers had opened the gates even of elite institutions to us barbarians.

Among newly perceived discrepancies were the following. First, not only had estimations of literary merit varied wildly across historical eras; they differed from one professor's classroom to the next. The Shelley person bickered with the Wordsworthian; the Emersonian scoffed at the Thoreauvian. Second, it was impossible to reconcile an American literature that enunciated universal truths with one that responded to uniquely American motifs. Third, assertions that one's interpretation was "correct" accompanied diametrically opposed readings; nor could it be ignored that truly correct readings, once produced, would terminate the practice of academic literary criticism. Since our livelihoods depended on this practice, the claim to correctness could only be a rhetorical front for the activity of endless, endlessly publishable interpretation.

It took me longer to see how many so-called universal truths were in fact male. But, helped by the work of Kate Millett and Simone de Beauvoir and other early second-wave feminist writers, I eventually recognized (as I wrote in *Woman's Fiction*) that critics of American literature favored things male—favored whaling ships rather than sewing circles as symbols of human community; preferred satires on domineering mothers, shrewish wives, or betraying mistresses to those on tyrannical fathers, abusive husbands, or philandering suitors; sympathized with the crises of the adolescent male while scorning the parallel crises of young women. More narrowly, as a Hawthorne scholar, I observed critics strenuously warping *The Scarlet Letter* to center on Dimmesdale because they could not imagine a major literary work, less still any work written by a classic male author, with a female protagonist.

My revisionary efforts in American (i.e., United States) literary history began when widespread recognition of these many discrepancies signaled an opportunity to do useful work rather than leave the profession. (At that time, being a divorced mother with two small children to care about, I couldn't afford to leave; the personal is political, and a lot more.) The essays in this book are all products of those efforts. Part 1 collects some forays into the center of national literary history that focus on material ignored in or suppressed by that center. They range from close reading ("The Short Happy Life of Francis Macomber") to literary contextualization (*The Last of the Mohicans*) and author biography (Hawthorne and his mother) to analysis of larger schemes by which disparate texts and authors have conventionally been connected in a nationalist literary-historical narrative: the romance-novel distinction, the self-in-the-wilderness myth, the myth of New England origins.

Part 2 collects provisional contributions to our understanding of writing by American women; they are meant to revise the narrative of white American women's literary history that is already partly written. This narrative assigns women writers before the Civil War to a domestic sentimental tradition, simultaneously comfortable and irksome, which actually overlooks a substantial body of other kinds of writing by American women before the twentieth century. Since my *Woman's Fiction* has—understandably—been used to equate women's writing with the domestic enterprise, I feel a particular revisionary responsibility here.

Actually, *Woman's Fiction* was conceived as a formal study, concentrating on one particular, plot-defined antebellum genre (from which *Uncle Tom's Cabin,* now taken as a touchstone of female domestic sentimentality, is explicitly excluded). By calling the study woman's, not women's, fiction, I meant to dissociate any essentialist idea of "woman" from the literary producers *of* this story, however it might apply to the representations *in* the story. My statement that this genre absorbed the full energies of almost all the women novelists in America for fifty years was inaccurate, however: Few women writers were novelists exclusively, and, at least in the 1820s, they wrote more historical than domestic novels. The essays in part 2, all written since 1990, reflect my enlarged understanding of American women's literary discourse before the Civil War.

The two essays in part 3 engage polemically with issues affecting feminist attempts at revisionary history. "The Madwoman and Her Languages," reprinted here in its 1987 redaction, originated as a talk in 1982. This was a year after *Critical Inquiry* published its special 1981 issue on "Writing and Sexual Difference," an event that Jane Gallop takes to mark a "breakthrough" in feminist criticism. I well remember my dismay at that title, whose totalizing "difference" seemed to ignore or undo everything that 1970s feminism was about. For me, then, this breakthrough represented the overcoming or undermining of feminism via discourses (especially Freudian and Lacanian psychoanalysis) that were constitutively misogynist. Matricide was the essay's not-very-hidden motif.

Ten years later feminist theory has laboriously rediscovered multiplicity and differences within "woman," while remaining in thrall to psychoanalytic approaches that negate women in advance. (Phyllis Grosskurth, writing in the *New York Review of Books* for 24 October 1991, expresses the hope that "in time women will find that they need Freud less and less," observing that they would "strengthen their cause if they ceased reacting against this brilliant but drastically limited theorist and struck out on their own.") Feminist theory also continues to vex itself with the question that confronted feminism from the beginning—whether to stress differences between or solidarity among women, a question that cannot be answered from the standpoint of theory but only of practice. Early second-wave feminist activists assumed that one had to do both and pursued one or the other goal as circumstances seemed to call for.

But by including the first-person pronoun in the essay's subtitle, I meant from the start to identify it as a personal statement, not a manifesto. Ten years later, though I still don't do feminist literary theory, I more clearly see how useful the practice of feminist literary theory is for those who do. Especially for younger women in academia, it has opened a valuable space for collective and individual work. Being opposed to anti-intellectualism in any form, I would rather be with theory than against it insofar as antitheory equates to old-boy know-nothingism. Of course, theory does a certain amount of anti-intellectual posturing of its own.

The essay "Matters for Interpretation" is about feminist pedagogy. It argues that feminist teaching controlled by the "woman's voice" paradigm is reductively complicit with a model of men-only speech. My liberal feminism instructs me that women, who differ among themselves, will likely differ from each other in how they speak. I do not want to deny women access to any kind of speech, including speech stereotypically thought of as "male." Since I am concerned with classroom practice, studenticide is the essay's not-very-hidden motif.

The feminist moment, of which this collection is the cry, is—insofar as I understand it—one of broad-ranging attack on liberal feminist individualism from both the Right and the Left. Postmodernist deconstructionist approaches call individualism a pernicious myth, culturalist Marxists call it a pernicious reality. Either way, the collapsing of antithetical definitions of *individualism* into one term—individualism as unique identity or as mass atomism—makes the attack incoherent. For me it's distressing to see feminists attempting to discredit the *L*-word that has legitimated us. Without denying that individualism has problems that feminism is particularly well situated to expose—and should make a point of exposing—I believe that feminism in the Western world (the world in which it originated) is an Enlightenment (and a middle-class) phenomenon. Women in all cultures have been defined as less than persons, however personhood is culturally defined; since the Enlightenment, however, it has been possible to think of ways that women might become persons. The promise is not fully realized for any woman, and such realization as there is has been unevenly distributed, but tardiness and unevenness do not negate it. On the contrary, they have created feminism. In my view a feminist concept of personhood in the United States omitting women from "we the people" will only return women to the status of less than persons.

Feminism and individualism, finally, were not invented by individuals. Like literature, they were and are dynamic cultural and historical group events. In the essays collected here, as in *Woman's Fiction* and *Novels, Readers, and Reviewers,* I try to approach "literature" and "criticism" as social composites in which individual acts are connected to, enabled by, defined by, and contributory to various collective—by no means harmoniously collective—discourses. My aim as a feminist literary historian would be to write ever more contextually, to mime more accurately, though never "correctly" (since context is infinite), the variously relational production of all individual literary work.

Acknowledgments

Versions of the chapters in this book were published as essays during the 1980s and early 1990s. Chapters 1, 3, 4, and 13 reprint the essays much as they originally appeared; the rest have been substantially revised. I thank the journals and publishers collectively for permission to reprint and acknowledge them individually as follows:

"Melodramas of Beset Manhood: How Theories of American Fiction Exclude Women Authors," *American Quarterly* 33 (1981): 123–139; "Nathaniel Hawthorne and His Mother: A Biographical Speculation," *American Literature* 54 (1982): 1–27, published by Duke University Press, reprinted by permission of the publisher; "Concepts of the Romance in Hawthorne's America," *Nineteenth-Century Fiction* 38 (1984): 426–443, copyright 1984 by the Regents of the University of California, reprinted by permission; "The Madwoman and Her Languages: Why I Don't Do Feminist Literary Theory" (originally published in a special issue of *Tulsa Studies in Women's Literature* in 1984), from *Feminist Issues in Literary Scholarship*, ed. Shari Benstock (Bloomington: Indiana University Press, 1987), 45–61; "Matters for Interpretation: Feminism and the Teaching of Literature," appearing in an earlier form as "The Feminist Teacher of Literature: Feminist or Teacher?" *Papers in Language and Literature* 24 (1988): 245–264; "Early Histories of American Literature: A Chapter in the Institution of New England," *American Literary History* 1 (1989): 459–488; "The Myth of the Myth of Southern Womanhood," *Hebrew University Studies in Literature and the Arts* 18 (1990): 27–47; "The Ann Sisters: Elizabeth Peabody's Gendered Millennialism," *American Literary History* 3 (1991): 27–45, reprinted by permission of Oxford University Press; "Reinventing Lydia Sigourney," *American Literature* 62 (1990): 385–404, published by Duke University Press, reprinted by permission of the publisher; "Sarah Hale, Political Writer," appearing in an earlier form as "Onward Christian Women: Sarah J. Hale's History of the World," *New England Quarterly* 63 (1990): 249–270; "Women and the Republic: Emma Willard's Rhetoric of History," *American Quarterly* 43 (1991): 1–23; "'Actually, I Felt Sorry for the Lion': Reading Hemingway's 'The Short Happy Life of Francis Macomber,'" appearing in an earlier form as "'Actually, I Felt Sorry for the Lion': A Feminist Reads 'The Short Happy Life of Francis Macomber,'" from *New Critical Approaches to the Short Stories of Ernest Hemingway*, ed. Jackson J. Benson (Durham, N.C.: Duke University Press, 1990), 112–120, 467–468, reprinted by permission of the publisher; "From Enlightenment to Victorian: Toward a Narrative of American Women Writers Writing History," published as "Between Enlightenment and Victorian," *Critical Inquiry* 19 (1991): 22–41; "Putting Women in Their Place: *The Last of the Mohicans* and Other Indian Stories," appearing in an earlier form as "How Men and Women Wrote Indian Stories" in *New Critical Essays on "The Last of the Mohicans,"* ed. H. Daniel Peck (New York: Cambridge University Press, 1992), 67–86.

I want to thank without naming the friends and colleagues who thought this work worth collecting. I hope the result proves them correct.

Feminism
and American
Literary History

Part 1

Revising Old American Literary History

1
Melodramas of Beset Manhood
How Theories of American Fiction
Exclude Women Authors

This essay is about American literary criticism rather than American literature. It proceeds from the assumption that we never read American literature directly or freely but always through the perspective allowed by theories. Theories account for the inclusion and exclusion of texts in anthologies, and theories account for the way we read them. My concern is with the fact that the theories controlling our reading of American literature have led to the exclusion of women authors from the canon.

Let me use my own practice as a case in point. In 1977 there was published a collection of essays on images of women in major British and American literature, to which I contributed.[1] The American field was divided chronologically among six critics, with four essays covering literature written prior to World War II. Taking seriously the charge that we were to focus only on the major figures, the four of us—working quite independently of each other—selected altogether only four women writers. Three of these were from the earliest period, a period which predates the novel: the poet Anne Bradstreet and the two diarists Mary Rowlandson and Sarah Kemble Knight. The fourth was Emily Dickinson. For the period between 1865 and 1940 no women were cited at all. The message that we—who were taking women as our subject—conveyed was clear: There have been almost no major women writers in America; the major novelists have all been men.

Now when we wrote our essays we were not undertaking to reread all American literature and make our own decisions as to who the major authors were. That is the point: We accepted the going canon of major authors. As late as 1977, that canon did not include any women novelists. Yet the critic who goes beyond what is accepted and tries to look at the totality of literary production in America quickly discovers that women authors have been active since the earliest days of settlement. Commercially and numerically, they have probably dominated American literature since the

middle of the nineteenth century. As long ago as 1854, Nathaniel Hawthorne complained to his publisher about the "damned mob of scribbling
women" whose writings—he fondly imagined—were diverting the public
from his own.

Names and figures help make this dominance clear. In the years between
1774 and 1799—from the calling of the First Continental Congress to the
close of the eighteenth century—a total of thirty-eight original works of
fiction were published in this country.[2] Nine of these, appearing pseudonymously or anonymously, have not yet been attributed to any author. The
remaining twenty-nine are the work of eighteen individuals, of whom four
are women. One of these women, Susannah Rowson, wrote six of them,
or more than a fifth of the total. Her most popular work, *Charlotte* (also
known as *Charlotte Temple*), was printed three times in the decade it was
published, nineteen times between 1800 and 1810, and eighty times by the
middle of the nineteenth century. A novel by a second of the four women,
Hannah Foster, was called *The Coquette* and had thirty editions by the mid
nineteenth century. *Uncle Tom's Cabin,* by a woman, is probably the all-time
biggest seller in American history. A woman, Mrs. E.D.E.N. Southworth,
was probably the most widely read novelist in the nineteenth century. How
is it possible for a critic or historian of American literature to leave these
books, and these authors, out of the picture?

I see three partial explanations for the critical invisibility of the many
active women authors in America. The first is simple bias. The critic does
not like the idea of women as writers, does not believe that women can be
writers, and hence does not see them even when they are right before his
eyes. His theory or his standards may well be nonsexist, but his practice is
not. Certainly, an *a priori* resistance to recognizing women authors as serious writers has functioned powerfully in the mind-set of a number of influential critics. One can amusingly demonstrate the inconsistencies between
standard and practice in such critics, show how their minds slip out of gear
when they are confronted with a woman author. But this is only a partial
explanation.

A second possibility is that, in fact, women have not written the kind of
work that we call "excellent," for reasons that are connected with their
gender although separable from it. This is a reasonable possibility. For example, suppose we required a dense texture of classical allusion in all works
that we called excellent. Then the restriction of a formal classical education
to men would have the effect of restricting authorship of excellent literature
to men. Women would not have written excellent literature because social
conditions hindered them. The explanation, though gender connected,
would not be gender per se.

The point here is that the notion of the artist, or of excellence, has efficacy
in a given time and reflects social realities. The idea of "good" literature is

not only a personal preference, it is also a cultural preference. We can all think of species of women's literature that do not aim in any way to achieve literary excellence as society defines it: for example, the "Harlequin Romances." Until recently, only a tiny proportion of literary women aspired to artistry and literary excellence in the terms defined by their own culture. There tended to be a sort of immediacy in the ambitions of literary women leading them to professionalism rather than artistry, by choice as well as by social pressure and opportunity. The gender-related restrictions were really operative, and the responsible critic cannot ignore them. But again, these restrictions are only partly explanatory.

There are, finally, I believe, gender-related restrictions that do not arise out of cultural realities contemporary with the writing woman but out of later critical theories. These theories may follow naturally from cultural realities pertinent to their own time, but they impose their concerns anachronistically, after the fact, on an earlier period. If one accepts current theories of American literature, one accepts as a consequence—perhaps not deliberately but nevertheless inevitably—a literature that is essentially male. This is the partial explanation that I shall now develop.

Let us begin where the earliest theories of American literature begin, with the hypothesis that American literature is to be judged less by its form than by its content. Hypothetically, one ascertains literary excellence by comparing a writer's work with standards of performance that have been established by earlier authors, where formal mastery and innovation are paramount. But from its historical beginnings, American literary criticism has assumed that literature produced in this nation would have to be groundbreaking, equal to the challenge of the new nation, and completely original. Therefore, it could not be judged by referring it back to earlier achievements. The earliest American literary critics began to talk about the "most American" work rather than the "best" work because they knew no way to find out the best other than by comparing American with British writing. Such a criticism struck them as both unfair and unpatriotic. We had thrown off the political shackles of England; it would not do for us to be servile in our literature. Until a tradition of American literature developed its own inherent forms, the early critic looked for a standard of "Americanness" rather than a standard of excellence. Inevitably, perhaps, it came to seem that the quality of Americanness, whatever it might be, *constituted* literary excellence for American authors. Beginning as a nationalistic enterprise, American literary criticism and theory has retained a nationalist orientation to this day.

Of course, the idea of Americanness is even more vulnerable to subjectivity than the idea of the best. When they speak of "most American," critics seldom mean the statistically most representative or most typical, the most read or the most sold. They have some qualitative essence in mind, and frequently their work develops as an explanation of this idea of American rather than a description and evaluation of selected authors. The predictable recurrence of the term *America,* or *American,* in works of literary criticism treating a dozen or fewer authors indicates that the critic has chosen his authors on the basis of their conformity to his idea of what is truly American. For examples: *American Renaissance, The Romance in America, Symbolism and American Literature, Form and Fable in American Fiction, The American Adam, The American Novel and Its Tradition, The Place of Style in American Literature* (a subtitle), *The Poetics of American Fiction* (another subtitle). But an idea of what is American is no more than an idea, needing demonstration. The critic all too frequently ends up using his chosen authors as demonstrations of Americanness, arguing through them to his definition.

So Marius Bewley explains in *The Eccentric Design* that "for the American artist there was no social surface responsive to his touch. The scene was crude, even beyond successful satire," but later, in a concluding chapter titled "The Americanness of the American Novel," he agrees that "this 'tradition' as I have set it up here has no room for the so-called realists and naturalists."[3] F. O. Matthiessen, whose *American Renaissance* enshrines five authors, explains that "the one common denominator of my five writers, uniting even Hawthorne and Whitman, was their devotion to the possibilities of democracy."[4] The jointly written *Literary History of the United States* proclaims in its "address to the reader" that American literary history "will be a history of the books of the great and the near-great writers in a literature which is most revealing when studied as a by-product of American experience."[5] And Joel Porte announces confidently in *The Romance in America* that

> students of American literature . . . have provided a solid theoretical basis for establishing that the rise and growth of fiction in this country is dominated by our authors' conscious adherence to a tradition of non-realistic romance sharply at variance with the broadly novelistic mainstream of English writing. When there has been disagreement among recent critics as to the contours of American fiction, it has usually disputed, not the existence per se of a romance tradition, but rather the question of which authors, themes, and stylistic strategies *deserve* to be placed with certainty at the heart of that tradition.[6]

Before he is through, the critic has had to insist that some works in America are much more American than others, and he is as busy excluding certain writers as "un-American" as he is including others. Such a proceeding in the political arena would be extremely suspect, but in criticism it has been the method of choice. Its final result goes far beyond the conclusion that only a handful of American works are very good. *That* statement is one we might agree with, since very good work is rare in any field. But it is odd indeed to argue that only a handful of American works are really · American.[7]

Despite the theoretical room for an infinite number of definitions of Americanness, critics have generally agreed on it—although the shifting canon suggests that agreement may be a matter of fad rather than fixed objective qualities.[8] First, America as a nation must be the ultimate subject of the work. The author must be writing about aspects of experience and character that are American only, setting Americans off from other people and the country from other nations. The author must be writing his story specifically to display these aspects, to meditate on them, and to derive from them some generalizations and conclusions about "the" American experience. To Matthiessen the topic is the possibilities of democracy; Sacvan Bercovitch (in *The Puritan Origins of the American Self*) finds it in American identity. Such content excludes, at one extreme, stories about universals, aspects of experience common to people in a variety of times and places— mutability, mortality, love, childhood, family, betrayal, loss. Innocence versus experience is an admissible theme *only* if innocence is the essence of the American character, for example.

But at the other extreme, the call for an overview of America means that detailed, circumstantial portrayals of some aspect of American life are also, peculiarly, inappropriate: stories of wealthy New Yorkers, Yugoslavian immigrants, Southern rustics. Jay B. Hubbell rather ingratiatingly admits as much when he writes, "in both my teaching and my research I had a special interest in literature as a reflection of American life and thought. This circumstance may explain in part why I found it difficult to appreciate the merits of the expatriates and why I was slow in doing justice to some of the New Critics. I was repelled by the sordid subject matter found in some of the novels written by Dreiser, Dos Passos, Faulkner, and some others."[9] Richard Poirier writes that "the books which in my view constitute a distinctive American tradition . . . resist within their pages forces of environment that otherwise dominate the world," and he distinguishes this kind from "the fiction of Mrs. Wharton, Dreiser, or Howells."[10] The *Literary History of the United States* explains that "historically, [Edith Wharton] is likely to survive as the memorialist of a dying aristocracy."[11] And so on. These exclusions abound in all the works that form the stable core of American literary criticism at this time.

Along with Matthiessen, the most influential exponent of this exclusive Americanness is Lionel Trilling, and his work has particular applicability because it concentrates on the novel form. Here is a famous passage from his 1940 essay "Reality in America," in which Trilling is criticizing Vernon Parrington's selection of authors in *Main Currents in American Thought:*

> A culture is not a flow, nor even a confluence: the form of its existence is struggle—or at least debate—it is nothing if not a dialectic. And in any culture there are likely to be certain artists who contain a large part of the dialectic within themselves, their meaning and power lying in their contradictions: they contain within themselves, it may be said, the very essence of the culture. To throw out Poe because he cannot be conveniently fitted into a theory of American culture . . . to find his gloom to be merely personal and eccentric . . . as Hawthorne's was . . . to judge Melville's response to American life to be less noble than that of Bryant or of Greeley, to speak of Henry James as an escapist . . . this is not merely to be mistaken in aesthetic judgment. Rather it is to examine without attention and from the point of view of a limited and essentially arrogant conception of reality the documents which are in some respects the most suggestive testimony to what America was and is, and of course to get no answer from them.[12]

Trilling's immediate purpose is to exclude Greeley and Bryant from the list of major authors and to include Poe, Melville, Hawthorne, and James. We probably share Trilling's aesthetic judgment. But note that he does not base his judgment on aesthetic grounds; indeed, he dismisses aesthetic judgment with the word *merely*. He argues that Parrington has picked the wrong artists because he doesn't understand the culture. Culture is his real concern.

But what makes Trilling's notion of culture more valid than Parrington's? Trilling really has no argument; he resorts to such value-laden rhetoric as "a limited and essentially arrogant conception of reality" precisely because he cannot objectively establish his version of culture over Parrington's. For the moment, there are two significant conclusions to draw from this quotation. First, the disagreement is over the nature of our culture. Second, there is no disagreement over the value of literature—it is valued as a set of "documents" which provide "suggestive testimony to what America was and is."

One might think that an approach like this which is subjective, circular, and in some sense nonliterary, or even antiliterary, would not have had much effect. But clearly Trilling was simply carrying on a long-standing tradition of searching for cultural essence, and his essays gave the search a decided and influential direction toward the notion of cultural essence as some sort of tension. Trilling succeeded in getting rid of Bryant and Greeley, and his choice of authors is still dominant. They all turn out—and not by accident—to be white, middle-class, male, of Anglo-Saxon derivation, or at least from an ancestry which had settled in this country before the big waves of immigration which began around the middle of the nineteenth century. In every case, however, the decision made by these men to become professional authors pushed them slightly to one side of the group to which they belonged. This slight alienation permitted them to belong, and yet not to belong, to the so-called mainstream. These two aspects of their situation—their membership in the dominant middle-class, white, Anglo-Saxon group and their modest alienation from it—defined their boundaries, enabling them to "contain within themselves" the "contradictions" that, in Trilling's view, constitute the "very essence of the culture." I will call the literature they produced, which Trilling assesses so highly, a "consensus criticism of the consensus."

This idea plainly excludes many groups, but it might not seem necessarily to exclude women. In fact, nineteenth-century women authors were overwhelmingly white, middle-class, and Anglo-Saxon in origin. Something more than what is overtly stated by Trilling (and others cited below) is added to exclude them. What critics have done is to assume, for reasons shortly to be expounded, that the women writers invariably represented the consensus, rather than the criticism of it; to assume that their gender made them part of the consensus in a way that prevented them from partaking in the criticism. The presence of these women and their works is acknowledged in literary theory and history as an impediment and obstacle, that which the essential American literature had to criticize as its chief task.

So, in his lively and influential book of 1960, *Love and Death in the American Novel*, Leslie Fiedler describes women authors as creators of the "flagrantly bad best-seller" against which "our best fictionists"—all male—have had to struggle for "their integrity and their livelihoods."[13] And in a 1978 reader's introduction to an edition of Charles Brockden Brown's *Wieland*, Sydney J. Krause and S. W. Reid write as follows:

> What it meant for Brown personally, and belles lettres in America historically, that he should have decided to write professionally is a story unto itself. Americans simply had no great appetite for serious literature in the early decades of the Republic—certainly nothing of the sort with which they devoured . . . the ubiquitous melodramas of beset womanhood, "tales of truth," like Susanna Rowson's *Charlotte Temple* and Hannah Foster's *The Coquette*.[14]

There you see what has happened to the woman writer. She has entered literary history as the enemy. The phrase "tales of truth" is put in quotes by the critics, as though to cast doubt on the very notion that a "melodrama of beset womanhood" could be either true or important. At the same time, ironically, they are proposing for our serious consideration, as a candidate for intellectually engaging literature, a highly melodramatic novel with an improbable plot, inconsistent characterizations, and excesses of style that have posed tremendous problems for all students of Charles Brockden Brown. But by this strategy it becomes possible to begin major American fiction historically with male rather than female authors. The certainty here that stories about women could not contain the essence of American culture means that the matter of American experience is inherently male. And this makes it unlikely that American women would write fiction encompassing such experience. I suggest that the theoretical model of a story which may become the vehicle of cultural essence is: "a melodrama of beset manhood." This melodrama is presented in a fiction which, as we will later see, can be taken as representative of the author's literary experience, his struggle for integrity and livelihood against flagrantly bad best-sellers written by women. Personally beset in a way that epitomizes the tensions of our culture, the male author produces his melodramatic testimony to our culture's essence—so the theory goes.

Remember that the search for cultural essence demands a relatively uncircumstantial kind of fiction, one that concentrates on national universals (if I may be pardoned the paradox). This search has identified a sort of nonrealistic narrative, a romance, a story free to catch an essential, idealized American character, to intensify his essence and convey his experience in a way that ignores details of an actual social milieu. This nonrealistic or antisocial aspect of American fiction is noted—as a fault—by Trilling in a 1947 essay, "Manners, Morals, and the Novel." Curiously, Trilling here attacks the same group of writers he had rescued from Parrington in "Reality in America." But, never doubting that his selection represents "the" American authors, he goes ahead with the task that really interests him—criticising the culture through its representative authors:

> The novel in America diverges from its classic [i.e., British] intention which . . . is the investigation of the problem of reality beginning in the social field. The fact is that American writers of genius have not turned their minds to society. Poe and Melville were quite apart from it; the reality they sought was only tangential to society. Hawthorne was acute when he insisted that he did not write novels but romances—he thus expressed his awareness of the lack of social texture in his work. . . . In America in the nineteenth century, Henry James was alone in knowing that to scale the moral and aesthetic heights in the novel one had to use the ladder of social observation.[15]

Within a few years after publication of Trilling's essay a group of Americanists took its rather disapproving description of American novelists and found in this nonrealism or romanticism the essentially American quality they had been seeking. The idea of essential Americanness then developed in such influential works of criticism as *Virgin Land* by Henry Nash Smith (1950), *Symbolism and American Literature* by Charles Feidelson (1953), *The American Adam* by R.W.B. Lewis (1955), *The American Novel and its Tradition* by Richard Chase (1957), and *Form and Fable in American Fiction* by Daniel G. Hoffman (1961). These works, and others like them, were of sufficiently high critical quality, and sufficiently like each other, to compel assent to the picture of American literature which they presented. They used sophisticated New Critical, close-reading techniques to identify a myth of America which had nothing to do with the classical fictionist's task of chronicling probable people in recognizable social situations.

The myth narrates a confrontation of the American individual, the pure

American self divorced from specific social circumstances, with the promise offered by the idea of America. This promise is the deeply romantic one that in this new land, untrammeled by history and social accident, a person will be able to achieve complete self-definition. Behind this promise is the assurance that individuals come before society, that they exist in some meaningful sense prior to, and apart from, societies in which they happen to find themselves. The myth also holds that, as something artificial and secondary to human nature, society exerts an unmitigatedly destructive pressure on individuality. To depict it at any length would be a waste of artistic time, and there is only one way to relate it to the individual—as an adversary.

One may believe all this and yet look in vain for a way to tell a believable story that could free the protagonist from society or offer the promise of such freedom, because nowhere on earth do individuals live apart from social groups. But in America, given the original reality of large tracts of wilderness, the idea seems less a fantasy, more possible in reality or at least more believable in literary treatment. Thus it is that the essential quality of America comes to reside in its unsettled wilderness (i.e., unsettled by white people) and the opportunities such wilderness offers the individual as the medium on which he may inscribe, unhindered, his own destiny and his own nature.

As the nineteenth century wore on and settlements spread across the wilderness, the struggle of the individual against society became more and more central to the myth; where, let's say, Thoreau could leave in chapter 1 of *Walden,* Huckleberry Finn has still not made his break by the end of chapter 42 (the conclusion) of the book that bears his name. Yet one finds a struggle against society as early as the earliest Leatherstocking tale (*The Pioneers* [1823]). In a sense, this supposed promise of America has always been known to be delusory. Certainly, by the twentieth century the myth has been transmuted into an avowedly hopeless quest for unencumbered space (Kerouac's *On the Road*), or the evocation of flight for its own sake (Updike's *Rabbit, Run* and Bellow's *Henderson the Rain King*), or as pathetic acknowledgment of loss—for example, the close of Fitzgerald's *The Great Gatsby* where the narrator Nick Carraway summons up "the old island here that flowered once for Dutch sailors' eyes—a fresh, green breast of the new world . . . the last and greatest of all human dreams" where man is "face to face for the last time in history with something commensurate to his capacity for wonder."

We are all very familiar with this myth of America in its various fashionings, and, owing to the selective vision that has presented this myth to us as the whole story, many of us are unaware of how much besides it has been created by literary Americans. Keeping our eyes on this myth, we need to ask whether anything about it puts it outside women's reach. In one sense, and on one level, the answer is no. The subject of this myth is supposed to stand for human nature, and, if men and women share a common human nature, then all can respond to its values, its promises, and its frustrations. And in fact, as a teacher, I find women students responsive to the myth insofar as its protagonist is concerned. It is true, of course, that, in order to represent some kind of believable flight into the wilderness, one must select a protagonist with a certain believable mobility, and mobility has until recently been a male prerogative in our society. Nevertheless, relatively few men are actually mobile to the extent demanded by the story, and hence the story is really not much more vicarious, in this regard, for women than for men. The problem is thus not to be located in the protagonist or his gender per se; the problem is with the other participants in his story—the entrammeling society and the promising landscape. For both of these are depicted in unmistakably feminine terms, and this gives a sexual character to the protagonist's story which does, indeed, limit its applicability to women. And this sexual definition has melodramatic, misogynist implications.

In these stories the encroaching, constricting, destroying society is represented with particular urgency in the figure of one or more women. There are several possible reasons why this might be so. It seems to be a fact of life that we all—women and men alike—experience social conventions and responsibilities and obligations first in the persons of women, since women are entrusted by society with the task of rearing young children. Not until he reaches mid-adolescence does the male connect up with other males whose primary task is socialization, but at about this time—if he is heterosexual—his lovers and spouses become the agents of a permanent socialization and domestication. Thus, although women are not the source of social power, they are experienced as such. And although not all women are engaged in socializing the young, the young do not encounter women who are not. So from the point of view of the young man, the only kind of women who exist are entrappers and domesticators.

For heterosexual man these socializing women are also the locus of powerful attraction. First, because everybody has social and conventional instincts; second, because his deepest emotional attachments are to women. This attraction gives urgency and depth to the protagonist's rejection of society. To do it he must project onto the woman those attractions that he feels and cast her in the melodramatic role of temptress, antagonist, obstacle—a character whose mission in life seems to be to ensnare him and deflect him from life's important purposes of self-discovery and self-assertion. (A Puritan would have said: from communion with Divinity.) As Richard Chase writes in *The American Novel and Its Tradition*, "The myth requires celibacy." It is partly against his own sexual urges that the male must struggle, and so he perceives the socializing and domesticating woman as a doubly powerful threat; for this reason, Chase goes on to state, neither

Cooper nor "any other American novelist until the age of James and Edith Wharton" could imagine "a fully developed woman of sexual age."[16] Yet in making this statement, Chase is talking about his myth rather than Cooper's. (One should add that, for a homosexual male, the demands of society that he link himself for life to a woman make for a particularly misogynist version of this aspect of the American myth, for the hero is propelled not by a rejected attraction but by true revulsion.) Both heterosexual and homosexual versions of the myth cooperate with the hero's perceptions and validate the notion of woman as threat.

Such a portrayal of women is likely to be uncongenial, if not basically incomprehensible, to a woman. It is not likely that women will write books in which women play this part, and it is by no means the case that most novels by American men reproduce such a scheme. Even major male authors prominent in the canon have other ways of depicting women: for example, Cooper's *Pathfinder* and *The Pioneers,* Hemingway's *For Whom the Bell Tolls,* Fitzgerald's *The Beautiful and The Damned.* The novels of Henry James and William Dean Howells pose a continual challenge to the masculinist bias of American critical theory. And in one work—*The Scarlet Letter*—a "fully developed woman of sexual age" who is the novel's protagonist has been admitted into the canon but only by virtue of strenuous critical revisions of the text which remove Hester Prynne from the center of the novel and make her subordinate to Arthur Dimmesdale.

So Leslie Fiedler, in *Love and Death in the American Novel,* writes this of *The Scarlet Letter:*

> It is certainly true, in terms of the plot, that Chillingworth drives the minister toward confession and penance, while Hester would have lured him to evasion and flight. But this means, for all of Hawthorne's equivocations, that the eternal feminine does not draw us on toward grace, rather that the woman promises only madness and damnation. . . . [Hester] is the female temptress of Puritan mythology, but also, though sullied, the secular madonna of sentimental Protestantism.[17]

In the rhetorical "us" Fiedler presumes that all readers are men, that the novel is an act of communication among and about males. His characterization of Hester as one or another myth or image makes it impossible for the novel to be in any way about Hester as a human being. Giving the novel so highly specific a gender reference, Fiedler makes it inaccessible to women and limits its reference to men in comparison to the issues that Hawthorne was treating in the story. Not the least of these issues was, precisely, the human reference of a woman's tale.

Amusingly, then, since he has produced this warped reading, Fiedler goes on to condemn the novel for its sexual immaturity. *The Scarlet Letter* is integrated into Fiedler's general exposure of the inadequacies of the American male—inadequacies that, as his treatment of Hester shows, he holds women responsible for. The melodrama here is not Hawthorne's but Fiedler's—the American critic's melodrama of beset manhood. Of course, women authors as major writers are notably and inevitably absent from Fiedler's chronicle.

In fact, many books by women—including such major authors as Edith Wharton, Ellen Glasgow, and Willa Cather—project a version of the particular myth we are speaking of but cast the main character as a woman. When a woman takes the central role it follows naturally that the socializer and domesticator will be a man. This is the situation in *The Scarlet Letter.* Hester is beset by the male reigning oligarchy and by Dimmesdale, who passively tempts her and is responsible for fathering her child. Thereafter, Hester (as the myth requires) elects celibacy, as do many heroines in versions of this myth by women: Thea in Cather's *The Song of the Lark,* Dorinda in Glasgow's *Barren Ground,* Anna Leath in Wharton's *The Reef.* But what is written in the criticism about these celibate women? They are said to be untrue to the imperatives of their gender, which require marriage, childbearing, domesticity. Instead of being read as a woman's version of the myth, such novels are read as stories of the frustration of female nature. Stories of female frustration are not perceived as commenting on, or containing, the essence of our culture, and so we do not find them in the canon.

So the role of entrapper and impediment in the melodrama of beset manhood is reserved for women. Also the role of the beckoning wilderness, the attractive landscape, is given a deeply feminine quality. Landscape is deeply imbued with female qualities, as society is—but where society is menacing and destructive, landscape is compliant and supportive. It has the attributes simultaneously of a virginal bride and a nonthreatening mother; its female qualities are articulated with respect to a male angle of vision: What can nature do for me, asks the hero, what can it give me?

Of course, nature has been feminine and maternal from time immemorial, and Henry Nash Smith's *Virgin Land* picks up a timeless archetype in its title. The basic nature of the image leads one to forget about its potential for imbuing with sexual meanings any story in which it is used, and the gender implications of a female landscape have only recently begun to be studied. Recently, Annette Kolodny has studied the traditional canon from this approach.[18] She theorizes that the hero, fleeing a society that has been imagined as feminine, then imposes on nature some ideas of women which, no longer subject to the correcting influence of real-life experience, become more and more fantastic. The fantasies are infantile, concerned with power, mastery, and total gratification: the all-nurturing mother, the all-passive bride. Whether one accepts all the Freudian or Jungian implications of the argument, one cannot deny the way in which heroes of American myth turn to nature as sweetheart and nurturer, anticipating the satisfaction of all desires through her and including among these the desires for mastery and power. A familiar passage that captures these ideas is one already quoted: Carraway's evocation of the "fresh green breast" of the New World. The fresh greenness is the virginity that offers itself to the sailors, but the breast promises maternal solace and delight. *The Great Gatsby* contains our two images of women: While Carraway evokes the impossible dream of a maternal landscape, he blames a nonmaternal woman, the socialite Daisy, for her failure to satisfy Gatsby's desires. The true adversary, however, is Tom Buchanan, but he is hidden, as it were, behind Daisy's skirts.

I have said that women are not likely to cast themselves as antagonists in a man's story; they are even less likely, I suggest, to cast themselves as virgin land. The lack of fit between their own experience and the fictional role assigned to them is even greater in the second instance than in the first. If women portray themselves as brides or mothers, it will not be in terms of the mythic landscape. If a woman puts a female construction on nature—as she certainly must from time to time, given the archetypal female resonance of the image—she is likely to write of it as more active, or to stress its destruction or violation. On the other hand, she might adjust the heroic myth to her own psyche by making nature out to be male—as, for example, Willa Cather seems to do in *O Pioneers!* But a violated landscape or a male nature does not fit the essential American pattern as critics have defined it, and hence these literary images occur in an obscurity that criticism cannot see. Thus, one has an almost classic example of the double bind. When the woman writer creates a story that conforms to the expected myth, it is not recognized for what it is because of a superfluous sexual specialization in the myth as it is entertained in the critics' minds. (Needless to say, many male novelists also entertain this version of the myth and do not find the masculinist bias with which they imbue it to be superfluous. It is possible that some of these novelists, especially those who write in an era in which literary criticism is a powerful influence, have formed their ideas from their reading in criticism.) But if she does not conform to the myth, she is understood to be writing minor or trivial literature.

Two remaining points can be treated much more briefly. The description of the artist and of the act of writing which emerges when the critic uses the basic American story as his starting point contains many attributes of the basic story itself. This description raises the exclusion of women to a more abstract, theoretical—and perhaps more pernicious—level. Fundamentally, the idea is that the artist writing a story of this essential American kind is engaging in a task very much like the one performed by his mythic hero. In effect, the artist writing his narrative is imitating the mythic encounter of hero and possibility in the safe confines of his study; or, reversing the temporal order, one might see that mythic encounter of hero and possibility as a projection of the artist's situation.

Although this idea is greatly in vogue at the moment, it has a history.

Here, for example, is Richard Chase representing the activity of writing in metaphors of discovery and exploration, as though the writer were a hero in the landscape: "The American novel has usually seemed content to explore . . . the remarkable and in some ways unexampled territories of life in the New World and to reflect its anomalies and dilemmas. It has . . . wanted . . . to discover a new place and a new state of mind." [19] Richard Poirier takes the idea further:

> The most interesting American books are an image of the creation of America itself. . . . They carry the metaphoric burden of a great dream of freedom—of the expansion of national consciousness into the vast spaces of a continent and the absorption of those spaces into ourselves. . . . The classic American writers try through style temporarily to free the hero (and the reader) from systems, to free them from the pressures of time, biology, economics, and from the social forces which are ultimately the undoing of American heroes and quite often of their creators. . . . The strangeness of American fiction has . . . to do . . . with the environment [the novelist] tries to create for his hero, usually his surrogate. [20]

The implicit union of creator and protagonist is made specific and overt at the end of Poirier's passage here. The ideas of Poirier and Chase, and others like them, are summed up in an anthology called *Theories of American Literature,* edited by Donald M. Kartiganer and Malcolm A. Griffith. The editors write, "It is as if with each new work our writers feel they must invent again the complete world of a literary form." (Yet the true subject is not what the writers feel but what the critics think they feel.) "Such a condition of nearly absolute freedom to create has appeared to our authors both as possibility and liability, an utter openness suggesting limitless opportunity for the imagination, or an enormous vacancy in which they create from nothing. For some it has meant an opportunity to play Adam, to assume the role of an original namer of experience." [21] One sees in this passage the transference of the American myth from the Adamic hero *in* the story to the Adamic creator *of* the story and the reinterpretation of the American myth as a metaphor for the American artist's situation.

This myth of artistic creation, assimilating the act of writing novels to the Adamic myth, imposes on artistic creation all the gender-based restrictions that I have already examined in that myth. The key to identifying an "Adamic writer" is the formal appearance, or, more precisely, the *informal* appearance, of his novel. The unconventionality is interpreted as a direct representation of the open-ended experience of exploring and taming the wilderness as well as a rejection of "society" as it is incorporated in conventional literary forms. There is no place for a woman author in this scheme. Her roles in the drama of creation are those allotted to her in a male melodrama: Either she is to be silent, like nature, or she is the creator of conventional works, the spokesperson of society. What she might do as an innovator in her own right is not to be perceived.

In recent years some refinements of critical theory coming from the Yale and Johns Hopkins and Columbia schools have added a new variant to the idea of creation as a male province. I quote from a 1979 book entitled *Home as Found* by Eric Sundquist. The author takes the idea that in writing a novel the artist is really writing a narrative about himself and proposes this addition:

> Writing a narrative about oneself may represent an extremity of Oedipal usur- pation or identification, a bizarre act of self-fathering. . . . American authors have been particularly obsessed with *fathering* a tradition of their own, with becoming their "own sires." . . . The struggle . . . is central to the crisis of representation, and hence of style, that allows American authors to find in their own fantasies those of a nation and to make of those fantasies a compelling and instructive literature.[22]

These remarks derive clearly from the work of such critics as Harold Bloom, as any reader of recent critical theory will note. The point for our purpose is the facile translation of the verb *to author* into the verb *to father*, with the profound gender restrictions of that translation unacknowledged. Accord- ing to this formulation, insofar as the author writes about a character who is his surrogate—which, apparently, he always does—he is trying to be- come his own father.

We can scarcely deny that men think a good deal about, and are pro- foundly affected by, relations with their fathers. The theme of fathers and sons is perennial in world literature. Somewhat more spaciously, we rec- ognize that intergenerational conflict, usually perceived from the point of view of the young, is a recurrent literary theme, especially in egalitarian cultures. Certainly, this idea involves the question of authority, and "au- thority" is a notion related to that of "the author." And there is some gender-specific significance involved since authority in most cultures that we know tends to be invested in adult males. But the theory has built from these useful and true observations to a restriction of literary creation to a sort of therapeutic act that can only be performed by men. If literature is the attempt to *father* oneself by the author, then every act of writing by a woman is both perverse and absurd. And, of course, it is bound to fail.

Since this particular theory of the act of writing is drawn from psy- chological assumptions that are not specific to American literature, it may be argued that there is no need to confine it to American authors. In fact, Harold Bloom's *Anxiety of Influence*, defining literature as a struggle between fathers and sons, or the struggle of sons to escape from their fa- thers, is about British literature. And so is Edward Said's book *Beginnings*, which chronicles the history of the nineteenth-century British novel as exemplification of what he calls "filiation." His discussion omits Jane Austen, George Eliot, all three Brontë sisters, Elizabeth Gaskell, Mrs. Humphrey Ward—not a sign of a woman author is found in his treatment of Victorian fiction. The result is a revisionist approach to British fiction recasting it in the accepted image of the American myth. Ironically, just at the time that feminist critics are discovering more and more important women, the critical theorists have seized upon a theory that allows the women less and less presence. This observation points up just how significantly the critic is engaged in the act of *creating* literature.

Ironically, then, one concludes that, in pushing the theory of American fiction to this extreme, critics have "deconstructed" it by creating a tool with no particular American reference. In pursuit of the uniquely American they have arrived at a place where Americanness has vanished into the depths of what is alleged to be the universal male psyche. The theory of American fiction has boiled down to the phrase in my title: a melodrama of beset manhood. What a reduction this is of the enormous variety of fiction written in this country, by both women and men! And, ironically, nothing could be further removed from Trilling's idea of the artist as embodiment of a culture. As in the working out of all theories, its weakest link has found it out and broken the chain.

2

Putting Women in Their Place

The Last of the Mohicans and Other
Indian Stories

In 1971 I published an "images of women" study of James Fenimore Cooper's Leatherstocking tales, placing character in a structural and ideological framework.[1] Arguing that Cooper's female depictions were more diverse than previous criticism had recognized, I described supposed defects in the treatment of women as effects of Cooper's theme—"contrasting modes of thought as they are brought into play in the establishment of an American civilization"—as that theme was controlled by his social conservatism.

"Women," I continued, "are not full members of the societies Cooper depicts; his cultures are composed entirely of males. Women are, however, the chief signs, the language of social communication between males; in the exchange of women among themselves men create ties and bonds, the social structures that are their civilizations. Without women there can be relationships like the friendship of Natty and Chingachgook, profoundly resonant with personal feeling and meaning, yet entirely without social significance. With women there are classes, societies, civilization. Though Cooper's women have no power over his men, they are vital for man's civilization, and thus man has to take them along wherever he goes, and at whatever cost. The chief 'statement' of the social language is, of course, marriage, which is shown in Cooper's Leatherstocking stories as a transaction between males, where the giving away of women creates a rhetoric of group membership and exclusions. The content of the marriage statement is deeply conservative: Marriage takes place within the boundaries of the group. Neither extending or modifying the social structure, it confirms the group's previous membership, and tightens the group's solidarity and exclusiveness.

"In Cooper's conservative view of society, no person is a 'person' in the romantic or existential sense wherein he exists for his own ends, and wherein the group's ultimate purpose is to facilitate self-development and fulfillment. On the contrary, the chief 'existent' is the group, and the idea of personhood is only rudimentarily developed. It is largely from a conflict between the social and romantic senses of 'personhood' that a character like Natty Bumppo draws his continuing strength and interest. Women, as signs and objects in the society—as the mortar rather than the bricks of it—are even less persons than men are, and Cooper's depiction of them is controlled by the issue of their social use. Marriage rather than love is the matrix of his 'romances,' which are not truly romances because the sentimental interest in the heroine's feelings is largely absent. Absent, too, is the genteel romancer's guiding faith that marriage is both a personal epiphany and a social good. Cooper does not dispute this belief; the matter is simply not of interest to him."

I wound up this summary by observing that Cooper chiefly "divides women into those who can be married and those who cannot. One can also distinguish in his handling of women, as well as in the psychologies of the women themselves, some vaguely sensed stress between woman-as-person and woman-as-object. This stress is particularly evident in the contrast between Cora and Alice Munro" in *The Last of the Mohicans.* The essay concluded by noting that Cooper's "rigid hierarchical view of society eclipses the romantic sympathies which he embodies in loners and outcasts" and that order in the Leatherstocking tales "is achieved only at the cost of a social submission that falls with particular completeness and severity on the women."

Twenty years later I would attribute Cooper's practice to Enlightenment republicanism not incipient structural anthropology. If I were writing that essay now, I would analyze female character in the Leatherstocking tales as the product of two representational modes—a classical mode in which "character" in the sense of unique individuals does not exist, and a romantic mode in which the uniqueness of the individual is the very point of the characterization. I would argue that, because American civilization tends to deny women the individualism that it supposedly cultivates as a national trait, a clash of representational modes would emerge sharply in female depiction.

In the analysis to follow, however, I emphasize the structural frame rather than the production of individual character. The 1826 *Last of the Mohicans* is set during the French and Indian wars on a terrain that was not yet the United States. Its subject is a collision of cultures not over incompatible belief systems but over land. Cooper assumes indeed that needs for land and space override all belief systems in determining human action, bringing different cultures together in that spectacle of hostilities which comprises world history. Since war is the chief way in which cultures interact, no group can survive unless it differentiates the labor of men and women according to the fundamental difference in physical strength between the sexes. To Cooper nothing more, and nothing less, than difference in physical strength determines the relative sexual roles in all cultures, and this is the focus of his treatment of gender in *The Last of the Mohicans.*

Before considering what led him to this focus, and why he handled it as he did, it is useful to recall some basic facts about the outpouring of American historical novels in the 1820s. Inspired by the American success of Sir Walter Scott's Waverley novels, as well as by the successful outcome of the War of 1812 (the "second war with England," as it was called in its own time), these novels sought to establish and popularize a nationalistic narrative of American history. Critics of the 1820s, however, tended to call all historical fiction "Indian stories," because American Indians figured centrally in all the settings featured in American historical fiction: Puritan New England, the American Revolution, and the frontier. These novels were looking back, to be sure, but they were also involved with the fraught contemporary issues of Indian policy. The 1820s was the decade, after all, in which "Indian removal" became the law of the land. The novels were necessarily taking part in debates over American Indian policy, and no doubt the vogue of the historical novel subsided in part when these debates were concluded.[2]

The Indian story did not require—indeed, aesthetically speaking, unless it was to take the shape of melodrama, it precluded—making Euroamericans all good and Indians all bad. Sympathetic Indians, however, were always viewed through a moral lens, in which Euroamerican culture was a higher form of civilization, and through a historical lens, in which higher forms of civilization were destined to supplant lower. It was impossible, therefore, to instantiate an ultimate Indian victory or a future civilization in which American Indian and European cultures either merged or were contained pluralistically in one polity. The only remaining possibility—that American Indians might assimilate to a dominant Euroculture—was often imagined but always dismissed, chiefly through Indian characters who themselves reject this option. The figure of the "vanishing Indian," although not invariably a euphemism for extermination, showed that Indians needed their own space, beyond white surveillance, to survive.

Indian stories, alert to the presence of women readers, identified the elevated condition of women within white culture as the most important difference between it and Indian culture. Indian men, the argument went, used their superior strength to exploit their women, white men to protect them. As Ruth explains concisely to her daughter in Cooper's 1829 *Wept of Wishton-Wish*, Indians, "of wild and fierce habits," know little "of our manner of life. Woman is not cherished as among the people of thy father's race, for force of body is more regarded than kinder ties."[3] The formula of the historical novel involves attaching a fictional love story to real historical events; some Indian stories—including *The Last of the Mohicans* and the other novels to be discussed here—used love stories to question whether white and American Indian civilizations might be conjoined through marriages between white women and Indian men. Could Indian men learn to see white women as white men saw them, there was some hope for bringing them—and along with them, Indian women—into white society. In their resolutions, however, Indian love plots discarded this possibility, showing that white women forced to marry Indians were in no position to represent white civilization and that white women choosing to marry Indians had already rejected it. Either way, white women married to Indians became Indians. The stories maintained, then, that if they were to represent the higher state that differentiated white from American Indian civilization, white women had to remain within white society's protective and defining boundaries.

Indian warfare is over in Cooper's first-written Leatherstocking story, the 1823 *Pioneers,* which takes place in mid-state New York during 1793–94; only one aged Indian—who will become the lordly Chingachgook in *The Last of the Mohicans*—remains in the area. Nevertheless, the story turns on a question of land which develops in constant reference to the dispossessed American Indians and raises the possibility of Indian-white marriage. The heiress-heroine in the wilderness has no suitor, but there is a very handsome and exceptionally well-bred young man in the vicinity to whom she is evidently attracted. He, however, is thought to be a grandson of Chingachgook. Ultimately, the plot reveals that he is the grandson of an American Tory not an American Indian; marriage bridges the post-Revolutionary gap between England and the United States rather than the chasm between two groups of Americans competing for the same space.

No less than men, women writers eschewed stories that brought Indians into white society through marriage.[4] Equally with male writers, they represented Indian and white cultures as incompatible, accepting—indeed, welcoming—their role as representative of the pinnacle of white civilization. They used the historical novel to raise a different issue, a gender issue—to suggest that, if white women were what men claimed, their social role should be more active: They should do as well as be. Lydia Maria Child's 1824 *Hobomok* and Catharine Maria Sedgwick's 1827 *Hope Leslie,* carefully (albeit differently) distance their protagonists from the Indians. Cooper, revising Child in *The Last of the Mohicans,* is less concerned with her representations of Indians per se than with her depictions of white women, but he is not worried about how she represents individuals so much as about her dangerously mistaken view of generic female power. He is resisting or rejecting the fantasy of women's novels that women's elevated place in white society is a function of a spiritual power by which male physical force can be countered, contained, and even disarmed. Responding to

Hobomok, and responded to in turn by Sedgwick's *Hope Leslie*, *The Last of the Mohicans* is a node in a literary network wherein white authors debated each other on the topic of male and female as well as the topic of whites and American Indians.

Child was moved to compose her 1824 *Hobomok* when she read an essay by John Gorham Palfrey about the 1820 verse epic *Yamoyden* by James East-burn and Robert Sands in an old issue of the prestigious *North American Review*. *Yamoyden* is set during King Philip's War, and Philip is its hero.[5] The associated love plot features Nora, a Puritan whose marriage to the Indian Yamoyden—even though he is friendly to the colonists and a Chris-tian—has led her father to disown her. In the tumult of interracial and in-tertribal war Yamoyden is killed by an Indian bullet aimed at Nora's father, Nora dies of grief and exhaustion by his side, and the remorseful and belat-edly forgiving father adopts their child. It would have falsified history to make King Philip the victor in this conflict, but the fictional Nora's story could have gone either way. Authorial choice killed her off along with Yamoyden.

In typical 1820s review style Palfrey summarized *Yamoyden*'s plot book by book, quoted from it extensively, and criticized it freely. He said little about *Yamoyden*'s love story but much about its history. He attributed the poem's heroic view of King Philip to Irving's sentimental sketch of the Wampanoag leader rather than to "any graver authority" and complained that the New York authors had "gone out of their way to throw a gauntlet to New England." To their sympathy for Philip's cause he countered that, "politically speaking, Philip had perhaps a right to attempt to rid the coun-try of his English neighbours; but, politically speaking, they had an equal right to keep their ground, if they could." And he took several pages to celebrate the early New England (male) character, inviting New England authors to accept *Yamoyden*'s challenge and write about Puritan, not Indian, heroes.[6]

In *Hobomok* Child responded ingeniously and—as Carolyn Karcher has pointed out in her introduction to the novel—subversively to Palfrey's call. A framing preface offers the book as "a New England novel" and refers humorously to Scott's *Waverley* and three Cooper novels: "A novel! . . . When Waverley is galloping over hill and dale, faster and more successful than Alexander's conquering sword? Even the American ground is occu-pied. 'The Spy' is lurking in every closet,—the mind is every where sup-plied with 'Pioneers' on the land, and is soon likely to be with 'Pilots' on the deep."[7]

The frame presents a male speaker, who adopts a jocose masculine style characterized by competitive, martial imagery. Thus, the work openly identifies itself with narrative precursors by men, affiliating with them in amicable contest and inviting readers to notice deviations from the models it has named. But because the persona is established as male, the reader is not prepared for the novel's gender inflections.

Hobomok takes place between 1629 and 1633, so early in the history of New England settlement that no major war between American Indians and whites had yet been fought. It typifies the New England male in the heroine's father, Roger Conant, a historical figure who had broken away from the Plymouth colony and settled, along with other dissenters from the dissenters, at Naumkeag (later Salem). By no means the filiopietistic representation that Palfrey had asked for, Conant is rather a tyrannical, bigoted, ill-bred patriarch who has selfishly transported his delicate, aristocratic Anglican wife and daughter Mary from their comfortable life in England. During the novel's course Mrs. Conant dies from accumulated New World hardships. Mary, deprived of her mother, her friends (one dies, another marries and moves away), and her Anglican lover (who is banished from the house by her father and then presumed lost at sea), becomes increasingly distraught. Her father's unrelenting harshness, his immersion in abstract doctrinal controversy, and his lack of sympathy for Mary drive her to the extraordinary step of asking the friendly Indian Hobomok, who has long worshipped her from afar, to marry her. But three years later she rejoins the white community, without stigma and with her son, to marry Charles Brown, her first love, who was not dead after all. When Charles turns up Hobomok—knowing that Mary has never ceased to love him—divorces her, Indian-style, and elects to "vanish" into the forest. The contrite patriarch becomes a doting grandfather to Mary's son, who, adopted and renamed by Charles, ceases to be Indian.

Child revises *Yamoyden*'s plot so that the heroine does not have to die for marrying an Indian. She also lets the Indian husband live but denies him a place in white society. In Hobomok's chivalric heroism as well as other traits he is a good Indian, indeed, but by no means representative. He is far more spiritual than most Indians (his religion of nature is appraised by the author as the most one can hope for without Christian revelation), and he is friendly to the English from the start. Moreover, Hobomok loves Mary *because she is a white woman* and is especially elevated through this love. In sum, he cannot serve as a figure for investigating white treatment of American Indians because he is so carefully set apart from Indians-as-such. Although Child was later to write on behalf of the American Indians, white-Indian relations are not her focus here. As Karcher has observed, her target is white men's (or New England Puritan men's) treatment of their women. The book equates Puritanism with the worst aspects of New England's historical legacy. It comprises a liberal Protestant—a Unitarian—attack on old-style Calvinism and is an Indian story that is not about Indians.

Puritan doctrinal disputatiousness is depicted in considerable detail throughout the novel.[8] Conant is cruel to Mary mainly because she accepts her mother's latitudinarianism and loves an Anglican. The kinder paternal treatment that would have prevented Mary's calamitous marriage is identical to religious tolerance, which Conant realizes after the fact. Hobomok, then, is merely a pawn in Mary's ultimately successful struggle for paternal recognition and love. Her mad marriage allowed her to escape Conant's plan for her to marry a doctrinally correct blockhead, with whom her future could only repeat her mother's repressed and overworked life.

In larger historical terms *Hobomok* gives women power to reform white society by changing men as Mary changes her father. (The theme is repeated in a comic subplot centered on Mary's lower-class friend Sally.) The novel implies that if women's values were implemented a more tolerant, more imaginative, more gracious civil state than the one instituted in America by Puritan men would come into being. Actually, the novel implies that such a civil state has already come into being in New England, for this is a *historical* novel about the softening of the male Puritan heart. As Michael Davitt Bell has written in his treatment of New England historical romance, the heroine, "in disagreeing with the intolerance of the fathers, establishes the basis of the new society."[9]

Cooper, though no admirer of New England patriarchy himself, seems to have been piqued by *Hobomok*'s gender representations. *The Last of the Mohicans* implicitly disparages Child's novel as a juvenile and potentially harmful fantasy and replaces it with a story based on the hard truths of history. The novel denies that women have influenced world or national events and uses the romanticizing of American Indians in women's novels as evidence of their unfitness for the cultural power to which they were apparently aspiring. Cooper's many-stranded argument depends on the fundamental claim that his novels represent Indian warfare and Indian nature realistically while women's novels represent nothing but ignorant feminine imagination. The gender distinction is crucial to Cooper's idea of authorship. Men could produce realism because they faced reality directly; women could produce only schoolgirl romance because they were protected—by men—from the ceaseless struggle through which civilization is instituted and maintained as well as from the savagery that made and makes such struggle necessary. Ironically, the protection that women would reject in order to become more active in the world is exactly what has enabled them to imagine the Utopian alternative that they mistake for truth. Cooper says to women authors and readers that only men can write truthfully, even when the subject is women.

The Last of the Mohicans, then, is much more focused on women's place in the polity than *The Pioneers.* It takes up the question of sexual relations between American Indian men and white women that *The Pioneers* had only played with. Through the unlike sisters Cora and Alice the novel images two ways of writing women into the story of white colonization of the North American continent. The images develop in a context where any possible connection between a sympathetic white (or quasi-white, since Cora is partly black) woman and a friendly noble Indian is nullified in advance by the reality of intractable enmity between their cultures. The opposition of Cora and Alice permits consideration of how an embattled civilization might use such active traits as outspoken bravery, firmness, intelligence, self-possession, and eloquence in a woman. By developing these attributes in a woman whom it then discards for one who has been socially constructed as an object, the novel demonstrates that in a woman these traits are no use at all. In contrast, although Alice's extreme passivity constantly endangers her and her companions, it turns out that by preserving this woman a high civilization signifies itself. In *The Last of the Mohicans* the white man does not need a woman fighting by his side to inspire him, still less a woman mediating between him and the Indian enemy; he needs a woman to fight *for* and *about*. White women therefore serve their civilization by sacrificing dreams of independence, repressing sexual fantasies, and acknowledging how lucky they are to be the prize possessions of white men.

In effect, *The Last of the Mohicans* rejects the woman-centered structure of *Hobomok* and reclaims the Indian story for white males. At the novel's center is Duncan Heyward, a very white white man. Cooper goes to sometimes awkward lengths to place Duncan in every scene and to narrate all the action, except for the massacre at Fort William Henry, from his perspective. Formally speaking, then, he is the readers' surrogate, marking out the position from which readers would view the action if they were in the book. Except for a few forays into Cora's thoughts, Cooper limits his representations of subjectivity to Duncan: We learn about Duncan's feelings, his attention, his painful doubt, his hope, his confidence; his hearing, his fancies; his shame, his uneasiness; his interest, his belief.[10] He is also the patriarch's lieutenant and heir—that is, the present and future protector of American women and, accordingly, the protector and progenitor of American civilization. His chosen consort, in turn, will be the mother of America, so the plot has to ensure her survival. The plot need not necessarily, however, eliminate the woman he does *not* choose. By saving Alice and killing off Cora along with her likely spouse, Cooper demonstrates that citizens of the future republic are to be whites only.

For a long time it was critically fashionable to explain Duncan's lack of interest in Cora, Magua and Uncas's attraction to her, as functions of the exotic sexuality of her mixed blood. White men, the explanation went, fear sex, and nonwhite men like it. The extraordinary and un-self-conscious sexism and racism of this interpretation was, perhaps, excusable since the point of this criticism was less to analyze Cooper than to remasculinize the undersexed white male, but the implicit oversexualization of women and

Indians according to some Lawrentian symbolization of "tainted blood" far exceeds the plot's boundaries. It would be possible today to sophisticate this unselfconscious replication of racialist theories into a deconstructivist post-colonialist feminist analysis of Cora as the overdetermined scapegoated representation of all the book's (and Cooper's) others—blacks, American Indians, women—but this analysis does not speak to Cooper's novel in its historical moment. In that novel Duncan is already in love with Alice before he learns from Munro that Cora's mother was remotely descended from black slaves. Neither Magua nor Uncas ever knows anything about Cora's "blood," and in any event Magua thinks poorly of blacks: "'The spirit that made men, coloured them differently,' commenced the subtle Huron. 'Some are blacker than the sluggish bear. These he said should be slaves; and he ordered them to work for ever, like the beaver. You may hear them groan, when the south wind blows, louder than the lowing buffaloes, along the shores of the great salt lake, where the big canoes come and go with them in droves'" (300–301).

Finally, Cora is morally stainless. The plot would be incoherent if she were not. Cora is not sexually attracted to Indians-as-such, covertly or sub-consciously, although she *is* devoid of racial prejudice. Through various muted but telltale signs (sighs, blushes) Cooper shows the reader that Cora consciously, unrequitedly, loves *Duncan*. Her maidenly purity is on exhibit throughout the novel and forms the crux of the contest between Uncas and Magua. When she is lustfully appraised by Magua—"Her eyes sunk with shame under an impression, that, for the first time, they had encountered an expression that no chaste female might endure" (105)—not Cora, but Magua and his typical Indian view of women are the narrator targets. Magua has already been unfavorably characterized through his scorn for white men's treatment of women: "The pale-faces make themselves dogs to their women . . . and when they want to eat, their warriors must lay aside the tomahawk to feed their laziness" (42). These words bode ill for any white woman who might become his victim. Magua's open display of lust for Cora expresses this same low opinion of women, not some unrepressed primitive appreciation of female sexuality. Finally, if Magua were indeed to have been characterized as a villain attracted to the white man's woman, he would have lusted for Alice, nor Cora.

Cora's mixed blood is not psychologically symbolic, since Cooper's char-acters are not psychological, interiorized entities. Concerned with cultures, civilizations, societies, he represents persons as constituents of social bodies. Cora, the beloved daughter of a father who married women of two different races, stands for the possibility of an American future in which the races were combined into one new social body. Her already mixed blood, were it to be mixed again with an American Indian's, would produce triracial chil-dren—the incarnate "e pluribus unum" of the American national seal.

Given the novelistic convention that requires the romantic pairing of youthful characters, and given Duncan's preference for Alice, the plot constantly invites readers to find a man for Cora. Because there is no second eligible white male in the novel, because Cora's blood is mixed and she has no race prejudice (she alone among white characters refuses to judge American Indians on the basis of skin color), it seems possible that her mate might be an Indian. The heroicized representation of Uncas makes him the right Indian.

Quickly the plot divides into parallel quests: Duncan's to rescue Alice, Uncas's to rescue Cora. Magua is the villain of both actions, but he is a different villain in each because he desires Cora, not Alice. In contrast to Uncas, the ayptical Indian who desires her idealistically, like a civilized man, Magua desires her instrumentally, like a savage. The romantic outcome, then, toward which this second action might be moving is for Uncas to kill Magua and rescue Cora and for Cora to fall in love with and marry him. Everything following the massacre at Fort William Henry in chapter 17 anticipates this conclusion. Uncas, brave and stalwart from the first, is inspired to feats of overreaching heroism by his love for Cora, and when he arrives at the Delaware village he is installed as the great chief of a resurgent American Indian nation that could, perhaps, flourish and co-exist with whites on the North American continent. "Bad" whites (French) and "Bad" Indians (Hurons) would be eliminated; "good" representatives of the two races—English and Delaware—would become one family through marriage to sisters.

That, Cooper says sternly and punitively, is fantasy. We all know what really happened; we know how history turned out. This is a historical novel, not a romance. Uncas is not a "real" Indian but a fantasy. The real Indian is Magua.

Before pursuing this point it is necessary to backtrack to consider what—if Cora's lack of racial purity is not deployed for psychosexual excitation in *The Last of the Mohicans* but to speculate on the possibility of a cross-cultural citizenry in the United States—her failure to inspire love in Duncan might mean. Duncan's good-bye to the two sisters in chapter 15 provides a clue: "'God bless you in every fortune, noble—Cora—I may, and must call you. . . . In every fortune, I know you will be an ornament and honour to your sex. Alice, adieu'—his tone changed from admiration to tenderness—'adieu, Alice; we shall soon meet again'" (150). The dictionary tells us that to admire is to think highly of, which implies that the person so thought of is higher than the person who does the thinking, hence in no need of help from that person. Tenderness, in contrast, is the solicitude and concern called out in a stronger person by the appeal of one who is weaker; it is a response to the expression of need. Admiration is a heroic emotion, tenderness a sentimental one that often involves—perhaps requires—some kind of possessiveness. The relationship of "love," in which white men and women are paired asymmetrically, involves just this male response of protective and possessive tenderness toward a female who must be correspondingly weak and dependent.

Alice is thus a lovable woman, being artless, thoughtless, childlike, cheerful, and incompetent. She clings to Duncan "with the dependency of an infant" and is drawn into the cavern by Cora in a "nearly insensible" state (80), a "trembling weeper" on her firmer sister's maternal bosom (82). She regards Duncan with a look of "infantile dependency" (108). She looks "like some beautiful emblem of the wounded delicacy of her sex, devoid of animation, and yet keenly conscious" (110). During the retreat from Fort William Henry she drops "senseless on the earth," and her dead faint enables Magua to abduct her and hence lure Cora to eventual doom (177–178). When Duncan finds Alice in captivity she is trembling "in a manner which betrayed her inability to stand" (259); "helpless" to follow him (262), she has to be carried out of the cave (263), a "precious burthen" (264), later a "precious and nearly insensible burthen" (303).

And despite all this weakness—because of it, really—she survives. It is Cora, the noble-minded maiden, the paragon of fortitude, who ends up a "burthen" carried to her grave by a bevy of Delaware women. Alice's very tenderness and softness—her constant need to be tended, watched over, taken care of—finally save her; Cora's very strength—her firmness, boldness, fortitude, and thoughtfulness—doom her. In the white world a woman's weakness is her strength, inspiring men like Duncan, the representative of Anglo-American civilization, to fight for her. Cora shares the male perception of Alice: "I need not tell you to cherish the treasure you will possess," she says to Duncan (316) when she leaves as Magua's captive.

Alice's fitness to be loved by men in white culture does not translate to anything that an Indian—even a "good" Indian—can understand; she is of no interest to Magua *or* to Uncas. Magua uses her captivity as a lure for Cora and is happy to release her when he secures the prize he is really after. Alice would be a burden, but no treasure, to an Indian male. The gendered interrelation of dependency and protection called "love" does not exist among Indians. This does not mean, however, that women and men are more nearly equal in American Indian culture. Magua, out for revenge against Munro by treating his daughter like an Indian, finds Alice unsuitable, but he certainly does not appreciate Cora for the qualities that make her admirable to the representative white male, Duncan Heyward. Apart from his possible intuition of Munro's preference for Cora, Magua appreciates her strength and fortitude because they fit her to draw water, hoe corn, cook venison, and bind up his battle wounds (105). Women in Indian societies are no less possessions, but much more beasts of burden, slaves, than in white.

Implicitly criticizing Magua's Indian attitude toward women, Cooper endorses white woman's interest in love and in love stories. *The Last of the Mohicans* maintains that love in the Western sense is very much *in* a woman's interest but insists that such love is only to be encountered in the civilization that has invented it. The novel rejects women's fantasies of Indian lovers on the basis of a historicist conviction that love is a white cultural construction existing only in white society.

It could be objected to this line of interpretation that Magua is only one individual, not a generic "Indian." What about Uncas? But in *The Last of the Mohicans* Magua, not Uncas, is the generic Indian. Magua's identity with his kind is established by naming him with a simple variant of his tribe's name—Maqua—which, in turn, applies to the whole Iroquois confederacy. He succeeds in controlling his fiercely democratic, always potentially anarchistic, people because he skillfully voices what they already believe. Magua is heroicized as a Miltonian Prince of Darkness, but he is only one of many diabolic and demonic Indian figures who, emerging from the gloom of the forest with satanic yells, display virtually supernatural abilities to materialize and dematerialize.

More mundanely, Cora's plea to Tamenund, sage of the friendly Delawares, is rejected in terms showing that for women there is no difference between contending American Indian cultures: "Girl, what woulds't thou! A great warrior takes thee to wife. Go—thy race will not end" (313). Finally, we are instructed that Uncas's sympathetic and sentimental side (which is what enables him to love and admire Cora for herself) "elevated him far above the intelligence, and advanced him probably centuries before the practices of his nation" (115). Thus, Uncas is a fit partner for Cora not because he is like an Indian but because, in crucial ways, he is unlike an Indian. He is simultaneously the last of his kind and unlike his kind.

Cora leaves the Delaware camp as Magua's "passive captive" (317). The words alert us to the reality in *The Last of the Mohicans* that her admirable firmness and boldness and fortitude come to nothing when cultures collide. The captive Cora is as abject as Alice. Hawk-eye—the Leatherstocking—describes both women indifferently as "harmless things," "flowers," "tender blossoms" (46), "gentle ones" (127, 138); the narrator speaks of both women's "fragile forms" (93, 261). From these two authoritative perspectives the women are interchangeable. In the warrior world of *The Last of the Mohicans* no degree of difference between Cora and Alice will finally transform Cora into a man who can fight and kill. Since she is not a man, she can only be a woman. When Magua proposes to exchange Cora for Hawk-eye, the scout replies, "It would be an unequal exchange, to give a warrior, in the prime of his age and usefulness, for the best woman on the frontiers" (314). The inferior physical strength of a woman makes anatomy her destiny, because in war the issue is simply brute force.[11]

But if Indians customarily felt even a fraction of white reverence for womanhood, the story implies, neither the final fictional catastrophe nor yet the historically real massacre at Fort William Henry would have taken place. In a sense the catastrophe simply repeats the massacre, which is the novel's rhetorical and thematic centerpiece. Among a variety of possible incidents in the historical sources he drew on for his account, Cooper selected a scene of wanton woman killing to epitomize the whole. Indians greedy for finery, overcome by blood lust, and desperate for scalps to demonstrate their manhood do not hesitate to slaughter women. The relative helplessness of the women simply makes them easier victims. If the scene has special horror for white readers, this must be because they make a distinction that American Indian culture does not.

Thus, Cooper places the story of his two women in a world at war, makes the plot of *The Last of the Mohicans* exemplify that world, and brings its lesson home to white women. Everything within the plot's enclosure resonates with the combat that surrounds and occasions it. The battle for possession of the entire continent makes the entire continent a scene of bloodshed, with no certain safety anywhere. The action progresses as a series of retreats from one supposedly safe space to another, each refuge quickly and repetitiously turning into a battlefield.

The particular combat, too, is shown to be global in its reach. The French and Indian wars were a territorial struggle between whites, with American Indian tribes traditionally hostile to each other enlisted on opposing sides. The victorious French do not themselves carry out the massacre at Fort William Henry but openly allow it to take place. Each culture fights according to its own rules; all are equally warlike. War is inevitable when different groups aspire to the same territory, and the particular narrative moment is extracted from a series that originated when whites invaded the American continent.

It was then that the French and English "united to rob the untutored possessors of its wooded scenery of their native right" to the land and the Dutch deployed liquor to cheat the Indians of both land and dignity (12). This historical reading identifies Magua as the novel's chief victim as well as its chief villain. "Is it justice to make evil, and then punish for it!" he exclaims rhetorically to Cora, and she—like other white characters in Indian stories confronted by arguments they cannot counter—simply has to remain silent (103).

Cora's silence implies less the justness of the American Indian side than that justice is irrelevant to the reality that the novel urges on its readers. Dreams of domesticated Indians and peacefully cohabiting settlements are constituents of a silly girlish imagination—an imagination, perhaps, that would be typical in a young woman like Alice, who is so pleased to sing hymns too loudly with David Gamut in the wilderness. But this imagination, though charming and certainly an appropriate expression of female inexperience, is not harmless, because its illusion of safety creates vulnerability, just as the noisy harmony alerts hostile Indians to the whereabouts of the white party. The fancy that Indians will nobly vanish into the forest like Hobomok after they have been so badly cheated and treated—will do so out of love and admiration for what a white woman represents—is especially silly from Cooper's perspective. The kind of woman that civilization has created and protects is useful only when she *is* protected; should a woman like this attempt to act on the basis of what she believes about the world, the result could only be disaster. One goal of the repeated scenes of breached security in *The Last of the Mohicans* may be to undermine the fantasies that underlie civilized (hence unworldly) women's attempts to intervene in the world.

The assumption that men's depictions of a warrior world are realistic for all times and places while women's more pacific representations are always and everywhere dangerously Utopian institutes gender distinction at a fundamental narrative level. This claim to superior realism on the grounds of greater worldliness, of course, characterizes much men's writing throughout American history, from Cooper to Mark Twain and Ernest Hemingway and beyond. And that Cooper had women's narratives in mind when writing *The Last of the Mohicans* is bluntly asserted in his preface to the first edition of the book, which announces that the story relates "to matters which may not be universally understood, especially by the more imaginative sex, some of whom, under the impression that it is a fiction, may be induced to read the book," and which inveighs against readers "who find a strange gratification in spending more of their time in making books, than of their money in buying them" (1). The preface concludes by advising "all young ladies, whose ideas are usually limited by the four walls of a comfortable drawing room," to avoid *The Last of the Mohicans* since, "after they have read the book, they will surely pronounce it shocking" (4).

Sedgwick's *Hope Leslie,* published a year after *The Last of the Mohicans,* might have been subtitled *The Last of the Pequods,* so closely did it invoke its precursor while spiritedly challenging it. The challenge begins with the preface, which cheerfully grants that this novel—like all novels—is not history but fiction and implicitly mocks Cooper's insistence that his own story is anything different. Throughout her novel Sedgwick parallels Cooper's male severity and rigidity with a feminine sprightliness, and Hope Leslie, her heroine, is a young woman with a decided taste for fun and laughter. More somberly, Sedgwick denies that any account of Indians and whites told from an exclusive white viewpoint can be true and, by promising an Indian perspective, actually suggests that her own account is more historical than Cooper's. This beginning is followed up by the surprising representation of the Uncas figure as an American Indian woman, a depiction that cannot but bring strongly to the reader's mind the functional absence of Indian women from Cooper's narrative. (They were also lacking in *Hobomok,* however, so that not only Cooper is being revised here.) *Hope Leslie* quickly raises the possibility of two Indian-white marriages and allows one of them to take place.

After an exposition the novel begins in New England immediately after the Pequod war, which is pushed back a year in order to conflate it with other historical events. The first seven chapters take place on the frontier and feature Indian massacres, daring rescues, and escapes. It looks like a typical Indian story except for two striking modifications: It narrates the massacre that ended the Pequod war from the Pequod perspective, and it includes an audacious sex-role reversal, having the young hero Everell Fletcher (the Duncan Heyward figure) saved by the Pocahontas-like intervention of Magawisca, who is the daughter of the defeated Pequod chief. The conflict in Magawisca's heart between love for Everell (and his family, to which she had been indentured after being captured) and love for her father suggests a possible outcome like the marriage between Poncahontas and John Rolfe. But because, in rescuing her, Magawisca's father massacres most of the Fletcher household—including women and babies—New England history takes a different turn from Virginia history and augurs a different future. Enabling Everell to escape from her father (a deed leading to the loss of her arm as she deflects a blow aimed at Everell), Magawisca does not save him for herself but for white culture and the white heroine Hope Leslie.

As the Indians pursue their way through the wilderness, Sedgwick archly promises to refrain from describing, "step by step, the progress of the Indian fugitives," since their "sagacity in traversing their native forests" has been "so well described in a recent popular work, that their usages have become familiar as household words, and nothing remains but to shelter defects of skill and knowledge under the veil of silence."[12] Following this pointed allusion to *The Last of the Mohicans,* she goes on to do what, presumably, she does have the skill and knowledge to do (perhaps what the less aristocratic Cooper cannot do?): describe civilized society. The second part of *Hope Leslie* takes place in Boston several years later and seems almost a different work, combining a drawing-room comedy of romantic misunderstanding with a Gothic melodrama wherein the villainous Catholic Philip Gardiner masquerades as a Puritan to conceal his nefarious designs on Hope, who supplants Magawisca as the object of reader interest and of Everell's affections.

Magawisca's appearance in Boston, however, reinstalls the Indian/woman connection because she brings Hope news of her sister Faith, who has married Magawisca's brother Oneco. In the intervening years Magawisca has become irremediably Indian, so there is no longer any question of marriage between her and Everell. Faith, too, is lost to white society, having become wholly Indianized by her marriage. She is different from Magawisca, however, to whom she is contrasted much like Alice to Cora; one is intractably independent, the other completely dependent on her male protector and provider. This very dependency makes Faith immune to white culture's attempts to reclaim her; she wants only to be with Oneco.

In another ingenious reversal of Cooper the novel features the capture and rescue of these two *Indian* women. Faith is kidnapped by the Puritan establishment and incarcerated in Governor Winthrop's mansion to be deprogrammed; eventually, Oneco arrives in disguise—just as Duncan disguised himself to get to Alice—and carries her off. Magawisca is unjustly accused of fomenting Indian hostility against the Puritans and imprisoned. In a scene recalling the escape of Natty Bumppo from prison in *The Pioneers* Hope and Everell get her out—but this comes after a trial scene where Magawisca uncompromisingly rejects white culture: "Take my own word, I am your enemy; the sun-beam and the shadow cannot mingle. The white man cometh—the Indian vanisheth. Can we grasp in friendship the hand raised to strike us?" (292).

When Hope and Everell plead with her to "return and dwell with us" she replies: "My own people have been spoiled—we cannot take as a gift that which is our own—the law of vengeance is written on our hearts—you say you have a written rule of forgiveness—it may be better—if ye would be guided by it—it is not for us—the Indian and the white man can no more mingle, and become one, than day and night" (330). Criticizing white people for violating their own law of forgiveness, she exempts the Indians from the law because it is a white, not an Indian, construct. She could defend herself by pointing out that she was not guilty as charged but prefers to insist Indians are not subject to white law. In defining American Indian tribes as independent nations (like the Cherokees when suing the State of Georgia), Magawisca's defense forecloses the possibility of their aggregation with any future United States.

Faith Leslie's marriage to Oneco is also a rejection of the white world. "No speak Yengeese" are the first—virtually the only—words she speaks to Hope; alas for sisterhood, her "final departure" does not "seriously disturb" Hope's happiness. "There had been nothing in the intercourse of the sisters to excite Hope's affections. Faith had been spiritless, woe-begone—a soulless body—and had repelled, with sullen indifference, all Hope's efforts to win her love" (338). Thus, *Hope Leslie* presents Indians as beyond the reach of white attempts to acculturate them, while proposing no alternatives except acculturation and removal. Sedgwick's three surviving Pequods and Faith voluntarily "vanish" into the western forests. Beyond the white horizon, out of the line of white sight, they (like Hobomok) are never heard from again. Hence the novel's innovations—its noble woman savage and its white woman permanently married to an Indian—serve no culturally radical purpose. In mocking Cooper's martial hysteria *Hope Leslie* proposes that Indian removal need not have been, nor need be in the future, so bloody: The Indians will be willing or at least acquiescing agents of their own removal.

Even as it shows mistreatment of American Indians by whites, *Hope Leslie* enunciates values that are clearly white and Christian. The second half of *Hope Leslie*, like *Hobomok*, is more about women and the New England patriarchy than about whites and American Indians. And it tells the same New England story that *Hobomok* did of Puritan severity moderating under woman's liberal influence. Hope, having helped Magawisca escape from jail, should be severely punished, but Governor Winthrop declines to act harshly. His mildness, called out by a woman's principled heterodoxy, historicizes the New England errand into the wilderness by showing that over time the Puritans would overcome their initial narrow-mindedness and develop a progressive, enlightened, yet still Protestant culture. (Unfortunately for feminist readings of the novel, the most despicable and intransigently Puritan character is a lower-class woman servant who perishes in Boston Harbor along with Sir Philip.)

In Cooper's 1828 *The Prairie* the passive woman was a much more grotesque figure than Alice, and the active woman was a much more healthy, ordinary person than Cora. In his 1829 non-Leatherstocking *The Wept of Wish-ton-Wish* Cooper wrote his only New England Indian story. Set during King Philip's War, the novel portrays a white-Indian marriage like the marriage of Faith and Oneco; unlike Sedgwick, Cooper does not allow this couple to survive, but, like her, he represents that marriage as a loss of the white woman's selfhood. After a hiatus Cooper produced two more works in the Leatherstocking series—*The Pathfinder* (1840) and *The Deerslayer* (1841)—both of which make white women more important than the earlier books, give them much more active roles and create important American Indian women characters. *The Pathfinder* even allows a woman to bear arms. Cooper was apparently recognizing that castigating and denigrating women readers—who comprised the main audience for all kinds of fiction—was not the best strategy for selling books to them. Still he continued to represent a world structured by cultural groups that were always in potentially violent and unforgiving competition with each other for scarce goods. It may have been Magawisca and Faith Leslie who showed him that martial white women, Indian-white marriage, and Indian women could exist within the scope of this worldview. The evidence of *Hope Leslie* suggested that the alarm he manifested in *The Last of the Mohicans* was excessive. After all, no radical undermining of white society would eventuate if its women got more of the action.

Nathaniel Hawthorne and His Mother

A Biographical Speculation

Every student of Nathaniel Hawthorne's work and life knows that he wrote *The Scarlet Letter* because he lost his job at the Salem Custom House. He told the world so in his autobiographical preface to the novel "The Custom-House," and all later biographers have followed his lead while filling out the details.[1] But the sequence of events Hawthorne chronicles in the preface explains no more than how he came to be free to write and offers no factual basis for understanding what he wrote. To be sure, his angry and defiant heroine might express some of his own humiliation and rage. To write a story that favored the outcast so heavily against the establishment might have been an act of sweet revenge on the author's powerful enemies.

I

But such connections are remote. The essence of Hester's character and story (not to mention Dimmesdale's) is untouched. Why did Hawthorne pick a woman protagonist? Why a lone woman? Why a mother? To the extent that we seek biographical explanations for such choices we are probably always limited to surmise rather than certain knowledge. But it seems fair to say that the biographical accounts we now have do not offer hypotheses that engage with these questions.

Another event occurred in Hawthorne's life at the same time, exactly, that he was dismissed from the customhouse. On 30 July 1849, only six days after the new surveyor was appointed, his mother died. Her health had long been fragile, but she had lived to be sixty-nine years old. She was residing in Hawthorne's house (as were his two sisters, both unmarried) when she succumbed to a sudden, relatively brief illness, which took the author by surprise. He was greatly affected by her death, coming near to a "brain fever" after her burial on 2 August. Six days later he was writing for the first time of leaving Salem, "this abominable city," forever, as indeed he was to do after finishing *The Scarlet Letter*. By early September he had recovered from his illness and begun *The Scarlet Letter,* working with an intensity that almost frightened his wife and with a speed that brought the book to completion before the year ended. He was inspired as he had never been before, or was to be again.[2]

Common sense suggests that a work following so immediately on the death of a mother, featuring a heroine who is a mother (and whose status as a mother is absolutely central to her situation), might very likely be inspired by that death and consist, in its autobiographical substance, of a complex memorial to that mother. But one looks virtually in vain for a biographical analysis of *The Scarlet Letter* which pursues such a suggestion.[3] One looks in vain for a reliable, comprehensive account of Hawthorne's mother and his relationship with her. Instead, we have a long-standing and unreliable tradition about her which seems impervious to countervailing evidence. This tradition permits critics to accuse her of a grotesque, pernicious role in his life or, alternatively, to deny her any role at all.

Mark Van Doren, one of the few skeptics, described the situation well: "His mother has long been the subject of a sentimental legend which no evidence supports. She is supposed, soon after her husband's death, to have shut herself away not only from the world but from the Mannings [her natal family] and her own children. There are hints of a darkened room where she takes her meals alone, says nothing, and mourns 'in a Hindoo seclusion' the irreparable sadness of her lot. It appears on the contrary that she was an excellent cook, an attentive mother, and an interesting talker about things past and present. Her son's childhood letters to her, a number of which survive, are addressed to no such awful stranger as the legend suggests."[4] Van Doren could have added that some of her letters also survive, showing an active, outward-looking disposition and betraying no hint of reclusiveness. But despite evidence accumulated and publicized by such scholars as Norman Holmes Pearson, Randall Stewart, Manning Hawthorne, and Gloria Ehrlich, the legend persists in newer biographies.[5] Thus, when we look for Hawthorne's mother we have to make our way past a legend constructed, it seems, to deny access.

It is not hard to understand why the legend endures. It has Hawthorne's own authority behind it as well as the endorsement of his wife, his sister-in-law, and his son. For those seeking a reason for Hawthorne's supposed lifelong feelings of gloom and alienation both the maternal rejection and her example of seclusion seem to provide clues. Such early biographers as George Woodberry, Lloyd Morris, Herbert Gorman, Robert Cantwell, and Newton Arvin depended heavily on the legend to explain the oddities of Hawthorne's imagination and his fiction. To other biographers seeking (for various reasons) to connect Hawthorne to the father he never knew and the father's family he had nothing to do with, her alleged absence allowed them to follow their preferences by writing her out of his life altogether. Among such biographers, one must include Randall Stewart, Hubert Hoeltje, Arlin Turner, and James R. Mellow.

It is not especially difficult to understand the motives of Hawthorne's surviving family in transmitting to the public a misrepresentation of his mother. This misrepresentation operated to their advantage, as we shall see; and in any case they would not have been likely to go against a story originating with Hawthorne himself. It is very puzzling, however, to make out Hawthorne's own motives in this case. But it is important to try to do so, for every conscious misrepresentation points to something hidden. Hawthorne seems to have been trying to hide not merely the actual role that his mother had played in his life but also the fact that she had a role at all. Such a denial—completely unnecessary in those innocent pre-Freudian days—only suggests that her role must have been very large indeed.

The legend made its first appearance of record in his early love letters to Sophia Peabody, where he writes of his mother's and sisters' eccentric reclusiveness and the morbid atmosphere in their house, which he calls "Castle Dismal." (The phrase later became a favorite of Sophia's.) Later he resisted Sophia's urgings that he make their engagement known by citing "the strange reserve, in regard to matters of feeling, that has always existed among us. We are conscious of one another's feelings, always; but there seems to be a tacit law, that our deepest heart-concernments are not to be spoken of."[6]

These sentences have carried a good deal of weight with biographers, who have taken them at face value instead of observing their highly literary character. They need to be examined for the equivocations of their rhetoric—the unallowable equation of an engagement with deepest, private "heart-concernments," for example. And, while asserting the existence of "a strange reserve," these lines imply a group of people deeply attuned to one another's moods and hence, possibly, an understanding beyond the need for speech. In any event people who are always conscious of one another's feelings must be in more or less constant contact. A particular irony of this letter is the way Hawthorne offers up its obfuscation to Sophia as exemplary of how he can gush out freely to her and to her only.

In sum what we seem to have here is an instance of a lover's strategy, to claim that nobody understands him and thereby appear both more needy and more interesting in the beloved's eyes, all the while giving her the pleasure of enacting the heroine's role in his romantic drama. "Mine ownest," he wrote her on 4 October 1840, addressing her as though they were already married,

> Here sits thy husband in his old accustomed chamber, where he used to sit in years gone by. . . . Sometimes (for I had no wife then to keep my heart warm) it seemed as if I were already in the grave, with only life enough to be chilled

and benumbed . . . till at length a certain Dove was revealed to me, in the shadow of a seclusion as deep as my own had been. . . . So now I begin to understand why I was imprisoned so many years in this lonely chamber, and why I could never break through the viewless bolts and bars. (*Letters,* 15:494–495)

Sophia's limpid, unsophisticated imagination accepted the lover's hyperbole as literal truth, as Hawthorne expected—for he was aware of, and attracted to, the transparent sensibility that seemed the very opposite of his own. "I tell thee these things," he wrote, "in order that my Dove, into whose infinite depths the sunshine falls continually, may perceive what a cloudy veil stretches over the abyss of my nature" (*Letters,* 15:495). Her simple sincerity guaranteed that she would mistake the veil for the abyss. And as a result of her mistake, she transmitted the legend through conversations and letters until it became an article of family faith.

Sophia was apparently not the only one to whom Hawthorne talked in this vein in the years before his marriage. When Julian Hawthorne was preparing a biography of his parents in the early 1880s he asked Elizabeth Peabody, Sophia's sister, to write up her recollection of Hawthorne during the period of his courtship. (Peabody had sought Hawthorne out after the publication of *Twice-Told Tales* [1837] and had introduced him to her sister Sophia.) Her memories can be questioned, since they pertain to a period almost fifty years behind her, but the statements she attributed to Hawthorne resemble those he wrote to Sophia. He is represented as saying,

"We do not live at our house, we only vegetate. Elizabeth [Hawthorne's older sister] never leaves her den; I have mine in the upper story, to which they always bring my meals, setting them down in a waiter at my door, which is always locked." "Don't you even see your mother?" said I. "Yes," said he, "in our little parlour. She comes and sits down with me and Louisa [Hawthorne's younger sister] after tea—and sometimes Louisa and I drink tea together. My mother and Elizabeth each take their meals in their rooms. My mother has never sat down to table with anybody, since my father's death." I said, "Do you think it is healthy to live so separated?" "Certainly not—it is no life at all—it is the misfortune of my life. It has produced a morbid consciousness that paralyzes my powers."[7]

Peabody then goes on to describe the reclusive widow Hawthorne who, through Julian Hawthorne's biography, found her way into the common understanding of Hawthorne's life. But in the very same description she comments on the widow in a manner that undercuts her own account. "Widow Hawthorne always looked as if she had walked out of an old picture, with her ancient costume, and a face of lovely sensibility, and great brightness—for she did not *seem* at all a victim of morbid sensibility, notwithstanding her all but Hindoo self-devotion to the manes of her husband. She was a person of fine understanding and a very cultivated mind."[8] It takes no great acumen to observe that Elizabeth Peabody could not have

known how the widow "always" looked or characterize her fine and cultivated sensibility if she had seldom left her bedroom. Indeed, the revealing
phrase "she did not *seem* at all a victim of morbid sensibility" shows that
Peabody's theories of Elizabeth Hathorne did not mesh with her memories.

Julian Hawthorne was a shrewd and tactful man who doubtless perceived
discrepancies in the material he had before him. However, given the filial
respect that was his announced motive in writing *Nathaniel Hawthorne and
His Wife,* he could not contradict views of events maintained by his parents.
He transmitted much of Elizabeth Peabody's account, and, building from
its description of the widow's reclusiveness, he attributed Hawthorne's
alienated temperament to the mother's unnatural behavior. Hawthorne
"was brought up," Julian wrote,

> under what might be considered special disadvantages. His mother, a woman
> of fine gifts but of extreme sensibility, lost her husband in her twenty-eighth
> year; and, from an exaggerated, almost Hindoo-like construction of the law of
> seclusion which the public taste of that day imposed upon widows, she with-
> drew entirely from society, and permitted the habit of solitude to grow upon
> her to such a degree that she actually remained a strict hermit to the end of her
> long life, or for more than forty years after Captain Hawthorne's death. . . . It
> is saying much for the sanity and healthfulness of the minds of these three
> children, that their loneliness distorted their judgment, their perception of the
> relation of things, so little as it did. (*Hawthorne and His Wife,* 1:4–5)

Only a few pages further on Julian approves Widow Hawthorne's views
on education and credits her with shaping her son's literary sensibilities by
encouraging him to read poetry, romance, and allegory. And he prints recollections by other informants which contradict the legend implicitly. He
never engages with the inconsistencies in his narrative. He needs the widow's morbidity for his thesis that Hawthorne was saved as man and artist
through marriage to Sophia. The story that Julian's father had invented as
an ardent lover is respectfully promulgated by a dutiful son.

Perhaps the damage done to Elizabeth Hathorne's reputation resulted inadvertently from Hawthorne's campaign to win Sophia. But, unquestionably, there is malice and hostility expressed toward her in the particular
legend Hawthorne devised. In some obscure manner she is held accountable
for Hawthorne's incarceration in the Castle Dismal. In the fairy-tale structure of the legend (a variant of "Beauty and the Beast," perhaps) she is
allocated the role of the enchanter whose evil spell must be undone by the
greater power of Sophia's beneficence. While the structure is demonstrably
out of keeping with known facts, it might well be an accurate, though necessarily figural, dramatization of Hawthorne's inner reality. If so, then its
representation of the mother as absent actually masks an oppressive sense
of her presence in his psychic world. But known facts do not permit us to
characterize Elizabeth Hathorne as domineering and possessive. The pres-

ence that is symbolized, then, is the presence of Hawthorne's own deep attachment to his mother.

II

Elizabeth Clarke Manning was born in 1780, the third of nine children of Miriam Lord (b. 1748) and Richard Manning (b. 1755). The other children were Mary, b. 1777; William, b. 1778; Richard, b. 1782; Robert, b. 1784; Maria, b. 1786; John, b. 1788; Priscilla, b. 1790; and Samuel, b. 1791: a total of five boys and four girls, all surviving to adulthood. The Mannings were a close-knit and late-marrying family who lived together in a large plain wooden house on Herbert Street in Salem. The head of the family, Richard Manning, began his working life as a blacksmith and progressed to owning a stagecoach line. Through this and other enterprises, including land investments, he built a comfortable estate.

Although none of the Manning children attended college—Nathaniel Hawthorne would be the first of the line to do so—there was considerable interest in education among them, and all (including Elizabeth) received some schooling. As adults, they were avid readers. Their religious views inclined toward the liberal, as they belonged to the Unitarian church. (Elizabeth and her sister Mary joined the Congregational church in 1806, however.) Elizabeth was the first to leave the Manning household, marrying Nathaniel Hathorne—as the name was then spelled—on 2 August 1801, when she was twenty-one years old. Hathorne, a sea captain, was five years older than she and had probably known her for some time because he lived across the back fence in a house on Union Street, where she moved upon marriage. There is evidence of a courtship of some duration: On a voyage two years earlier Nathaniel had written couplets to his "dear Betsey." The notebook in which these verses were inscribed became in time the property of his son, who copied over one of his father's amatory couplets: "In the Midest of all these dire allarms / I'll think dear Betsey on thy Charms." [9]

The household to which Elizabeth moved was presided over by Nathaniel's mother, a widow, and his two unmarried sisters also lived there. He and his brother Daniel, also a seafaring man, lived at home when they were on shore, which was seldom. He left for sea very shortly after his marriage and was away when Elizabeth bore her first child on 7 March 1802, a daughter also named Elizabeth, though commonly called Ebe.

The date of Ebe's birth was barely seven months after that of her parents' marriage. The significance of this seven-month's child has escaped notice, or at least mention, by virtually all of Hawthorne's biographers. But it could hardly have escaped the notice of the three women with whom Elizabeth was now domiciled, nor could it have been insignificant to them. Perhaps they were models for the hostile chorus of women at the beginning of *The Scarlet Letter*. For, if the historian Carl N. Degler is correct, "bridal pregnancies" in nineteenth-century America appear to have been quite rare—well under 10 percent—and, as evidence of sexual relations outside marriage, led to social stigma, which "fell like a hammer" on the errant.[10] Certainly among conservative segments of Salem society, including quite probably the old-fashioned and pious Hathornes, Elizabeth would have been harshly judged. The daughter Ebe grew up into a strikingly independent, only partially socialized woman, much as though she had been exempted from normal social expectations by those entrusted with rearing her. It is not improbable that Hawthorne's depiction of the wild Pearl had as much to do with his memory of Ebe as a child as with his observations of his own daughter Una.

Nathaniel Hathorne, Jr., was born on 4 July 1803; his father was again away at sea. A third child, Maria Louisa (called Louisa) arrived on 9 January 1808, barely two weeks after the father had again set sail, this time on what proved to be his last voyage. Early in the spring of that year he died of a fever in Surinam. He left Elizabeth a widow at the age of twenty-eight, with children aged six and four and an infant of a few months. In seven years of married life he had spent little more than seven months in Salem and had been absent from home at the births of all his children. We need hardly look further for sources of the image of a socially stigmatized woman abandoned to bear and rear her child alone.

Elizabeth, however, did not have to deal with her harsh lot alone, although support did not come from the Hathornes. Only a few months after receiving word of her husband's death she returned permanently to the Mannings. It was only prudent for her to do so, since the Hathornes were not well off and she had inherited nothing from Nathaniel. The Mannings were lower on the social scale than the Hathornes, but they were prospering, and the family included several vigorous men to look after its interest and conduct its business.

In addition, there is evidence of bad feeling between Elizabeth and her husband's family. Aunt Peabody in her recollection to Julian Hawthorne wrote that Elizabeth "was not happily affected by her husband's family— the Hathornes being of a very sharp and stern individuality—and when not cultivated, this appeared in oddity of temper."[11] Peabody's syntax is defective here, but her intent is to characterize the Hathornes as people who had, through want of cultivation, let a naturally stern individualism turn to oddness and eccentricity. It may well be that they, rather than Hawthorne's mother, went in for solitude. In any event, after she left them, Elizabeth Hathorne made little effort to keep up contacts, notwithstanding their continued proximity. Nor is any effort at relationship recorded from their side. On an occasional Sunday young Nathaniel went over and read the Bible in his grandmother's parlor, and the difference between that household of sharp and stern eccentrics and the cooperative Mannings must have been imaginatively striking.

The failure of the Hathornes to pursue a relationship with Elizabeth seems stranger than her defection from them, because in losing her they lost grandchildren who bore their name. But perhaps Elizabeth's misstep had disqualified her children as Hathornes in their eyes. Perhaps they viewed her as a social interloper, a female conniver using a woman's age-old trick to entrap a husband. Perhaps their old-fashioned piety led them to perceive her as sinful and fallen. Perhaps the causes of the falling-out were banal. But however it came about, it is impossible that Nathaniel Hawthorne could have absorbed any other perspective on this rift than that of his mother. Through his later readings in New England history he came to associate the early Puritans with the Hathornes, and this association may go far to explain the severity with which he turns their judging natures back on themselves. The Puritans versus a defenseless woman equalled the Hathornes versus his mother. If his mother herself suffered some sense of guilt or shame under the judgment, then her psychological turmoil filtering into her son's consciousness might linger to provide a model for Hester's complex ambivalences. In any event I should suppose that some heightened response to her situation underlies the poignant depiction of Hester's duress in *The Scarlet Letter*.

Of course, much would have been beyond his childish understanding. He would have to be old enough to mesh a knowledge of wedding and birth dates with a knowledge of biological processes before he could relate his mother's guilt, her children, and her separation from the Hathornes in one logical structure. But the aura of mystery—of the uncanny—which accompanies so many "adult doings" in his fiction from "My Kinsman, Major Molineux" to *The Marble Faun* may be an expression of just that deeply impressed early sense of bewilderment.

As he became more knowing, Hawthorne may have come to feel some guilt himself—guilt over siding with his mother, if she was indeed in the wrong, and guilt over carrying the name of people (perhaps sharing their traits) who had repudiated his mother for the sin of bearing children. *He* was one of those children, and when later in his life he was reading New England history and found a variant spelling of the paternal name— Hawthorne instead of Hathorne—his adoption of that orthography may have been a gesture of counterrepudiation.

Elizabeth's return to the Mannings has been seen as the first step in an intensifying withdrawal, but in fact the Mannings were much more in the world than the Hathornes, and there were enough of them to be a world in themselves. In 1808 the entire clan was intact at Herbert Street. This means that ten people were living there, ranging from Mrs. Manning, who was then sixty years old, to Samuel, who at age seventeen was only eleven years older than Hawthorne's sister Ebe. These numbers alone suggest an explanation for Hawthorne's love of solitude; he must have had almost none of it in his boyhood. The addition of Elizabeth and her three children to the Herbert Street group brought the total living in that house to an incredible (by modern middle-class standards) fourteen.

The three children were apparently regarded as a joint family charge, and their futures were discussed and determined upon by all. After the senior Manning died in 1813 and Richard settled in Raymond, Maine, to manage family property there the business head of the Mannings became Robert, while Mary ran the household. Given the limited biological understanding of the child, young Hawthorne probably never missed his dead father consciously, and since there were male heads of the Manning household in abundance he probably never grasped, at any level, the fact that he was lacking a father until he was beyond childhood. At the best this lack could only have been grasped intellectually, for in his emotional world he had several. The evidence is that he missed not one more father but a home that might be presided over by his *mother* without the intervention of any other adult. For a while this seemed likely: Elizabeth considered settling near Richard in Maine and running her own farm. She actually tried this way of life on and off for six years, and, though Hawthorne often had to stay behind in Salem for his schooling, he was anxious for her to make Raymond her permanent residence.

"I hope, Dear Mother," he wrote from Salem on 19 June 1821,

> that you will not be tempted by any entreaties to return to Salem to live. You can never have so much comfort here as you now enjoy. You are now undisputed mistress of your own House. Here you would have to submit to the authority of Miss Manning. If you remove to Salem, I shall have no Mother to return to during the College vacations. . . . If you remain where you are, think how delightfully the time will pass with all your children around you, shut out from the world with nothing to disturb us. It will be a second garden of Eden. (*Letters,* 15:150)

Two elements of Hawthorne's imagery are noteworthy. First, Raymond was at that time not a garden but a forest setting (although, perhaps not insignificantly, a rose bush grew before Elizabeth Hathorne's door).[12] Ever after, Hawthorne visualized Eden not as a garden but a forest, albeit that vision was often obscured by subsequent grief and loss in his fiction. Too, the "first" Garden of Eden had no children in it, while Hawthorne's second Eden conspicuously lacks an Adam. If Hawthorne secretly casts himself in Adam's role, then he is his mother's son and lover both. For him Eden is a benign matriarchy.

A year earlier he had written to his mother expressing reluctance to go to college and, more generally, to grow up. "Oh how I wish I was again with you, with nothing to do but go a gunning. But the happiest days of my life are gone. Why was I not a girl that I might have been pinned all my life to my mother's apron" (*Letters*, 15:117). Given the conspicuous gun image, Hawthorne is not complaining about his gender but about social rules that force a boy out of the Garden of Eden into the cold patriarchal world while permitting a girl to remain enclosed in the maternal paradise. The search for the lost *mother*, rather than the lost father, underlies much of the story patterning in his mature fiction, as does the scheme of flight from the patriarchy. The idea of the matriarchy retained a powerful hold on his imagination throughout life, and he could only view patriarchal social organizations—the only kind he knew, though others could be dreamed of—with enmity.

The enmity may owe its origins precisely to Elizabeth's return to Salem. Hawthorne may have been hurt and angry that his mother disregarded his wishes in favor of her siblings' entreaties. He may have resented his failure to conform her life to his plans; a residue of bitterness may have indeed affected his relation to her after he graduated from Bowdoin and had to come back to Herbert Street instead of Raymond. But he could fault the Mannings too. Hawthorne was glad enough to leave Herbert Street when he was married, but in fact he never felt at home again.[13] Home was mother.

By 1825 the Manning family had suffered from time and circumstance. Only six were still living at Herbert Street when Hawthorne came back from Bowdoin, although some of the others were domiciled close by. Briefly, the senior Richard Manning had died in 1813, his son Richard had gone to live in Maine, and John had disappeared the same year (presumably lost at sea). Maria died in 1814. Priscilla married in 1817 and Robert in 1824; both moved out but remained in Salem. When Hawthorne was married in 1842 the household had been so far depleted as to consist only of his mother and two sisters. Mrs. Manning died in 1826, William went into bachelor quarters, and Samuel died in 1833. At the time that Hawthorne was stressing his solitude to the Peabody sisters, Mary was still living at Herbert Street, but she died in 1841. Robert died in 1842.

The probable cumulative effect of all these deaths on Hawthorne has never been appreciated, possibly because he said and wrote little about them. Whatever their effects on him, however, they must have been disastrous for Elizabeth, who had made her whole life within the family circle. It is useful to remember that when Hawthorne was married she was mourning for the sister to whom she had been closest and was soon to lose a brother. If she seemed somewhat reclusive in the years when the Peabody sisters came to know her, it may have been merely because she was sad. Or because she did not change with her changing world: She was approaching the age of sixty and may have seen no way to fill the void that her departing siblings created. She did remain close to her surviving sister Priscilla (Mrs. Dike) and to Robert's widow, Rebecca.

In the years that Hawthorne was living at Herbert Street after graduation he may well have been the obscurest man of letters in America (as he poetically characterized himself), but he certainly could not have been the most solitary. He may indeed have had to resort to such devices as taking meals in his room and locking his door in order to get some writing done in that busy house. Still he walked and visited, went on trips with his uncle Samuel, worked on a magazine in Boston (with help from Ebe). He shared his literary plans and agonized over his failures with his mother and sisters. Ebe selected books for him from the Salem Athenaeum. The three knew about his anonymous first novel *Fanshawe,* although Sophia never learned of it. Ebe was able partly to reconstruct many years later the early aborted projects for framed collections of short stories. All three women helped him to collect copies of the pieces printed in *Twice-Told Tales* and to prepare the manuscript for publication.[14] Louisa made him a shirt when he went to Brook Farm, while Elizabeth sewed buttons on his trousers and rejoiced in Osgood's flattering portrait of her son which he had made for her. Louisa, who carried on most of the correspondence with him while he was at the farm, bemoaned the infrequency of his letters and visits in a manner that suggests ordinary family intimacy.[15] That Hawthorne was much petted and greatly adored he implicitly admits (Castle Dismal notwithstanding) in a letter to Sophia gently chiding her for having taken offense at something he had written earlier: "Dearest, I beseech you grant me freedom to be careless and wayward—for I have had such freedom all my life" (*Letters,* 15:332).

When Hawthorne fell in love with Sophia Peabody late in 1838 he was thirty-five years old. No evidence survives about whether his mother and sisters had hoped that he would marry, or wished him to remain single or simply hoped for his happiness whatever he did. Given their general fondness, the last is the most likely possibility. Certainly, however, they never expected him to *conceal* an attachment, and when he finally announced his engagement a scant month before his wedding Ebe at least was angered beyond the ability to forgive or to rejoice in his happiness. She wrote to Sophia:

> Your approaching union with my brother makes it incumbent upon me to offer you the assurances of my sincere desire for your mutual happiness. With regard to my sister and myself, I hope nothing will ever occur to render your future intercourse with us other than agreeable, particularly as it need not be so frequent or so close as to require more than reciprocal good will, if we do not happen to suit each other in our new relationship. I write thus plainly, because my brother has desired me to say only what was true; though I do not recognize his right so to speak of truth, after keeping us so long in ignorance of this

affair. But I do believe him when he says that this was not in accordance with your wishes, for such concealment must naturally be unpleasant, and besides, what I know of your amiable disposition convinces me that you would not give us unnecessary pain. It was especially due to my mother that she should long ago have been made acquainted with the engagement of her only son.[16]

To some degree Ebe never forgave her brother for his deviousness. "We were in those [early] days almost absolutely obedient to him," she wrote to Julian. "I do not quite approve of either obedience or concealment" (*Hawthorne and His Wife*, 1:124–125). And despite her comment about Sophia's amiable disposition, she never warmed to her brother's wife. "I might as well tell you that [Sophia] is the only human being whom I really dislike," a late letter to relatives said. "Though she is dead, that makes no difference. I could have lived with her in apparent peace, but I could not have lived long; the constraint would have killed me." [17] Perhaps Hawthorne's having chosen so timidly conventional a woman caused Ebe to reassess his character.

But Elizabeth responded in a different way, as Hawthorne wrote to Sophia:

> Sweetest, scarcely had I arrived here, when our mother came out of her chamber, looking better and more cheerful than I have seen her this some time, and enquired about the health and well-being of my Dove! Very kindly, too. Then was thy husband's heart much lightened; for I knew that almost every agitating circumstance of her life had hitherto cost her a fit of sickness; and I knew not but it might be so now. Foolish me, to doubt that my mother's love would be wise, like all other genuine love! . . . Now I am very happy—happier than my naughtiness deserves. . . . At first her heart was troubled, because she knew that much of outward as well as inward fitness was requisite to secure thy foolish husband's peace; but, gradually and quietly, God has taught her that all is good, and so, thou dearest wife, we shall have her fullest blessing and concurrence. (*Letters*, 15:628–629)

Despite his mother's loving acceptance, Hawthorne's concealment had done her a great wrong, and he knew it. His little boy's confession of naughtiness refers to more than that concealment, however. He was also confessing the naughtiness of his involvement with Sophia to his mother. And, too (what he did not confess), there was the naughtiness of the way in which he had misrepresented her and his relation with her, to the Peabody sisters (and perhaps to others as well). In fact, I surmise that his complex sense of acting in bad faith toward Elizabeth led him to desire concealment; this concealment became another act of bad faith, in a chain of the sort that Hawthorne's fiction sets out so knowingly. Indeed, for the rest of his life Hawthorne was caught by that act of bad faith since he was never able to rectify it, except in the oblique language of his fiction.

And I suspect that more than lies about Castle Dismal and solitary meals burdened Hawthorne's conscience. The constellation of images in which he represented his case to Sophia suggested, as I have said above, that Sophia was to save him from and substitute for his mother. The image of the one woman annihilates the image of the other; on the inner stage, where the image is the person, to let Sophia rescue him is to kill his mother. No evidence exists to suggest that Sophia or Elizabeth regarded each other as rivals; the narrative Hawthorne projected derives (to the extent that it is sincere) from his own emotions and not fact. The narrative suggests—what the belated adolescent quality of his romance with Sophia tends to confirm—that his attachment to Elizabeth was so deep and pervasive that he experienced his love for another woman as doing some kind of violence to her, as a killing infidelity. At the same time, if Hawthorne blamed her for his long years of "enchantment" in the Herbert Street house while the world of adult sexual relationships passed him by, then he must also assuredly have *wanted* to kill her to gain his freedom. And so on, through the complex layers of the heart that Hawthorne knew so well.

Sophia probably caught no glimmer of these depths in his talk of naughtiness, but we can see that she was not entirely satisfied with his explanations because she later worked out a tale that made Ebe (conveniently) the culprit in the concealment. Obligingly, though in revealing language, Julian transmitted her explanation: Ebe, wishing to come between the two lovers, let Hawthorne know that "news of his relation with Miss Sophia would give [Elizabeth] a shock that might endanger her life." As a loving son, Hawthorne was naturally "not prepared to face the idea of defying and perhaps 'killing' his mother" (*Hawthorne and His Wife,* 1:196–197). This story does not withstand a moment's scrutiny. Ebe could not have forestalled the announcement of an engagement that she didn't know about; her blunt nature was incompatible with concealment; and, of course, Hawthorne knew how his mother was likely to react as well as Ebe did. But if *Ebe* had not persuaded Hawthorne that his engagement would kill his mother, he had probably persuaded himself.

Elizabeth declined to be killed, however, and hence not even a temporary break in her relations with Hawthorne actually took place. Granted, she did not attend his wedding, but there are other explanations for this than hostility. During his sojourn at the Old Manse he had more than one occasion to return to Salem, and inevitably he stayed at Herbert Street, dining and chatting with his mother and sisters, as his letters to Sophia record. When he returned with Sophia and his child Una to Salem upon being appointed to the customhouse, he took up residence in Herbert Street while looking for his own home. He did this as a matter of course. The stay lasted several months—longer than anticipated—and seems to have produced tension. But we must remember that Sophia never became a favorite with the three women, nor did she greatly care for them. We find her writing to her mother in January of 1846, for example, that "on many accounts it would be inconvenient to remain in this house. Madame Hawthorne and Louisa are too much out of health to take care of a child, and I do not like to have Una in the constant presence of unhealthy persons. I have never let her go into Madame Hawthorne's mysterious chamber since November, partly on this account, and partly because it is so much colder than the nursery, and has no carpet on it" (*Hawthorne and His Wife*, 1:307–308). A woman who regarded her husband's closest female relatives only as babysitters, described them as "unhealthy persons," and kept her child out of grandmother's room for many weeks because it lacked a carpet cannot be imagined to have encouraged family intimacy. It seems clear that a major goal on Sophia's part was to preserve the autonomy of her own new family.

Nevertheless, when a house (on Mall Street) that finally suited them was found it was determined that Elizabeth, Ebe, and Louisa should join them permanently. The house, Sophia wrote to her mother, fortunately had a suite of rooms

> wholly distant from ours so that we shall only meet when we choose to do so. Madame Hawthorne is so uninterfering, of so much delicacy, that I shall never know she is near excepting when I wish it; and she has so much kindness and sense and spirit she will be a great resource in emergencies. . . . It is no small satisfaction to know that Mrs. Hawthorne's remainder of life will be glorified by the presence of these children [Julian had been born] and of her own son. I am so glad to win her out of the Castle Dismal, and from the mysterious chamber, into which no mortal ever peeped till Una was born and Julian—for they alone entered the penetralia. Into that chamber the sun never shines. Into these rooms in Mall Street it blazes without stint. (*Hawthorne and His Wife*, 1:314)

One wonders how Sophia knew so much about Elizabeth's room if none but the little children had ever entered it or what opportunities the widow would have had to show her kindness, sense, and spirit if she herself never left it. Indeed, Sophia's obtuseness is equalled only by her complacency (or is some complex defensiveness working itself out here?). What sort of rescue would it be for "Madame Hawthorne" if her lot was to wait in her chamber until called on for help in an emergency?

However, Elizabeth Hathorne had her own kind of spunk, it seems. She made her presence known after all. She began to cook items of food for Hawthorne that he had loved as a boy and even to carry bowls of coffee to him in his study as he sat writing. Though Sophia was appalled, Hawthorne made no objection. Sophia unbent so far, finally, as to obtain from Elizabeth a recipe for an Indian pudding of which her husband was especially fond.[18]

Hawthorne's feelings about his mother in the years after his marriage are not recoverable, for he spoke of these personal matters only to Sophia and then necessarily in a highly oblique language designed as much to veil as reveal. Sophia regularly read his journal, and therefore he had to compose his entries with her expectations in mind. Nevertheless, we can be sure that the threatened loss of his position at the customhouse after the election of 1848 must have been particularly horrifying because he had assumed responsibility for his mother's welfare and undertaken to make a home for her "remainder of life." While he could be sure that the surviving Mannings would provide for her (as they did for Ebe and Louisa after Elizabeth's death), the question was not her physical or even psychological welfare but his own.

Certainly, then, her sudden serious illness and death at just the moment when he became unable to provide for her must have seemed profoundly significant to a man who felt so strongly the force that the inner life exerted on the outer world. It is in the context of a host of like thoughts, which he would not articulate plainly, that we must read his extraordinary journal entry penned the day before his mother died:

> I love my mother; but there has been, ever since my boyhood, a sort of coldness of intercourse between us, such as is apt to come between persons of strong feelings, if they are not managed rightly. I did not expect to be much moved at the time—that is to say, not to feel any overpowering emotion struggling, just then—though I knew that I should deeply remember and regret her. Mrs. Dike was in the chamber. Louisa pointed to a chair near the bed, but I was moved to kneel down close by my mother, and take her hand. She knew me, but could only murmur a few indistinct words—among which I understood an injunction to take care of my sisters. Mrs. Dike left the chamber, and then I found the tears slowly gathering in my eyes. I tried to keep them down; but it would not be—I kept filling up, till, for a few moments, I shook with sobs. For a long time, I knelt there, holding her hand; and surely it is the darkest hour I ever lived. Afterwards, I stood by the open window, and looked through the crevice of the curtain. . . . I saw my little Una of the golden locks, looking very beautiful; and so full of spirit and life, that she was life itself. And then I looked at my poor dying mother; and seemed to see the whole of human existence at once, standing in the dusty midst of it. (*Centenary*, 8:429)

Though constrained to repeat the legend of coldness since boyhood (which his boyhood letters so decisively refute), and to finish this entry with an expression of hope in the afterlife suitable for Sophia's eyes, Hawthorne nevertheless permits the depths of his grief to come to light. Connecting Una to his mother through himself, and making this linked chain of three comprise the whole of human existence, he effectively expunges Sophia from the record, makes Una his mother's child, and hence makes his mother both wife and mother to him. But these were not his last words on the subject. His real tribute to her, and to her influence, was to come in *The Scarlet Letter*.

III

The Scarlet Letter cannot be called a work of autobiography or even biography as we use these terms to refer to recognizable literary genres. But this discussion is meant to demonstrate the way in which it, along with "The Custom-House," contains autobiographical and biographical material (his mother's biography) and is engendered specifically by Hawthorne's experience of his mother's death. It is not inaccurate to describe *The Scarlet Letter* as Hawthorne's response to his mother's death. This response is composed of a number of elements difficult to extricate separately from the one dense texture of the romance. The fact that the woman it writes about is dead is paramount, for her death provides the motive for writing and also the freedom to write. The consciously articulated intentions of *The Scarlet Letter*, one might say, are to rescue its heroine from the oblivion of death and to rectify the injustices that were done to her in life, and both of these intentions take death as their starting point.

It is possible, within the elegiac frame of the work, to point to several autobiographical and biographical strands, some pertaining to the mother herself, some to the mother and son, and some to the son alone. First, *The Scarlet Letter* makes a noble attempt to realize the mother as a separate person with an independent existence in her own right; such an attempt represents the son's very belated recognition that his mother was a human being with her own life and consciousness, something more than a figure in his own carpet. As a youth of seventeen begging his mother to live in Maine, Hawthorne had his own Garden of Eden in mind, but he never doubted that his ideal would be hers also and that a life shut off from the world with her children would content her. Perhaps as a mature man he began to know better.

Yet in realizing the separate individuality, he must make Hester a mother, for that is what Elizabeth inescapably was not only as part of his reality but as part of hers also. So he tries to understand what motherhood might mean for a person who does have, as all human beings do, a sense of independent existence. The way in which Pearl both impinges on and defines her mother's selfhood vividly dramatizes the claims that children make on their mothers.

Yet even as he strives to provide Hester with an independent existence as the center of her own world, Hawthorne maintains a double focus. Events in *The Scarlet Letter* never work themselves free of the constant voice of the narrator. We are always aware that the character Hester depends for her reality on the act of narrative generosity which is creating her. Here Hawthorne reverses the biological relation of mother and child and becomes the creator of his mother. It seems to me that such a reversal not only underlies all representational art but also responds to a specific set of wishes in the particular author writing at this particular time—the wish to be free of life-long dependency on maternal power, the wish to have one's mother all to oneself (even if that possession can be attained only after death).

But—another twist in the cable—Hester's instant-by-instant dependence on the narrator-author is reversed again in the testimony of "The Custom-House" where "Hester" is defined as a creative force *outside* the romance which is responsible for his inspiration and his ability to write about her. Thus, there is a transcending symbiosis of symbol and artist, mother and son—each created by the other and each dependent on the other for artistic life: the artist dependent on the image which inspires him and the image dependent on the artist for representation.

There is, finally, an inevitable gap between the image and the being who has inspired it and whom it represents; the image is the refraction of the mother's influence in the son's psychic world. And so the work becomes an ambitious attempt to give his mother her own reality and bring to life her image in his mind as well and somehow to keep these distinct. Mediating between the two intentions of biography and autobiography, Hawthorne as narrator creates a structure in which the identities of the two subjects alternately assert themselves independently and then merge into a larger unity. The unity is best symbolized in the icon of mother and child—Divine Maternity—which is thrust on our attention in the first scaffold scene of *The Scarlet Letter*.

Beyond this complex personal intention, Hawthorne is also concerned to make his romance a public document, and hence much of the work of his text goes into generalizing, extending, and depersonalizing the meaning of his core images. The maternal symbol at the heart of *The Scarlet Letter* is contained within a sophisticated narrative structure, and this structure is distanced from the reader by the prefatory "Custom-House" essay. The personal meanings of the romance are processed though a sequence of narrators (the narrator of "The Custom-House" is not identical to the narrator of *The Scarlet Letter*) who are deeply aware of what, in "The Custom-House," Hawthorne refers to as the reader's right—the reader's right not to have unwanted confidences forced upon him.

Some of the resemblances between Hester's and Elizabeth's stories will, I hope, already be evident from the account provided of her life: the questionable circumstances of their children's births, their repudiation by those assigned society's judging function, the absence of spouse and abandonment of the child entirely to the mother. Facing down Hester's critics and overcoming presumed reader resistance to her, Hawthorne goes beyond forgiveness to complete acquittal. The chief agency of Hester's exoneration is

Pearl. Although the narrative perspective is resolutely adult, it silently privileges Pearl's point of view toward her mother over all the others. Her very existence is the narrative's first and last fact, and it legitimizes the act of her mother which engendered her. We cannot doubt that Pearl has a right to be and hence cannot fault the mother for bringing her into existence.

Essentially, too, Pearl is her mother's child only. Though society and Hester are aware that a man participated in the act, Pearl has no sense of this necessity, and hers is the view that the reader is forced to adopt. That is, we know that Hester has had a lover, but we never really "know" that Pearl has a father. Through Pearl and because of her, then, Hester takes precedence over Dimmesdale and over the society that tries to put him and his cohorts at the organizing center of the fictional world. The world of the romance is organized around her. Matriarchy prevails. Autobiographically speaking, Hawthorne identifies himself once and for all as his *mother's* child.

To be sure Hester pays a high price for her legitimation, the price of confinement within her motherhood for most of her life. Throughout the romance she is virtually never separated from Pearl; the image she represents, we remember, is inextricably linked to maternity rather than selfhood or even womanhood. The brookside scene in the forest, for all its multiple possibilities of interpretation, dramatizes at some basic level the need of the child to possess the mother all to herself. Pearl recognizes at once through the mother's changed appearance, as Hester blossoms out into relation with Dimmesdale, that the mother is no longer merely and entirely her mother. She cannot abide this. Imperiously, she requires that Hester reassume motherhood as her sole reality before she will return to her. The *A* at this point means only maternity: The complex, bewildering, and ambiguous set of events which have set Hester's course for life are ultimately reduced to the "sin" of having given birth to a child.

The tensions between Hester's motherhood and personhood, between the needs of her own life and the needs of her child, between the person herself and the figure in the son's tale, are resolved at a higher level of the story than Pearl's perceptions. The narrator, taking the roles of her prophet, son, and lover simultaneously, creates an image now responsive to its own rhythms and now to the rhythms of the two beings who impinge on her—Pearl, her figured child, and the author-narrator, who in many respects is her child grown up. The image to which both subscribe, and within which they enclose Hester, is the Garden of Eden, the benign matriarchy.

One is reminded not only of Hawthorne's adolescent letters but of a lengthy passage from "Main Street," which is the only tale we are sure that Hawthorne meant to include along with *The Scarlet Letter* in the larger collection he was originally planning. "Main Street" is a rapid survey of New

England history, and it begins before the patriarchy comes to impose its civilization on Western soil, with the timeless land existing under the rule of a woman:

> You perceive, at a glance, that this is the ancient and primitive wood,—the ever-youthful and venerably old,—verdant with new twigs, yet hoary, as it were, with the snowfall of innumerable years, that have accumulated upon its intermingled branches. The white man's axe has never smitten a single tree; his footstep has never crumpled a single one of the withered leaves, which all the autumns since the flood have been harvesting beneath. Yet, see! along through the vista of impending boughs, there is already a faintly-traced path. . . . What footsteps can have worn this half-seen path? Hark! Do we not hear them now rustling softly over the leaves? We discern an Indian woman—a majestic and queenly woman, or else her spectral image does not represent her truly—for this is the great Squaw Sachem, whose rule, with that of her sons, extends from Mystic to Agawam. That red chief, who stalks by her side, is Wappa-cowet, her second husband, the priest and magician. (*Centenary*, 11:50–51)

The white man—adulthood for the race—has arrived, and the happy days of mother rule retreat to legend and imagination. But within imagination their existence is powerful and pervasive. *The Scarlet Letter* is Hawthorne's testimony to the existence of that inner world ruled over by a woman. The woman in that inner world could never die.

The Scarlet Letter is the only one of Hawthorne's long romances whose origin can be attributed to a specific autobiographical impulse. Alerted by the kinds of concerns it manifests, one can, however, perceive certain biographical implications in the others. Although there is not a trace of the Squaw Sachem in *The House of the Seven Gables,* this is a quintessential family story whose deepest meaning resides, ultimately, precisely in her absence. For it tells a tale of the submersion of individual identity and the total loss of happiness and freedom in a male-ruled household. The reason why the alternatives of Pyncheon and Maule can provide no resolution to the excesses of the other is that each remains in essence a patriarchy. Eliminating Pyncheon, the hero Holgrave has nothing to substitute but—himself. One can interpret the families of Pyncheon and Maule as Hathorne and Manning, respectively, the run-down aristocrats and the rising laborers, and recall that neither permitted Elizabeth to be mistress in her own house. From another vantage point the Pyncheon house can be seen as an amalgamation of *both* Hathorne and Manning into a composite figure of hated family oppression, an overwhelming symbol of patriarchal usurpation. In sum the repudiation of father and fathers imaged forth as a minor point in *The Scarlet Letter* as it defended Hester's priority here becomes the central autobiographical statement.

In this context Phoebe can be only Sophia, as indeed we are asked to understand by other indications (Hawthorne frequently called Sophia Phoebe).

Her role in the rescue, or failed rescue, plot is only superficial, however. She is fundamentally unequal to the other powers in the story and at crucial points in the narrative is shown to be susceptible to victimization by them. Hawthorne, I think, is here beginning to realize, or at least to signify, that Sophia was having far less efficacy in his life than he had originally expected.

That the simplicity of Sophia's imagination was more and more seeming like shallowness rather than infinite depths is more overtly suggested in *The Blithedale Romance* and *The Marble Faun*. In both romances the hated male rulers are abetted, albeit without much awareness, by female figures whose task is to supplant or discredit a more matriarchal or maternal type. (It must be granted that in *The Blithedale Romance* the matriarchal type is badly flawed, as she is to a lesser degree in *The Marble Faun,* so no possibility for restoring the matriarchy is seriously represented in either romance.) In *The Blithedale Romance* this dovelike supplanter appears at the beginning as part of the degraded urban complex that the narrator-protagonist wishes to reject for a pastoral ideal. The proper Arcadian values are established at once when the narrator finds Zenobia ruling over Blithedale, but her initial matronly and queenlike authority is systematically undercut and discredited by the collusion of all the other characters until she is driven to suicide. The dove is left in command of the field. But the survivors of the battle are merely the walking wounded, and her lifelong task is to nurse and guard them—a parody of matriarchy, making *Blithedale* in some sense the dark inverse of *The Scarlet Letter.*

Something similar happens in the tortured symbolism and obscure narrative line of *The Marble Faun,* where Kenyon's election of Hilda, the dove transmuted into a steely virgin, is equivalent to retreat from the complexities of an adult world. Hilda's cutting simplifications and platitudes masquerade as a worldview which the sculptor, finding himself unable to deal with the implications of adult relations between the sexes, gladly espouses. The babyland to which Kenyon and Hilda are returning at the end of the romance is nothing like the ageless forest presided over by the Indian Queen, who, disguised in this romance as Venus, has been rejected by Kenyon on the campagna in favor of Hilda. But Hawthorne does not blame Sophia.

Toward the close of his literary career Hawthorne, working up his English essays for publication, inserted a passage into "Outside Glimpses of English Poverty" for which there is no notebook source:

> Nothing, as I remember, smote me with more grief and pity . . . than to hear a gaunt and ragged mother priding herself on the pretty ways of her ragged and skinny infant, just as a young matron might, when she invites her lady-friends to admire her plump, white-robed darling in the nursery. Indeed, no womanly characteristic seemed to have altogether perished out of these poor souls. It was the very same creature whose tender torments make the rapture

of our young days, whom we love, cherish, and protect, and rely upon in life and death, and whom we delight to see beautify her beauty with rich robes and set it off with jewels. (*Centenary*, 10:283)

The image goes beyond the gaunt and ragged mother, beyond the young matron, and even beyond Elizabeth Hathorne to the archetype, the Magna Mater enthroned in a blaze of jewels in her son's imagination. Even at this late date the imagination remains centrally possessed of and by her image. Elizabeth had been dead for fourteen years. Hawthorne would be dead within a year himself. In this ardent image he indicates that her presence will survive with him to the end.

4

Concepts of the Romance in Hawthorne's America

Perhaps the single most powerful theoretical concept in modern American literary history and criticism has been that of the "romance" as a distinct and defining American fictional form. It has been a concept indispensable for constructing a canon of major works; membership in the romance category has been a significant criterion for inclusion or exclusion. Accordingly, the issue of whether or not a given work can be demonstrated to be a romance has become important in critical analysis and controversy. The idea of romance as a specific and specifically American genre mediates between a conviction that literature and the works comprising it are valuable in themselves, important human achievements worthy of study, and a simultaneous rejection of merely formalist, aesthetic, or affective modes of assessment and analysis. Much as they loved literature and were dedicated to it, major post–World War II critics located its significance or seriousness in the enhanced cultural understanding it might be brought to provide. In the (revealing) words of the *Literary History of the United States,* ours is "a literature which is most revealing when studied as a by-product of the American experience."[1] The term *by-product* speaks volumes.

From the earliest days of the republic literary critics had sought to encourage and defend an American literature, and debate over whether or not such a literature would be defined by its national qualities raged on through the 1830s (although it lapsed thereafter).[2] Whether consciously or not, the scholars contributing to the *Literary History of the United States* incorporated the traditions of American literary nationalism into their study, and in so doing they reflected the critical habits of their decade, habits under whose aegis the works that we read and study and teach today were assembled and made coherent. To look in literature for the essence of "the American experience" was necessarily to seek for something that could be found in the literature of no other nation and, indeed, to identify nationality as the basis of literary creation. But since literature is not, or should not be, merely an envelope for message, that "something" had to be a form. Most specialists in American literature have accepted the idea that in the absence of history (or a sense of history) as well as a social field, our literature has consistently taken an ahistorical, mythical shape for which the term *romance* is formally and historically appropriate.

The study most responsible for establishing this distinction was, of course, Richard Chase's *The American Novel and its Tradition*.[3] In that enormously influential book Chase differentiated the American from the British "novel"—or, more properly, the *truly* American from the British novel—by saying that there was an observable American variant more properly called a romance. In doing this he drew on ideas expounded earlier by Lionel Trilling in his 1940 *Partisan Review* article on V. L. Parrington.[4] Trilling's essay argued that the social thinness of early American life made the dense realistic novel associated with English authors either impossible to write in America or untrue to American experience (reality) if it was in fact written. Henry Nash Smith's *Virgin Land* and R. W. B. Lewis's *The American Adam* had also contributed to the construction of the idea that there was a singularly American work as well as what it was like,[5] but it was Chase who labeled it, and a proliferation of subsequent studies arguing that this or that work is or is not an American romance suggests that the label may have become more important than the contents.

When Chase distinguished *romance* from *novel* he assumed that the two terms already had different meanings; his usage, one might say, applied common and broad definitions to a restricted field, no doubt making the term *romance* a little sharper, more focused than it was in everyday parlance but still relying on a well-understood definitional consensus. What is more he indicated that the definitional distinction he was drawing on had existed in America for a long time and had in fact entered into the historical production of the type of fiction he was now identifying; in support of this position he offered statements by William Gilmore Simms (his preface to the 1853 revision of *The Yemassee*—although Chase, citing only the original date of the work's publication, created the impression that Simms had written his preface in 1835) and Nathaniel Hawthorne (his 1851 preface to *The House of the Seven Gables*). These statements, especially Hawthorne's, provided good evidence that major authors in a key developmental period in American literary history were consciously striving to create fictions that were not novels and that they were doing so according to a distinction current in their own time.

When a writer calls his work a Romance [Hawthorne wrote], it need hardly be observed that he wishes to claim a certain latitude, both as to its fashion and material, which he would not have felt himself entitled to assume, had he professed to be writing a Novel. The latter form of composition is presumed to aim at a very minute fidelity, not merely to the possible, but to the probable and ordinary course of man's experience. The former—while, as a work of art, it must rigidly subject itself to laws, and while it sins unpardonably, so far as it may swerve aside from the truth of the human heart—has fairly a right to present that truth under circumstances, to a great extent, of the writer's own choosing or creation. If he think fit, also, he may so manage his atmospherical medium as to bring out or mellow the lights and deepen and enrich the shadows of the picture. He will be wise, no doubt, to make a very moderate use of the privileges here stated, and, especially, to mingle the Marvellous rather as a slight, delicate, and evanescent flavor, than as any portion of the actual substance of the dish offered to the Public. He can hardly be said, however, to commit a literary crime, even if he disregard this caution.[6]

Such phrases as "it need hardly be observed" and "is presumed to" lull the unwary into believing that Hawthorne was indeed working within categories known to and shared by his contemporaries. A self-aware tradition of American romance was said to have originated in the practice of Charles Brockden Brown (Chase wrote: "in the writings of Brockden Brown, Cooper, and Simms we have the first difficult steps in the adaptation of English romance to American conditions and needs," a comment that suggests authorial intention; and Leslie Fiedler, who referred to Brown throughout *Love and Death in the American Novel,* called him "the inventor of the American writer").[7] The tradition stretched down to Faulkner and beyond, involving all our major authors in a massive effort to create a "real" American literature. In fact, such involvement can be taken as a sign and measure of authorial seriousness and hence of a work's suitability for serious critical analysis.

But a study of those texts in which ideas about fiction current in Hawthorne's time are most often discernible—specifically, reviews of long fiction appearing between 1820 and 1860 in a variety of major American magazines[8]—reveals what we after all might have expected: that Hawthorne's distinction between *romance* and *novel,* a distinction which has carried so much weight for subsequent criticism, was idiosyncratic, his own. In fact, the term *romance* turns out to have been used so broadly and so inconsistently in the era that in any given instance of trying to fix its meaning the critic or writer was evidently indulging in a creative rather than a descriptive activity.

It is important, though perhaps not immediately central to my argument here, to observe that the location of the uniquely American in the romance form involves a silent slide from literature in general to literature as fiction. It is certainly a result of that slide that so many nonfiction works, like *Walden* or *Nature,* have been treated as though they were fiction, a treatment that obscures the (possible) generic determinants that it supposes to be un-important or nonexistent. By 1840, to be sure, the novel had established itself as the most popular of literary forms. Some were claiming that it was the best form, others that it was the form most suited to the age. Successful novelists were certainly the preeminent literary celebrities. But few in that time would have been willing to restrict a definition of literature to its man-ifestations in fiction.[9] But it is central to an understanding of the term *romance* in this period to understand that, in an ambience in which a variety of now obsolete genre distinctions were employed, the term *romance* was deployed in the main, indeed massively so, simply as a synonym for the term *novel*.[10] Let me cite several from among hundreds and hundreds of possible examples.

From the *North American Review:* Cooper "has laid the foundations of American romance, and is really the first who has deserved the appellation of a distinguished novel writer" (July 1822); a review in July 1825 discussed ten "Recent American Novels," two of which included the word *romance* in their subtitles; a review of Italian "romances" in April 1838 alternately spoke of the "historical novel" and the "historical romance"; an October 1856 review of new popular "novels" began, "with the romance which stands at the head of our list" and ended, "we have selected these three novels from the multitude about us"; an April 1859 review of a novel by Bulwer commented that "there are so many different ways of doing one or the other of these things through the medium of a good romance, that the novel which fails of them all cannot redeem itself"; and a review in October 1859 described *Adam Bede* as "a romance of common life."

From the *New York Review:* "the common prejudice of sober men against novels is well founded. . . . But romance may become, and often is, an impressive medium for the transmission of truth" (April 1839). From the *Literary World: Lady Alice* is "considerably above the common level of mod-ern Romances. . . . It is a genuine novel, with a plot and a catastrophe" (21 July 1849); "it is very hard work nowadays for the novelist to construct an effective romance out of those meagre materials which, fifty years ago, were considered all-sufficient" (17 August 1850). From *Graham's:* "some of the most deleterious books we have are romances. . . . Hence, in criticising a novel, it becomes important to examine the tendency of the work" (May 1848); *Vanity Fair* is "one of the most striking novels of the season. It bears little resemblance in tone, spirit, and object, to the other popular romances of the day" (November 1848); a May 1850 review described *The Scarlet Letter* as "a beautiful and touching romance" and asserted that readers "will hardly be prepared for a novel of so much tragic interest and tragic power"; a review of *Westward Ho!* in July 1855 spoke of "the evident intention of the novelist" which "the romance evinces"; Charles Reade, it noted in August

1855, "is not merely a romancer, but a man of vigorous and original individuality, and his novels are not only good, but . . . ."

On 2 June 1838 the *New York Mirror* reviewed a new "novel" happily not "executed in the worst style of modern romances." *Knickerbocker* for October 1838 observed that "we live in such a novel-reading age, that every work of romance, possessing more than ordinary excellence, is seized on with avidity, and made popular at once." A review in the same journal in June 1843 began: "In the romance before us, as in his previous novels, Mr. Fay. . . ." *Peterson's,* July 1846, commented that "the author of this novel is favorably known to the public. . . . The present story is exceedingly well told; and, like all the author's romances, teaches a moral lesson." In August 1851 it called a book "one of the very best works of romance that has appeared since Christmas, a period, it must be remembered, fertile in superior novels." In May 1860 it noted the publication of *The Marble Faun:* "a new romance by Hawthorne is always an event. . . . The novel is, in one sense, an art-novel."

On a female character in a new fiction the *Christian Examiner* for July 1843 observed that "a little more of human imperfection would have made her more interesting to all but thorough-bred novel readers, who expect, as a matter of course, to pursue one such 'faultless monster' through the mazes of romance." *Harper's* for November 1850 introduced "a new romance by the author of *Talbot and Vernon*. . . . Like the previous work of the same author, the novel is intended. . . ." In June 1854 it wrote of a work's "interest as a novel—which is guaranteed by a plot of high-wrought romance." From the *Atlantic,* May 1858: "novelists recognize that Nature is a better romance-maker than the fancy. . . . Sometimes, indeed, a daring romance-writer ventures. . . ." In a review in December 1859, *Sword and Gown: A Novel* is characterized as "rather a brilliant sketch than a finely finished romance." The *Democratic Review* for September 1850 introduced *Moneypenny; or, the Heart of the World,* a book subtitled *A Romance of the Present Day,* with a comment about "the range of subjects accessible to the American novelist."

Examples could be greatly multiplied, but I hope that these show how the terms were used interchangeably throughout the period of Hawthorne's development in a variety of journals. There were reviews and essays, however, which did make an effort to discriminate between the two terms, but the distinction varied from review to review and, whatever it was, was often abandoned even within individual reviews. In many cases the distinction appears to be entirely ad hoc: The reviewer is developing an idiosyncratic scheme and calls on these two words to make a point in a classification that is not duplicated in other critical writings.

Knickerbocker, for example, announced in August 1838 that under "the head of novels" there are "but two recognized divisions,—namely, the novel, properly so called, and the historical romance"; in October of that year it explained that the novel implied "only fiction," whereas the historical romance was bound by fidelity to personages who had actually existed or events that had actually taken place. The *Southern Literary Messenger* in a June 1847 review made a similar distinction between the novel and the *historical* romance: "In the *novel*, all this is bad enough, but it becomes intolerable in those *romances* which, blending history with fiction, aim to portray the renowned characters of other ages."

The *Southern Literary Messenger* again, in a long essay on Hawthorne in June 1851 (by Henry T. Tuckerman), distinguished "two distinct kinds of fiction, or narrative literature, which for want of more apt terms, we may call the melo-dramatic and the meditative; the former is in a great degree mechanical, and deals chiefly with incidents and adventure; a few types of character, . . . approved scenic material and what are called effective situations, make up the story; the other species, on the contrary, is modelled upon no external pattern, but seems evolved from the author's mind." Avoiding the terms *novel* and *romance*, the essay distinguishes outer and inner fiction but leaves entirely out of the picture the leading form that contemporary fictitious narrative was usually thought to take, the unmelodramatic narrative of everyday life.

In March 1842 a reviewer writing on Dickens in the *Christian Examiner* preceded his evaluation with a long general disquisition on fiction, distinguishing epic, pastoral, novel, and romance. The novel "deals primarily with events, and makes character subsidiary. Its aim is to replace the lost thread of cause and effect, to bind actions to their legitimate consequences." The romance mingles all the other forms of fiction, combining "the stately epic tread of heroes on an elevated stage, with the passion and sentiment of the tragic muse. It borrows the tenderness of the pastoral . . . while with the novel its plot turns on the principle of retributive justice." This is not a particularly useful or acute distinction. Indeed, it is difficult to know just what works the reviewer might have had in mind to exemplify his description of the romance, but the comment shows how reviewers setting out to distinguish romance from novel were likely to invent their distinction on the spot. This means that a critic or student looking for a historically current distinction between *novel* and *romance* in Hawthorne's time should probably turn last to those essays in which the formulation of such a distinction is featured.

In September 1850 the *American Review,* writing on Bulwer, also felt impelled to expatiate on the general nature of fiction and stated that, "as a preliminary step" to a criticism, "it will be necessary to set forth briefly the recognized ideal of a Novel, and to distinguish it from the Romance. This is a task demanded by the present scheme of criticism, and not out of place in correcting a prevailing error of the day, which tends to call every fiction a novel." It described the novel as "a picture of society, a delineation of manners, increased in interest and effect by the aid of plot and incident. . . . Vastly more than other fiction it requires to be philosophic and scrutinizing." In contrast, the romance was "a panorama of outward life" which "surveys men and manners in mass, avoids all analytic investigations of character, and deals for the most part in broad and free strokes," with plots that are "rarely complicated," thoughts that are "never above the comprehension of the most ordinary minds." The romance is "vivid, startling, and fond of effect," the romancer "essentially objective. Nothing that he relates conveys the bias of his own mind." The novel is a more descriptive, more analytic, and more subjective mode than the romance, but close examination of the distinction shows that this is not a true contrast; different and unrelated qualities are discussed for the two genres.

Again, *Putnam's* in October 1854 featured a long essay on "Novels: Their Meaning and Mission." The author commented (and I quote at length here) that

> there is no more unfortunate circumstance than the lack of an appropriate and experienced name for that kind of composition to which we are necessitated, in lieu of a better, to affix the appellation, Novels, Romances, etc. They are total misnomers, every one of them. The fact is, that the thing has repeatedly changed, while the name has not, and thus thing and name are mutual contradictions. . . . The terms "Novel" and "Romance," though often confounded—are, in a general signification, analogous to the philosophico-metaphysical divisions, "Imagination," and "Fancy." . . . The term Romance is indicative of a *combination* of wonderful deeds and darings . . . while novel . . . carries the idea of an Art-creation; not an accretion of circumstances and particulars from without, but an inly production of the mind in its highest imagining or *poetic* moods.

This identification of the novel rather than the romance with an inward creation is strikingly unlike the modern view.

Yet another instance appears in an "Easy Chair" in the June 1858 *Harper's*, distinguishing "novels of society," in which "it is the picture of life and the development of character that interest us, and not the fate of the people," from "a love story, or a proper romance," whose "point is the concurrence of every circumstance to the union or separation of the lovers. They may be, in themselves, but names and shades, but the description of where they were and what they did must be very absolute and distinct." Using *romance* to mean a love story, *Harper's* employs the term in a familiar manner; equating *romance* with plot, *novel* with character and description, it makes another familiar distinction; blending the two, it is idiosyncratic. *Harper's* made a similar point, but in inconsistent if not incoherent terminology, in a June 1859 comment: "the novel is interesting, philosophically, as illustrating completely the style of romance which depends upon the delineation of character for its interest rather than on the progress and development of a story. It is unquestionably the higher kind of novel—but equally without question it is less popular." This passage notably makes a distinction twice and twice erases it within the confines of two sentences: The novel is a form of romance, the romance a form of novel, and the two modes are distinct. Interesting, too, is the perception that, insofar as the two forms can be distinguished, the romance is the more popular.

The literary discourse on romances and novels, to complicate matters still further, though at one extreme characterized by total interchangeability of the terms and at the other by total definitional anarchy, also contains two "mainstream" definitions in the sense that, in a preponderance of essays and reviews in which one can see an operative distinction, one or the other of these usages obtains. One of these definitions incorporates a history of fiction (is diachronic) while the other schematizes existing fiction (is synchronic). In the diachronic mode of writing the novel is seen as a modern form of romance, which is the overform, the generic name for narrative fiction over time. In the synchronic mode the generic name for narrative fiction is the novel, and the romance is one type of the genre. If we put these two modes together, we come up with a discourse in which romance is a type of novel which is in turn a modern type of romance. No doubt a great deal of confusion can be attributed to this merging of two different approaches to fiction.

Authority for both of these typifying schemes stems from a single source, Walter Scott's long essay on romance in volume 6 of the 1824 supplement to the *Encyclopaedia Brittanica*. Scott began his survey by deconstructing a prior authority, Samuel Johnson, who had defined *romance* as "a military fable of the middle ages; a tale of wild adventures in love and chivalry." Scott wrote that "the 'wild adventures' is almost the only absolutely essential ingredient in Johnson's definition. We would be rather inclined to describe a *Romance* as 'a fictitious narrative in prose or verse; the interest of which turns upon marvellous and uncommon incidents.'" Scott's purpose in making this new definition, he openly allowed, was to facilitate a contrast "to the kindred term *Novel*, which Johnson has described as 'a smooth tale, generally of love'; but which we would rather define as 'a fictitious narrative, differing from the romance, because accommodated to the ordinary train of human events, and the modern state of society.'" Scott then produced an elaborate history of the romance, not the novel, and his essay shows that he regarded the novel as a modern form of the romance *even though* he had described them as contrasting modes. Thus, Scott simultaneously posits *romance* as an overarching historical and generic term and as one term in an atemporal binary opposition. To confuse matters further the eighth edition of the *Brittanica,* published in America in 1859, incorporated

Scott's essay into volume 19 and added a postscript on "modern romance and novel." The novel was there identified as a modern form that replaced not the old romance but the *drama*.

Following Scott, when reviewers before 1860 laid out a history of prose fiction they generally used the term *romance* to refer to the form throughout the ages and the term *novel* to imply a modern type distinguished by its concentration on the ordinary and the contemporary. Then they slid into using the term *romance* to mean premodern types of novels, those produced in the past century which depended on supernatural and marvelous events to resolve their plots and to achieve their effects. What they did *not* do in this approach was to use the term *romance* to refer to any contemporary work; inevitably, the word *romance* was associated with older works. As *Harper's* observed in a notice in July 1857, "Derby and Jackson have tempted the throng of novel-readers to fall back on the ancient favorites of their grandmothers by the publication of a neat edition of the world-famous romances of Mrs. Radcliffe, and Jane Porter's *Thaddeus of Warsaw* and *Scottish Chiefs*. It is a curious experiment to try the effect of these high-spiced productions of a past age on readers who have been trained in the school of nature and reality, as successfully illustrated by Scott and Cooper."

At the same time when the term was used to refer to a contemporary work in a way that singled that work out from the overclass of novels, then it referred to works of fiction which were especially exciting, stirring, dramatic, action packed, thrilling. The highly wrought modern fiction, the sensation novel, and the painfully exciting story were described as romances to suggest that the reader would find passion, intensity, thrilling interest. (This synchronic distinction may be thought of as derived from the diachronic one but need not be.) For example, in a review of *The Heirs of Derwentwater* by E. L. Blanchard on 24 May 1851, the *Literary World* wrote that "the book possesses much of the *material* of a true romance. An intricate plot skillfully developed; an unflagging interest pervading every chapter, from the initial to the final; characters and incidents, far removed from the common-place, challenge our attention, if not our admiration. It is a tale of the dark and fearful school of Sue and Reynolds; a picture of life in which the foreground figures are blackened with crime or shrouded in gloom." In July 1860 *Peterson's* wrote of Maria Cummins's *El Fureidis,* a highly rhetorical oriental tale set in Syria, that "strictly speaking, the work is a romance, not a novel. As a romance it will be generally more acceptable than if it was a novel." *Godey's* wrote about *The Lone Dove* in November 1850: "As a romance, or rather rhapsody, this volume can claim some rare attractions. It is strange, wild, wonderful, and fantastic."

Given this general association of the romance, when it was distinguishable from the novel, with the highly wrought, the heavily plotted, the ornately rhetorical, the tremendously exciting, and the relentlessly exterior, it seems clear that Hawthorne's work would not fall into the category. And indeed, his works, with one exception, were not described as romances in his own lifetime, and this is so despite his own insistence on such a classification for them. Of course, before *The Scarlet Letter* Hawthorne had written exclusively in the short form, and the short form was considered to be inherently ephemeral, if not trivial—"writers of a light character are so accustomed to look only upon what appears fair and good . . . that we are startled in the class of composition chosen by Hawthorne with these revelations," the *Democratic Review* had observed of his work in April 1845—and hence not the object of close reviewer attention. Thus, the issue of the genre in which he was working did not seriously arise before 1850, and it arose in part within the context that Hawthorne created for it by his repeated claim that he was writing romances rather than novels. Yet if his short works had been unlike romances because of their interiority, slow pacing, relative lack of action, and heavy proportion of meditative prose, and if *The House of the Seven Gables* departed in significant ways from Hawthorne's earlier practice, surely it did so in the direction of a greater contemporary realism and attention to surface finish, attributes that would create works different from but no more romancelike (in his age's terms) than his earlier fiction.

Since, however, Hawthorne himself persisted in labeling his works with the term *romance,* the reviewers did devote some commentary to the issue, commentary showing that they found his definition idiosyncratic and by no means accepted it as properly descriptive of his achievement.

A reviewer for the *Literary World* wrote on 26 April 1851:

> In the preface to this work . . . Mr. Hawthorne establishes a separation between the demands of the novel and the romance, and under the privilege of the latter, sets up his claim to a certain degree of license in the treatment of the characters and incidents of his coming story. This license, those acquainted with the writer's previous works will readily understand to be in the direction of the spiritualities of the piece, in favor of a process semi-allegorical, by which an acute analysis may be wrought out and the truth of feeling be minutely elaborated; an apology, in fact, for the preference of character to action.

This review shows that to understand what Hawthorne meant by his distinction, one had to know his previous works; in terms of a current distinction, however, the novel rather than the romance was associated with character.

Knickerbocker, alone among the journals, called *The Scarlet Letter* "a psychological romance" (May 1850), but the qualifying adjective served to identify a unique literary product rather than one belonging to a common form. And the *Christian Examiner,* reviewing *The Marble Faun* in May 1860, wrote:

We doubt if Romance be the fit title of the story. . . . Here, where, as we are carried along in the order of external circumstances, we follow still more closely the course of moral struggles and exigencies, and find, in the playing out of the drama, our interest engaged, more than in any outward bearing and action, in the passionate strife, with its catastrophes of evil or issues of good, which marks the temptation and the developing of human spirits, we question whether the addition of "The Romance of Monte Beni" belongs to the name. . . . The query, however, must not be thought the mere criticism of the title, but as put in the interest of a profound admiration for the thoughtful and serious spirit, and the skillful subtlety in the treatment.

In brief, insofar as Hawthorne's use of the term *romance* to signal something to his readers did, in fact, convey something out of the lexical welter surrounding the word, it was inaccurate. Readers would expect intensity, passion, excitement, and thrills resulting from ornate rhetorical treatment and from a focus on outer action. Hawthorne did not deliver these.

It is interesting to speculate why, in this atmosphere of definitional chaos, and in the evidence of a lack of fit between Hawthorne's label and the public understanding of the meaning of that label, Hawthorne made the distinction, why he claimed that it was common parlance, and why he so firmly insisted on the membership of his works in this genre. A few possible explanations come to mind, although I confess that they do not satisfy me. Given his well-known desire for popularity and his penchant for artistic subterfuge, it is certainly possible that he was intentionally misleading potential readers, taking advantage of definitional confusion to make claims for his work which would not stand up in the reading but would entice a reader into purchasing his book. Literary history is full of examples of authors misrepresenting their works as a means of insinuating them into the public arena. One can picture, not without amusement, Hawthorne (himself amused) imagining the reader turning to *The House of the Seven Gables* for breathless excitement, plenty of action, and numerous scenes of highly wrought passion, only to meet Miss Hepzibah and her cent shop in the first chapter and then to follow a narrative whose adventurous climax involves two old people taking a brief railway trip. If Hawthorne could not write as the public wanted, he could at least pretend to (and perhaps derive some enjoyment from the pretense).

Another possibility is that he was invoking the authority of Scott—more precisely, the first paragraph of Scott's essay in the *Brittanica*—to justify the inclusion of the "marvellous" in his story. But if this was his purpose, he was invoking a dated authority to justify the use of fictional strategies that were everywhere agreed to be obsolete. For the specifically supernatural appurtenances of eighteenth-century fiction were, reviewers concurred as early as 1820, no longer acceptable to fiction lovers of modern times. "A giant, a wizard, or spirit . . . makes but a sorry figure in a modern story, in which the author affects any regard to probability," the *North American Review* had observed in a review of Cooper's *Pilot* in April 1824; yet now, more than a quarter century later, Hawthorne was presenting readers with a story whose action was supposedly controlled by a wizard's curse.

The point is not so much that this sort of fictional strategy was being characterized as out of date as early as the years of Hawthorne's youth, when his own literary tastes were being formed and his literary ambition solidified (and that this obsolescence was hugely furthered through the achievement of his idol and exemplar Scott). It is, rather, the corollary—that the public had no taste for it. If, that is to say, Hawthorne understood the general discourse about fiction—not only at midcentury but as it had evolved throughout his lifetime—his invocation of a form both obsolete and unattractive looks like an act of deliberate self-sabotage insofar as literary success was concerned.

But one sticks at the fact that in Hawthorne's own terms—if the "marvelous" was the one ingredient that separated novel from romance to him—*The House of Seven Gables* was the least romantic, the most "novelistic" of his fictions to that date (taking novel to be a probable fiction of everyday life, as Hawthorne describes it in the preface to *The House of the Seven Gables*). Since the novel, so understood, was *the* form of the age, one wonders why he sacrificed the possibility of claiming novel status for this particular work.

What he was clearly not doing, however, was invoking the romance genre as a means of classifying his work as a particularly American creation. (And, subtle as his imagination was, he could certainly have had no idea that his definition would serve in the next century to identify a peculiarly American form and to place his own work at the very center of an American literary tradition.) If anything, he did the reverse. Indeed, Richard Chase was manifestly wrong when he wrote, "as we see from the prefaces to his longer fictions, particularly *The Marble Faun,* Hawthorne was no less convinced than Cooper and Simms that romance, rather than the novel, was the predestined form of American narrative."[11] What Hawthorne in fact insisted on in that preface was precisely the opposite: The difficulty if not impossibility of writing a romance in America:

> Italy, as the site of his Romance, was chiefly valuable to him as affording a sort of poetic or fairy precinct, where actualities would not be so terribly insisted upon, as they are, and must needs be, in America. No author, without a trial, can conceive of the difficulty of writing a Romance about a country where there is no shadow, no antiquity, no mystery, no picturesque and gloomy wrong, nor anything but a common-place prosperity, in broad and simple daylight, as is happily the case with my dear native land. It will be very long, I trust, before romance-writers may find congenial and easily handled themes either in the annals of our stalwart Republic, or in any characteristic and prob-

able events of our individual lives. Romance and poetry, like ivy, lichens, and wall-flowers, need Ruin to make them grow. [12]

Almost unquestionably, Hawthorne is here suggesting that there is something un- or at least non-American in his imagination, in its attraction to themes and events that seemingly have so little pertinence to the ongoing national life. (It is probably worth noting, too, that Simm's preface to *The Yemassee,* while it did see the romance—as he defined it—as well suited to America, did not see this nation as having an exclusive claim on it and that Cooper for his part did not refer to his works as romances.) Whatever claims Hawthorne made or implied for his work, and however accurate or inaccurate one may judge them to be, and whatever the motives behind his claims, he did not present his work as distinctly American in its nature. As far back as his uncompleted *Story Teller's Story,* composed in the early 1830s, and his sequel *Legends of the Province House,* he had portrayed the addict of unrealities as an aberrant American type, a pebble on the banks of the stream of its modern life. He may well have thought (or hoped) that he was a representative American artist and therefore that the artist in America was generally a social outcast, a modern ahead of his time. He may have believed that the nation needed the correcting voices of outcast artists. But he did not conclude that the condition of such artists is representative of the American experience more generally, that what Hawthorne saw was the distillation of what his compatriots saw. Indeed, if he thought of his work as a corrective to the easy optimism and superficiality of American attitudes, it would be destructive to his position to present it as mainstream. Yet observe that in the preface to *The Marble Faun* he wrote that America had no shadow, not that it had a shadow that it had failed to recognize and therefore needed the artist's teachings. Of course, in view of the imminence of the Civil War his words may have been ironic; historically, however, there is little evidence that Hawthorne perceived slavery as a shadow or a hereditary wrong.

Works with ruins and castles and ancient wrongs had long since been noticed in the nationalist press specifically for their lack of distinctive American character. For example, according to the *North American Review* for July 1824, Charles Brockden Brown could not be said "to have produced an American novel. So far from exhibiting any thing of our native character and manners, his agents are not beings of this world; but those dark monsters of the imagination, which the will of the master may conjure up with an equal horror in the shadows of an American forest, or amidst the gloom of long galleries and vaulted aisles. His works have nothing American but American topography about them." (Brown, as noted above, is now taken to be the first practitioner of the American romance.) This review shows concern with the specific nature of Americanness as it might be manifested in fiction and implies that the "romance" (if that is what Brown was writing—the review did not use the term) was not at all American. It also suggests that Brown's form, whatever it was appropriately called, was not the novel. It follows as at least a possibility—one that Hawthorne's preface to *The Marble Faun* raises again more than thirty years later—that the novel rather than the romance (insofar as the two forms are distinguishable) is the form appropriate to American experience. In other words the general American idea of the literary form appropriate to its national character at the time Hawthorne was writing was precisely the novel as distinct from the romance, insofar as such a distinction was made. As the July 1824 *North American Review* explained, the "*Americanism* of American novels" is to be constituted by treatment of "our native character and manners," by "strong graphic delineations of [the nation's] bold and beautiful scenery, and of its men and manners, as they really exist, or have at some time existed"; people approaching a work represented as "an American novel" would "expect to find the familiar manners, habits, and dialects of those immediately about them." Novel, not romance—always remembering that *romance* was at best a fuzzy term—was the appropriate American form but, again, not an exclusively American form. The distinctness of an American literature would lie in its choice of American settings, its treatment of American subjects.

The consensus, of course, is not necessarily correct. But to the extent that consensus itself is the issue, Hawthorne in his own day was seen neither as the romance writer he claimed to be nor as the essentially representative writer he has come to be. While retrospective understanding is certainly the task of historical scholarship, it is important not only for our understanding of Hawthorne's practice but also for that of American literary development in general that we see how the idea of American romance now controlling so much American literary study is a recent invention.

5

"Actually, I Felt Sorry for the Lion"

Reading Hemingway's "The Short Happy Life of Francis Macomber"

Feminist literary critics are not responsible for the view that Ernest Hemingway's work is deeply antiwoman in its values. Nor are they responsible for reading his life and his self-presentation into his works. On the contrary, feminists who follow these lines have only accepted the standard arguments of Hemingway criticism. Their innovation is to view these values, and the author who supposedly endorses them, as defective rather than admirable.

The conventional interpretation of Hemingway's depiction of women runs like this: In his prizing above all the cause of a manhood confirmed by male bonding and achieved by participation in war or, when war is not available, in blood sports, he casts all but the most passive, submissive, and silent women as corrupting or destructive. Only those women characters who accept their place in Hemingway's universe as a lower order of being than men—with the functions of waiting *on* them when they are around and waiting *for* them when they are elsewhere—help men achieve masculine selfhood and thereby win the author's approval.

The increasing evidence of Hemingway's deeply troubled relation to his own sexual identity does not require a revision of this approach; indeed, it might be expected that the author would cling all the harder to an ethos because it was achieved with such difficulty.[1] Even so, interpretations of particular Hemingway fictions as less than firmly "machismo" have been published over the years, recently with increasing frequency. Stories like "Cat in the Rain" and "Hills like White Elephants," for example, are now regularly read as presenting the woman character's point of view sympathetically and attributing her plight to male insensitivity and egotism.[2]

But "The Short Happy Life of Francis Macomber" resists such interpretive strategies because it has been a keystone of the standard approach. For those critics who see Hemingway's work as a significant site of the "bitch-woman" figure, Margot Macomber along with Brett Ashley in *The Sun also*

Rises are always the two outstanding examples. Brett, with her irresistible combination of sexual allure and sexual appetite, creates competition, hence disharmony and antagonism, among men who would otherwise bond. And her wiles undermine the hard-boiled approach to life that men achieve and sustain with such difficulty. As for Margot, she commits adultery virtually under her husband's nose and then kills him at the very moment when his belated entrance into manhood (through blood sport and male bonding) threatens her dominance. It is not surprising that a feminist short story anthology has featured it, through four editions, as a leading example of the "bitch" stereotype.[3] Nevertheless, it seems to me that the anthology accepts without question a reading that is likely more the critics' than the author's construction.

Although the technique of scanning men's writings for evidence of male chauvinism has largely vanished from feminist criticism, feminists are certainly not obliged to read Hemingway sympathetically merely to make him acceptable to an audience that is aware of the policing functions of hostile feminine portraiture. If it seems that Hemingway "really" represented Margot as a murderous bitch, one must say so. (And in fact, there *are* murderou. women in the world, although calling them bitches is to construct them in an already misogynist textual world.) But I have found that student readers unaware of the standard interpretation of "The Short Happy Life of Francis Macomber," who also know little or nothing about the Hemingway my tique, may in fact see the story differently, see it in a way responsive to the formal play of narrative voices and points of view in the text as well as to the twists of its plot.[4] It is for them that I want to propose a different approach to the story.

At the outset "The Short Happy Life of Francis Macomber" represents and voices a number of subject positions; it then tells a story in which all but one are silenced, in which this progressive silencing is the main event. The lexicon and syntax (the discourse) of "The Short Happy Life of Francis Macomber" belong mainly to the narrator, but the story is focalized through five perspectives, including: the narrator, an omniscient though taciturn presence; Robert Wilson, the white hunter; Francis Macomber, his employer; Margot Macomber, the wife of Francis; and a lion. Of these the lion's is especially important and has been especially neglected.[5]

The narrative of "The Short Happy Life of Francis Macomber" begins in the middle of the action, at lunch after the killing of the lion and before the hunting of the buffalo. If we were to reorder the narrative chronologically, we would start with the lion's voice, whose initiating function is reflexively marked in the text: "It had *started* the night before when he had wakened and heard the lion roaring somewhere up along the river."[6] Narrative time is then manipulated so that the lion takes almost half of the narrative space to die, and when the group returns to camp after killing him (on the eighteenth page of a thirty-four page story, at which point we return from the flashback to the opening of the narrative proper) the narrator reflexively marks the closure: "That was the story of the lion" (120).

The dead lion continues to exert his presence in the story, however, and his point of view, which has been used to present much of the hunt and slaughter, is now transferred to Margot. She registers her husband's cowardice, Wilson's brutality, and the interdependence of the two as epitomized in the lion's fate. She also recognizes that animals in the so-called wild are not true adversaries or antagonists, because they are so massively overpowered by the men's technology—their guns, their cars. She sees the safari as a sham, its participants as hypocrites. Wilson, who makes his living by manipulating the appearances of mortal danger for the titillation of his clients, is anxious to suppress her point of view, and at the end of the plot he succeeds.

But that he did not fully succeed outside of the plot may be surmised from the urgency with which the first generation of male critics felt the need to continue his work. Another Wilson, name of Edmund, set the tone by praising the "Short Happy Life" as "a terrific fable of the impossible civilized woman who despises the civilized man for his failure in initiative and nerve and then jealously tries to break him down as soon as he begins to exhibit any." And later in his career the increasingly self-protective author himself adopted this interpretation, telling an interviewer in 1953, for example—seventeen years after the story was published—that "Francis' wife hates him because he's a coward. . . . But when he gets his guts back, she fears him so much she has to kill him—shoots him in the back of the head."[7]

Of course Margot Macomber shoots and kills her husband. There is no doubt of that whatsoever. But it should be equally clear that she does so accidentally. Here is the relevant passage, in which a buffalo charges at Macomber and Wilson:

> Wilson had ducked to one side to get in a shoulder shot. Macomber had stood solid and shot for the nose, shooting a touch high each time and hitting the heavy horns, splintering and chipping them like hitting a slate roof, and Mrs. Macomber, in the car, had shot at the buffalo with the 6.5 Mannlicher as it seemed about to gore Macomber and had hit her husband about two inches up and a little to one side of the base of his skull. (135)

Now no reader has ever doubted that Wilson did, indeed, duck aside for a shoulder shot or that Macomber did, indeed, stand tall and shoot high. The text affords no basis for dismissing as unreliable one, and only one, clause in this omniscient narrator's report—the one that says Margot shot *at the buffalo*. What is more, as an essay by John Howell and Charles Lawler points out, a homicidal Margot had no *need* to shoot her husband at this moment. They write, "if she had wanted her husband dead, the bull seemed about to do that job for her."[8] Of course, Margot Macomber might be so stupid as not to have noticed what the bull was about to do. But whatever her defects of intelligence—and one could well argue that shooting at the buffalo is a stupid move—it is precisely the bull's charge, her husband's mortal danger, that drives her to action.

Now if Margot was shooting at the buffalo, not her husband, then she was shooting to save her husband not to kill him. So that if Margot's bitchiness entails her eventual murderousness, then she is no bitch. Her bad press is attributable to the critics' desire to identify what they *take* to be Wilson's ethical code with the story's values, and hence with Hemingway's values. In pursuit of this aim they must reduce the multivocal narration of "The Short Happy Life of Francis Macomber" to Wilson's monologue, which is precisely what Wilson himself does.

Carlos Baker's reading in *Hemingway: The Writer as Artist* is paradigmatic of the argument that one understands "The Short Happy Life" correctly as an endorsement of Wilson's values:

> Easily the most unscrupulous of Hemingway's fictional females, Margot Macomber covets her husband's money but values even more her power over him. To Wilson, the Macombers' paid white hunter, who is drawn very reluctantly into the emotional mess of a wrecked marriage, Margot exemplifies most of the American wives he has met in the course of his professional life. Although his perspectives are limited to the international sporting set, the indictment is severe. These women, he reflects, are "the hardest in the world; the hardest, the cruelest, the most predatory, and the most attractive, and their men have softened or gone to pieces nervously as they have hardened."[9]

To Baker Wilson's subjective and self-serving indictment of Margot and other women like her is an objective description that the reader should accept as true. He describes Wilson as a "yardstick figure," a "fine characterization," the man "free of woman and of fear," the "standard of manhood towards which Macomber rises."[10] By contrast, Kenneth Lynn's *Hemingway*, though not the first study to call Wilson a brute, makes clearer than any other interpretation what Wilson's motive is for accusing Margot of premeditated murder.[11] He is blackmailing her. For in the chase preceding the buffalo kill Wilson has allowed a pursuit of the animals by automobile, something that is illegal and that Margot knows is illegal. Unwisely, as it turns out, she flaunts her knowledge:

> "I didn't know you were allowed to shoot them from cars though."
> "No one shot from cars," said Wilson coldly.
> "I mean chase them from cars."
> "Wouldn't ordinarily," Wilson said. "Seemed sporting enough to me though

while we were doing it. . . . Wouldn't mention it to any one though. It's illegal if that's what you mean." . . .

"What would happen if they heard about it in Nairobi?"

"I'd lose my license for one thing. . . . I'd be out of business." (128–129)

Wilson's behavior here puts in question more than his adherence to the laws of the hunt, to the code of the fraternity of white hunters. Soon he is shown justifying this illegality on the grounds of its crucial contribution toward making the cowardly Macomber into a brave man. "Beggar had probably been afraid all his life. Don't know what started it. But over now. Hadn't had time to be afraid with the buff. That and being angry too. Motor car too. Motor cars made it familiar. Be a damn fire eater now" (132). But if Macomber has been tricked into bravery, what exactly has Wilson accomplished?

The illegal car chase is not the only questionable tactic Wilson uses in his program to make Macomber think himself a brave man. Wilson also uses a gun so powerful that he calls it a "cannon." (According to Lynn, the supposed real-life model for Wilson, Philip Percival, said that this type of rifle was so powerful that its use on safaris was unsportsmanlike and that, therefore, he never carried one.) [12] With this unsportsmanlike cannon, Wilson in effect kills every single animal that is killed in the story—killings that cannot be done cleanly or well done by any means since this kind of gun cannot kill cleanly. What is more, Wilson is far less skillful a hunter than he claims to be.

Look first at the buffalo hunt, whose action is the last third of the story. (Following Aristotle's instructions, we may divide the story's action thus: beginning, the botched killing of the lion; middle, the repercussions of that botch on the party of three; end, the compensatory killing of buffalo.) First, Macomber downs one of three bulls (bull #1) and is told by Wilson that he has killed it. But Wilson is either mistaken or he is lying. If he has made a mistake, it is one that the skillful hunter he is supposed to be would not have made, and it is a life-threatening one, lulling all members of the group into a false sense of security, which later allows the wounded but far-from-dead bull to make an unexpected charge and, thus, to become the indirect cause of Macomber's death. If he is lying, then Wilson is cynically endangering the group in order to flatter his employer. We are not ever to know whether Wilson was cynical or merely stupid, but we do know that bull #1 is not killed until after Macomber is dead, when he is killed by Wilson. [13]

After having downed bull #1 Macomber shoots at bull #2. His first shot hits the animal but does not drop him; his second shot misses altogether. Wilson now shoots, downing the animal for Macomber to finish off later. So much for bull #2. Then both men fire at but miss bull #3, who runs away. A second illegal car chase, however, gives them a second chance.

Macomber fires at the bull five times—*five!*—to no effect. Then Wilson shoots with a deafening roar; the bull staggers and goes down (127). Bull #3, like bull #2, is incapacitated by Wilson so that Macomber can safely kill it. True, in some sense it is Macomber who kills but certainly not in the brave white hunter sense that is supposedly the code by which Wilson lives and which he is supposedly dedicated to instilling in, or at least offering to, his clients. In that lofty sense Macomber didn't kill any of the buffalo.

Wilson killed them all, and he killed the lion as well. Wilson is a "white hunter," a professional organizer and guide of private safaris. He "hunted for a certain clientele" and has no hesitation in accepting the standards of that clientele "as long as they were hiring him" (125). Since from time to time the women on these outings make sexual advances, he carries "a double size cot on safari to accommodate any windfalls he might receive" (125). If money has corrupted both Margot Macomber and Francis Macomber, it has equally corrupted Wilson, who lives off them and their kind by catering to their illusions of power. These illusions are gender based: The men imagine they are heroically brave, the women that they are seductively attractive. The phrase "hunted for" may be applied to Wilson in two senses: He hunts on behalf of his clients; he also hunts them, they are his prey.

According to his interior monologue, Wilson accepts his clients' standards "in all except the shooting"; "he had his own standards about the killing and they could live up to them or get some one else to hunt them" (125). Live *up* to them: to standards that, as we see, allow for chasing buffalo illegally in cars and shooting them with megaguns so that the client can kill them without danger. The chief illusion above all to which Wilson caters—the illusion that he in large measure creates—is that the safari is dangerous. Margot sees through the illusion—although to her cost she does not see through the illusion that flatters her own sexual vanity. " 'It seemed very unfair to me,' Margot said, 'chasing those big helpless things in a motor car' " (129). Unquestionably, this needling of the two men is tactless—in traditional terms it is unwomanly; certainly, Margot's freedom of speech is part of what makes her a bitch in critics' eyes. Nevertheless, what she says about the safari, to her eventual cost, corresponds with what the text presents as true.

The killing of the lion looks very different when we look at it through Margot's eyes, seeing Wilson as a man paid for eliciting from his (male) clients the simulacrum of courage and thus presenting them with an illusion of their own manly heroism. This killing is focalized through Francis Macomber's perceptions as follows:

> He heard the *ca-ra-wong!* of Wilson's big rifle, and again in a second crashing *carawong!* and turning saw the lion, horrible-looking now, with half his head seeming to be gone, crawling toward Wilson in the edge of the tall grass while the red-faced man worked the bolt on the short ugly rifle and aimed carefully

as another blasting *carawong!* came from the muzzle, and the crawling, heavy, yellow bulk of the lion stiffened and the huge, mutilated head slid forward. (119)

By the time that this ghoulish event transpires the lion is already virtually dead:

> sick with the wound through his full belly, and weakening with the wound through his lungs that brought a thin foamy red to his mouth each time he breathed. His flanks were wet and hot and flies were on the little opening the solid bullets had made in his tawny hide, and his big yellow eyes, narrowed with hate, looked straight ahead, only blinking when the pain came as he breathed, and his claws dug in the soft baked earth. All of him, pain, sickness, hatred and all of his remaining strength, was tightening into an absolute concentration for a rush. (118)

Since nothing in the story quite equals the physical immediacy and power of this description, it is surprising that in all the published criticism only Howell and Lawler identify the lion for what he is—the true standard of courage in the story, which amounts to persistence in the face of certain death.[14]

At any rate, Wilson fires three shots into this more than half-dead animal's head and face. Margot, sitting in the car, has "been able to see the whole thing"—both Macomber's cowardly flight *and* Wilson's killing (119). That to her these two acts are parts of a whole we realize when recalling what she had said to Wilson at lunch: "I want *so* to see you perform again. You were lovely this morning. That is if blowing things' heads off is lovely" (108).

Now moving forward again to Margot Macomber sitting in the car during the buffalo chase, we see her as she sees that "there was no change in Wilson. She saw Wilson as she had seen him the day before when she had first realized what his great talent was. But she saw the change in Francis Macomber now" (132). What was it that Margot, the day before, had realized Wilson's "great talent" to be? A talent for "blowing things' heads off." We may infer, indeed—just as conventional criticism would have it—that Margot sees her husband in the process of becoming a man like Wilson. "You're both talking rot. . . . Just because you've chased some helpless animals in a motor car you talk like heroes," she says, including both of them in her assessment (132). But the man that she sees Wilson as is no mighty hero; he's a bully and a fraud.

If Margot thinks that Macomber is becoming another Wilson, then her attempt to save her husband from the buffalo at just that moment is a quixotic gesture. If heroism consists in acting against one's interest on behalf of certain socially inculcated loyalties, one might even call this act heroic. Certainly, her represented interests, like her spontaneous expression of sympathy, align her with the animals, not with men like Wilson. That in shooting to save her husband from the buffalo she has acted against her own interests is made clear by the story's trick ending, and, of course, it is a trick, in the tradition of Guy de Maupassant, when the intended act backfires—one might say backfires almost literally—in every respect.

Before the incident with the lion Margot Macomber has not been represented as hostile to hunting: "'You'll kill him marvelously,' she said [and this passage is presented without irony], 'I know you will. I'm awfully anxious to see it'" (112). She comes to hate hunting when, in fact, she sees it. She sees that Macomber, with Wilson and his gun behind him, is never in real danger. She sees that a matter of life and death for the animal is a wasteful war game for men. The text implicitly endorses her judgment by giving the lion himself the last word on his wounding and death:

> That was the story of the lion. Macomber did not know how the lion had felt before he started his rush, nor during it when the unbelievable smash of the .505 with a muzzle velocity of two tons had hit him in the mouth, nor what kept him coming after that, when the second ripping crash had smashed his hind quarters and he had come crawling on toward the crashing, blasting thing that had destroyed him. Wilson knew something about it and only expressed it by saying, "damned fine lion." (120)

Macomber knows nothing about the lion; Wilson knows something but much less than he thinks he does; Margot knows much more. She does *not* know, however—what the text through which she is constructed shows— that she is in the same position as the lion in relation to these men, imagined to be dangerous, in fact a powerless victim, as "buffaloed" by the men as the buffalo. She has an illusion of freedom or power that is expressed occasionally in infidelities to her husband and frequently in her freedom of speech. But infidelities do not free her so much as circulate her within an economy of male power, while the narrow limits of her freedom of speech become clear at the story's end, when Wilson shuts her up. The knowledge that she lacks might have led to more circumspection had she possessed it—just as better-instructed animals might have done a better job of protecting themselves had they recognized their own helplessness.

In other words, Margot's great mistake is to imagine herself equivalent to these men when, in fact, they are far more powerful than she is and she "exists" only by their sufferance. Nevertheless, we are not meant to think that Macomber's newfound bravery would have resulted in his leaving his wife or that Margot imagines so; as Wilson thinks when he first perceives Macomber's newfound bravery: "probably meant the end of cuckoldry too. Well, that would be a damned good thing. Damned good thing" (132). What we are to anticipate is the establishment of a marriage conducted according to more traditional patterns of overt male dominance and female subservience. Thus, in shooting at the buffalo Margot is acceding to tradition rather than rejecting it, and her extreme vulnerability when she is without a husband is well represented at the story's end, when she must beg Wilson's indulgence. This story shows the "emancipated woman" to be a cultural fiction equivalent to the "wild animal."

I noted earlier that student readers unconstrained by the conventional interpretation of "The Short Happy Life," who additionally know little or nothing about Hemingway and hence have no prior ideas about his supposed values, do indeed see the story as a multivocal structure in which Wilson by no means occupies the author's place. Here is part of a transcript of an introductory fiction class where I observed an apprentice teacher attempt to instill the conventional interpretation.

"Does Margot Macomber kill her husband?" he asks. "Wilson *thinks* she does," is the cagey answer. But is Wilson right, the teacher pursues. "It says"—it, not Hemingway—"that she shot *at* the buffalo," a student responds. The teacher's attempts to answer the question against Margot by defining Wilson's values as the moral center of the story elicit scattered counterevidence of his inconsistencies. Nobody much *likes* Wilson. "Well," the teacher concedes, "it's true that, intentionally or not, Hemingway at times does undercut his point [his point here taken for granted as something prior to the story rather than emerging from this reading of it]—whom *can* you like in this story?"

Silence.

Then a woman student—the first woman to enter the discussion—speaks up: "Actually, I felt sorry for the lion."

This is not what the teacher anticipated. He responds, far too quickly for reflection: "Now you sound like Margot." The student laughs softly and nervously; she does not speak again.

Here, then, a male in authority (to the undergraduate student, the T.A. [teaching assistant] is authority, since he controls the course grade) silences a woman by, in effect, assuming Wilson's voice and casting her in the role of Margot; if we are not sure whom to care for in the story, it is at least sure that we may not care for *her.* To accuse a woman of being like Margot is to silence her indeed, to return her to the role of submissive woman. The story's plot is reenacted, in a nonfatal but deeply political (and I think destructive) fashion, right in the classroom. The teacher's ire reflects the discomfort of the enfranchised when the silenced start to talk.

Apart from the politics of the situation, I would hold that this woman, in resisting the interpretation of the story that allows Wilson to bully us into his perspective, was not resisting or misreading the story so much as she was hearing the voices that are constructed in it—above all, the voice of the lion that occupies so much of its space. For the lion, and Margot too, do have voices in "The Short Happy Life of Francis Macomber." And whatever Hemingway himself came eventually to say about the story, attentive readers should hear them. Otherwise, reading "The Short Happy Life of Francis Macomber" becomes an episode of indoctrination into an ethos, a self-styled male ethos, whose murderous hypocrisies and inconsistencies are precisely the matters that the text exposes and asks us to consider.

6

Early Histories
of American Literature

A Chapter in the Institution
of New England

When, in the second decade of the twentieth century, academics defined a field of study called "American literature," they did so by appropriating and sophisticating a nationalistic narrative already available in the many American literary history schoolbooks that had been published between 1882 and 1912. Putnam's; Houghton Mifflin; Ginn; American Book Company; Silver, Burdett; Macmillan; Henry Holt; A. C. McClurg; Scribner's; Harper; D. C. Heath; D. Appleton—these and other publishers commissioned American literary histories for high school and college use and kept them in circulation through frequent revisions and updatings.[1]

These textbooks aimed to succeed in the lucrative but competitive textbook market by constructing literary history in a shape compatible with the recognized aims of public schooling: forming character and ensuring patriotism in a motley, fractious population.[2] As one literary historian explained, American literature "is valuable to the young student and future citizen of the Republic just in proportion as it seems to mirror our American ideals and as it shall have a tendency to build up the reader into a worthy citizenship."[3] Most of the textbooks were written by professors of New England origin employed at elite colleges. They routinely cribbed from each other and meshed with handbooks, anthologies, memoirs, and biographies (many compiled by the same professors) to create the tendentious narrative that eventually launched the academic field and continues to influence it.

Narrating history in a shape to further the purposes of schooling, the textbook writers featured authors as culture-heroes whose lives and works displayed the virtues and accomplishments of an Anglo-Saxon United States founded by New England Puritans. This representation was expressly derived from national history as it had been iterated throughout the nineteenth century in a variety of forms, chiefly in connection with the New England Whig political project.[4] The story that they told, simply put, is this: In the face of numerous obstacles a legitimate American literary culture had developed in New England soon after 1830. *Literary* here means "belletristic," literature written for its own sake. No sermons or political documents qualified. *Culture* means a social scene wherein the production of belles lettres was encouraged, its producers esteemed, and the cultural products themselves widely circulated and appreciated. The story showed how this country, at first hostile or indifferent to belles lettres and lacking entirely in literary culture, came to develop both.

This literary culture, according to the story, emerged in New England among groups of Cambridge and Concord authors linked socially through the amenities of Boston, where a powerful publishing and critical apparatus supported them and circulated their writings around the nation. The main authors—Emerson, Hawthorne, Lowell, Longfellow, Holmes, and Whittier—were descendants of Puritans and had accomplished the remarkable task of adapting Puritan values to literary goals. The result was a literature combining beauty with moral strength. The histories encouraged respect, veneration, and gratitude toward these men who had achieved American literature on behalf of the rest of us and implied that affiliation with them would assimilate the reader to the national culture they represented and displayed.

It is important to stress that this story is not false. It is, rather, just one of the several stories that might have been told, and it was told for a reason. The earlier Whig project of installing New England as the originary site of the American nation was intended frankly to unify the unformed and scattered American people under the aegis of New England by anchoring national history in that region. Conservative New England leaders knew all too well that the nation was an artifice undergirded by no single national character type. They insisted passionately, and I think believed, that the nation's future peace, progress, and prosperity required a commonalty that, if it did not exist, had at once to be invented. By originating American history in New England and proclaiming the carefully edited New England Puritan as the national type, they hoped to stimulate all citizens to develop (or at least revere) those qualities they thought the nation needed to survive: self-reliance, self-control, and acceptance of hierarchy. Of course, it was no accident that these qualities were, or were thought to be, aspects of New England character.

Intellectual leaders saw almost at once that the public, or common, schools could be important to this nation-building process. Common schools, designed for children whose parents could not afford private instruction, had been established throughout New England early on, but, while local governments were required to run them, attendance was not required. The number of such schools increased greatly during the 1830s, when the first significant wave of non-English immigrants arrived on

American shores. By no accident, both Connecticut and Massachusetts established boards of education in 1837, in the decade when a substantial Irish population settled in the Northeast and, more specifically, in the panic year of disproportionate suffering among the working poor.[5] New England educational reformers, led by the Whigs Horace Mann of Massachusetts and Henry Barnard of Connecticut, forthrightly theorized the school as a socially conservative force. The expanded and rigorously standardized pedagogical apparatus they hoped to put in place was meant to school young people for a long time and turn them out as literate, rational, reliable citizens who understood and exemplified national values.[6]

Indirectly but not incidentally, this educational program required many teachers and textbooks—textbooks for teachers to use, textbooks for teachers to learn from. Publishers, the largest segment of whose business had always been textbooks, quickly became ardent supporters of educational reform. It was not apparent at first, however, that belles lettres had a place in this system. Mann perceived literacy as the foundation of republicanism but distrusted imaginative literature, especially for young people; Barnard thought that the King James Bible was sufficient for all classroom reading needs.[7] Insofar as American belles lettres—or belles lettres of any sort—entered the schools in the antebellum era, it did so only through extracts in compilations like McGuffey's. Pared to their obviously declarative content, these extracts enunciated patriotic, moral, and Protestant Christian sentiments and, in true Whig fashion, attributed the enlightened, prosperous, independent, intelligent, Protestant Christian, honest, hard working, sober, and moral American character—along with the republican institutions that were the organic emanations of such a character—to New England Puritan origins.[8]

In the last two decades of the nineteenth century educators responded to the revived specters of cultural chaos and social violence accompanying mass immigration and industrialization, predictably, by advocating yet more schooling. Industrialization, creating enormous new wealth and distributing it unequally, had produced a large class of urban poor, many of whose members were immigrants. Lured to this country mainly by the prospect of economic advantage, they found themselves packed into wretched slums where, it was imagined, they were ripe for Socialist or anarchist propaganda. The educational establishment latched onto this situation opportunistically, proposing to Americanize these people by teaching their children, making long-lasting public education compulsory for all children. This project called for more teachers, more textbooks, and more subjects to fill up all this required time. Since history, the chief subject through which American values were disseminated in antebellum schools, had been overcast by the shadow of the Civil War, a new subject was needed as the centerpiece. American belles lettres emerged as its substitute.

Since none of this advocacy was covert, no New Historicist detective work is required to unearth it. It was frankly argued that a literature authored by native-born Americans—preferably of several generations' descent—composed in English, expressing American values and representing American themes and events, was now the subject most likely to Americanize immigrant youth. Certainly, nothing was more suited to deflect the (usually foreign-born) poor from their desire to have a substantial piece of the country's settled wealth than exposure to an idealism from whose lofty perspective the materialist struggle would seem unworthy. As for an increasingly disaffected native-born rural population, its moribund patriotism might be revitalized through the spectacle of great literature written by people whose lineage and values they shared. The old textbook compilations were inadequate for this ambitious new enterprise. One needed to teach literature, not merely declaim it; teaching called for a thoughtful arrangement of the material accompanied by an apparatus of clarifying histories and guidebooks.

The publishing company most prepared to further this programmatic and professional approach to teaching literature in the schools was Houghton Mifflin, which held the copyright to all the Cambridge-Concord authors, authors who had, in fact, already been well established before the Civil War. The antebellum roles of this company and its predecessor, Ticknor and Fields, in promoting New England authors and establishing the first national canon, are well known.[9] We can see the company at work in an 1888 convention address to teachers on the place of literature in the schools, delivered by Horace Scudder, director of Houghton Mifflin's recently established Education Department and reprinted in a Riverside Press pamphlet. Scudder praised the common schools system as the safeguard of the American way and observed that the system was now responding in two different but equally appropriate ways to "the danger which threatens the nation"—a danger described alternatively as "the relations of labor to well-being" and "the cry of Labor in Poverty."[10] One response was industrial (i.e., vocational) education to enable students to earn a living wage; the second was literary education, to reconcile them to genteel poverty by stressing the primacy of spiritual over material values. Since the nation was now too religiously diverse to use the King James Bible as a school text, spirituality had to be sought in other places. The best substitute, Scudder claimed, was literature, in which, above all other cultural forms, spirituality was fully and richly "enshrined" (33).

Scudder added that the spirituality of American literature had a particularly national aspect. Its well-born authors were examples of the highest type of American—men who had chosen the spiritual way in the face of the powerful material temptations of American life. "The lives and songs of Bryant, Emerson, Longfellow, Whittier, Holmes, and Lowell have an imperishable value regarded as exponents of national life"; along with Hawthorne, Irving, and Cooper, who "associate with them in spiritual power," they have been the "consummate flower of American life"; through their works "spiritual light most surely and immediately may penetrate our common schools" (25–26).

Houghton Mifflin brought out extracts and short works by these standard authors in its inexpensive Riverside Literature Series pamphlets, designed especially for the elementary schools.[11] But the firm also enhanced and sophisticated this offering as early as 1883, when it published a historically organized primer of American literature by Charles Richardson to guide the students' reception of the important authors. And as more and more people needed to know about these authors in order to teach them, textbooks for higher levels of schooling developed apace. Whereas textbooks for very young children put more emphasis on idealized biographies of individual authors, textbooks for higher education were invariably literary histories. Though Houghton Mifflin benefited most from the study of copyrighted primary texts, all publishers could enter the market for literary histories.

The literary histories did not content themselves with sketching a view in which American character traits, although originally established by Puritan Anglo-Saxons, were within the reach of all. In the climate of racialism characterizing the last decades of the nineteenth century they tended to attach these traits to "real" Anglo-Saxons, in part by playing up the strictly English origins of the American nation. Thereby they instructed classrooms of children of non-English ancestry in the virtue of deference to Anglo-Saxon traits more than in the acquisition of Anglo-Saxon traits themselves. This important point was often left implicit, but it certainly comes through strongly when a historian asserts that American literature can never be anything other than "the literature of a part of the English people, under new geographical and political conditions" (Richardson, 1:1). In a cruel paradox non–Anglo-Saxons could become American only insofar as they accepted the connection between Americanness and an Anglo-Saxon racial lineage.[12]

Emphasis on English precedence served the historical plot as well, for it allowed historians freely to concede that the literature of the United States was belated and inferior to English literature and then to use this very backwardness as the starting point of their story. That literature had been produced at all in the United States—this was the whole happy point, the triumphant occasion for the celebration of American literature in school. The celebrated works did not need to be masterpieces; it was enough that they were certifiably belletristic and that there were enough of them written by enough authors to constitute a recognizable social phenomenon. Their status as aesthetic objects allowed the history to be written, but the history focused on the social context that enabled them rather than on the aesthetic property of the individual works. Authors who worked in solitude, like Charles Brockden Brown, merited notice only as instances of the *failure* of literary culture to develop, bringing out by contrast the very different situation in New England.

Warming to their trials-and-triumph plot, the opening pages of these texts gleefully specified the many difficulties that any would-be literary culture in America faced, including: no unique national language; no primitive era in national history; the geographical isolation of the nation and its resulting tardy exposure to European intellectual currents; (alternatively) the too-rapid transport to these shores of the superior literatures of England and the Continent; the all-absorbing material hardships of American life.

Yet these obstacles were minor compared to the unliterary character of early Anglo-Americans themselves in their two incarnations as hedonistic Virginia Cavalier and dour New England Puritan. It was hardly surprising, then, that—as all the histories agreed—no literary culture developed in America before the nineteenth century. On the contrary, the surprise was rather that it had developed at all. To make its belatedness all the more salient historians routinely denigrated the literary quality of whatever early American writings they chose to acknowledge. "The literature of the Colonial age in Virginia is so scanty and uninteresting as to deserve little attention" (Pattee, 15). The literature of Virginia "during these early years is comparatively meager and poor" (Bronson, 11). "If pure literature be the test, there is very little, after all, to detain us," in colonial New England (Burton, 3–4); Puritan literature is "hopeless" from the "point of view of intrinsic aesthetic value" (Trent, 2). "The Day of Doom," like the *Bay Psalm Book* and Anne Bradstreet's poems, is not literature; "the student notes it only as a curiosity, and as a pitiful indication of the literary poverty of the days and the land in which it was popular" (Richardson, 2:6–7).

Since all agreed that American literary culture finally established itself in New England, the plot moved American writing toward belles lettres and toward New England simultaneously. Moses Coit Tyler's two scholarly volumes on Colonial literature, published in 1878, was the chief source for the other historians. (His two volumes on the literature of the American Revolution did not appear until 1897, and his plan to write a complete history of American literature was never realized.) Ignoring his own announced plan to trace "the rise of American literature at the several isolated colonial centres" until when, in 1765, "the scattered voices of the thirteen colonies were for the first time brought together and blended in one great resolute utterance," Tyler quickly reduced the Colonies to two: "during the first epoch in the history of American literature, there were but two localities which produced in the English language anything that can be called literature: Virginia and New England" (Tyler, 1:v, 80). There was nothing new in Tyler's dichotomizing; as early as the 1820s, Charles A. Goodrich, author of the most popular of all antebellum schoolbook United States histories, had produced national history as the story of two colonies; "In Virginia, the free and licentious manners of society produce a government unsteady and capricious. This government re-acts upon their manners, and aids rather than checks their licentiousness. On the contrary, in New-England, the severe puritanical manners of the people produce a rigid, energetic government, and this government returns its puritanical influence back upon the manners of the people."[13]

Everybody followed Tyler because he himself was a follower. "All our northern colonies developed from those planted in Massachusetts, and all our southern from that planted in Virginia" (Wendell and Greenough, 25). "Such literary activity as existed was divided at first between Virginia and New England" (Burton, 2); Virginia and Massachusetts are the "fountain heads of all that is strongest in our national and our literary history" (Pattee, 10).

Next Tyler narrowed the field further by announcing that Virginia produced no literature after the first twenty years of settlement (1:80). He gave New England about two-thirds of the space in each of his volumes and used much of the non–New England space to speculate on why literature written elsewhere was scanty and poor. (Reserving Franklin for treatment in the volumes on the Revolution, Tyler allotted him only two pages.) Tyler's thoroughly conventional explanations of Southern inadequacy appeared in other literary histories as well. "Conditions of life in the Colonial South were distinctly unfavorable to any great achievements in literature" (Pancoast, 20). "Colonial Virginia lacked the mental stimulus of life in towns and cities, where mind kindles mind by contact; if books were written, it was difficult to get them printed; and if they were printed, there were few people to read them. In such conditions the production of a large body of literature is not to be expected" (Bronson, 14). "With no metropolis to furnish the needed contact of mind with mind, with material needs making large drains upon their energy, with the chase and other rural sports satisfying their rudimentary instincts for pleasure, and, above all, with no deep-seated artistic impulses and few inherited literary traditions and aspirations," Virginians naturally "produced little literature and developed little culture of importance" (Trent, 6). "The Virginia gentleman preferred field sports and indoor social diversions to letters" (Burton, 3).

As if to emphasize the point, the historians all chose John Smith as the greatest Virginia writer. In shorter histories he was the *only* Virginia writer. Smith's brief sojourn in North America proved that Virginians were not serious about founding a nation and, thus, implied that their writing was not really American. One text observed that Smith "never ceased to be an

Englishman" and was probably included in American literary history books because of the "paucity of readable colonial books and writers" (Trent, 3–4).

According to Tyler, New England was literary because it was intellectual, by which he meant idealistic, interested in ideas that are ideals. Virginians "came here chiefly for some material benefit," New Englanders "chiefly for an ideal benefit. In its inception New England was not an agricultural community, nor a manufacturing community, nor a trading community: It was a thinking community" (Tyler, 1:98). Again other historians fell in line. "Concentration of population" in New England "stimulated intellectual activity and made easier the establishment of common schools"; the level of intelligence "was very high, and there was from the first a literary class, composed chiefly of clergymen and magistrates, who had the capacity, learning, and industry to write many books" (Bronson, 16–17). Contrasting "the high average of intelligence and character among the New England colonists" with "the idle, profligate, and disorderly elements which entered into the making of Virginia" a textbook called Massachusetts "the most intellectual of all the Colonies"; it was there that popular education, "the only foundation on which a republic such as ours can safely rest, was begun" (Pancoast, 24–25).

New England, in fact, "produced so large a proportion of American books during the seventeenth century that we hardly need consider the rest of the colonies" (Wendell and Greenough, 33–34). But even though New England alone produced literature, it was by no means unrepresentative. Far from it. For those who did not write also did not stay, did not establish our American institutions, and did not multiply across the continent. "The settlers of Massachusetts differed from the early Virginians in almost every respect. They did not seek America for worldly gain; they were not adventurers cast up by the tide of chance, nor were they carried across the sea by a wave of popular enthusiasm. They were earnest and prayerful, prone to act only after mature deliberation, and they had come to America *to stay*" (Pattee, 19).

The high seriousness of the New England Colonialists was interpreted (with a little help from Matthew Arnold and other racial theorists of the day) as a defining quality of the Anglo-Saxon mind. This mind believes that there is a "necessary connection between art *and* ethics" so that "between two books of equal literary merit, but unequal purpose, it gives greater and more lasting favor to the more useful book" (Richardson, 1:339–340). The English inheritance of moral seriousness in the New England Puritan which first made the American nation possible later gave American literature its distinct character. Without William Bradford and John Winthrop "we could not have had Emerson and Hawthorne" (Richardson, 1:12).

If American literature, when it developed, could not be anything other than didactic and moralistic, the historical problem, however, was that at the start New Englanders were so moralistic and didactic that they could produce no literature—no belles lettres—at all. Richardson, the first historian who took the story up to the present day, asserted that "Puritan theology in New England could no more produce poetry than it could paint a Sistine Madonna. Its theological force was intense, but it was neither gracious nor serene . . . of the poetic art it had not an idea" (2:1); and that New England "was virtually blind to the infinite vision which makes life worth living, and inspires religion, philosophy, literature, and arts, and science to struggle toward a more perfect expression" (2:284). More mildly, another wrote that, "while the tone of New England was conspicuously intellectual, and while conditions favorable to the encouragement of the intellect were by no means lacking, the whole mental life was cramped by an almost complete devotion to questions of theology and point of doctrine" (Pancoast, 28). So if it was true that we could not have had Hawthorne and Emerson without Bradford and Winthrop, it was still a question how we could have had them *with* Bradford and Winthrop. Nothing less than a transformation of the New England character was required, one in which morality and didacticism were freed from theology and dogma on the one hand and merged with beauty and artistic craft on the other. In a word, it was necessary to produce secular Puritans before New England could produce literature.

In the historical narrative offered by our first literary historians disconsolate belles lettres wandered from region to region, finding no resting place except briefly in New York, until at last New England, prepared by the Unitarians, welcomed and transformed it, through its own intense spirituality and moral earnestness, into something truly national. In this union of (feminine?) literature with (masculine?) New England, belles lettres was uplifted, and New England was softened and beautified. "The mission of all the great New England writers of this age was to make individuals freer, more cultivated, more self-reliant, more kindly, more spiritual. Puritan energy and spirituality spoke through them all" (Halleck, 268).

Skipping rapidly past Jefferson and Washington, as well as Franklin and Brockden Brown, the historians agreed that the first true national literary culture was established in New York. "The 'rosy fingers' of this long-expected dawn were first to brighten the skies above the Hudson" (Richardson, 2:23–24). Irving, the first American author whom we enjoy reading, is "the father of our American prose," who stands "at the threshold of the greater period of our literature" (Pancoast, 116). Irving, of course, did not stand at the threshold alone; a gregarious man, he was a member of the Knickerbocker School. The emergence of a school, rather than of a singular, gifted writer, signified the belated formation of a true, if frivolous, literary culture. Secular, commercial New York was the right place to hatch an American literature because it was open to the liberal currents streaming across the Atlantic, but it could not nurture such a literature into maturity. For in that city, "then as now," an "excess of the commercial spirit over the intellectual and artistic" hindered true literary achievement (Bronson, 112–113), and literature was produced from the first as "an article of trade" (Woodberry, 65). Knickerbocker writing was "urbane and elegant rather than profound or forcible" (Higginson and Boynton, 83). Except for Bryant, the one New Englander among them, the Knickerbockers "placed the chief emphasis on the power to entertain" (Halleck, 109); they were "a band of young New Yorkers attempting, with the exception of Bryant, nothing very earnest nor very wise, but working on human materials in the artistic spirit for the artistic end of pure delight" (Bates, 106). Bryant alone charged his work with "that depth of moral power that was his heritage from Puritanism, and marked in the next generation the literature of New England, setting it off from the literature of New York" (Woodberry, 59).

Since New Yorkers "never dealt with deeply significant matters," only New England could produce "the serious literature of America" (Wendell and Greenough, 184–185). But New England in the Knickerbocker age "lagged behind" New York because of a "narrowness and lack of general cultivation which resulted from the strictness of its religion" (Pancoast, 159). The region could not play "that leading part in the purely literary development of the country which it afterward assumed. It had no names to match against those of Irving and Cooper" (Beers, 115). Something had to intervene before there could be a "transfer of the leadership from New York to New England" (Pattee, 196). What intervened was the particularly New England response to the European liberalism that had created Knickerbockers in New York—not a Knickerbocker school but a theological movement that, "though not immediately contributory to the finer kinds of literature, prepared the way, by its clarifying and stimulating influences, for the eminent writers of the next generation. This was the Unitarian revolt against Puritan orthodoxy. . . . That we do now possess a national literature, is in great part due to the influence of Channing and his associates" (Beers, 115, 118). The Unitarian movement emancipated "the New England mind from these narrow ideas" and led to "the rise of the greatest group of writers the country has yet produced" (Pancoast, 159).

The underlying New England character endured through this "mental revolution which changed the whole character of New England and turned into new channels the current of its thought and literature" (Pattee, 196). Thus, the literature it eventually produced was

> a characteristic outbreak of the mighty moral passion of New England. A Knickerbocker literature, essentially artistic and entertaining, was not for her. When her great hour of utterance came, it was the old Puritan flood of idealism

broken loose again. The liberalization of theology through Channing and Parker, the European influences brought to bear upon American thought and taste by Allston and Dana, Everett and Ticknor, Longfellow and Lowell, resulted in that New England renascence whose supreme achievements were the Transcendental essays and poems of Emerson, and the mysterious romances of Nathaniel Hawthorne. (Bates, 117–118)

The Unitarians had rejected Puritanism while preserving the Puritans' "deep reserves of poetry, and capacity for independent thought" (Pancoast, 161). Then,

> released from the weight of formalism and asceticism, and at the same time quickened and uplifted by influences of a most congenial and stimulating character, the New England mind ceased to expend itself wholly on theology, and asserted through a group of great writers those literary powers which had been so long suppressed. In its great literary epoch, the reserve power, the stored-up energy and repressed sympathies of New England, first found an adequate outlet in literature. (Pancoast, 164)

The central New England writer, corresponding to Irving in New York, was the man deemed most responsible for moving beyond Unitarianism into a literary utterance separated from any particular doctrinal program and hence transforming Puritanism itself into literature. Emerson was this writer. His centralization is not, as many present-day Americanists believe, a twentieth-century construction: It coexists with the institution of New England in American literary history, which is to say, with the institution of American literature itself. One text called him "the foremost representative of the powerful influence which New England has exerted on American life and on American literature" (Matthews, 93). Another put him "in the center of the remarkable little group of New England writers who stood for God and country, who were idealists, yet thoroughly of the soil, into whose words the very genius of their land seems to have passed" (Burton, 135). A third said that Emerson, though not necessarily "a greater writer than any of the men who surrounded him," was "most representative of the whole movement" and "the most influential in shaping its form and character" (Pancoast, 165). A fourth called Emerson "the most eminent figure among the Transcendentalists, if not indeed in all the literary history of America" (Wendell and Greenough, 254). And still another said he was the "foremost figure of the age. . . . Puritanism, the old search for God in New England, ended in him; and he became its medium at its culminating moment of vision and freedom" (Woodberry, 83, 92).

But again, Emerson was not merely the ideal center of a national literature; he was the actual, historical center of a group of many like-minded men and a few women (Margaret Fuller and Harriet Beecher Stowe), all actively and deliberately engaged in building American literature and all exemplary, in different ways, of the New England mind. Six in particular—Longfellow, Emerson, Hawthorne, Whittier, Lowell, and Holmes—"constitute a large part of the strength and beauty of American literature." Historians stressed that these were not only New Englanders but were also Massachusetts residents, all but one born in Massachusetts, and that most of them lived in or near Boston or Cambridge. They did so to remind students that:

> New England had from colonial days been the intellectual and literary leader of the country; Massachusetts was the head of New England, and Boston was the eye of Massachusetts. By heredity, tradition, and acquired momentum the Bay State still kept the lead in mental activity; Unitarianism and the Transcendental movement added an intellectual freedom and freshness not elsewhere attained so early in like degree; and Harvard College, its roots now deep in the past, bore in larger measure with every succeeding year the beautiful fruit of a ripe culture. (Bronson, 177)

"As they grew up and began to write, these authors became friends; and their friendship lasted with their lives" (Matthews, 124). Concord was one of two "spiritual suburbs of Boston"; the other was Cambridge, where the university scholar could live "withdrawn in an academic retirement" yet "within easy reach of a great city, with its literary and social clubs, its theaters, lecture courses, public meetings, dinner parties" (Beers, 161). Pattee, Wendell, and other historians specified elements of the network besides Harvard: the Saturday Club, the *North American Review,* the Lowell Institute, the *Atlantic Monthly,* Ticknor and Fields. No solitary could have been the center of a literary history whose purpose was to show the emergence of a literary culture, no matter what his literary gifts. It was, indeed, Emerson's gifts for society, his demonstrable place in both Concord and Boston circles, that fitted him for the central role that he was made to play in American literary history.

The six major writers, in fact, were each central to the project in a different way, and the histories frequently represented them as quasi-allegorical personifications of some aspect of what, even in these pre-Millerian days, was called the New England mind. The basic scheme installed Whittier as the Reformer, Longfellow as the Poet, Holmes as the Wit, Lowell as Man of Letters, Emerson as Teacher or Philosopher (a designation that may explain his especial popularity with educators), and Hawthorne as Artist. The histories acknowledged other writers than the key figures and disposed them in different ways on the peripheries of their narrative. Occasionally, historians signaled toward a large anonymous group of texts by mentioning the need to elevate youthful taste above them. The didactic, sensational, and sentimental work that almost certainly comprised most of what was read in nineteenth-century America besides journalism and religious writing had no place in these narratives. In fact, the obliteration of such writings, along with the literary centers that supported them—New York and Philadelphia—was evidently an aim of this historical project.[14]

Historians did, however, name two other types of writers, which I will distinguish as minor and marginal. Minor writers were the lesser adherents of the schools that produced the major writers. Fitz-Greene Halleck and Rodman Drake as Knickerbockers; Margaret Fuller, Bronson Alcott, and Henry David Thoreau as Transcendentalists—these are among the names that most often recur as minor figures. Their shortcomings highlighted the major writers' excellences, while their presence in the narrative once again emphasized the cultural aspect of literary production.

Not so with two disruptive American figures, Poe and Whitman, who could not be left out of the narrative because English and European critics esteemed them highly. It became a challenge to plot a story that acknowledged them in order to exclude them. They were cast as pretenders—writers who were not "really" American—and thus as foils to the central authors. Emerson could oppose Poe or Whitman; Hawthorne was particularly useful to counter Poe, and Longfellow to counter Whitman.

Typical commentary on Poe runs like this: Poe has been "admired, imitated, and translated as hardly another of the native writers," which is an "interesting and curious" fact, because Poe "is not representatively American at all." His work "has no local color, and it does not reflect our native ideas or ideals; it tells little or nothing of the soil whence it springs, of the civilization behind it" (Burton, 66). Poe seems "out of place in American literature, like an importation from the Old World," teaching no lesson and writing only "to chill the blood by mere revolting physical horror" (Pattee, 172, 181). His "place in our literature is one of peculiar isolation," as he "wanders in his unsettled and struggling career from city to city"—a cosmopolitan, a wandering Jew, who "stands essentially alone" (Pancoast, 263–264).

But insofar as Poe was judged a real artist by sophisticated European critics, denying him a role in American literature might make the historians seem parochial. Since "in place of moral feeling he had the artistic conscience" (Beers, 213), they looked for a New England writer who had moral feeling *and* artistic conscience. They found that figure in Hawthorne, whom they always described as the "artist" in the New England group. To be sure, the Hawthorne who is made to play this role is not an isolated figure; his love of solitude is offset by his deep roots in New England literary culture, both as a descendant of the Puritans, whose deeds he records and whose temperament he shares, and as an active participant in the New England Renaissance, friend of Longfellow, resident of Concord, member of the Saturday Club, an author published by Ticknor and Fields and the *Atlantic*.

We read, then, that Poe "cannot affect our whole lives as does a Hawthorne in prose, nor can his eye sweep from zenith to nadir in the poetic vision of Emerson" (Richardson, 2:136). "The tragedy in Hawthorne is a spiritual one, while Poe calls in the aid of material forces"; if Poe's poetry "had the sweet home feeling of Longfellow or the moral fervor of Whittier, he might have been a greater poet than either" (Beers, 218–219). Both Poe and Hawthorne were "dwellers in the dusk, but the shadow that haunted Poe crept from the charnel-house, while Hawthorne's, sprung from the sinful heart of man, showed still a glint of heaven" (Bates, 299). "Poe lavished on things comparatively superficial those great intellectual resources which Hawthorne reverently husbanded and used. That there is something behind even genius to make or mar it, this is the lesson of the two lives" (Higginson and Boynton, 209). "From whatever cause, Poe's life and character, when placed beside that of Longfellow or of Lowell, stand out in sharp and tragic contrast." His work shows how "the worship of beauty entirely for itself, dissociated from any sense of design or regard for essential and ethical value, inevitably degrades the worshiper" (Fisher, 255). As Hawthorne's shadow, Poe entered largely into the way in which literary histories represented Hawthorne as a blend of Poe-like qualities tempered by New Englandism.

Whitman challenged the internal coherence of the historical account even more than Poe because, as a self-styled democratic poet, he laid claim to a quality that some had identified with the United States since Tocqueville. Actually, the word *democracy* seldom appeared in American literary histories before 1900, given their Whig orientation. But throughout the life of this genre, the histories countered Whitman's claim to be a people's poet by pointing out that the people themselves ignored or rejected him. And they chose the beloved patrician Longfellow to withstand him.

"A poet in whom a whole nation declines to find its likeness cannot be regarded as representative" (Woodberry, 243). "Of all our poets, he is really the least simple, the most meretricious; and this is the reason why the honest consciousness of the classes which he most celebrates—the drover, the teamster, the soldier—has never been reached by his songs" (Higginson and Boynton, 233). His work is "as utterly removed from the people as he himself was close to them in his daily life. The scholars Longfellow and Lowell are the poets of thousands of humble homes; Whitman is as yet the admiration of a little clique among the most cultured upper class. Called the founder of a national American literature, by a singular irony he is better known to the intellectual aristocracy of England than among the people of his own land" (Pancoast, 301–302). When the "barbaric yawp" of Walt Whitman was heard in the land "the American public, so far as it heeded him at all, was affronted, and with right good reason" (Bates, 199). Longfellow, the "most widely read and loved of American poets" contrasts sharply with "such a 'cosmic' singer as Whitman, who is still practically unknown to the 'fierce democracy' to which he has addressed himself"; "Whittier and Longfellow, the poets of conscience and feeling, are the darlings of the American people. The admiration, and even the knowledge of Whitman, are mostly esoteric, confined to the literary class" (Beers, 162, 165, 236). The representation of Longfellow as the genial, beloved, and immensely popular poet had much to do with his function as a defense against Whitman, just as Hawthorne's representation was in part a creation of the specter of Poe.

Poe and Whitman failed as writers, the historians urged, because internally they lacked national traits and externally they lacked a sustaining literary culture. These two lacks were not unrelated. If they had been more "American," they would have been more successful. In this way, the idea of success entered the narrative obliquely; the truly American writer will be recognized by his culture and find an honored place in it. Some historians identified Poe as a Southerner, others as a New Yorker, but all agreed that he was in essence a rootless wanderer. It could not be denied that Whitman was a New York City man; despite his native ancestry, historians described him as though he were an unassimilated immigrant, one who voiced values that the institution of American literature in the schools was designed to obliterate. "One begins to see why Whitman has been so much more eagerly welcomed abroad than at home. His conception of equality, utterly ignoring values, is not that of American democracy, but rather that of European. His democracy, in short, is the least native which has ever found voice in our country" (Wendell and Greenough, 375).

Toward the end of the thirty-year period encompassed by these history books attitudes toward Poe and Whitman began to soften. Woodberry, who had written a biography of Poe, ranked him with Bryant, Irving, Cooper, Emerson, Hawthorne, Longfellow, and Lowell in the "first class" of authors "whom the nation as a whole regards as its greatest writers in pure literature" (203). Trent observed that Poe's "fame has been so steadily rising in America that it is becoming possible for critics of standing to hold that Hawthorne's superiority to him is not a settled point" (376). Halleck recorded that Poe had an "almost world-wide reputation for the part which he played in developing the modern short story" (299) and, comparing Hawthorne, who "saw everything in the light of moral consequence," to Poe, who "cared nothing for moral issues," even suggested that it was a Puritan literary criticism that faulted Poe (306). And as his reputation rose, Poe's unworldly purity became more a matter for critical notice.

Whitman called for reassessment as the usefulness of the term *democracy* for the American system became more manifest. In light of the origins of the new immigrants Whitman—who had been careful to remind readers in

"Song of Myself" that he was "born here of parents born here from parents the same, and their parents the same"—was reinterpreted as a visionary ahead of his time, whose lack of reception among the populace showed that democracy had not yet arrived. In a move that prefigured Matthiessen some now saw him as an idealist, a lesser Emerson. Thus, though the winds of change rippled over the surface, the New England anchorage held firm.

The brief celebration with which literary histories in the 1880s ended their didactic narrative became, over the thirty years in which the genre flourished, an ever longer and more conflicted coda. Appearing first when the great New England generation was finishing its work, the literary histories had attempted to institutionalize the work of that generation as the achievement of a long-prefigured literary project. Thirty years later the achievement could only be seen as ephemeral; no second generation of New Englanders was carrying on the tradition, which meant in effect that no tradition had been established after all. Not through the works of the New England writers themselves, but in the stories that literary histories told about them in the classroom, a New England literary tradition was installed nationwide.

Perceiving that New England had "lost its long monopoly" (Beers, 260), most historians saw the contemporary scene as a time of diffuseness in which literary activity, dispersed across the continent as well as among a very large number of independent, entrepreneurial writers, had lost definition as well as excellence. There was nothing in the present moment like the "sharply defined group of which Emerson, Hawthorne, Longfellow, Whittier, Holmes, and Lowell were the leaders"; amidst a "host of bookmakers" no one now attained "the stature of Longfellow and Hawthorne, and the other leaders of the early school. It is a period of minor poets and novelists" (Pattee, 345). "Although there have never been so many authors as there are to-day, and although the average of literary skill is probably higher than ever before, there is now no towering figure and no dominating personality. And those who are at the head of American literature in the end of the nineteenth century are not men of the same general type as the greatly-gifted New Englanders whom they succeeded; and their aims and their ideals are not the same" (Matthews, 229). At present there is a "halt of our literary genius"; the "field is open, and calls loudly for new champions" (Woodberry, 252, 253).

In their conclusions historians pointed regularly to: a striking increase in the production of long and short fiction along with a decrease in poetry; the dominance of the school of realism in fiction, with Henry James and William Dean Howells as its chief practitioners and advocates; the development of a distinct type of humorous literature; and—decentralization and diffusion notwithstanding—the rise (or return) of New York City as the chief

American literary center. The association of Boston with the spiritual, New York with the material, had explained why the Knickerbockers failed to produce major literature. Now, as literature slipped out of Boston's control, these associations led to the doleful suggestion that the motive force of history itself had changed and was becoming material. (Henry Adams was soon to be canonized as a literary artist precisely to score this point.) American men of letters, "sucked in ever greater numbers into the vortex of New York . . . are spun about, like mere bankers and brokers, in the whirl"; today's literature "is abundant, varied, clever, but if genius is among us, it walks unrecognized" (Bates, 130). Now that New York was the country's literary center novels and poems have "become mere commercial commodities . . . manufactured in cold blood at specified times, at specified rates, and while fierce competition has greatly raised the standard of mere literary art, it has not breathed into the product that indefinable *something,* the presence of which makes work immortal" (Pattee, 350).

As we have seen, it was chiefly fear of the materialization of American values, or, more precisely, fear of the spread of materialist goals to people who could not hope to satisfy their ambitions without thorough renovation of the social system—"the relation of labor to well-being" as Scudder had phrased it—which shaped these literary history textbooks in the first place. Canvassing the contemporary scene for hopeful signs that the tradition would continue, historians inevitably translated the question "Will American literature remain, or again become, true to the American spirit?" into the question "Who are the heirs to the New England Renaissance (Wendell's phrase) and where can we find them?" Isolated New England local colorists conveyed at best a diminished and unacculturated version of the earlier period. Realists and naturalists were often skillful, but their implication in the worst tendencies of American life made them thoroughly ineligible. Their very skill became the reason for an attack on intellectualism as un-American; this attack meshed with the long-standing distrust of pure aestheticism to produce an ideal of American literature as a body of writing neither overly intelligent nor overly accomplished: a moral literature for a moral people.

The historians found what they were looking for, at least provisionally, in a nebulous rural West populated mainly by Saxons along with some Germans who, as Teutons, shared the requisite racial heritage. Here might be the locus of a future American literature. They saw a new dawn first, tentatively, in Bret Harte and then more certainly in Mark Twain and Abraham Lincoln. Wendell's American literary history of 1901 had concluded with an elegy on "The Decline of New England" and an attack on Whitman; the coauthored textbook version he produced in 1907 ended by celebrating Mark Twain. Another textbook closed with Lincoln, "a conservative, not a radical force, one proceeding from the democratic West, not from old aristocratic Boston," and "a fitting and auspicious name with which to close an account of the development of American literature" (Trent, 578–579).

The Cambridge History of American Literature, which both contributed to and reflected the ongoing construction of American literature as an academic profession, was structured to reflect the expertise of individual professors, and it parceled out the field into separate scholarly properties rather than telling a historical story.[15] It is no wonder then that its chapters "mainly read like isolated essays in a collection printed without benefit of transitions and continuity"; and yet, even so, an implicit if unexamined narrative remained "obvious" in its conventional periodization and choice of major authors (Vanderbilt, 156). In a move that seems to have been meant to free them from the traditional narrative's constraints the scholars of the *Cambridge History* expanded the definition of American literature beyond the belletristic to consider it as an expression of the national intellectual life. But in so doing, they were led to a much higher estimation of the historical importance of the New England Colonial and Revolutionary periods in our literature, so that the basis of the origins narrative was actually strengthened. Vernon Parrington's *Main Currents in American Thought* depended on the narrative of prefiguration and fulfillment that had been instituted as the historical basis of American literary study and, indeed, restated it at the very moment that it declined to confine American literature to belles lettres. Nor had this narrative frame been escaped in the attacks launched on the professors by men like John Macy or Van Wyck Brooks. For they did not deny that the professors accurately recorded the history of what American literature had been—they argued, rather, that it was time to escape from American literary history, to start American literature anew. What Macy and Brooks clearly grasped, however, was the essentially conservative motive involved in a program to anchor literature to nationalistic history.

If, however, belles lettres was no longer the point of the story, and different authors had become central figures in American literature, and some of the New Englanders were written out of the narrative, and emphasis shifted from the achievements of a literary culture to those of solitary individuals, how could it be that a new historical narrative did not replace the old? With the Puritan and Revolutionary periods valued more highly than they had been in the old literary histories, and installed even more tenaciously as the origins of American literature, there was really no other story to tell. And, therefore, canonical change was much less far-reaching than it appeared to those advocating it. Their newly canonical authors were still white and Anglo-Saxon; many of them were also New Englanders. They admired Thoreau and a New Englandized Whitman and an Anglo-Saxon Mark Twain. Removing the Cambridge group from the center, they left the Concord group at the pinnacle. Non–New Englanders were added to the canon

only if they could be assimilated to this still New England center, still preferably as a matter of racial inheritance but at least as a matter of shared
ideology.[16] The equivalence of the New England and national characters
remained the guiding principle of American literary studies, with or without the protective sheathing of a narrative specifically about belles lettres
and literary culture as a social formation.

Perry Miller studied literature as intellectual history rather than belles
lettres; his work appears in many respects to be a sophisticated rewriting of
Tyler. And practitioners in the field of early American literature continue to
argue for the importance of their field on the ground that the texts they
study are the basis of later American literature. As for F. O. Matthiessen,
his *American Renaissance* appropriated and revised Wendell's catchy phrase
with something that looked much broader, but his American Renaissance,
though more democratic than Wendell's, was no less New Englandish in
tone. He eliminated Cambridge but kept Concord. Emerson was detached
from Longfellow but buttressed by Thoreau and a Whitman who was not a
sensual urban working-class poet but a Transcendental idealist. Melville
moved to the literary center not as a New Yorker but as friend and soul
mate to Hawthorne. And Emerson and Hawthorne repeated their traditional roles as New England philosopher and New England artist, respectively. Matthiessen's oft-noted omission of Poe indicates—notwithstanding
the elaborate aesthetic apparatus of *American Renaissance*—that American
literature is the place to look for national ideals, not for fancy writing. Not
until Edward H. Davidson represented Poe as a moral writer—the double,
not the opposite, of Hawthorne—did that writer win his firm place in the
canon.[17]

The myth critics with their frontier vision attempted more deliberately
than Matthiessen to escape the New England narrative. But as we have seen,
the western solution had already emerged in the 1890s (so did Turner's frontier thesis of American history) as a way to reject aspects of American life
that the New Englanders had also been used to reject—the city, industry,
commerce, mass culture, immigrants, along with their attendant literary
movements. The frontier in 1950s myth criticism served similar purposes.
Though again devaluing the genteel social networks of antebellum Boston,
such criticism apothesized lonely and intransigent New England types, like
Thoreau or—what would otherwise seem an extraordinary anomaly—
Emily Dickinson. The mythic frontiersman existed on a mythic frontier
that could be anywhere. As the frontier became a metaphor, New England
was released from its geographical specificity and identified with the state
of mind represented by the frontier myth, an allegory of the American.[18]
Likewise, scholars who proposed to study the literature of the South argued
that, since New England had become as crass and commercial and full of
the foreign born as New York, only the South was left to represent what an

earlier New England had stood for.[19] Even feminists have affiliated with New England by tracing a canon of American women writers back to the foremother Anne Bradstreet and then moving it forward to the present through Emily Dickinson.

Between the continuing supposition that the vision articulated by American authors necessarily presents a New England perspective and the still functioning (though increasingly attenuated) preference for writers of actual New England descent, the originary narrative of American literary history remains in place, even among many who earnestly wish to escape it. Although explanations for this tenacity must certainly include institutional inertia and professional vested interest, there are structural reasons as well for the likelihood that some form of the known story will continue to dominate critical writing and teaching.

Three reasons seem to me especially important to stress. First, scholars considering how the field might be revised are not considering alternatives to America as the field's subject; rather, most revisionary hypotheses are offered as improvements in our understanding of America. To take two out of countless possible examples. When Annette Kolodny refers to the literary historian's longing to tell "a coherent, integrated story about our literary past" the pronoun *our* can only refer to we-the-people and, thus, invoke a collective unified national body already in existence prior to what is written about it; and when Philip Gura launches a thoroughgoing attack on the New England focus of Colonial literary studies he refers throughout his polemic to a totalized America as the focus of Colonialists' interest.[20]

Second, to assert, to demonstrate, that the New England origins narrative of American literature is a discursive construction is not to demonstrate that it is unreal. Having structured the field from the first and exerted influence for more than one hundred years, the New England origins narrative is intensely real; it cannot be wished away. It would be a gesture of astonishing naïveté for the very scholars who claim that reality is significantly textual to act as though textuality were not after all a determinant of material practices. This narrative has indoctrinated literally millions of students as well as teachers, writers, and scholars; it may be disputed, it may be displaced, but it cannot be erased without perpetrating a censoring of the historical record that nullifies any historicist purpose.

There is, finally, the didactic imperative to teach literature for social purposes. To the extent that American literature teaching is practiced for the ultimate aims of forming student character and producing better citizens it incorporates familiar nationalistic aims. The much touted revisionary Heath anthology of American literature, for example, is a passionately nationalistic, patriotic document. No matter how radical or revolutionary the teachers' aims may be, and no matter how deeply teachers feel these aims, if they hope to produce better Americans, a better America, or even just a better understanding of the *real* America, then the supposedly suppressed or over-turned Whig project continues in full force. The more resolutely the teacher insists on a politically engaged pedagogical and critical practice, the more Whiggishly the teacher follows the trail marked out by the first American literary historians.

Part 2

Writing New American Literary History

7

From Enlightenment to Victorian

Toward a Narrative of American Women Writers Writing History

Addressing the commencement class at Litchfield Female Academy on 29 October 1818, the veteran educator Sarah Pierce (who had founded the academy in 1792) explained why women should be schooled. True, "the employments of man and woman are so dissimilar that no one will pretend to say that an education for these employments must be conducted upon the same plan"; nonetheless, "the discipline of the minds, the formation of those intellectual habits which are necessary to one sex are equally so to the other. The difference in their employments requires a difference of personal qualifications but not a difference of intellectual exertion."[1] The implicit, enabling claim that women are capable of an intellectual training "equally" demanding with men's features a precept that Enlightenment (more precisely, Cartesian) thought made possible: that mind has no sex.[2] Linking and repeating the concepts and terms *necessity, employments,* and *difference,* Pierce invokes a human scene in which gender correlates with forms of labor rather than forms of intellect. Her focus is women's work, not women's minds.

Pierce is typical of a generation of post-Revolutionary American educators who based their reformist program for women on two axioms: that Universal Reason was equally a property of men and women and that the success of the Revolution—the establishment of the American republic—demanded new kinds of women's work. From their perspective all Americans had to work at conserving and building the new nation, performing tasks that differed according to class, gender, and marital status. Assuming that every married woman would be a mother, the educators claimed that, as well as bearing children, republican mothers were required to instruct them, in ways congruent with their "station," in the virtues that would sustain the nation and the patriotism that would defend it. Manifestly, ignorant women could not instruct others, hence the need to educate them.[3]

Pierce, however, extends this family-bound ideology of republican motherhood to project a public destiny for women as teachers of the entire nation, even of the world. In an essay on patriotism she starts out conventionally enough:

> Greece and Rome ceased to rule the world when their citizens became corrupted by luxury and sloth. It is indispensable to the existence of a republic to be moral and religious. Who then can calculate the beneficial effects resulting from the early habits of piety and morality planted by maternal wisdom upon the rising generation. And may we not hope that the daughters of America will imitate the example of the Spartan and Roman matrons in the day of their glory, who taught their children to love their country beyond every earthly object, even their own lives.

But then she moves on: "May we not hope that by cultivating the solid rather than the ornamental branches of education, our young women will emulate their sisters in Europe in moral and intellectual acquirements [so] that on this side of the Atlantic Hannah Mores and Mrs. Sherwoods will arise to instruct and enlighten the world" (*C*, 218, 219).

Only fifteen years after Pierce expressed this notion of sexually differentiated national labor, her nephew and successor John Pierce Brace set out a rationale for women's education in which patriotic cultural work played no part and women's intellects were strikingly circumscribed. His commencement address at Litchfield on 23 October 1832 assured his listeners that

> our object has been, not to make learned ladies, or skilful metaphysical reasoners, or deep-read scholars in physical science: there is a more useful, tho less exalted, and less brilliant station that woman must occupy; there are duties of incalculable importance that she must perform: that station is home; these duties, are the alleviation of the trials of her parents; the soothing of the labours and fatigues of her partner; and the education for time and eternity of the next generation of immortal beings.

> [For such station and duties] the formation of character; the acquisition of correct habits; the controul of tempers, and the restraint of appetites; the discipline of mind, that will lead to perseverance and industry, to order and system hereafter, are of more importance than the principles of science, than the refinements of manners, or the elegancies of Literature. (*C*, 305)

Brace's summary shares some surface features with Pierce's words but lacks her commitment to women's minds as well as her authorizing concept of universal, ungendered Reason. And it also lacks the concept of urgent republicanism through which, for Pierce, Reason was given gendered work do to. In his rhetoric these concepts have been overwritten and overridden by an ideal of female character for whom Reason is not important, a character whose gaze turns in toward the home rather than out from it and hence has no connection to the republic or the world.

I see in these differences a cultural shift from post-Revolutionary Enlightenment to Victorian ideologies. Another way of representing this shift might go as follows: Whereas by the 1850s American women's writings had become invested in (though by no means wholly subsumed by) the production of domestic fiction, in the 1820s they had centered on nationalist historical fiction, while from the 1790s through the second decade of the nineteenth century they had chiefly comprised various forms of history writing to which fiction was marginal. The first two generations of American women writers, born before 1790—a group that includes Sarah Pierce, Hannah Adams, Ann Eliza Bleecker, Hannah Mather Crocker, Margaretta Bleecker Faugeres, Deborah Norris Logan, Judith Sargent Murray, Sarah Wentworth Morton, Mercy Otis Warren, Emma Willard, and even the former novelist Susanna Rowson after she founded a girls' school in Boston—were activated or enabled by an Enlightenment republicanism whose tenets guaranteed women intellectual parity with men and offered them the chance to serve their nation if they developed their minds.

The American Enlightenment women named here seem to have perceived logocentrism as what in some sense it assuredly was: the key to their literary empowerment.[4] They stand in striking contrast to the leading textualist-feminist theorists of our own cultural moment, who blame Western logocentrism for disempowering women by identifying them with body while constructing reason and language as male. Such theory, often and inaccurately called "French feminism," has been written about ad infinitum; notwithstanding its proclaimed antilogocentrism, the approach actually valorizes, even fetishizes, language, aiming above all to permit the writing of that which it believes has been hitherto silenced or is only now coming into being. From the perspective of this essay it is unfortunate that these aims seem to require muting or denaturing as "male identified," false, or dishonest (criticisms with a peculiarly Victorian inflection) so much of what women have already written and continue to write.[5]

From a different perspective contemporary feminist political theorists have assailed a totalized construction of Enlightenment liberal or republican thought for inscribing the male body on the supposedly universal concept of citizenship, thereby covertly denying to women what it supposedly offered to all.[6] The extensive material traces of women's Enlightenment practice already comprise a counterargument. My work here does not judge (or tries not to judge) this practice from a contemporary standpoint of what is and what is not emancipatory for "women." I am concerned, however, only with writing and that nebulous, correlated articulation of the public sphere defined through print—a sphere that enables women to imagine themselves out of their bodies. The logocentric key allowed homebound women to enter that sphere and participate in its woman-centered and general political discourses.[7]

A particular advantage of logocentrism to these early American women writers was that they did not have to deny the supposedly obvious or natural differences between male and female bodies, although they did have to name them. The obvious differences that they recognized, which they derived again from their emphasis on labor and action, were women's unique reproductive capacity and their relative bodily weakness. While these women readily conceded that they belonged to the weaker sex, *weaker* is all—merely and totally—that they conceded. Taking the moral high ground, they analyzed the historically documentable willingness of women to present their bodies as sites for male visual pleasure or consumerist display as an effect of the false devaluing of women's minds typical of aristocratic or feudal or pagan—that is, pre-Enlightenment, prerepublican—ideologies. The fact that mind and body were distinct meant that the weaker body did not imply a weaker mind.

From the labor-intensive perspective of a world of small social structures and economic scarcity they perceived bearing, birthing, and suckling children as taxing, necessary physical labor imposed on women by nature or an inscrutable God, and they accepted the idea that whatever additional work women took on had to comport with child rearing. Child rearing itself, however, could be defined in different ways: It could be mere physical nurture, or it might be far more complex intellectual work. And now, thanks to print technology, it seemed also that the reach of intellectual homework could extend far beyond one's own young children. Then, if it was rational to maximize every human being's contribution to the social good, and especially necessary to do so in a new and vulnerable nation, differences in body strength between the sexes could suggest a division of labor where men did more physical, women more intellectual work. In other words, the inarguably greater physical strength of men and the duties that such strength imposed on them might be used to legitimate women as intellectual workers. With respect to republican employment, men could perform the various tasks involved in physically building the nation, including waging its wars, and women the various tasks involved in the ideological acculturation of its citizenry. It was to this effect that Hannah Mather Crocker, an American Enlightenment feminist, observed that "men have less time for observation," and "therefore men's calculations in society must be more slow and less sure than women's, as applied to government."[8]

The earliest American women's writing emerged from and took part in just this discursive expansion.[9] In particular, it underlay a powerful cultural representation of the American woman citizen contributing to the polity through patriotic—and, even more specifically, through historical— writing. Insofar as our present-day definition of literature, or, more generally, of writing, is limited to poem, play, story, and novel—and insofar as the feminist enterprise of recovering women's writing emphasizes private, putatively unpublished forms like journal, diary, and letters—we have been instructed to perceive women writers as largely sealed off from public discourse, working outside the public sphere. To notice the prevalence of history writing, therefore—even though it is likely not, by present-day standards, "good" history—is to begin to see how often and how openly American women have written in public forms for public purposes. We then recover a different sort of writing woman from the madwoman in the attic and acquire materials to begin constructing a different narrative of American women's literary history. I do not mean, of course, to suggest that there were and are no madwomen in attics or that women have not been silenced or that we have all been able to write when and as we wanted (assuming that we knew or know our wishes). The existence of highly visible alternative female discursive practices, however, limits the applicability of this reigning paradigm.

The examples of Deborah Norris Logan (1761–1839), Mercy Otis Warren (1728–1814), and Hannah Adams (1755–1831)—none of them educators—will stand here for the larger phenomenon. Logan did not start writing until the second decade of the nineteenth century. In 1814 she discovered disorderly heaps of correspondence between William Penn and his agent, her husband's grandfather, in the attic of the Logan homestead and set about arranging, transcribing, and annotating this material. After her husband George died in 1821 she wrote a memoir of his life defending his politics. She presented the original correspondence and her annotated transcriptions, along with a memoir of her husband, to the American Philosophical Society, where they at once became basic sources for early Pennsylvania history. Warren published in the 1770s, brought out a collection of poems and plays in 1790, and completed a substantial history of the American Revolution around 1791, which she published in 1805. Adams was the first American professional woman of letters, perhaps the first American professional *person* of letters, having turned to writing after the Revolution to support herself. Her historical dictionary of religious sects appeared in 1784 and had several reissues; among other works, she published a history of New England (1799) and a history of the Jews (1812).[10] None of these three wrote or published pseudonymously.

As a particularly heavily mediated cultural activity, history writing in the early Republic required of its male and female practitioners alike such traits as a comparatively high level of literacy, access to large numbers of fairly costly books, and considerable political self-consciousness. (Later the wide availability of precursor and inexpensive, popularly written history books made it much easier for women to embark on history writing.) All three women possessed these cultural traits. All three accepted an Enlightenment notion of history as progressive and, taking the United States as the nation most favored by history, justified their history writing in historical terms as the outcome of the twinned principles of republican patriotism and universal Reason that I have already identified. All three presented themselves as instantiations of the American woman as the American Revolution had produced her. Indeed, most of the American women who did this kind of work authorized it as a specifically American phenomenon and derived from this sense of exceptional national enablement the nationalist/patriotic agenda that their writings then go on to feature.

Given the imagined sexual division of labor based on brute strength that I have outlined, one is not surprised to find Logan, Warren, and Adams conceptualizing written history as the record of the rise and fall of "nations" through the hard masculine work of war and diplomacy. *Nation,* as Eric Hobsbawm and others have reminded us, is a problematic term, but for these women it did not seem so. Nations, to them, were aggregations of peoples constituted by geography and war into governed units. The idea that print was actually constitutive of the nation—as scholars like Benedict Anderson and Michael Warner propose—would not have accorded with these women's self-understanding, but that print participated crucially in nation building was precisely the reason why they were writing.[11] For if women's lesser bodily strength situated them as spectators rather than agents of historical deeds, the role of witness did not prevent them from writing about what they had seen. On the contrary, it could be maintained that this privileged role virtually compelled them to testify. Was it not the obligation of the witness, precisely, to testify? Placing the agonistic domain of force outside their sphere, women appropriated all the more energetically for themselves—feminized from the start—the reflective yet public domain of writing. If one granted that women's and men's minds were alike, notwithstanding the difference in bodies, one could partition the labor of history between the sexes to make men out to be the soldiers and statesmen, women the scribes, transmitters, and, ultimately, the philosophers of history.

These early forms of women's history writing, then, reproduce men's physical activity *in* history as women's writing *of* history. The doubling of men's physical labor by women's mental labor created parallel, distinct tasks that converged to accomplish the national destiny and—these were Protestant Christians as well as patriotic women—God's plan. This stress on doubling meant that they were not historians of women. Nor did they strive to invent a woman's language. They wrote confidently as women but, like men, consistent with their beliefs that neither mind nor language (by which mind makes itself known and effective) were sexed. To have developed either a generically female history or a specifically feminine writing style in this context would have been to embody and genderize mind—as, very likely, these women thought it was already embodied and genderized in the novel, a genre which most of them emphatically rejected.

While they share this conjunction of Enlightenment with American republican themes, the works of Logan, Warren, and Adams are differently inflected by the rhetoric of other cultural fields: family for Logan, politics (in the customary sense of the word) for Warren, religion for Adams. These inflections produce somewhat different representations of female national identity among the three. Logan comes across as a traditional goodwife, motivated to write the achievements of her husband and his family into the historical record. Warren offers herself to the nation as a generalized republican mother—a public mother conveying republican values to the next generation of Americans at large by reminding them of their history. Adams, writing for the market, is neither wife nor mother but a liberal Protestant empowered by religious zeal, a proto–Unitarian Evangelical.[12]

Although Logan did not publish, the public intentions of her writing are obvious, and the gift of her manuscripts to the American Philosophical Society placed them effectively in the public domain. At the outset of her memoir of her husband's life Logan sets herself up as both loyal wife and veracious historian: "I have thought it to be my duty for the information of his family and posterity, but without any view whatever to the publication of the present work, to attempt some biographical notices of his life and character. . . . the only claim to attention which I can urge will be the uncommon disinterestedness, patriotism, and integrity of the character whose delineation I am about to attempt and the strict regard to veracity which shall guide my pen in this undertaking."[13]

As she worked to install the Logan family at the center of Pennsylvania history, Deborah Logan moved smoothly from family to regional and national narrative. "In contemplating the sudden rise of Pennsylvania to her present state of wealth, strength, and resources, the mind becomes curious to trace the steps of such prosperity; and I flatter myself that I am performing an acceptable service to my fellow-citizens in discovering to their view some of the remote rills and fountains which are the sources of the majestic river we now survey."[14] Logan's reference to the curiosity of an ungendered Enlightenment mind makes mind as much a motive for writing as her status as wife. Nor is patriotism absent: "perhaps it is not going too far to call the original frame of Government designed by William Penn for his Province, and the preliminary discourse affixed to it, the fountains from which have emanated most of those streams of political wisdom which now flow through every part of united America, diffusing civil and religious liberty, and favouring the expansion of happiness and virtue."[15]

During the quasi war of 1798 George Logan had taken it on himself to go to France and negotiate privately with the French government on behalf of the United States. This behavior put him under suspicion of treason and led to the passage of the so-called Logan Law forbidding private citizens to negotiate for their governments. Since she was not witness to her husband's experiences in France, Logan writes this crucial part of her memoir as the record of his absence and of the effect of this absence on her own life, in effect making herself the historical subject. "Were it proper here to speak of myself," she writes, "I could say a great deal, with the strictest truth, of the infinite anxiety of mind which I underwent at this period," then goes on to say precisely a great deal.

> I could not help being appalled with a sense of the difficulties which he would have to surmount, and the clamour which would be raised upon his departure; so that, when he left me indeed, I was as completely miserable as I could be whilst innocent myself and united to a man whose honour I knew to be without a stain. But I found it necessary, by a strong effort, to control my feelings. I must now crave permission to relate what was my own situation, and what were the events which occurred to me during the perilous time of my husband's absence.[16]

Along with vivid sketches of her encounters with, and character assessments of, Franklin, Jefferson, Washington, Lafayette, and other prominent men, Logan offers her own as well as her husband's views on the political achievements and currents of the times. Her account, both in its showing and telling, presents the writer, and implicitly all women, as double witness to historical actions that are performed by men: Women see what men do and also experience the effects of what men do as the determinants of their own lives. In the role of family historians many other United States women besides Deborah Logan have compiled archives that do not naively transcribe but complexly respond to a sense of history as simultaneously event and record as well as self-consciously exercising their felt or assumed responsibilities to history.[17]

Mercy Otis Warren lived amid revolutionary politics all her adult life. Her home in Plymouth was a gathering place for patriots, and she served the cause early on by writing dramatic satires of the royal Massachusetts government. Throughout her life she remained equally distrustful of inherited privilege and democratic mobs. Placing republicanism ahead of nationhood, she held that the United States deserved to survive only if it survived as a republic. The two blank-verse historical tragedies in her collection *Poems Dramatic and Miscellaneous* (1790) are object lessons in how republics fail. For her, as for innumerable other like-minded ideologues, republican survival depended on the frail reed of citizen virtue. Hence women's task of inculcating virtue possessed momentous political significance.

Warren's 1805 *History of the Rise, Progress and Termination of the American Revolution, Interspersed with Biographical, Political and Moral Observations* is a crabby, tendentious, outspoken work whose melodramatic narrative presents the monarchist British as monsters and the republican Americans as paragons. Its greatest attractions today will probably be its "observations," which range widely over human affairs and from which one may extract the author's self-reflexive justification for the public undertaking of the *History*. The work opens, for example, with self-justification:

> At a period when every manly arm was occupied, and every trait of talent or activity engaged, either in the cabinet or the field, apprehensive, that amidst the sudden convulsions, crowded scenes, and rapid changes, that flowed in quick succession, many circumstances might escape the more busy and active members of society, I have been induced to improve the leisure Providence had lent, to record as they passed, in the following pages, the new and unexperienced events exhibited in a land previously blessed with peace, liberty, simplicity, and virtue. . . . The solemnity that covered every countenance, when contemplating the sword uplifted, and the horrors of civil war rushing to habitations not inured to scenes of rapine and misery; even to the quiet cottage, where only concord and affection had reigned; stimulated to observation a mind that had not yielded to the assertion, that all political attentions lay out of the road of female life.[18]

What leads Warren to write—what requires her to write—is the conjunction of (1) a mind unwilling to accept politics as a solidly male sphere, (2) a crisis that extends into the specifically female sphere because it imperils the "quiet cottage," and (3) a particularly privileged spectator position that is gendered, since all the men in her group were too busy making war to witness it.

Nor is this all. Her womanly obligation to teach the young also calls for the *History:* "Nor need it cause a blush to acknowledge, a detail was preserved with a view of transmitting it to the rising youth of my country, some of them in infancy, others in the European world, while the most interesting events lowered over their native land" (*H*, 1:xliii). Warren presents herself here in the double aspect of both a gendered (blushing) body and an ungendered mind, whose gender-determined labor is circularly to inculcate, in this case through the production of a deeply felt history that only she can write, the republican values and virtues that will safeguard her body and authorize her mind.

Since both her brother James Otis and her husband, James Warren, were active in patriot politics (her husband, for example, was president of the Provincial Congress of Massachusetts) Warren, like Logan, probably had family reasons for writing the *History*. But except for one passionate excursus on her brother, she mutes the family note, stressing patriotism not family ties. Her own self-representation accordingly rewrites the homebound republican mother as the mother-teacher of her country—as the republican public mother. In this crucial trope the public and private spheres are so thoroughly intermingled, at least on the rhetoric level, that there can be no possible demarcation of their boundaries.

Nor is this all. At one point in the *History* Warren expresses hope that readers will not object to the various digressions "on the moral conduct of man, on religious opinion or persecutions, and the motives by which mankind are actuated in their various pursuits" which punctuate her account. These, she continues, "are more congenial to the taste, inclination, and sex of the writer, than a detail of the rough and terrific scenes of war. Nor will a serious or philosophic mind be displeased with such an interlude, which may serve as a temporary resting-post to the weary traveller, who has trodden over the field of carnage, until the soul is sickened by a view of the absurdity and cruelty of his own species" (*H*, 1:339). The apology calls attention to, genderizes, and valorizes the narrator's habitual practice. The commentary improves the narrative by intellectualizing it and improves readers by instructing them in the meaning and morality of events. This product of a "serious or philosophic mind," this better kind of writing, is associated with the female.

From Warren's republican perspective the gendered deployment of labor that follows from differential physical strength allows upper-class women to develop their intellectual abilities while demanding that such abilities be used for the public good. When representing women in the war years, which she does only occasionally, Warren tellingly focuses on the very bodily weakness that disqualifies them from physical participation in warlike activities and exposes them—literally—to the violence of war. The patriotic behavior of the ladies of South Carolina, for a mild example, was "resented by the officers of the [British] army, who themselves affronted them, and exposed them to insults of every kind, instead of defending the tender and helpless sex, as is justly expected, and required by the laws of civilization and humanity" (*H*, 2:449). The murder of Jane McCrea is a more horrific instance; representations of female tenderness and helplessness across all social classes underwrite the melodramatic depictions of insult, rape, and murder which constitute the only narrative of how women were "in" the Revolution that Warren seems able to imagine.[19]

These sado-erotic images are consistent with Warren's standpoint. She speaks on behalf of the domestic confines within which women are freed from the vulnerability of their weaker bodies and thereby liberated to observe, reflect, comment, and teach. The dominance of men on the basis of superior strength is taken for granted, making it rational for women to search for male protectors, to differentiate good men from bad ones. Believing that only the republican form of government valued domesticity and protected women from violence in principle, Warren gives women particular reason to be loyal and grateful republican citizens and enacts her own loyalty and gratitude by writing in praise of the republican nation, by participating in the nation's intellectual work. Warren's *History* can be seen as the end product of gendered labor performed by a woman on behalf of the form of government that had given her precisely this intellectual work to do. In the *History* Warren gives back to the republic the fruits of the republic's gift to her.

Hannah Adams's self-presentation as historian is significantly differentiated from that of Logan and Warren by her experience, as an unmarried woman, in a market economy. For her the fact that mind has no sex is of crucial importance if one needs to exchange one's abilities for cash, for by her own account she was exceptionally physically debilitated (and exceptionally psychologically timid), even for a woman. While not entirely physically untaxing—if, that is, women's minds are equal to men's—writing becomes the one arena in which she has a chance to succeed as well as an arena in which she does not need to be on display. The equality of men's and women's minds is the burden of the publisher's preface to her 1791 *View of Religions:* "if an invidious comparison between the sexes is in any respect justifiable, it cannot be grounded upon a defect of natural ability, but upon the different, and perhaps faulty mode of female education; for under similar culture, and with equal advantages, it is far from being certain, that the female mind would not admit a measure of improvement, which would at least equal, and perhaps in many instances eclipse, the boasted glory of the other sex." [20]

In her posthumously published memoir Adams allegorizes her life to show how self-education overcomes bad habits, as though feminizing Franklin's *Autobiography.* Although warped by the inconsistent attentions of an invalid mother and spoiled by too much novel reading in girlhood, Adams is saved when she is introduced to Latin, Greek, geography, and logic by men boarding at her father's house. She overcomes the degraded mental gendering of pre-Enlightenment times and rises—not into a man's world but into the pan-gendered world of logocentrism that has hitherto been reserved for men only. She studies these subjects "with indescribable pleasure and avidity." Religious history, encountered in a manuscript owned by one of these same boarders, inspired a particularly "ardent curiosity" which she gratified by "assiduously" reading every book on the subject that she could find. Then, "disgusted with the want of candor" in authors who gave "the most unfavorable description of the denominations they disliked," she "formed a plan" for herself and began the notebook compilation eventually published as her *View of Religions.* [21]

In this account Adams dwells on the impediments of her physical and intellectual feebleness, the latter the effect of an unsystematic and mainly sentimental literary education. "Reading much religious controversy must be extremely trying to a female, whose mind, instead of being strengthened by those studies which exercise the judgment, and give stability to the character, is debilitated by reading romances and novels, which are addressed to the fancy and imagination, and are calculated to heighten the feelings." [22] She insists that she turned to professional writing only because standard women's wage-earning work was beyond her: She was an untalented needle-woman and lacked the energy for teaching.

Finally, however, she shows that even the compelling need to make a living did not justify her professional work. Even as she deplores her feminine susceptibility to emotional excitement, she uses that very excitement, that "ardent curiosity," to authorize public writing. For her no less than for Logan and Warren, writing demanded an affective as well as a purely intellectual rationalization and an end product that could be interpreted as womanly employment performed on behalf of the nation. None of these women hold an ideology of romantic selfhood that makes mere possession of intellectual capabilities sufficient reason for publicly expressing them. Some kind of caring, some form of love, is also required: For Logan it was the love of husband, for Warren the love of republicanism, and for Adams the love of Christ.

Adams proposes that her *View of Religions* might help save Christianity from its own rancorous, parochial sectarianism, a sectarianism that exposes it to Enlightenment skepticism, even to atheism. Authorized by a universal Reason that transcends gender, Adams implements that belief in the service of a historical, developing Christianity whose progress is threatened. The United States—the nation that has overthrown English tyranny and rejected French atheism—is the potential site of a future-perfect Christianity, a Christianity that exceeds the doctrines of any of its sects, a transdoctrinal and ultimately transhistorical Christianity: in a word, the millennium. As with so many women throughout American life—whose work has been doubly erased from the record through the historiographical rupture between religion and politics *and* the absence of women in such histories of religion in America as exist—patriotic Christian activism justifies Adams's departure from, or her expansion of, the woman's sphere.[23]

Adams's 1799 *Summary History of New England* was the first codification and synthesis of the numerous scattered and individual regional New England histories, most of which predated the Revolution. Rewriting New England history from a post-Revolutionary perspective (and depending heavily on—indeed, openly cribbing from—David Ramsey's itself plagiarized history of the Revolution for that part of the narrative), the *Summary History* makes explicit the line that these earlier histories could only prefigure. To wit: New England history was controlled by Divine intentions that overrode or overruled those of the settlers themselves. She sees New England as the core of the United States and sees the United States from the vantage point of that eighteenth-century millennialism according to which God's intentions comprised, at that historical moment, the establishment of a republican form of government on the North American continent.[24]

In her condensed and rewritten textbook derived from the New England history Adams underscores this Providentialism, representing herself in what would prove to be an influential Christianized version of the republican public mother:

> Reviewing the history of New England and the late American Revolution, we find the wonders of divine Providence rising conspicuous in every scene. . . . Pious minds perceive with grateful admiration the controuling hand of Providence rendering every event subservient to the liberty and independence of the United States. . . . This highly favoured people ought to raise their minds in fervent aspirations, that their fair prospects may never be reversed by a temper of disunion, or a spirit of anarchy prevailing among the people, but that genuine liberty, united with order and good government, may diffuse their blessings through the widely extended union.[25]

Adams displays the combination of liberal, albeit highly pietistic, Christianity with conservative politics that characterized the New England Federalist elite, and it was indeed a group of Federalist politicians who eventually provided an annuity for her, linking their quarrel with the Calvinist Jedidiah Morse to his threat to bring out a textbook rival to Adams's.[26] My point here is not so much that active and outspoken American women are frequently politically conservative (a fact that we contemporary feminists find difficult to understand or accept but which is, nonetheless, true) but that, already in this early period, even the profoundly conservative Federalists had no objection to supporting and publicizing a woman's intellectual work whose views coincided with theirs.

Federalist patronage also made it possible for Adams to write her substantial, implicitly providential *History of the Jews* (1812). This study builds slowly and painstakingly through masses of historical material, much of it surprisingly gory in view of Adams's stress on her own timidity. The detail is controlled by an implicit narrative in which the United States figures as the place where the dispersed Jewish nation is finding sanctuary and support and hence reconstituting itself. This means that the conversion of the Jews is most likely to happen in the United States, proof that the United States is the nation selected by Providence to bring in the millennium, since, one remembers, the conversion of the Jews is a precondition for its arrival.

I have all too briefly described three writers who are recognizably pre-Victorian in their Enlightenment refusal to see mind as affected by its connection to a gendered body. In the most general terms the Victorian ideology of women's intellect rejects the sexless mind, elevates the value of spirituality over intellect, and associates women with spirituality. Accepting some idea of essential embodiment, ideologues of Victorian womanhood attempt to minimize negative implications of this idea by insisting that minds as embodied in the two sexes are incommensurable. Women are not less intellectual but differently intellectual, *qualitatively* different from men. While continuing to differentiate bodies in Enlightenment terms, that is, on the basis of physical strength, such ideology transforms woman's physical weakness into a sign of spirituality through the mediating idea of ethereality. A weaker body equals less body, and less body equals more spirit. The more spirit, the more godlike—so that, in its extreme formulation, woman, in her lesser body, becomes the invisible Christian God incarnate.[27]

This shift is obviously one of many ideological alterations as well as an array of socioeconomic changes in the years between, say, 1820 and 1860—changes that were bringing into being a middle class that had not earlier existed. The shift involved a gamut of responses to the reality of middle-class women's physical labor, responses that tended to converge, however, in two ways. First, they defined working-class women, and frequently upper-class women as well, out of the sex altogether—working-class women because they possessed masculine bodies, upper-class women because they were obsessed with bodily adornment.[28] Second, they attempted in practical terms to lessen the physical dimension of middle-class women's labor. More and more, the work of middle-class women was deemed to be wholly intellectual, even as the idea of what counted as intellectual for women changed. The shift to sexually divergent bodies also correlates to increasing preoccupation with psychology and the inner life, the return (or reaffirmation) of fiction as women's chosen literary form, and the identification of a supposedly apolitical character formation as the appropriate subject of the literature women wrote and read.[29]

That men generally had a mechanical understanding of the mundane outer world, women a transcendent intuitive grasp of the immaterial realm within and beyond, was seen to be the obvious result of their naturally different kinds of body. And there are connected shifts in the terms of religious discourse, from rationalist to emotive spirituality, which allowed Victorian American women to appropriate religion far more thoroughly than Hannah Adams had dreamed of doing. An appropriation, spiritualization, and embodiment of the Romantic idea of intuitive reason in the female form may be noted in the utterance of many prominent Victorian American women of letters, including Sarah J. Hale, Margaret Fuller, Elizabeth Peabody, Lydia M. Child, and Harriet Beecher Stowe.[30] Among them, women who came to adulthood in the 1820s, when the political ideology of republican womanhood continued to exert power, expressed themselves with particular force; their Victorianism supplemented and complicated rather than supplanted their Enlightenment republicanism.

For those ardent Victorian women republicans who believed that history was in some sense progressive, and that the United States was the most progressive nation, it came to seem that progress was toward an ever greater spiritualization (or, more narrowly, toward an ever greater Christianization) of the material world, evidence for which could be seen (circularly) in the increasing influence of women on the life of the nation and even the life of the world. This historical view underlies Sarah Hale's 1852 compendium

Woman's Record, where, as Hale explained in the preface, "Those who hold the doctrine of equality will be no doubt shocked to hear that I am convinced the difference between the constructive genius of man and woman is the result of an organic difference in the operations of their minds." Whereas woman inhabits "the world of life, not of things," man "models the world of matter."[31] By contrast, Judith Sargent Murray, one of the two Enlightenment-era historians of women-as-such, had based her account on claims of equality: Scrutiny of the historical record showed women to be equally brave, equally intelligent, equally articulate, equally loyal (and so on) as men.[32] The passionate opposition of many women like Hale to women's suffrage (women who, from "our" perspective, ought to have taken a different position) stemmed from their alarm over suffragist women's rejection of opportunities and responsibilities that a feminized and feminizing world had—at last!—made available to them.[33]

Combining the idea of women's spiritualized intellect with the idea of a historical movement toward the progressively more spiritual, this group of American women looked for signs of a specifically female role in history, signs that they assumed would not have been readily visible before history and women arrived at their present stage of development—in other words, to begin thinking both about the history of women and about history *as* the history of women. From hybrid Enlightenment-Victorian ideology emerged the notion of a separate woman's culture undergirded by a distinctively female mentality, which, it was claimed, had existed silently throughout history but whose moment of historical vocality had come in the nineteenth-century republic of America. This complex of ideas authorized numerous published compendia of celebrated women, of which *Woman's Record* was the most ambitious, as well as many ventures into a woman's kind of historical fiction that placed plausible, although imaginary, heroines in real historical situations and gave them influential roles therein.[34]

Victorian American women across the spectrum of political belief authorized their various public interventions throughout the antebellum period by means of appeals to this essentialist ideology. The idea of a sexless mind, which had enabled an earlier generation of active literary women to enter the public scene, did not work for the group of women who became articulate after 1820. There are numerous possible explanations for this development; two seem relevant here. First, although the Enlightenment stance did not foreclose women's bodily appearance in the public scene, it did not authorize it. At the historical moment when women wanted to become, or were compelled to become, bodily participants in public activities it would be necessary to develop a different rationale or to connect the sexless mind to the sexed body in some new configuration. Second, as the techniques of disseminating print images improved dramatically, ever more graphic representations of women's bodies entered the print arena itself, where they might have exerted some counterpull to the sexless spectacle of women represented by print letters. Neither development necessitated rejecting the concept of a universal, ungendered mind, but they complicated it.

Victorian American women, however, refused to give up the ground that they stood on thanks to their Enlightenment predecessors. They did not reject the appropriation of history writing and of history itself that had been accomplished on behalf of women by the earlier generation because they produced history writing in great quantities. They made women's supposed spirituality the basis for defining women as agents of historical progress, installing them ever more centrally in history, extending, not relinquishing, their grasp on history. Their talk of women's domesticity and women's sphere was conducted, in implicitly historicized rhetoric, in the public space of print culture. They expanded the project of history writing into a range of literary modes as a staple of their literary production. And in this writing—no matter how they represented women—they continued to write as women, but like men. They continued, that is, to claim reason and public language as constituents of their humanity.

8

Women and the Republic
Emma Willard's Rhetoric
of History

Although we celebrate the first woman poet in America for her personal and confessional lyrics, Anne Bradstreet was praised in her own day for writing history. *The Four Monarchies,* the lengthy centerpiece of her 1640 *Tenth Muse,* is a rhymed history of the kingdoms of Assyria, Persia, Greece, and Rome. A century and a half later, when the first generation of national writers began working, most of the literary women of the period—Hannah Adams, Ann Eliza Bleecker, Sarah Wentworth Morton, Judith Sargent Murray, Sarah Pierce, Susanna Rowson, and Mercy Otis Warren—wrote historical poems, plays, fictions, narratives, and textbooks, some to the virtual exclusion of anything else.

The history writing activity of this first group was continued by over a hundred literary women working between 1800 and 1860. The number suggests that such writing must have figured importantly in the way women approached and entered the public realms of action and literature as well as the ways in which they represented their own proper sphere of behavior. In writing history women were evidently engaging in an overtly public literary practice with political implications. In so doing, they made "woman" a nondomestic participant *in* history and crucially blurred the supposedly sacrosanct boundaries between the private and public.[1]

As all scholars of antebellum American discourse have agreed, history held the place of honor in the cultural hierarchy of literary modes, and knowledge of history was thought essential to an educated republican citizenry. That the survival of the republic required educated women as well as educated men became a rationale for establishing numerous post-Revolutionary female academies in which women were supposedly trained to understand their obligations as republican mothers. While never doubting that women's activities would center on home duties, the Enlightenment ideology of republican motherhood—unlike the sentimental Victorian maternalism that supplanted it—defined those activities as educated efforts of the head rather than untutored effusions of the heart. Under the banner of the Enlightenment tenet that mind had no sex, educators of American women argued that women, who had to understand republicanism and America's place in the world to fulfill their gendered work of instructing children in and keeping spouses true to republican principles, were fully capable of acquiring the education they needed.[2] And since universal history formed the repository within which examples of earlier republics were stored and since the nascent field of American history gave Americans the basis for understanding their own particular mission, it was history in particular that republican mothers needed to know.

As they studied history, women would discover that the need for educated women was itself a historical phenomenon, since it had not existed in earlier times. Experiencing the liberation and expansion of their intellects produced by this study, they would know firsthand the compelling advantages of republicanism for their own sex. Now, as the field of writing expanded to an extent that encouraged, indeed required, the presence of women in the print circuit, it stood to reason that literary women would define history writing as an appropriate field for their enterprise. And this enterprise would likely carry a very different literary meaning from their writing novels, at least in the early stages of our national history. If, as Cathy N. Davidson has argued, the early American novel was a form with potential countercultural force, then—as the common, invidious opposition between novel reading and history reading for women invites us to theorize—the study of history may be theorized as an attempt by the establishment to secure the allegiance of this marginalized population.[3] Whereas the novelistic spur to aimless narcissistic fantasizing kept women isolated and apart from the polity while exacerbating their discontents with that polity, the discipline of history joined them to the body politic by allowing them access to its core of knowledge and by giving them the sense that just to possess such knowledge was to help preserve the republic. The notable presence of women among the writers of popular history therefore points to a cultural scene in which gender is perceived as functioning within an overriding national identity—in which, one might say, gender is historicized by nationality. Women who wrote history were identifying themselves and their sex with the establishment.

The distinction between history and other forms of woman-centered discourse (novel, personal lyric) that I am stressing here became far less pressing when, thanks to Sir Walter Scott, a way was found to merge history with fiction. Antinovel sentiment among members of the cultural establishment abated strikingly and by no means coincidentally as the practice of historical fiction in the mode of Scott increasingly took hold. From the 1820s on, conventional strictures against novel reading for women were qualified by explicit exemptions of historical fiction from the forbidden field.[4] Historical fiction opened a new mode of history writing to American women, one that they pursued with zest, turning out historical novels in great numbers from the 1820s onwards. But alongside this development, women continued to produce nonfictional narrative histories in a variety of modes and for a variety of purposes.

The instance of Emma Willard (1787–1870) represents the double practice of educator and history writer common to many other women from the early national period, including Susanna Rowson, Sarah Pierce, Elizabeth Peabody and her daughter Elizabeth Palmer Peabody, Lydia Maria Child, Lydia Huntley Sigourney, Eliza Robbins, and (somewhat later) Augusta Berard. But Willard was uniquely successful in both domains. Troy Female Seminary, which she founded and directed for many years, has been well publicized; less well known are her history textbooks. These books, continuously republished and revised over almost fifty years, must have been a key source of historical knowledge for many thousands of Americans and, thus, in their own time might have had far broader cultural significance than the more focused achievement of the seminary.

Willard's American history textbook combined the two strands that students of republican thought have distinguished as "liberal" and "classical"— the former deeply committed to an expansionist, entrepreneurial, and imperial vision of the American future, the latter fearful of the "corruption" that would overtake a republic when citizens pursued private gain instead of public good—and thereby used the "classical" American past as a way to authorize the "liberal" American future.[5] Her *Universal History in Perspective* essayed the millennial task of demonstrating that the American republic was nothing less than the beginning of the fulfillment of a Divine plan for world peace. As for the position of women within the republic, Willard's own performance demonstrated that the properly educated woman could at one and the same time herself be a successful entrepreneur *and* serve her country in a way that transcended gender boundaries without overturning sexual difference. Her textbooks, that is to say, constituted an expansion of the work of republican motherhood, and the classical republican mother became a liberal economic success.

Like many New England girls from large farm families, Willard was a poorly educated local schoolteacher in her teenaged years.[6] As preceptress of a girls' academy in Middlebury, Vermont, in 1814, she was struck by the difference between what the men at Middlebury College were being taught and what she had received by way of an education, and she was outraged when her request to attend classes at Middlebury was denied. Acting out of a ferocious ambition whose origins can only be guessed at, she "formed the design of effecting an important change in education by the introduction of a grade of schools for women higher than any heretofore known. . . . I determined to inform myself, and increase my personal influence and fame as a teacher, calculating that, in this way, I might be sought for in other places, where influential men would carry my project before some Legislature, for the sake of obtaining a good school." [7]

The first result of that determination was a carefully composed and densely reasoned *Plan for Improving Female Education,* which she circulated among a large audience of influential citizens; when published in 1819 it came to the attention of city officials in Troy, New York, and led to the founding of the Troy Female Seminary in 1821, which Willard directed until 1838. The argument of the *Plan* derives entirely from the rhetoric of republican ideology, splicing an assertion of woman's intellectual and spiritual equality with men to an assertion of her gendered social duties in a republic. [8]

During the years that she presided at Troy, and later as she worked with Henry Barnard in the 1840s, Willard also wrote the successful history textbooks whose researching, revising, and updating occupied much of her time, permitted her to travel around the country and correspond with statesmen, and made her rich and famous. The number of editions of her various texts is impressive. In 1822 she brought out a brief (under one hundred pages) historically oriented *Ancient Geography,* which, sometimes bound separately and sometimes bound together with a modern geography text written by William Woodbridge, had over fourteen printings between its first appearance and its last in 1847. The substantial *History of the United States; or, Republic of America* (close to five hundred pages) was her bestseller, first published in 1828 and enjoying a total of fifty-three reprintings and revisions in regular and abridged versions between its first edition and its last in 1873; it was also translated into German and Spanish. In 1849 Willard published popular histories of the Mexican War and the settlement of California; in the latter she directly addressed emigrants on their way to the new state, loftily counseling them on principles of good government. These local histories were worked into revisions of her general American history textbook after 1850. The unabridged version, printed on heavy stock in a large format with a good binding and large print, was advertised by the publishers as suitable for academies and private libraries; the shorter school history, small print and small size, was offered to common schools. The intended audience for this history, then, was the entire literate population. [9]

Willard's *Universal History* was an even longer work than the American history. Appearing first in 1835, it had twenty-four reprintings up to its last edition in 1882; Willard also published a separate teachers' manual of world chronology to accompany it. Like the longer American history, *Universal History* was designed for private libraries as well as schools. Both histories in all their editions contained chronological charts and geographical maps. Notwithstanding that it was already a truism that "chronology and geography are the eyes of history" when Willard began her work, it appears that she was the first textbook historian in America to include historical maps in the book itself. This territorial visualization of history, derived in part from her earlier work as a geographer, had much to do with the way that she identified the nation with its political occupation of space.

When one approaches Willard's *Plan for Improving Female Education* and her textbooks as exercises in a rhetoric of history, her overriding commitment to republicanism and the extent to which an ideology of woman's place is articulated within the frame of that commitment become clear. Willard's thematics is consistently that of a filiopietistic patriotism uniting American men and women in a common republican heritage and differentiating them by the necessarily gendered tasks they must perform to serve the nation. They are necessarily gendered because, as Willard's long view so clearly shows, history is a record of incessant warfare, warfare requires warriors, and only men can be warriors. Men and women alike are required to subordinate themselves—*subordination* was one of Willard's favorite words—to the needs of their country but differences in bodily strength dictate that they do so in different ways.

Readers will better understand the dynamics of Willard's *Plan* as well as the more general trajectory of her aims if they rid themselves of the commonly held notion that Willard's chief educational project was to train professional teachers. Notwithstanding the transformation of the American class structure since the early nineteenth century as a predominantly rural economy gave way to an industrial one, it has always been the case that teachers originate in the middle to lower classes rather than the higher social strata. Now, as then, the daughters of the true elite are generally trained to become wives of elite men, not workers in their own right, while women teachers are recruited from groups whose women members need paid work for at least part of their lives. To educate women from such groups requires either economic sacrifice by their families or outside subvention. While Willard did support perhaps a tenth of her pupils on scholarships and train them as teachers, she had other plans for the remaining 90 percent.[10] Fowler, writing in 1861, observed that

> it was always Mrs. Willard's design to limit the number of teacher-scholars, so that the institution would not incur financial disaster by carrying too heavy a burden. And since normal schools, distinctively established and endowed, have removed the necessity of pursuing the system at the seminary, it has been for the most part abandoned, and its present pupils are generally from wealthy parents, and those whose object is to fit their daughters for private life.[11]

What might seem peculiar in this context but is actually the very point (although no commentator on Willard's work has noted it) is that the *Plan* solicited government funding to educate wealthy young women, which would seem quite unnecessary. Willard specifically attacked the current mode of educating the daughters of the wealthy, asserting that, unless the state paid the bill, curricular content would continue to be dictated by parents and women's education would never improve. Only if control of education was removed from the family and placed in the domain of the state can women be educated for the state:

> It is the duty of a government, to do all in its power to promote the present and future prosperity of the nation, over which it is placed. This prosperity will depend on the character of its citizens. The characters of these will be formed by their mothers; and it is through the mothers, that the government can control the characters of its future citizens, to form them such as will ensure their country's prosperity. If this is the case, then it is the duty of our present legislators to begin now, to form the characters of the next generation, by controlling that of the females, who are to be their mothers, while it is yet with them a season of improvement. (*Plan*, 16)

As Willard represents matters, the fashionably educated woman is not merely frivolous, she is downright dangerous to republican social order, threatening to dissipate the national wealth in idle luxury. This is no empty threat since history shows that it has happened before.

> In those great republics, which have fallen of themselves, the loss of republican manners and virtues, has been the invariable precursor, of their loss of the republican form of government. . . . It may be said, that the depravation of morals and manners, can be traced to the introduction of wealth, as its cause. But wealth will be introduced; even the iron laws of Lycurgus could not prevent it. Let us then inquire, if means may not be devised, to prevent its bringing with it the destruction of public virtue. May not these means be found in education? (*Plan*, 30)

The allusion to Lycurgus, the Spartan lawgiver, installs Willard's argument in a traditional historical narrative, while additionally demonstrating by her own example the value of historical knowledge to women. The rhetoric of Spartan self-sacrifice and patriotism was omnipresent in the Revolutionary and post-Revolutionary eras and, indeed, flourished in the Jacksonian period as well; yet Sparta, as its history was commonly understood, declined after the Peloponnesian War. As Sarah Pomeroy explains, "The simplicity and rigorousness of life in Sparta during the Archaic Age gradually gave way to a more relaxed and luxurious way of living," a "corruption of the earlier regime" for which "Greek and Roman writers tend to blame the women."[12] Willard, then, was here addressing the conundrum that, according to all students of republican discourse, has regularly vexed republican ideologists: the corruptive threat to virtue posed by wealth. Her proposition that national prosperity, though inevitable and desirable, nevertheless threatened the polity through its overliberated women was familiarized and naturalized by historical reference.

The *Plan* thus brings to the fore an anxiety-producing vision of female rapacity, appetite, and endless desire that would not be unfamiliar to its audience. It salves that anxiety by insisting that these female traits are to be understood not as an expression of the Eternal Woman but as the historical products of national affluence augmented by a misguided education in values of consumption and display. The *Plan* counts on the argument that, since women are historically and culturally produced, cultural interventions in history could produce them differently. Proper education could train them to conserve and transmit republican values *and* concrete, material wealth, both of which are necessary for national survival. By insisting that wealth (a public matter) and women's morals (a private matter) were one and by invoking a long tradition of historical commentary—much of it hostile to women—to support the argument, Willard's rhetoric obliterates the space between public and private spheres, between men's and women's proper areas of action (though not between distinctly proper *modes* of action). The rhetoric builds, however, not to an argument for protecting the republic by removing women from the public sphere but to the claim that women's informed participation in the national life can make the American republic, unlike all others, endure and flourish. Willard further blurs the public-private distinction by authorizing herself as a woman—and Willard always displayed her name prominently on everything she published—to enter the arenas of economic, historical, and political discourse through a public display of expertise subordinated to patriotism.

Willard's *Plan,* though centered on the elite women whose education she deemed most important for national prosperity (since they had access to the greatest segment of the nation's wealth), also briefly considers the place of other classes of women in the polity. It looks to women from a group in between the securely wealthy and the poor (what we would now call the middle class), wherein financial ups and downs are the order of the day, as a source for teachers for the elite girls' academies as well as all schools for young children of both sexes. To use such women as teachers is economically sound: "they would be likely to teach children better than the other sex; they could afford to do it cheaper; and those men who would otherwise be engaged in this employment might be at liberty to add to the wealth of the nation by any of those thousand occupations from which women are necessarily debarred" (*Plan,* 29). Deploying them as teachers will be doubly beneficial: Their self-support will help conserve existing national wealth while freeing up men for those activities by which wealth may be increased.

Between republican domesticity for the wealthy and salaried teaching for those in moderate circumstances, "laudable objects and employments, would be furnished for the great body of females, who are not kept by poverty from excesses" (*Plan,* 34). Members of a third group, poor women, are not a concern here because poverty, by definition, precludes them from either squandering or conserving. But for a fourth group, an anomalous subset of middle-class women, "master spirits, who must have pre-eminence, at whatever price they acquire it," women whose restless spirit, if left "without any virtuous road to eminence, is unsafe to community; for not unfrequently, are the secret springs of revolution, set in motion by their intrigues," Willard offers something "worthy of their ambition; to govern, and improve the seminaries for their sex" (*Plan,* 34).

Therefore, at every social level except the bottom of the scale, where necessity imposes its own discipline, Willard envisages education for women as a discipline that will implicate them constructively (from her perspective) in the political and economic advancement of the nation-state. The women who are produced by this discipline are by no means romantic, intuitive, nurturing; they do not resemble the products of a cult of true womanhood. They are disciplinarians, rulers, governors of themselves and of others. If, then, Willard's rhetoric has blurred the boundaries of the public and private spheres, so has it also blurred the boundaries of male and female sex typing. As all women (except the poor) are redefined as teachers—whether they teach at home or in the seminary, dame, or common school—the woman teacher in turn is redefined as the lawgiver and the law's embodiment: Woman becomes Lycurgus.

Indeed, discipline for its own sake, in the sense of developing rules and regulations for the purpose of providing training in obedience, was always a crucial aspect of Willard's educational program, and training women to punish the disobedient was also part of her project. Here, for example, is part of what she wrote to her teacher-trainee graduates:

> In every moral government, from that of the Father of mercies over his intelligent creatures, to that of a school mistress over her school, there must be punishment; for such a government presupposes a control over free agents, to be exercised by means of laws which they *can* obey, or *can* disobey. A law is a precept, to do, or abstain from a certain act, on a certain penalty. The law being disobeyed, the penalty must be enforced, or the law itself becomes a nullity. . . . It is necessary that [people] should be punished to PRESERVE THE SUPREMACY OF LAW. Without law there can be no rational government; all must be anarchy and violence—the weak at the mercy of the strong—the good subject to the bad. By whatever benefit government confers, all are bound, then, to uphold the laws.[13]

It was Willard's ambition that the Troy Female Seminary provide instruction in every academic area, and by 1832 the curriculum included several dozen subjects.[14] Her own commitment to history as the cornerstone of education is to be gauged by the rhetoric that permeates the historical textbooks. Edition after edition of the *Republic of America* and the *Universal History* insisted, just like the *Plan,* that only the practice of early republican virtue could control the centrifugal tendencies of expansion and that only repeated exposure to vivid representations of the Revolution could motivate republican practice. Her narratives of American history installed the Revolution as the expression of the nation's originary values as well as its actual point of origin and offered the experience of reading the narratives as occasions for students to assimilate those values and carry them forward. In the teachers' preface to the 1852 *Republic of America,* for example, Willard wrote:

> There are those, who rashly speak, as if in despair of the fortunes of our republic; because, they say, political virtue has declined. If so, then is there the more need to infuse patriotism into the breasts of the coming generation. And what is so likely to effect this national self-preservation, as to give our children, for their daily reading, and study, such a record of the sublime virtues of the worthies of our earliest day,—and of Washington and his compatriots, as shall leave its due impress? And what but the study of their dangers and toils,—their devotion of life and fortune, can make our posterity know, what our country, and our liberties have cost? And what but the History of our peculiar, and complicated fabric of government, by which, it may be examined, as piece by piece the structure was built up, can impart such a knowledge of the powers it gives, and the duties it enjoins, as will enable all our future citizens, to become its enlightened and judicious supporters?[15]

In composing and managing this public spectacle Willard from the first drew on and claimed to exemplify the image of republican womanhood, representing herself *literally* as a daughter of the republic. This representation had its basis in fact: The child of older parents, she was the daughter of a participant in the Revolution and had been reared on stirring tales of patriotism and Revolutionary valor.[16] Early editions of the *Republic of America* contained a poetic dedication to Willard's mother whereby Willard connected herself and her historical enterprise to the American Revolution as the moment of national origin.

> Accept this offering of a daughter's love,
> Dear, only, widowed parent; on whose brow
> Time-honoured, have full eighty winters shed
> The crown of glory.
>   Mother, few are left,
> Like thee, who felt the fire of freedom's holy time
> Pervade and purify the patriot breast.
> Thou wert within thy country's shattered bark,
> When, trusting Heaven, she rode the raging seas,
> And braved with dauntless, death-defying front,

The storm of war. With me retrace the scene,
Then view her peace, her wealth, her liberty, and fame:
And like the mariner, who gains the port
Almost unhoped-for, from the dangerous waves,
Thou can'st rejoice:—and thankful praise to God,
The Great Deliverer, which perchance I speak—
Thou, in thy pious heart, wilt deeply feel.[17]

The history text to come is represented by this poem as a loving daughter's offering to two mothers: her literal mother and her figurative mother, the American republic. To describe the nation during the Revolutionary War as a shattered bark on the raging seas (while hardly original) is to conflate all colonial settlement history into one image of the long struggle to secure a safe haven on the continent, a struggle that the Revolution achieves, thereby making national existence possible. The poem's conventional sequence of figures summarizes the nation's Providential success story. It is implicit that retellings of this story, histories, are becoming necessary because, as the Revolutionary generation ages—the group in whom the "fire" that should "pervade and purify the patriot breast" is kept alive by direct memory—that fire is likely to go out. Retracing the scene *with her mother,* fortuitously among the few who remain from that generation, Willard offers her book exactly as a site where a narrative of events can link readers *to* the Revolution and keep the fire burning. For Willard personally—or, rather, for Willard as she presents herself personally—the book manifests *her* patriot fire. A highly visible and carefully gendered filiopietism therefore sanctions Willard's activity as a writer of history.

It is not merely that Willard is proposing a gendered mode of doing history; she is also making the figure of the historian—herself—feminine. Let us assume that for Willard a properly supervised contact with "history," that is, with a well-designed and well-taught narrative of past events, will produce patriots of both sexes and thus contribute to national well-being; still patriot men and patriot women, differentiated by gender, must find expression for their patriotism in different acts. We would expect, perhaps, that her text would offer many examples of female patriots, but this is not the case. As in Mercy Otis Warren's history of the Revolution, Willard's national and world histories are overwhelmingly populated by males. The American history of 1831 contains a passing reference to Pocahontas, a brief disparagement of Anne Hutchinson, a paragraph on the murder of Jane McCrea. There are also approving words for the heroic elite women of Carolina who, during the Revolution, "refused their presence at every scene of gayety, sought out and relieved suffering soldiers, visited prison ships, descended into loathsome dungeons, encouraged their brothers and sons to fight" (*1831,* 239); and there is telling praise for Martha Washington as her husband's enabling helpmeet, as prudent in private, as her husband was in public affairs. In his absence, she presided over the domestic finances, and provided for the common household. . . . She had no caprices to disturb his affections, in that citadel of man's happiness, the conjugal relation. Thus it was owing to the talents and virtues of his wife, that Washington could give himself wholly to the dictates of that patriotism, which this virtuous pair mutually shared, and reciprocally invigorated. (*1831*, 240)

In the early 1840s, as the cult of Washington's mother took hold, Willard added her to the record as "a rare women, affectionate, judicious, firm and energetic" under whose "maternal guidance, and in the common school," Washington "developed those physical, intellectual, and moral elements, which formed his greatness."[18] The coupling of the common school and Washington's mother invokes the Willard schoolroom with its aim of producing teacher-mothers. Between the frugal helpmeet Martha—whose capable administration of Washington's estate (that it was originally her own estate is not mentioned) allows him to serve his country without going bankrupt—and the character-forming Mary, Washington's heroism is placed in a context of female support. This context, however, conventionally makes men the prominent actors in history, with women relegated to the narrative background. But through the use of history teaching as a basic tool in shaping men's characters and conserving national wealth, women may after all enter history directly through control of the representation of history itself. It is in this sense that one might think of history and the historian as both gendered female, as they had already been in Willard's dedicatory poem.[19]

One might observe that the dedication also genders the nation as a female. Feminine iconography for nations is so common and conventional that nothing necessarily follows from the practice here, but it is notable that in the introduction to early editions of the *Republic of America* such iconography leads to a melodramatic and sexualized argument for instructing America's future leaders in the history of the American Revolution:

England, seeking to make her filial child her slave, refuses to listen to her duteous pleadings, and applies the scourge. She deigns not to give even the privileges of civilized warfare, but sends forth the brand which lights the midnight fire over the heads of the sleeping family, and the tomahawk which cleaves the head of the infant in the presence of the mother. England also descends to base arts. She bribes, she flatters, she sows dissensions, she purchases treason, and she counterfeits money. In the conduct of France too, though gratitude rises in our hearts for her actual services, yet history compelled, though sometimes sorrowfully, to follow truth, must pronounce that in her conduct as a nation, there is nothing virtuous or generous. . . . How interesting, in her youthful simplicity, in her maiden purity, does America appear, contrasted with these old and wily nations. (*1831*, xvii)

Knowledge of this tale, Willard continues, is certain to "warm the young heart of the future statesman of America," who will be moved to say "my country was the most virtuous among the nations" and will "resolve, that when manhood shall have placed him among her guardians, he will watch the purity of her character with jealous tenderness, and sooner part with existence than be made the instrument of her degradation!" (*1831*, xvii).[20]

This rhetoric situates the future statesman of America in the national family like a *brother* dedicated to the purity of his sister. Note the melodramatic energy, the acute sense of danger, the implication that patriotic fervor is always necessary because innocence is never secure. The image of the statesman as a possible instrument of the nation's degradation fuses external and internal threats and sees threats everywhere. *Any* act whatsoever that put private interest over national well-being was collusive with the nation's enemies, who consisted of all the nations of the world who hoped that the republican experiment would fail. Since most nations of the world were antirepublican, the republic was extremely vulnerable. It was their awareness of this vulnerability that motivated the quarreling designers of the Constitution to compromise:

> That these great difficulties were compromised, holds up this convention, as an example to future times, of the triumph of strong patriotism and honest zeal for the public welfare, over party feeling and sectional prejudice. If the time shall ever come, when any American Congress, or convention, shall fail to compromise amicably, disputes, which conflicting interests must produce in this extensive republic; then will the day of its degeneracy have arrived, and its downfall be at hand. . . . The finger of history would point with scorn at such a body of men, while she contrasted them with the wise and honest patriots, who framed the constitution. (*1831*, 277–278)

The problems faced by the Founders could only intensify as the republic increased in size and diversity. Inevitable conflicts of interest could be settled peacefully only if statesmen held to a paramount ideal of national well-being. Ordinary people, too, had a role to play: "The government of the United States is acknowledged by the wise and good of other nations, to be the most free, impartial, and righteous government of the world; but all agree, that for such a government to be sustained many years, the principles of truth and righteousness, taught in the Holy Scripture, must be practised. *The rulers must govern in the fear of God, and the people obey the laws*" (*1852*, 15–16). Here an old-fashioned (for 1852) hierarchical republicanism, dividing the polity into law-abiding rulers and law-abiding people, the responsibility of one to make just laws and the other to obey them, becomes the salvation of the nation. The work of women who, as mothers and teachers, inculcate responsibility at home and in the schoolrooms of America becomes ever more crucial to the American future as the years go by.

Law was designed to protect the weak from the strong, and the special beauty of republican law was that it actually required that the strong protect the weak. But to Willard laws decreeing protection could not also decree equality. Her opposition to the woman's rights movement thus accords with the overarching vision of law and order which regulates her politics. The alternative to law and order is, simply, war.

War, as noted, dominates Willard's vision of history and her textbooks.[21] The 424 pages of the 1831 American history textbook include 48 pages on the French and Indian wars, 110 on the Revolution, and 78 on the War of 1812. More than half of the book, then, is explicit military history; another quarter of its pages deal with Indian wars and insurrections such as Bacon's Rebellion, Shay's Rebellion, and the Whiskey Rebellion. Similar proportions occur in other texts, except that the Mexican War—which excited her territorial imagination with an intensity second only to the Revolution— enlarges the military segment of the American histories after 1850. Willard is a fine narrator of military action and conspicuously at ease in assessing military blunders or brilliance. But although a woman may quite demonstrably *write* war, Willard insists that she cannot *fight* war. In a worldview that takes war as the fundamental condition of humankind this finally becomes the determining difference between the sexes. In war, which is all around us, women and children are the protected, not the protectors.

Indian warfare is Willard's core emblem of danger to American women, since Indians were believed to attack by surprise, destroy undefended homesteads, and massacre women and children. Indian warfare is connoted in Willard's description of "the brand which lights the midnight fire over the heads of the sleeping family, and the tomahawk which cleaves the head of the infant in the presence of the mother" (*1831*, xvii). Like the majority of the many women who wrote about American Indians in the antebellum years, she views the Indians as irredeemably savage and, as such, inimical to the civilization for which Providence had destined the American continent. Borrowing from Puritan historiography, she wrote in *1831*, in connection with the plague that decimated the American Indian population shortly before the Puritan landing, that

> it is a wonderful coincidence of events, that a disease of such unexampled mortality should have attacked, weakened, and humbled these powerful nations, at a time just preceding the arrival of our forefathers upon their shores. Had they remained in their full strength, it is evident, that with the small means which the first European emigrants possessed, they could not have effected a settlement. In this the undevout will perceive nothing but a happy fortuity; but the pious heart will delight to recognize and acknowledge a superintending Providence, whose time for exchanging, upon these shores, a savage for a civilized people, had now fully come. (*1831*, 15)[22]

Willard rang down her account of the Mexican War with a lament over the emotional and pecuniary costs of the venture and called for Christian governments to appoint respected veteran officers to meet and design an international Council of Peace. "Could this great errand of 'PEACE ON EARTH' be accomplished, and that by the instrumentality of this nation, then, with peculiar emphasis, might PROGRESS be made the watchword of the nineteenth century, and of the Republic of America."[23] But the millennium was not her subject, and along with her call for peace Willard's narrative bristled with partisan rhetoric: "Bitterly did the Mexicans reap the fruit of their former cruelties, by the almost superhuman energies put forth in fight by the Americans, and the unvarying success which it pleased the Almighty to give to their arms" (*Last Leaves*, 97).

In this context women's relation to the national well-being takes its most profoundly gendered form because it is the woman's body and its need to be protected in a world whose history is a chronicle of war among nations that makes gender distinctions necessary. Willard's melodrama of the brother-statesman defending his sister-nation identifies the national icon with the corporeal woman through their common relation to men, their shared need for male protection. As she had written in her *Ancient Geography* in connection with the rise of empires, "When men are so weak as to need protection, they must yield obedience to those from whom they receive it. They must in this case barter their liberty for their preservation; for mankind love power, and may be expected to exercise it where they can."[24] Gender distinction, though it might not follow from contemplation of the woman's body abstractly, rises inevitably from the connection of that body to a real history that expresses the working out of power relations based ultimately on physical force. The historical body—nation or woman— is subject to this discipline of history, and from Willard's point of view the physical superiority of men to women is so obvious as not to need rhetorical development. In this unspoken yet pervasive sense her histories are about the woman's body, notwithstanding the sparse population of historical women in her pages.[25]

Thus, while her melodrama appears to address only the future states*men* of America, it speaks obliquely to the sisters of those statesmen by a gendered image that places them in the position of the threatened nation and hence leads them to see the nation's protectors as *their* protectors also. Willard's conviction that war was the language in which nations habitually speak to each other underlies both the expansionist and the retractionist dimensions of her program for women in public.

The proportion of space devoted to war in Willard's *Universal History* exceeded that given over to it in the American history text. *Universal History* was a panorama of the rise of empires through conquest, destruction, and absorption of lesser tribes until they were conquered, destroyed, or absorbed by other empires. The lesson sporadically drawn from this spectacle was that Providence had successively favored one nation after another but that none had proved itself worthy of permanent prosperity. Now, clearly, the United States enjoyed Divine approval; so to Willard the point of *Universal History* for Americans was simply its display of examples to be avoided. Universal history

> is at this time particularly important to Americans, because to them the world are now looking for a response to the grand question, "Can the people govern themselves?" And, perhaps, the next twenty years will decide it for coming generations. Shall monarchy in its palaces, and aristocracy in its lordly halls, then exult, as it is told that America is passing through monarchy to despotism,—while mankind at large mourn, and reproach us that we have sealed their doom as well as our own, and that of our posterity? Or shall we continue to be that people, which of all others heretofore, or now existing, possess the most equitable government; and to whom national calamity is but as a phrase ill understood? A history of the past, no more extensive than that which is here presented, might make us understand that phrase, with a salutary fear.[26]

Willard's idea of women's education developed like her history textbooks in consonance with ideas of the nation in history and the role that women might play in forwarding national interests. She represented Troy Female Seminary as a womanly contribution to the future of the republic, as a manifestation of her own patriotism designed to create future patriots. She described her history writing as another such act. Ironically, perhaps, she became a celebrity, earned a great deal of money, and thereby installed an entrepreneurial, self-aggrandizing model of female activity even as she expounded subordination. As suggested at the outset, this peculiar conjunction is also characteristic of her historical rhetoric as it conjoins fealty to republican virtues with the goal of increasing national wealth and acreage. Readers may suppose that the congeniality of this conjunction to an audience, anxious to get on with the future while equally anxious not to lose a sense of the authorizing past, functioned to override whatever negative implications there may have been in a woman's articulating it.

9

The Ann Sisters

Elizabeth Peabody's Gendered Millennialism

It has been Elizabeth Palmer Peabody's fate to appear mainly at the periphery of American transcendentalism and romanticism. For many years critics cast her in the stock role of great-man groupie: whether as William Ellery Channing's amanuensis, Bronson Alcott's assistant, Horace Mann's confidante, Nathaniel Hawthorne's sister-in-law, or as overzealous publicist for Louis Kossuth, Josef Bem, and Friedrich Froebel. A line of criticism more sympathetic to Peabody's accomplishment has emerged in connection with the retrievalist project of academic feminism, but, unable to shift the center of discussion away from her contributions to the Transcendentalist agenda she is assumed to have shared, it has continued to marginalize her. Even an appreciative assessment finds her achievement to lie "not so much in her own intellectual gifts, though these were considerable, as in her ability to appreciate original thinking in others, draw it forth, publicize it, and transmit it."[1]

There are, to be sure, excellent and obvious reasons to place Peabody among the Transcendentalists. Insofar as there was such an entity as the "Transcendentalist Club," Peabody was a member. When she established herself as a publisher around 1840—probably a first for an American woman—she brought out Transcendental journals and pamphlets (among other works). But nevertheless, in her own terms Peabody was not a Transcendentalist at all. She followed the movement from the perspective of an unyielding evangelical Unitarianism and concluded that its revision of Unitarian belief stepped sideways rather than forward in history.[2] She criticized the Transcendentalists with increasing severity over the years for a radical individualism that, by rejecting explicitly Christian doctrine, rejected the human sociality that she believed was symbolized by Christ's mission on earth. From her perspective transcendentalism was dangerously unbalanced and potentially irreligious; borrowing Channing's word *egotheism* to describe it, she went well beyond him to call transcendentalism "the atheism of today."[3] Only Emerson, whose ideas she (mis)interpreted as identical to Channing's, was exempt from her condemnation. And she rejected Emerson's example—she quoted him as saying that "the only way to preach Christ *to this generation* is to say nothing about him personally" (*Reminiscences*, 380)—by invoking God or Jesus Christ on most of the pages that she turned out in a long lifetime of writing.

As a Unitarian, Peabody believed that Christ was human and divinely charged; from her perspective, if the Transcendentalists did not accept Christ's mediating necessity as the center of their religious creed, then they were not Christian. And if Peabody not only accepted but insisted on the necessity for Christ, then she was no Transcendentalist. There is more than a semantic distinction at stake here. It is easy to understand why even those—especially those—who want to take Peabody seriously prefer to call her a Transcendentalist, even if this nomenclature ignores the Christian overtext of her work and makes her, as it were, marginal to herself. To the extent that we critics inhabit a postmodern secular professional space we might appear embarrassingly naive if we presented a particular writer to the scholarly community by stressing the theological grounding of that writer's discourse.

But I am going to seize this moment of criticotheoretical return to history and describe Peabody as an important representative of antebellum New England literary culture precisely because she assimilated a range of nineteenth-century discursive trends to a project distinct from transcendentalism or romanticism—that of helping to establish Christ's kingdom on earth. Moreover, she conceived and described her project as an appropriately *womanly* undertaking and authorized her numerous interventions into the putatively male domains of theology, philosophy, and history on that basis. Because Peabody's invasion of the male sphere through religious self-authorization is by no means unique among women in American life, we may imagine that she centered herself less in a men's tradition than a women's.[4] At the same time, because her work was so resolutely intellectual, we may also see her as incorporating within the women's tradition an unwavering post-Enlightenment conviction that women's minds were the equal of men's.

To speak of establishing Christ's kingdom on earth is, of course, to imply millennialism, and to approach Peabody as a millennial thinker is to come to terms with her gendered religiosity and also better understand another neglected aspect of her writings: her intense concern with history. Most of Peabody's published work before the Civil War, and some of it afterward, are forms of history writing. Before 1860, when she committed herself almost entirely to the kindergarten movement, her concept of education had centered on teaching history, and she wrote several history textbooks to explain why. Her two longest critical essays—"The Spirit of the Hebrew Scriptures" (1834) and "The Dorian Measure" (1848)—applied a theory of symbolic language derived from her reading of Johann Gottfried von Herder to ancient texts in order to uncover the historical facts that the texts conveyed.

When she read Nathaniel Hawthorne's 1837 *Twice-Told Tales* she immediately imagined the author as an answer to her call for a genius to write about "the adventures of the settlers in North America, especially the stories of the Pilgrims," for the very young.[5] As we know, she encouraged him to write history for children and published his work in this line; as late as 1856, she was still plugging these stories and insisting that he could do no greater service to his country than to tell all its history in a similarly picturesque manner.[6] In 1852, to support Louis Kossuth's campaign in America, she wrote a history of the Austrian empire called *Crimes of the House of Austria against Mankind*. In fact, her instructed impulse when dealing with any philosophical or social issue was to frame it historically. Channing told her, "Your mind takes so opposite a direction from mine to come to the same result. You go back to the past for what I do not seek there, but in the future" (*Reminiscences*, 144).

The answer to the question "why this interest in history?" is self-evident if Peabody is a millennialist thinker. All expressions of Christian millennialism are necessarily historical, conceiving time as a "linear structure with a clear beginning and end," interpreting the present as a point on this line somewhere between the Revelation and the arrival of a period of "heavenly perfection on earth."[7] The question for all Christian millennialists was (or is): Where is that somewhere? Peabody's ambition was to encompass the entire historical record as a form of Divine speech in order to find the answer. "To deliver the mind from the thraldom of the present, and to prepare it to comprehend the future, the most obvious course is to open upon it the past, which is an assured gift of God to the race. Hence the importance of history" (*First Steps*, 1). "All history should be studied with reverence, as a *sacred* illustration of the providence of God"; "The events of history are God's conversation with man upon his nature, duties, and destiny"; "to study man in society, to the end of working his redemption from the organized evils that the elder world has bequeathed, is the paramount matter. . . . The chronological relation is God's disposition of events, every one of which is a *word* proceeding out of his mouth. Let us read *these words* as they lie in time, giving significance to each other."[8]

In this historical and historicizing project Peabody rejected the kind of millennialist practice that concentrated exclusively on Biblical exegesis. She also rejected the Transcendental turn to "Nature," which she saw as abrogating history altogether. The same religious conviction animated both rejections: She believed that God's full intentions concerning humankind were not inscribed either in depopulated nature or in the history of any single nation—not even the nation that had been favored with Revelation.

But if history encrypted the answer to the millennial question, it did so problematically, as Peabody recognized: To read all history as a record of divine intention called for vast scholarship and for mastery of decoding techniques appropriate to the range of historical documents. Accordingly, she became one of the most learned women of her day and one of the few American theorists of history male or female in the antebellum era. In doing so, she worked within the tradition of women history writers who had construed gender roles as giving women the advantage in reading and interpreting history while obliging them to implement this advantage. She wrote in 1832 that, "as history is the department of human knowledge which is more within the sphere of woman's attainment than any other, so the study of it is the most important to women, and has the most direct influence in forming them for the duties peculiar to their relations in life" (*First Steps,* 12–13), and fifty years later she repeated that, "as the art of life is the universal vocation of woman, history is what woman should read from youth to age, whatever else she does."[9]

As she later recalled or constructed it, Peabody took her commitment to a religiohistorical practice as well as her belief in the womanliness of such a practice from her mother, who brought up all her daughters to be teachers, "considering it the highest and the proper activity of every American woman who loved her country" ("My Experience," 722). The older Elizabeth Peabody ran a girls' school in Salem until about 1816 and published her own textbook of "Sacred History" in 1810, which she introduced with the hope that, "in this age of doubt and infidelity, every friend to the interest of human kind will, the Author flatters herself, view with favourable eye her attempt to disseminate among the young the knowledge of sacred history. Friends of religion must be armed for attacks against it."[10] Sacred history, one of the most prominent school subjects in the early national curriculum, comprised study of the Old and New Testaments as historically veracious documents. In this altogether conventional maternal discourse Elizabeth Peabody encountered the complete interfusion of history and religion, and, ultimately, she represented her mother as a woman sanctified through teaching.

This womanly ideal had, also, an intensely patriotic dimension that further valorized the idea of history. "I had been brought up by a devout, unconventional mother," Peabody reflected in 1880, "who had been educated to religion, like the Israelites of old, by the history of her country from the Pilgrim emigration to the Revolutionary war" (*Reminiscences,* 18). This mother taught that to educate children "morally and spiritually as well as intellectually" was "the most sacred of the duties of the children of the Pilgrims who founded the Republic to bless all the *nations* of the earth"

(*Reminiscences,* 40) and inspired Elizabeth Peabody to see teaching as a vocation—both opportunity and obligation—shared by the entire community of American Protestant women.

> [The] idea of the paramount importance of women to American civilization was with her the governing principle, and she wished to impart it to other women. The history of New England, by Miss Hannah Adams, was the first she gave in the historical course. She used to say it was the only history in modern times that seemed to be written on the principle of Sacred History, and loved to compare [the Hebrews] with the Pilgrim bands, who left the despotisms of Europe to plant a nation of freemen, by which all the nations of the earth were to be finally blessed. Born and brought up in the midst of a family all of whom devoted all their means to their country, in its birth struggle, she looked upon national life as God's education of mankind, and it was the pattern on which she modelled the education of every citizen. ("My Experience," 742)

From within this heavily charged pietistic atmosphere Peabody remembered herself as creating, as a very young child, a mythology of the Puritan emigration that constitutes, to my knowledge, a unique and poignantly gynocentric representation. "My ancestors knew themselves to be God's children, whom neither tyrannizing king nor priest had any right to prevent from going to him in prayer first hand," she began conventionally enough. They—but who are they?—

> left home and country and all the comforts of civilization, and trusted themselves in a frail vessel to be driven over a stormy ocean by the winds, at imminent peril from the waves below, which would have swallowed them up, had not God, who loved them, approved what they were doing, guided the ship . . . through the narrow opening of Plymouth Harbor to the rock where I still seem to see them streaming along, a procession of fair women in white robes as *sisters* (for so I had interpreted the word *ancestors,* who strangely enough were all named *Ann*). I still seem to see these holy women kneel down in the snow under the trees of the forest, and thank God for their safety from the perils of the sea; and then go to work in the sense of his very present help, and gather sticks to make a fire, and build shelters from the weather with the branches of the trees. Among these rude buildings my mother took pains to tell me that they built a schoolhouse where all the children were to be taught to read the Bible.[11]

A band of sanctified sisters who, under the benign stewardship and approving gaze of a loving father, worship him and introduce children to his name: Here is a feminine origins myth (as well as a myth of national origins) that invites interpretation from every theoretical standpoint. The millennialism to which the older Peabody initiated her daughter, then, while it is obviously akin to the standard republican millennialism described by historians, is also powerfully gendered. Apart from its sheer inspirational force, in more mundane terms such gender inflection allowed the Peabody women (and others like them) to insist that, while the republican political form made spiritual development possible, it did not guarantee it. Spiritual development within a republic was produced by the spiritual *progress* of its citizens, and progress was mediated through education, which at once instituted sociality as an element equal to individuality *and* called the particular faculties of women into productive play. It was women, holy women, who were entrusted with the responsibility of training up the young Christian republicans.

While Peabody's representation of women's role clearly connects to the paradigm of republican motherhood elaborated by historians Linda Kerber and Mary Beth Norton and associated with the Revolutionary generation, it is less purely political—or, rather, it cannot conceive of a politics apart from religion.[12] For Peabody and many other North American women born between 1790 and 1820 the discursive world of feminine ideology seems to have centered on a religiopolitical thematics associated with the American Revolution which these women were committed to transmitting and by the transmission of which they felt themselves ennobled. The home-centered and decorative Victorian ideology of womanhood associated with the later nationalist period also retains, in a great many instances, a dimension of religious and patriotic activism which commentators have frequently ignored, even when they have observed the protofeminist implications of this Victorian construct. On the one hand, scholarly investigations have separated politics (hence nationalism and patriotism) from religion; on the other, they have separated women's issues from general issues like the future of Christianity and the future of America.

Elizabeth Peabody's religious historicism was different from her mother's because it took into account and was shaped by post-Revolutionary developments in the religious climate of eastern Massachusetts as well as by her extensive reading in German romanticism. She agreed with many that Unitarianism was an advance within Christianity over Calvinism and that therefore Christianity had risen to a higher level in the United States after the Revolution than it had ever attained before anywhere in the world. Although she saw William Ellery Channing as the best articulator of the Unitarian creed, she never thought that he invented it. Rather, she saw Unitarianism as a stage in the unfolding of a historical-national text whose author was Divine.

Unitarianism, she wrote, though the "logical evolution of the Pilgrim emigration," was very far from what the Pilgrims themselves believed. In coming to America to put their beliefs into practice the Pilgrims rose above "the ground of the Calvinistic speculations, from which doubtless they started." But Roger Williams, not they, had established "the first community in Christendom—if not on earth—that separated Church and State." The separation between church and state did not pave the way for secularism but for a much more profound, because internally felt, religious faith; Williams "set free the moral sentiment, which had been deprived of its rights for ages" by an "ecclesiastical tyranny" from whose habits of thought the Pilgrim fathers were not entirely emancipated. The American and French revolutions comprised "further exertions of human power to realize the freedom and dignity of man, and had helped to give a new method to religious as well as political thinking" (*Reminiscences*, 27–28).

The simultaneous emergence of Unitarian belief and the American republic showed Peabody that for God politics and religion were one—that the glorious destiny of humankind was to be realized through the agency of nation-states governed by religious purpose. Curiously, but by no means coincidentally, human awareness of history had also emerged at the same time. The idea of history, therefore, was also historical, progressive, and ultimately Christian. "Does there not seem," she asked rhetorically, "to be something providential in the fact, that history first arose from the sleep of ages when America was discovered, and that, just when this great democracy is waking to self-consciousness, and needs to be taught how to dispose the elements of a new world into a truly Christian order, she takes up the telescope of critical observation?" (*Universal*, vii).

Although Peabody's scholarly historicism constitutes a sophistication of standard belief, the amalgam of Christian, historical, and nationalist that underlies it is altogether commonplace. All of the many antebellum universal and American history textbooks that I have examined offer versions of Protestant millennialism. They all intermingle secular and divine rhetoric, organize their narratives of universal and United States history as accounts of millennial progress, and take the Bible as a historical authority. While American history was taught in the schools far more often than universal history, it was universal history that Peabody preferred. This subject started with an account of Creation and the Hebrews based on the Old Testament, merged biblical and other narratives up to the crucifixion, represented modern history as the progress of Christianity furthered by Protestant republican governments and obstructed by despotisms (usually Catholic but also Oriental and Arab), and culminated in American history. To Peabody as historicist, American history could not be understood apart from its place in universal history. America was "the flower of the ages that have gone before" with "causal roots in all the ages of time previous"; it was ridiculous to teach it as "a fragment, and to those who do not know previous history" (*United States*, 5).

Chronology, always crucial to millennial analysis, was as necessary for weaving together sacred and secular accounts as for interpreting biblical prophecy. For one thing, obscure references in the Bible could be clarified (and their historical accuracy validated) by aligning their events with accounts in secular sources. For another, if God worked through nation-states, then the divine meaning of events could not be seen unless all the national histories were brought together in time. Christ might have been born at any time, for example. Why did he appear when he did? The question could not be answered sensibly unless one knew what else was happening when he arrived. The birth of Jesus, Peabody wrote, which "marks the turning-point of the history of the world, took place in a marked time. All the natural religions were dying," Rome was corrupt, and the Hebrew religion had deteriorated to a mere form. "The doctrine of spiritual freedom was now exhibited by a great life and death. . . . A new era for the human race began, that is not yet consummated" (*Universal*, 113). The coincidence of Christ's birth with the apogee of the corrupt Roman Empire was a commonplace, but Peabody's assertion that this birth was significant for "the doctrine of spiritual freedom" is manifestly liberal Unitarian.

Peabody, then, shared in her own way the conviction that chronology was much more than a pedagogic device for inserting history into childish memories, although its heuristic usefulness and its role in strengthening the memory were not to be ignored. Peabody differed from her American textbook writing contemporaries by embedding chronology within her theory of history as language, by defining it with some theoretical sophistication as the divine grammar. On the strength of her belief in the philosophic significance of chronology Peabody engaged in a vigorous campaign to publicize the system of Josef Bem, a campaign that led her to write textbooks of American and universal history applying Bem's principles and to lecture widely on his method.

Bem's method plotted historical events on a grid composed of years, decades, and centuries, assigning different colors to different nations. Peabody thought the method achieved two superlative results: First, it transformed time into space and allowed the student to see all of history at once very much as God could see it; second, and to much the same effect, it extracted events from secular texts composed by fallible or prejudiced historians and, thus, purified God's language. As Peabody expressed it, Bem's chronology "gives the outlines to the eye without human commentary" and allows the student "to supply from his own mind and conscience . . . the light of God's truth, wherein to view events in their relations to spiritual welfare" (*Universal*, v).[13]

The turn to an alinguistic philosophy of chronology represented, to some extent, Peabody's desire to escape from the limitations of a historical practice based on a philosophy of language which led her, from her earliest written textbooks in 1832 and 1833 on, to grapple with the textual nature of the historical record. Apart from the vague, inconsistent, incompatible, or nonexistent dates in ancient texts, including the Old and New Testaments, ancient languages were so highly metaphorical and symbolic that they often seemed to lack referential value and hence historical validity; they seemed to be merely myth or poetry. It was, therefore, primarily for the purpose of uncovering the historicity of ancient texts that in the 1830s Peabody had developed, or circulated, a theory of language that was itself historical. According to this theory, human beings in the earlier ages of the world had expressed themselves differently from the moderns. "In that vigorous era of the human mind when language could be created, all thought and fact would reappear in the mythical form" (*Polish-American,* 117). This meant that myth was not really myth but fact. Historicism promised that by understanding the perspective of the ancients one could paradoxically retrieve objective facts from their perspectival envelope, which was constituted by the cultural conventions of time and place through which history was represented.

Unlike Emerson, who drew on some of the same Herderian sources as Peabody for his theories of language—indeed, was introduced by Peabody to these sources—she did not plan to speak in symbols herself, nor did she want to apply symbolic techniques to the interpretation of nature.[14] She believed that the time had long passed for human beings to utter symbols ("Because we now learn words by rote, they are seldom to us what they were to those who first uttered them, inventing them as they spoke" [*Universal,* 116]) and, as we have seen, she distrusted nature worship for encouraging an antisocial egoism. But she was committed to the idea that one could understand past utterance, because her faith instructed her that it was necessary to do so and assured her that what was necessary would be provided for by a loving God. "To those who do not understand symbolic expression, the history of the earliest ages is a sealed book" (*Polish-American,* 118).

In *The Hebrews* Peabody had seen no contradiction in asserting that "the spirit of the several ages" could not "but breathe from their contemporaneous historians" and that the "unpractised mind" needed a "commentary" to assist it to "throw off present association, and enter completely into the genius, and state of mind of the people" (10, 57). Indeed, it would be her view that modern history writing, now enlightened by historicism, ought to be exactly that sort of commentary. "The Spirit of the Hebrew Scriptures," an ambitious essay published by the *Christian Examiner* in three parts during 1834, was a direct outgrowth of her attempt to provide this commentary for *The Hebrews.* The essay proposed to read the first books of Genesis as history in a way that would not put into question their status as revealed truth. Suppose that Moses did in fact have a revelation; wouldn't that revelation naturally take the form in which literature develops itself "in the ruder ages of the world? The earliest form of literature, is the historical Song. In all uncultivated countries, we find men following the instinct which prompts us to dwell on the glories of our forefathers, and singing their deeds in measure. For, it is this form of literature alone, which can be communicated to the people at large, before the art of writing is in general use."[15] Genesis, then, expresses a revelation that conveys historical facts and is couched in the historical form in order to fulfill Moses's particular historical purposes ("Spirit," 308). Properly apprehended, it is neither fable nor allegory but is history all the way through.

"The Spirit of the Hebrew Scriptures" may be seen in part as a sophisticated attempt to use historicism as a means of preserving the authority of the Bible and hence as Peabody's updating of her mother's commitment to sacred history, arming the friends of religion for attacks against it. The 1848 "Dorian Measure, with a Modern Application," is a far more socially ambitious piece of historical criticism, in which Peabody attempted to demonstrate among other things how Dorian (Spartan) worship of Apollo prefigured (but fell short of) an idea of human perfection, which would be actually realized in the life of Christ. She seems here to be extending Puritan techniques of typological exegesis to heathen texts. "The Dorian Measure" is partly an approving summary of Carl Otfried Muller's enthusiastically favorable history of the Dorians (1824) and partly an application of this history to the millennial prospects and responsibilities of the United States. Peabody accepted Muller's argument that a monotheistic Apollo worship dominated and shaped every aspect of Spartan life into a unity in which individual liberty and human sociality were inextricable. "The Dorians assumed that in a company of men guided by Apollo inhered a power which circumscribed the liberty of the individuals that composed it to the interests of the company as such; and that this social power must legitimate itself, by discharging a duty of which they had also the intuition, viz., that of unfolding each of its members into the harmonious exercise of his power." The Dorians are different from and superior to the Ionians (Athenians) because they make the social prior to the individual, recognizing that "the human being is socially dependent before he is individually conscious."[16]

The question for the present time was "whether there may not be a social organization which does as much justice to the Christian religion and philosophy as the Dorian state did to Apollo" ("Dorian," 102). Could Christ govern mankind as completely as Apollo governed the Dorians? If this was to come about, "religion must enspirit political forms as truly with *us* as with *them*, and an adequate education conserve them." Obviously, to any American the foundation of such a social organization already existed in the United States, for "it is our privilege to live under political forms that it is not difficult to trace quite immediately to our religion. . . . The fathers of the Federal Constitution built the temple, whose foundations the Pilgrims had laid" ("Dorian," 116).

But the Christian promise of the United States has not yet been fully realized, and that of humankind at large even less so. Moreover, the continual appearance in each generation of "a fresh mass of chaotic life, to be trained and cultivated by truth and beauty" means that process rather than product is the most that is to be hoped for "in this sphere." Nevertheless, "more and more approximation" to a millennial state "is to be looked for as the ages roll on," and education is both the means of approximation and of conserving whatever level humankind has already attained ("Dorian," 133). "The Dorian Measure" concludes with far-reaching recommendations about public education based on this argument.

Peabody's millennial vision identifies the highest level of progress with the United States and assumes that the example of the United States will enspirit other nations around the world. This identification of millennial history with the progress of a universal and Christianized republicanism underpins both her universal and United States history textbooks.

> For the first time in the *recorded* history of mankind, there is a nation whose government directly depends upon the mass of the people. . . . The Old World is covered with bad institutions which men have created, very often with positively good intentions, but on false notions, or at least, without large or profound ideas. These institutions have done infinite mischiefs, and are perpetuated and reproduced by the activity of the wicked and the passivity of the good. Whether the new world shall estimate and sift out these evils, or repeat these mistakes, depends on young Americans, who are now sitting in school rooms all over the country. (*United States,* 6, 8)

Peabody's republican millennialism does not dictate—indeed, it precludes—that the United States should engage in such imperialist enterprises as the Mexican War, expanding its territory to the Pacific Ocean, exterminating or removing the American Indians, or dispatching missionaries around the world. God's plan of free spiritual development could not be furthered by imposing Christianity on a resisting people; indeed, Christianity itself could not survive the attempt. Americans were, however, obliged to support those nations which, in the course of their own internal development, were attempting to overthrow despotism and establish a republic. Peabody's imagination was particularly captivated by the Hungarian Revolution, which she read as a sign that "the Anglo-Saxon race is not the only one whose life has blossomed out into constitutional liberty" as well as a confirmation that progress toward the millennium was still continuing and still discernible.[17]

Crimes of the House of Austria against Mankind, a ferocious attack on the Hapsburg dynasty, asserts that the United States had failed its millennial responsibility when it failed to support the Hungarian Revolution. Peabody excoriates the House of Hapsburg in terms derived from millennial descriptions of the Antichrist. And she sees the Hungarian Revolution as a war "unrivalled since the days, when Athens and Sparta, at the gate of Europe, stemmed that millions [*sic*] of Asia, that were threatening to overwhelm the only spot on Earth, where Freedom was self-conscious and intelligent. Indeed, the historian cannot fail to see a certain parallel between this crisis of the world's history, and that culminating point of antiquity, the world-renowned, time-honoured Persian war" (*Crimes*, 226). This parallel allows her to compare the United States invidiously with Sparta: "Where was Hungary's Sparta, even when the vanquished enemy rallied in still greater numbers and again stormed upon her? Did not the Earth contain an older republic, 'the model republic,' that might send a new Leonidas with some devoted 'three hundred'?" (*Crimes*, 229).

In compiling this narrative history from existing sources Peabody now encountered the historiographical dilemma of how to interpret what she called "conservative" history, history composed from the point of view of the oppressor. Whereas in dealing with ancient historiographical practices one needed only to learn how to understand symbolic language, in dealing with contemporary historians one was faced with outright falsification or erasure of the record, which raised different and far more vexing problems. Peabody lamented the absence of a history of Europe suitable for Americans "written from the republican point of view, a history of nations and not of their governors." Such a work would require "both genius and integrity of soul to conceive, and a vast industry properly to execute, the discovery of the exact truth being infinitely the greatest part of the labor required" (*Crimes*, 3, 4). "It has not been for the interest of monarchies of Europe to have the history of a republic understood. . . . In a history of Christian Europe, written from the American point of view, the republican nations of Poland, Hungary, and Switzerland would be done much more justice to than in any general history of Europe now extant" (*Universal*, 149).[18]

This gap between the written record and the "exact truth" introduces the problematic that a true history must be a republican history and can probably not be written until the whole world has become republican. At that point, when the millennium has arrived, historical texts will be transparent to the events they record, but at the same time, of course, they will not be necessary. "History" becomes, at this point, the art of the impossible. This is perhaps why the prospect of extricating a pure facticity via Bem's method seemed so appealing.

I have been describing Peabody's practice as a historical and bibliophilic practice, conducted for over a quarter of a century—between 1832 and 1859—without much change beyond a steady enlargement of range and growing self-confidence of voice. In 1859, however, a decided change of direction appears in her work. This is when she learned about the work of Friedrich Froebel in kindergarten education, and from then until the end of her life she worked as a highly influential proponent of kindergarten education in the United States. This rupture in Peabody's life may be connected to ruptures in the national life; the Civil War makes an obvious analogue.

Notwithstanding the claims of some of her biographers that Peabody was a staunch abolitionist, evidence of antislavery activity in her life is sparse before 1859.[19] Her United States history dealt extensively with the wrongs done to American Indians, but about slavery she said only that "a book intended for the public schools of all the United States, is not the place for discussion of a subject so vital to the interests of the Union as the slavery question" (*United States*, 308). In *Reminiscences* she concedes that she lagged behind Channing in antislavery sentiment because the Abolitionist attack on the Constitution appalled her. How was the United States to fulfill its appointed role if there *were* no United States? Like many republicans, she saw disunion as a greater evil than slavery and went out of her way not to consider how the presence of slavery in the republic might undercut American representations to be at the forefront of Christian history. Moreover, many of the European historians whom she read and admired held racialist beliefs. Her idolized Sparta was a slave society. Muller's explanations that the Dorians had inherited helot slaves when they invaded Sparta and that, anyway, the helots were racially different from the Dorians could easily be applied to the situation of the United States when the drafters of the Constitution compromised on the issue of slavery.

To say that, as the Civil War came on, she became more of an abolitionist, then, is not to say much; so did most New England intellectuals. More pertinent is to say that, as the Civil War came on, she lost some of her taste for history as well as some of her faith in the future of the United States. It is, thus, through the Civil War, about which she says little in her postwar writings, that I would explain the permanent detour into the kindergarten.

As war approached, Peabody saw at first less the scandal of slavery than the scandal of Americans putting their sectional and material interests ahead of the national union. The fragile balance of individualism and sociality had been upset. This is probably why she became increasingly outspoken in criticism of the Transcendentalists, whose egotism she had always deplored, a criticism that culminated with the 1859 naming of transcendentalism as "the atheism of today." (Perhaps she equated transcendentalism with abolitionism, but could not attack the latter directly.) The only remedy she could envision was more of what was lacking—an intense education in sociality begun early in life. The idea of the kindergarten—with its stress on socializing young human beings into relation with each other and benign authority rather than on developing their independent intellects—arrived at exactly this likely crisis to restore her belief that women had an important role to play in bringing about the millennium, even if they could not prevent the Civil War. It could even be imagined that failure to institutionalize women's role in society was part of what caused the war. "To be a kindergartner is the perfect development of womanliness—a working with God at the very fountain of artistic and intellectual power and moral character"

(*Lectures*, 13). The kindergarten was the institutionalization and profession-alization of women's millennial mission.

For Peabody to theorize women's particular fitness for kindergarten edu-cation as a product of an essential motherliness that corrects male egotism looks like a clearly reactionary effort to remove women from the public sphere and confine them to the nursery—and it certainly retreats from the intellectual representation of womanhood which she had long stood for. It constitutes the feminine by inherent difference as well as by socially differ-ent tasks and thus belatedly Victorianizes Peabody's feminine ideology. At the same time, however, as the kindergarten is not a private space, Peabody advocates a public, professional version of traditionally female domestic ac-tivities. Moreover, it was only after the Civil War that Peabody became a supporter of women's rights. She recalled that when asked to sign a women's rights petition in 1837 she had "replied that it seemed to me women could take and were allowed to take any course they were fitted for, if they chose, and I said that I would change the title Women's Rights for that of *Women's Duties,* which, if thoroughly understood by them, would involve their hav-ing the correlative rights, without anybody's disputing or hindering." But, she added, "I have ever since been learning that the Woman's Rights party was an inevitable protest of those who had the forecasting thoughts against laws, customs, and growing sentiments that operated to degrade woman and make her secondary to man in the serious work of life, which ought to include *noble politics*" ("My Experience," 741).

These changes, it seems to me, represent Peabody's relatively un–self-reflexive reconfiguration of ideas so as to preserve her earlier commitment to women's mission in circumstances that both differed from those in which the commitment was formed and illuminated, by hindsight, some earlier mis-takes and misunderstandings. The changes required a retreat from women's intellectuality in favor of a more heartfelt religiosity. While she continued to describe history as the study of choice for women, her postbellum enun-ciations involve a striking diminution of bibliophilia along with an augmen-tation of pietism. Except that the *Reminiscences of Channing* is a superb intellectual history of Boston in the 1820s, 1830s, and 1840s, she ceased to write history.

But there was no falling off of her lecturing, teaching, and writing ac-tivities for a cause she believed in and which she associated with a womanly mission. Her story of the sisters all named Ann is told in her *Lectures in the Training Schools for Kindergartners.* As she renarratized her life from the post–Civil War perspective, she saw that advocating the kindergarten was all along the mission for which she had been destined. "At the very time I am now speaking of (1825), Frederick Froebel was at Keilhau, engaged in writing his 'Education of Mankind,' which teaches what Dr. Channing and Miss Lowell had been teaching those mothers of Boston who 'had ears to hear'; namely, that in motherhood, conscious to itself of its divine vocation, and personally acted out with courage and faith, lies the secret of the redemption of the race from the accumulated evils of the past" (*Reminiscences*, 93).

Peabody's weaving of progressive and regressive, liberal and conservative, Enlightenment and Victorian standpoints into a postbellum logic is perhaps dominated by the phrase "noble politics," the phrase by which she justifies her support for women's suffrage. The phrase indicates her continuing commitment to a perfect nation inspired by holy women. The Civil War had reconstituted America and American history; the nation needed new works, new words, new women.

10

Reinventing Lydia Sigourney

If Lydia Howard Huntley Sigourney (1791–1865) had not existed, it would have been necessary to invent her. In fact, she *was* invented. As American women writers published in ever larger numbers before the Civil War, one of them was bound to be construed as an epitome of the specifically *female* author in her range of allowed achievements and required inadequacies. The prolific Sigourney was so well known from the late 1830s on that she would naturally become a candidate for this role. And much in her accomplishments and life history fitted her for it.

She was, as it happened, a poor, virtuous, essentially self-educated woman whose writing had originally been sponsored by one of the leading families in Hartford, Connecticut, and patronized by many other New England aristocrats.[1] She published pious poetry on domestic subjects in the major magazines and wrote for the Sunday School League. Having made a good marriage (from the social point of view), she faithfully performed her duties as wife, mother, and hostess, and she began to write for money only after financial reverses put the family under economic duress. She was, in short, a woman whose life could be used to show would-be literary women what they could do, what they should do, and also what they had better not do. Hers also was a life in which a modern success story of upward mobility through hard work and self-sacrifice led to an affirmation of traditional class structure.

The social construction of Lydia Sigourney began, then, in her own lifetime. And with Sigourney's canny participation it continued throughout her lifetime as well. For example, the prefatory "advertisement" to the 1815 *Moral Pieces in Prose and Verse,* which was written by Daniel Wadsworth, stresses the necessary haste with which she wrote: For the most part her compositions "arose from the impulse of the moment, at intervals of relaxation from such domestic employments, as the circumstances of the writer, and her parents, rendered indispensable." Thirty-two years later Sigourney's preface to the fifth (1847) edition of her *Select Poems* iterates the implications of that early notice; most of the poems in the book "were suggested by passing occasions, and partake of the nature of extemporaneous productions; all reveal by their brevity, the short periods of time allotted to their construction."[2] The poet encourages readers to think that she wrote only short poems and wrote them quickly; one would never guess from this preface that by 1847 she had also written (among other things) a four thousand-line historical epic in five cantos and two other historical poems, each over five hundred lines long.[3] Haste, perhaps; extemporaneous brevity, no.

But *Select Poems* collects mainly "the more popular poems which had appeared during several years in various periodicals" (*Letters,* 337). That is, this book, designed to recirculate such work as had already proved itself in the public arena, was directed to the preferences of audience rather than author. (Or the author preferences that it was directed toward were reputation building and money-making.) The incremental popularity of collections of the already popular (*Select Poems*—called simply *Poems* in its first edition of 1834—went through more than twenty-five editions during Sigourney's life) further consolidated a representation of the author based on her best-loved, or most widely known, poetry. The reappearance of these poems in anthologies like Rufus Griswold's or Caroline May's added to the effect. In sum, the Lydia Sigourney who was so often albeit so ambiguously and ambivalently praised in her own lifetime and has been so heartily calumniated subsequently, is a representation based on only some fraction of what she wrote and published. The Sigourney of the consolation elegy, the funerary poem, the Sigourney obsessed with dead children and dead mothers, has been constituted by a succession of critical audiences, each basing its commentary and opinion on an ever smaller segment of the author's published writings. Accordingly, even now, when writing by antebellum American women is more highly valued than it has been for a long time, the mere mention of Sigourney's name invokes a caricature: a mildly comical figure exemplifying the worst aspects of domestic sentimentalism.[4]

There is no Sigourney bibliography; many of her published books are difficult to find, and much if not most of the uncollected periodical material is probably now unrecoverable. But the surviving work does not show Sigourney as primarily a poet of mortuary verse. This is not to say that Sigourney did *not* write many poems about death, among which were poems about dead mothers and children. But such poems do not dominate even her poetic practice, and she also wrote significant quantities of prose. I count 16 elegies out of 114 pieces in her 1827 *Poems;* 50 out of 172 in the 1835 *Zinzendorff, and Other Poems;* 15 out of 115 in the 1841 *Pocahontas, and Other Poems;* and 32 out of 126 in *Select Poems,* already mentioned: Overall, this works out to 32 percent.[5] Perhaps in recognition of the popularity of this segment of her writing, Sigourney herself frequently called attention to it, as, for example in her preface to *Zinzendorff*, where she says that, "should it be objected that too great a proportion of [the poems] are elegiac, the required apology would fain clothe itself in the language of the gifted Lord Bacon:—If we listen to David's harp, we shall find as many hearse-like harmonies, as carols; and the pencil of Inspiration hath more labored to describe the afflictions of Job, than the felicities of Solomon" (6).

The category of elegy, or consolation poetry, or funerary verse, more-over, is a broad one, and one may discern within the Sigourney elegiac corpus three poetic subtypes. There are reflective memento mori poems deriving from some general observation in nature or the world; there are what I would want to call generic, or situational, elegies, whose subject is denoted as a member of a class rather than as an individual; and then there are elegies for named persons—memorial, or obituary, poems. One need go no further afield than the table of contents of *Zinzendorff* for examples of each type. "Death among the Trees" would appear to be (and is) a general reflection on the inevitability of death, as is "Thoughts for Mourners." "Death of the Wife of a Clergyman, during the Sickness of Her Husband," "Death of a Young Wife," "Burial of Two Young Sisters," "Death of a Young Lady at the Retreat for the Insane," "Farewell of a Missionary to Africa, at the Grave of his Wife and Child," and "Death of a Young Musi-cian" are situational elegies. "Funeral of Dr. Mason F. Cogswell," "Death of the Rev. Gordon Hall," "Death of Mrs. Harriet W. L. Winslow," "Death of a Son of the Late Honorable Fisher Ames," "Death of the Rev. Alfred Mitchell," and "Death of the Rev. W. C. Walton" are some of the specific memorials.

My distinctions here are not merely formal—or, rather, they are formal in Aristotle's sense of being configured with regard to an audience response. Each of the three kinds invokes a different type of occasion. (And as the titles above show, the subjects are by no means exclusively women and/or children.) The memento mori poem, which Sigourney practices the least, is an internal dialogue that dramatizes the persona's efforts to come to terms with death in general, with the death of a loved one, or with one's own inevitable death. Because it is meditative it is distanced from the immediacy of death. Thus, it bespeaks an interval of leisure, privacy, and solitude for the persona as well as any reader whose mental processes it may seek to guide and mime.

The generic and specific consolation poetry that Sigourney most often wrote, in contrast, is designed for immediate intervention at the moment of death or funeral. A generic elegy, like a greeting card, is available to the large number of people whose circumstances it suits at the moment; the memorial for a named person is designed to palliate the grief of a unique set of mourners. This set extends beyond close family to friends, acquaintances, or those who knew the dead person by name only. So newspaper obituaries serve us today. Thus, both the situational elegy and the obituary poem bespeak a public arena and a practical goal. They do not have time to expatiate on religious uncertainty, to exhibit the depth and extent of one's own grief, or to manage a personal catharsis; they aim to make suffering people feel better—and make them feel better fast. "Her muse has been a comforter to the mourner," Sarah Hale observed, and one necessary aspect of this comforting function is that the elegies are never about the speaker, always about others.[6]

Invariably, these useful poems designed specifically for Christians plug in a strong affirmation of the life to come. From the converging perspectives of high Victorianism and high modernism Sigourney's unsympathetic biographer Gordon Haight derides the intellectual simplicity of her religiosity, but *In Memoriam,* to which he invidiously compares Sigourney's elegiac corpus, was certainly not supposed to comfort any mourner besides its author.[7] Perhaps this other-directedness of Sigourney's elegiac voice also explains her minimal position in the narcissistic woman's poetic tradition developed by Cheryl Walker's *Nightingale's Burden,* a tradition centered on the topic of how hard it is to be a woman poet.[8] The activist and interventionist element in this elegiac poetry—an element that by all accounts succeeded in its intentions—would also seem to tell against Ann Douglas Wood's construal of Sigourney's death poetry: Its "heroine was herself, but emptied of conflict, sublimated, and desexualized . . . a small figure . . . seemingly submissive, submerged, half-hypnotized and half automaton," and also to qualify Richard Brodhead's recent Foucauldian speculations on the antebellum construction of women readers as isolated and passive consumers of mass-produced literary goods. Without denying that such a reading practice might have existed I would see it as only one of a range of practices; the memorial poem that forms part of the public occasion of the funeral and is then used, reused, and adapted by successive groups of mourners who find it pertinent implies another kind of reading.[9]

In terms of a self-conscious poetic practice Sigourney's elegies might be setting themselves against a male model of romantic egoism or a female stereotype of withdrawn narcissism. Thus, even were we to characterize Sigourney by her funerary verse alone, we would need a less homogeneous and implicitly contemptuous representation of her project. But her other poetry and her prose writings provide materials for the construction of a very different Sigourney. This different Sigourney is what I call a "republican public mother," a phrase applicable to the self-presentation of many literary women active in the early national years. Whereas the type of republican mother made familiar to us by historians of American women in the post-Revolutionary era (a woman who carries out her civic duties by training her children in patriotism and republican values) performs her activities in the home space, republican public mothers are public figures. As writers, they aim to enter the public sphere and influence the formation of public opinion. Sigourney's nonelegiac writings often take public positions and make public statements; she is no "sentimental domestic," to use Mary Kelley's phrase, by any means.[10]

Even where titles like *Letters to Young Ladies, Letters to Mothers,* and *Whispers to a Bride* might seem to imply the Victorian female world of love and ritual or the cult of true womanhood, the content reveals something much more political and much less emotional.[11] In these books Sigourney's domestic ideology is inseparable from patriotic and republican politics. In the often reprinted *Letters to Young Ladies,* for example, she writes that "the foundation of the unity and strength of all nations is laid in the discipline of well-ordered families; and the consistency and beauty of a well-balanced character may be resolved into the element of self-control"; and "to a republic, whose welfare depends on the intelligence, and virtue of the people, the character and habits of every member of its family are of value"; and "women possess an agency which the ancient republics never discovered"; and, finally, women, in return for all that America has given them, owe it to their country to give their "hands to every cause of peace and truth, encourage temperance and purity, oppose disorder and vice, be gentle teachers of wisdom and charity."[12] The motherly persona adopted by Sigourney in her advice books contains a significant Spartan element in her makeup, and her advice authorizes, indeed urges, women to move outside of the home when the cause is right.

Sigourney herself moved well beyond the halfway literature of domestic instruction (halfway, that is, between the private and public realms) into a clearly public sphere in her many historical writings. Like many women educators in the early years of the century—Sigourney taught school for several years before her marriage in 1819—Sigourney saw history as the core of a republican woman's education, so that in some sense the domestic preceptress and the historian are facets of the same female construction. In *Letters to Young Ladies* she wrote—quite conventionally—that fiction should be eschewed and history embraced: "history has ever been warmly commended to the attention of the young. It imparts knowledge of human nature and supplies lofty subjects for contemplation" (65). Her memoirs recalled her pleasure in unfolding with students "the broad annals of History. Seated in a circle, like a band of sisters, we traced in the afternoon, by the guidance of Rollin, the progress of ancient times, or the fall of buried empires" (*Letters,* 203). But as a writer rather than a teacher of history to girls, Sigourney is more directly part of the polity, for historical writings construct a view of the public sphere that extends well beyond women and aggressively comment on it.

It would appear, in fact, that well over half of what she published in both prose *and* poetry was historical in content, and it was also political—in a fairly conventional sense of the term—in implication. Through the learning, teaching, and writing of history Sigourney, like a number of other literary women between 1790 and the Civil War, enacted womanly behavior that in many ways nullified the distinction between public and private that operated so crucially in other contexts.[13]

The subject matter of Sigourney's historical writing falls into the four categories of: ancient and Biblical history; the local history of the region around Hartford, Norwich, and New London, Connecticut, from settlement through Revolution;[14] the American Revolution; and the history of the American Indians after the European arrival on the continent. Although she wrote numerous biographical sketches of exemplary women, she did not attempt to construct a separate history of women; indeed, her progressive Christian view suggested that women had only very recently emerged as a force in history. There is history in Sigourney's short poems and long poems, in sketches of varying length, in free-standing and embedded fictional narratives, and in a variety of nonfictional modes, including biography, narrative history, and children's textbooks designed for school or home use.[15]

The only work from this sizable segment of Sigourney's output previously excavated and analyzed is the 1824 *Sketch of Connecticut, Forty Years Since.*[16] An important essay by Sandra A. Zagarell claims that the *Sketch* is "quite directly concerned with the foundations and organization of public life," with a vision that "deliberately extended official definitions of the nation to imagine an America grounded in inclusiveness and communitarianism."[17] Since the sketch features real events from the past, I take it as a work of history which indeed has public intentions. But rather than psychologize those intentions, as Zagarell does, I would prefer to historicize them. When historicized, Sigourney's politics emerge as a self-conscious advocacy of the tenets of "classical" (i.e., conservative) republicanism in an age of increasing liberalism; as an urging of the merits of nonsectarian evangelical Christianity on an increasingly disputatious and fragmented religious scene; and as an effort to reconcile the civic with the spiritual realms in an amalgam of Christianity and republicanism.[18]

The *Sketch* is designed to celebrate the benevolent aristocratic widow Madam L——, whose charities and liberalities sustain a hierarchical republican community in productive harmony. Almost certainly, it would have been recognized as a political counterstatement to the Scotswoman Anne Grant's intensely Tory and anti–New England *Memoirs of an American Lady: With Sketches of Manners and Scenery in America, as They Existed Previous to the Revolution,* a work similarly configured around a benefactress recalled from childhood, which had its American publication in Boston in 1809. The real-life model for Sigourney's *Sketch* was Jerusha Talcot Lathrop, widow

of Daniel Lathrop, a prosperous druggist of Norwich. Until Madam Lathrop died in 1806 Sigourney's father, Ezekial Huntley, was gardener and
general handyman on her estate. After her death the family of a nephew,
Daniel Wadsworth, took an interest in the Huntleys and Lydia in particular
(see n. 1). Sigourney's own life story, then, would confirm to her the efficacy of a moral republicanism wherein the fortunate supported the virtuous
poor by giving them opportunities to support themselves.

This conservative republican theme is sounded at the very start of the
sketch with its evocation of the town of N——[Norwich] as site of "the
singular example of an aristocracy, less intent upon family aggrandizement,
than upon becoming illustrious in virtue" (4). Unlike other sections of the
country in the years immediately following the Revolution, there was no
"agitation" in Connecticut because "the body of the people trusted in the
wisdom of those heroes and sages of whom they had furnished their proportion. They believed that the hands, which had been strengthened to lay
the foundation of their liberty, amid the tempests of war, would be enabled
to complete the fabric, beneath the smiles of peace" (16). Madam L——'s
contribution to the fabric, as a woman of social prominence and fortune, is
to disburse appropriate charity and thereby maintain harmonious relations
among the social classes. She gives out money, food, clothing, jobs, and
advice to the deserving poor around her in return for their loyalty and
subordination.

Madam L——'s beneficence usually succeeds in producing a peaceful and
cohesive community and is especially effective with marginalized women.
As one impoverished woman is made to say, "what a blessed thing it is,
when the hearts of the rich are turned to give work to the poor, and assist
them to get the necessaries of life, for themselves and families" (73). But
with the American Indians the story is different. And nine of the eighteen
chapters of the *Sketch*—fully half of the book—are about the remnant of
the Mohegan tribe. In chapters 12 and 13 two tribal leaders—its chief and
its Christian minister—inform her that most members of the tribe have
decided to leave Norwich and move to the interior, where they will unite
with another tribe. This decision shows that Madam L——'s charities are
insufficient and beside the point where Indians are concerned. Individualistic Indians cannot accept a position at the bottom of a class hierarchy,
which is where the community of N—— places them. Their distaste for
settled agriculture makes it impossible for them to survive on their reservation, which "would have been more than adequate to their wants, had
they been assiduous in its cultivation" (31). Most of all, they believe—they
know—that the whites are determined to exterminate them (always except-
ing Madam L—— herself), and after experiencing a century and a half of
violence they have given up all thought of resisting. Their move is only a
stopgap. "Ere long, white men will cease to crush us, for we will cease to

be" (160). Occum, the minister, insists that Christianity holds promise for American Indians, but Robert Ashbow, the chief, counters that "Christianity is for white men" (161). As they depart, one young warrior asks despairingly, "Whither shall we go, and not hear the speech of the white man?" (173).

In fact, of the four historical subjects that most concerned Sigourney, the American Indians were foremost. The history of her own region and American Indian history were in some sense identical: The Pequod War had been waged there, the Mohegans had fought with English settlers first against the Pequods and then the Naragansetts, and the Mohegan chief Uncas was supposed to have given the land around Norwich to the English in exchange for protection from King Philip and other enemies. This meant that the establishment of the Christian American community which Sigourney extolled in the *Sketch of Connecticut* and elsewhere depended directly on white access to Indian land.

Sigourney drew from this history the moral conclusion that the Anglo-American national character was defined by how whites acquired the land they needed and what happened to the Indians afterward. In writing about the American Indians she confronted the insoluble narrative problem that, while three of her subjects were representable as comedies (the pagan world gave way to the Christian; the American Revolution was won by the right side; the Connecticut Valley fostered the most moral society ever known on earth), the fourth was an unmitigated tragedy. Sigourney also faced the insoluble *political* and *moral* problem that the triumphs of Christianity and republicanism in America were achieved at the cost of their own basic tenets. In destroying the American Indians rather than domesticating them, republicanism ignored its commitments to civic virtue and to the amelioration of the lot of the needy by the fortunate; Christianity neglected its imperatives of charity and of taking all souls as equals before God. Her historical writings are internally fractured because their attempt to affirm the progress of history is continually frustrated by the evident failure of Christian-republican ethics to meet the single most important test of the moral caliber of the American nation—the obligation to preserve the continent's "aborigines" by Christianizing them and integrating them into American society.

The *Sketch of Connecticut* concludes, for example, with three fantasy chapters given over to the story of Oriana, a beautiful white woman whose life has been saved in war by a Mohegan warrior who adopts her to replace his own dead daughter. In this allegory the historically documented Indian behavior of welcoming, feeding, and protecting the original white colonists wherever they set foot on American soil is reciprocated by Oriana's willingness to become their daughter and help Christianize them. At the same time the story neutralizes a widespread social fear that white people—especially women—adopted into American Indian tribes became hopelessly "Indian-ized." Oriana stays white, buoyed by a radical Christianity that leaves republican ideology, even as practiced by the exemplary Madam L——, completely out of the picture. Sigourney's fondness for this segment of the *Sketch* may be seen in the fact that she republished it as "Oriana" in her twice reprinted *Sketches*.[19]

In contrast to the imaginary Oriana's example, the core story of American Indian history after the European arrival presented in Sigourney's writings is one where Indian generosity is answered by European brutality. A para-digm of this narrative occurs in a short poem called "The Indian's Welcome to the Pilgrim Fathers," which appeared in *Zinzendorff* and reads in part:

> When sudden from the forest wide,
>   A red-brow'd chieftain came,
> With towering form, and haughty stride,
>   And eye like kindling flame:
> No wrath he breath'd, no conflict sought,
>   To no dark ambush drew,
> But simply *to the Old World brought,*
>   *The welcome of the New.*
>
> That *welcome* was a blast and ban
>   Upon thy race unborn.
> Was there no seer, thou fated Man!
>   Thy lavish zeal to warn?
> Thou in they fearless faith didst hail
>   A weak, invading band,
> But who shall heed thy children's wail,
>   Swept from their native land?
>   (47–48)

Sigourney's narratives of the American Indian disaster lead to the culmi-nating plea that her compatriots should return to the essence of republican and Christian doctrine and stop destroying the Indians by murder and relocation. But this plea undermines the affirmative dynamic of her other historical representations by substituting an implicit declension model of American and Christian history, and it does this without mitigating in the least the unrepublican and un-Christian carnage that has already taken place. From her historical perspective the cessation of American Indian destruction in the future—though it is much to be hoped for and though her writings are designed in part to further that goal—could not justify the erasure of past massacre. Whatever happened in the future, that is, it was necess-ary to remember what had happened in the past. Unwilling to adopt a tragic or ironic stance toward history (though she could not always avoid doing so), Sigourney could not accept the palliating conviction found in so many writings of the time that the destruction of the American Indians is merely inevitable. And convinced that a Christian must see the Indians as human kin, however "other" they may be, she cannot write a history in which their obliteration could be frankly presented as a sign of historical progress.

There is no honest way to resolve her dilemma, so Sigourney's Indian narratives typically end with a forthright contradiction. "We are struck with the prominence and discordance of some of the features in the character of our ancestors," she writes in a prose sketch called "The Fall of the Pequod." Boldness, cruelty, and "the piety to which they turned for sanction, even when the deed and motive seemed at variance," make a strange combination.

> The unresting vigilance with which they blotted out the very name of Pequod . . . was not less arbitrary than the dismemberment of Poland, and savored more of the policy of heathen Rome than of Christ. Mason, in common with the historians of that age, bitterly blamed the Indians for stratagems in war, but chose to adopt the creed he had denounced, and to prove himself an adept in the theory that he condemned. . . . The once-powerful aboriginal tribe . . . perished without a hand to write its epitaph: an emblem of the fate of that vanishing race to whom the brotherhood of the white man hath hitherto been as the kiss of Judas.[20]

No doubt, some might see prose like this as intellectually confused. But it could be equally described as intellectually forthcoming in a political setting where crude hypocrisy and debonair obfuscation were the order of the day.

"Traits of the Aborigines of America," which preceded the *Sketch of Connecticut* by two years, was Sigourney's first work about American Indians. Despite its bland title and its anonymous publication, this five-canto work of four thousand blank verse lines, with extensive scholarly annotation, is her longest and most ambitious poem, packed with classical references and historical allusion and dense with information about American Indian tribes.[21] While it ought to be considered a belated entry in the competition for "the" American epic, it is uniquely structured from the Indian point of view, and its narrative extends beyond the territorial United States to include the story of the continent from the Arctic circle to South America. This story, regardless of where it transpires, is always the same: The Indians welcome the newcomers and are exterminated.

Canto 1 begins with the Indians in undisturbed possession of the continent and then introduces a chronicle of incursion: "First, to their northern coast / Wander'd the Scandinavian" (1:253–254); after a while Columbus comes—the Indians thought he and his men were Gods,

> nor dream'd their secret aim
> Was theft and cruelty, to snatch the gold
> That sparkled in their streams, and bid their blood
> Stain those pure waters.
>
> (1:44–47)

Portuguese, French, Irish, English—everybody comes. Christians come too, bringing the potential benefit of their religion to the Indians. But that benefit does not develop because the Christians do not behave like Christians.

In canto 2, incursions become more extensive and frequent:

> Almost it seemed
> As if old Europe, weary of her load,
> Pour'd on a younger world her thousand sons
> In ceaseless deluge.
>
> (2:8–11)

The bulk of the canto narrates the life of John Smith, allowing the poet to provide a geography and history of most of the world through a chronicle of his travels. Pocahontas's rescue of him is compared to Pharaoh's daughter rescuing Moses—and with the same ultimately disastrous effect on her people:

> little thought
> The Indian Monarch, that his child's weak arm
> Fostered that colony, whose rising light
> Should quench his own forever.
>
> (2:1093–1096)

Sigourney vacillates between comic and tragic interpretations of the narrative and simultaneously avoids and intensifies both readings by focusing on the conversion and early death of Pocahontas herself. There is some unspecified and contradictory connection between the conversion and the death. On the one hand, it seems that Christianity itself is what kills Pocahontas; on the other, that, thanks to her conversion, she dies regenerate. The canto ends with brief attention to the founding of Pennsylvania, Delaware, and Florida, always from the vantage point of those who are forced out by European settlement:

> Pressing west
> O'er the vain barrier, and retreating tide
> Of Mississippi, spread our ancestors,
> Taking a goodly portion, with the sword,
> And with their bow.
>
> (2:1186–1190)

Canto 3 positions itself with the now outcast and understandably hostile Indians in their various forest refuges, describes many instances of savage warfare, and contains a ringing attack on whites for their instigatory barbarism as well as their hypocrisy in faulting the Indians.

> Who are these,
> Red from the bloody wine-press, with its stains
> Dark'ning their raiment? Yet I dare not ask
> Their clime and lineage, lest the accusing blasts,
> Waking the angry echoes, should reply
> "Thy Countrymen!"
>
> (3:905–910)

Sigourney's target here is the truism that Indians were naturally vengeful. She shows that they are naturally generous and reveals the truism as a white construction—part material (the Indians are responding self-defensively to white brutality) and part rhetorical (the Indians are often misrepresented as vengeful when their behavior is anything but).

Canto 4, the shortest in the poem, begins by praising the few missionaries—Eliot, Heckewelder—who went among the Indians to preach Christianity but gives most of its lines to Tuscarora, who mocks those of his tribe who want to convert:

> Behold! what glorious gifts
> Ye owe to white men. What good-will and peace
> They shed upon you! Exile and the sword!
> Poisons and rifled sepulchres! and see!
> They fain would fill the measure of their guilt
> With the dark cheat of that accursed faith
> Whose precepts justify *their* nameless crimes,
> *Your* countless woes.
>
> (4:348–354)

The point that Sigourney is after here is that the whites have created not only justifiable Indian hostility to them as a group but hostility as well to the Christianity that they claim to represent. The necessary task of joining with the Indians in brotherly love has been made infinitely more difficult by the white people's betrayal of their own religion.

Canto 5 then departs from the historical record to urge on Christian Americans the true obligations of their Christianity. "Make these foes your friends" (5:546–547). The narrator acknowledges that most living Indians are already demoralized and degraded and sees the possibility—albeit at some horrendous bloody cost to themselves—of the white's completely exterminating the Indians. But she argues vehemently that "our God hath made / All of one blood, who dwell upon the earth" (5:406–407); the only important difference between "red" and white people is that whites are (supposedly) Christian. Their very religion requires whites to Christianize the Indians. And when the Indians also become Christians, their justified desire for revenge will be set aside; they will then become an integral part of the American republic, and that republic, though no longer purely white, will be purely Christian.

Not the least interesting aspect of "Traits" is its continual recourse to references from what the era called "Universal History" in order simultaneously to heroicize the American Indians and deheroicize the Europeans. At various points in the poem the Indians are likened, for example, to "stern Regulus" (1:60); "the warlike Earl, stern Steward" (1:208); "the Scythian tribes" (1:224–225); "sublime Demosthenes" (2:143), "the impetuous Hannibal" (3:535); and "the stern, Spartan lords" (3:656). Sometimes Sigourney accompanies these comparisons with the lament that the Indians—equally valiant, noble, eloquent as these historical figures—are doomed to extinction *without a history* and hence to oblivion rather than remembrance. Sometimes she interrupts the Indian narrative for long accounts of historical carnage which far exceed anything that the American Indians have perpetrated:

> O'er the tow'rs
> Of lofty Ilion, wreck'd by Grecian wiles,
> Why does the dazzeled eye prolong its gaze
> In breathless interest, yet averts its glance
> Disgusted, and indignant, at the scenes of Indian stratagem?
> (3:721–726)

Sigourney's missionary perspective is, of course, culturally chauvinistic. It depends on an idea of the American Indians' likeness to whites rather than of their dignity in difference; it also assumes that American Indian culture is inferior to white because it is not Christian. But as we have seen, Sigourney is much more critical of white culture for failing to live up to its Christian ideals than of Indian culture with no such ideals to guide it. Overall, indeed, "Traits of the Aborigines" makes public demands on white American society that at the time were thoroughly Utopian. In the memoir written some forty years later Sigourney dryly observes that the poem "was singularly unpopular, there existing in the community no reciprocity with the subject." But her own views had not changed in the intervening years; "our injustice and hard-hearted policy with regard to the original owners of the soil has ever seemed to me one of our greatest national sins" (*Letters*, 327).

The poem that gives the *Zinzendorff* volume of 1835 its title is another work about Indians. The 584-line annotated poem in blank verse centers on the mission by Count Zinzendorff, founder of the radical Christian Moravian sect, to the Indians of the Wyoming valley in 1742. It praises Zinzendorff for going among Indians whose experience with whites makes them deeply suspicious of him.

> Sought he to grasp their lands?
> To search for gold? to found a mystic throne
> Of dangerous power?
>
> (lines 100–102)

Zinzendorff's peaceful persistence and his appeal to the women, children, and old people of the tribe, as well as the evidence of his remarkable escapes from plots against his life, persuade the Indian rulers to take his message seriously.

Sigourney begins this poem with a brief mention of a much-written-about incident, the 1778 massacre in the Wyoming Valley of Pennsylvania, when an alliance of Tory Pennsylvanians and American Indians slaughtered emigrant patriot settlers from Connecticut. She explains that white appropriation of Indian land in the decades before the massacre had created Indian hostility and thus was the actual historical cause of the massacre. Zinzendorff, in contrast, had gone among the Indians with only Christian motives. When, toward the end of the poem, the Indians are made to lament Zinzendorff's return to Europe, their grief is interpreted by the poet as prophetic of their future at the hands of people who will settle with self-aggrandizing rather than self-effacing intentions (lines 495–505). In brief, Zinzendorff's was the road not taken. The poem closes with an appeal to Christians to desist from sectarian controversy and unite in peaceful missionary activities among the Indians. There may still be time, the poem says, to reverse history's direction and bring Indians into the nation.

Sigourney wrote another piece about the Wyoming massacre, the "Legend of Pennsylvania," collected in *Myrtis*. She begins with the history that led to carnage. "The Connecticut colonists evinced their national courage and tenacity in defense of their homes, and what they deemed their legal possessions. The Pennsylvanians were equally inflexible in what they considered their antecedent rights. The Aborigines contended for their favorite dominion with a lion-like despair" (179). One disaster after another is represented in the destruction of families and registered in the responses of surviving women. At the story's end the last member of a once-thriving family of Connecticut pioneers in the valley joins the Moravians at Nazareth, living out the rest of her life as a teacher in the girls' school there. The Moravian sect had an interest in women's education and founded some of the earliest boarding schools for young women in the country, facts that endeared the group to Sigourney, who in later life looked back at her teaching years as the happiest she had known. In the poem Sigourney typically invokes the pacific and womanly alternative to carnage.

The mood of "Pocahontas," published in the 1841 volume *Pocahontas, and Other Poems,* is not hopeful. The 504-line poem, in fifty-six modified Spenserian stanzas, recounts the life of Pocahontas as a memorial to the

American Indian princess. Although by 1841 American literature was full of tributes to her, Sigourney puts a recognizable stamp on the story material. She begins as she had begun "Traits of the Aborigines," from an assumed American Indian perspective in the New World before the Europeans arrive. Apostrophizing the "clime of the West," she asks whether it was not "sweet, in cradled rest to lie, / And 'scape the ills that older regions know?" An entrance into history, long deferred, begins when the "roving hordes of savage men" look up to "behold a sail! another, and another!" She sounds her motif of Christian brotherhood: "What were thy secret thoughts, oh red-brow'd brother, / As toward the shore those white-wing'd wanderers press'd?" And when Powhatan, moved by his daughter's intercession, spares John Smith's life, Sigourney notes the ironic outcome of that event with the same comparison to Pharaoh's daughter that she had made in *Traits* (stanza 20).

"Thou wert the saviour of the Saxon vine, / And for this deed alone our praise and love are thine" (stanza 21) Sigourney says, once again stressing the self-destructive, ironically Christian tendency of the Indians to nurture and protect white intruders. Then, moving forward in time to the era of Indian surprise attacks on white settlements, she challenges the historians' accounts:

> ye, who hold of history's scroll the pen,
> Blame not too much those erring, red-brow'd men,
> Though nursed in wiles. Fear is the white-lipp'd sire
> Of subterfuge and treachery. 'Twere in vain
> To bid the soul be true, that writhes beneath his chain.
>
> (stanza 24)

The whites, answering Indian generosity with oppression and dislocation, created the vengeful Indians, whose behavior they now slander and use as a pretext for further incursions against them.

The poem then chronicles Pocahontas's capture, conversion, marriage, journey to England, and early death, but it refers beyond this personal narrative to another, larger narrative—especially when it returns at the end to the long view with which it began and addresses the American Indians en masse:

> I would ye were not, from your fathers' soil
>   Track'd like the dun wolf, ever in your breast
> The coal of vengeance and the curse of toil;
>   I would we had not to your mad lip prest
> The fiery poison-cup, nor on ye turn'd
>   The blood-tooth'd ban-dog, foaming, as he burn'd
> To tear your flesh; but thrown in kindness bless'd

The brother's arm around ye, as ye trod,
And led ye, sad of heart, to the bless'd Lamb of god.

(stanza 54)

I wish we hadn't, but we have—this is undoubtedly a weak, sentimental, acknowledgment of national crime, but at least it is an acknowledgment. Sigourney's conventional memorializing of Pocahontas, savior and servant of the whites, leads to an invocation of those nameless Indian dead who heroically *resisted* white incursion: "King, stately chief, and warrior-host are dead, / Nor remnant nor memorial left behind" (stanza 56). Sigourney's poem memorializes them as well as Pocahontas.

All history writing, in Sigourney's literary approach to it, is a memorial to the past—not the past made to live again, not even a representation of the past, but a memorial of it. (And this point allows us to think of her elegiac verse as another, individualized, form of history writing.) Her writing about American Indians can be seen as an attempt to influence the present moment in three ways. First, it argues for a sense of white responsibility toward the surviving remnants of Indian tribes; second, it tries to ensure that the Indian story became a part of American history no matter how badly the story reflected on the white conquerors; third, it insists that the Indians *were* Americans. Here her schooling in ancient history—with its chronicle of aggressor empires culminating in the mighty, yet decadent, Rome—served as a storehouse of parallels for interpreting and representing more recent history. The conventional classical references through which the Founders historicized their vision of a nation became, when Sigourney treated the American Indians, references rather to empire than to republic.

In the 1850s Sigourney turned her attention to the West and the New England pioneers who were settling it. A long poem from this decade, about a pioneer family from Connecticut settling in Ohio, features a stalwart Indian woman, whose medicinal skills save the life of one of the settler children, and the quasifictional, quasi-autobiographical *Lucy Howard's Journal* conjoins Lucy Howard, the New England heroine, with both a black and an Indian woman in an image of triracial (although inegalitarian) harmony.[22] The historical strain in her writing continues to the end of her life, when *Letters of Life* returns to the Norwich of her girlhood, the beloved Madam L——, and the memories of early republican Connecticut that had animated the *Sketch* of 1824. Whether Sigourney was a 'good" writer or not, she was obviously an important one in her own time, and we will understand that time much better if we abandon a social construction of Sigourney based on extremely limited awareness of her work. In particular, that a writer with so obviously public a program should come down to us as the most private and domesticated of antebellum women authors suggests the need to look again at the scope of antebellum women's writing.

11

Sarah Hale, Political Writer

Sarah Josepha Hale, author of poems, stories, sketches, a play, novels, and several home reference books, is remembered chiefly for her lengthy tenure (1837–77) as editor of *Godey's Lady's Book,* the most widely read women's magazine of its day. Using her position year after year to advance the doctrine of separate spheres for women and men, Hale is assumed by most critics to have exerted considerable influence on the gender ideology and cultural mores of the nineteenth-century American middle class.[1]

The doctrine of the separate spheres was once thought to reflect reality; now it is recognized as a rhetorical construct designed to intervene in cultural life but over whose content there was no consensus. Contemporary feminist scholars differ over their descriptions of the doctrine, their assessment of its liberating potential for women, and, therefore—explicitly or implicitly—their judgment of Hale's work.[2] Everybody agrees, however, that Hale was firmly committed to keeping women out of politics and that she used the concept of women's sphere to further this goal.

In *Declarations of Independence,* for example, Barbara Bardes and Suzanne Gossett cite an "Editor's Table" from the 1852 *Lady's Book* where Hale belittles the women's rights movement. Women should vote, she writes, "by influencing rightly the votes of men"; she quotes a woman "who, if women went to the polls, would be acknowledged as a leader," to the effect that, since she controls the seven votes of her husband and six sons, "why should I desire to cast one myself?"[3] Bardes and Gossett see the editorial as a nonpolitical document opposing women's involvement in politics. But such a reading assumes in advance that casting a ballot is the only way to be political, which, I would argue, is precisely the view that Hale is attacking here. Her editorial can (and in my view should) be read as pragmatically insisting that any issue to be decided at the polls is better served by seven votes than by one. Hale implies that it is shortsighted, selfish, and just plain bad politics for one woman to insist on casting a ballot in person when she can deliver seven votes by staying home. The position advanced here is certainly controversial, arguably illogical, but thoroughly political.

Again, Nicole Tonkovich Hoffman, who argues that Hale's work for women's education and women's occupations should be recognized as political, insists at the same time that Hale resisted such mainstream political issues as abolition and women's rights.[4] I would argue contrariwise that these two issues were extremely important to her in the 1850s—the "Editor's Table" discussed above, after all, is written in opposition to women's rights. The mammoth biographical and historical compendium *Woman's Record* (1853) is also explicitly and implicitly directed against that movement. As for abolition, two of the books Hale published in the early 1850s—a revised version of her 1827 novel *Northwood* (1852) and a historical novel *Liberia* (1853)—explicitly attacked it and supported colonization. Therefore, if women's rights and abolition are ipso facto political issues, Hale was very much an active political writer, at least in the decade before the Civil War. The problem, of course, is that from "our" point of view she argued for the wrong side in both instances.

My hypothesis here is simply that Hale was a profoundly political writer throughout her career. Born in New Hampshire in 1787, she was shaped intellectually, ideologically, and politically by the agitations and values of New England during the early republican era. From first to last she wrote on behalf of a vision of the United States as a Christian republic destined to lead the world into the millennium. She was not an individualist; she defined women and men in relation to each other, to the nation, and to the nation's goals. While she assumed that many human tasks would necessarily be allocated according to gender in any nation, she also saw the United States as uniquely responsive to female participation in the polity—this, indeed, was one of its claims to greatness. One field in which women might contribute to the national well-being was literature; illustrious foremothers like Mercy Otis Warren, Hannah Adams, Sarah Wentworth Morton, and Judith Sargent Murray testified amply to the compatibility of a literary career and womanly republican duties.

These convictions remained constant in Hale's work; others changed over time. Her views of appropriate gender activities, her very definitions of *man* and *woman,* altered dramatically, along the lines of a transformation from Enlightenment to Victorian ideologies that I have discussed earlier in this volume. Hale's writing in the late 1820s defined *woman* as a rational being, like *man.* In the enlightened republican patriarchy that Hale took the United States to be, woman's main tasks—the socially subordinate duties of helpmeet and mother—followed logically from her reproductive capacity and bodily weakness. By the eve of the Civil War Hale had come to define *woman* as a spiritual being, not at all like man, who had now become purely material; woman's tasks—no longer socially subordinate—were to harness and guide his brute force, to provide moral leadership for the nation and the world. Rationality had more or less disappeared from this picture; the nation—whether or not it had ever in fact functioned as a harmonious, hierarchical commonwealth—was now perceived as a scene threatened by atomistic fragmentation and chaotic competition. In this scene *woman* was redefined as man's opposite and alternative; she was, therefore, enjoined from action that simply replicated his behavior. If, in cultural terms, Victorianism is supplanting Enlightenment thinking here, it is not difficult to infer specific historical and political pressures behind the transformation. National survival remains Hale's obsession.

In the discussion that follows I am going to talk about Hale's independent writings rather than her work as editor of the *Lady's Book,* although I suspect that the journal would reflect similar continuities and changes. Her first novel, *Northwood, A Tale of New England* (1827), was about national identity and republican politics. It centers on the disparities and divisions between North and South and proposes to unite the nation by instituting a New England hegemony over the South. In line with the republican vision of a nation as constituted by the character and virtue of its citizens Hale assumes that the United States must have one character and identifies New England as the source of that character. The colonization of the South by New England is accomplished by sending the technical hero of the book, Sidney Romilly of New Hampshire, South to be adopted by a wealthy aunt and uncle.[5] The real hero of the book, however, is Sidney's father, Squire Romilly, the patriarch who embodies the ideal republican character. Allowing Sidney to go South is his rational decision to subordinate parental affection to Sidney's future welfare, since the family cannot afford to send him to college. But the nation is served as well: The underdeveloped South becomes a fair field for the industry and virtue of a surplus New England population, whose activity in turn incorporates it into the nation.

Northwood develops a bildungsroman around Sidney, who has to return North as a young man for further character development as well as to find a New England bride to help him plant a new England dynasty in the South; it also contains a few love stories. The first thirteen of the thirty chapters in the 1827 novel, however, contain little story material, and even the late-developing romances are subordinated to such discursive aims as describing the ideal American woman. Much of the book surveys New England life and character through a technique of interweaving narrator description and commentary with the male characters' political and patriotic discussion. As Lawrence Buell observes, its "return of the native" device creates a "comparatist but still essentially Yankee perspective" that allows Hale to anatomize "New England character and institutions from both an insider's and an outsider's angle of vision."[6] Moreover, since the returning Sidney is accompanied by an English friend, Hale is able to work her comparison three ways; if she partitions the nation to contrast North and South, she unifies it to contrast the United States with England.

Bardes and Gossett observe that "the world of political ideas, which is discussed at length in *Northwood,* is the world of men," and their point is well taken to the extent that the discussants of these ideas in the book are, indeed, male characters.[7] It is certainly reasonable to expect that, if a book is situating women within the field of politics, it will show them engaging in political discussion; this does not happen in *Northwood.* The lengthy encomiums on the female New England character focus on rationality, self-control, industry, frugality—to be sure, precisely the traits that are valued in men and hence not constitutive of sexual difference—but at no time do women appear to function in the public, political world. But Hale represents the domestic world within which women operate as resonant with political significance in every detail. The Romilly women, for example, enunciate political statements by wearing clothes made from American fabrics and preparing food and drink from native produce. When the Englishman Mr. Frankford laughingly asks Squire Romilly if he imagines "that currant wine or ginger-beer are at all connected with the preservation of your liberties," the squire reminds him of the significance of tea in American-English history (*Northwood,* 94).

More generally, republican ideology held obsessively to the conviction that luxury and extravagance were destructive to citizen virtue and national independence and believed that extravagant women in particular had been responsible throughout history for the fall of nations. (This point of view has not disappeared, as residual political criticism of Nancy Reagan's extravagance makes clear.) The prudent young American woman preserves and contributes to the national welfare when she is frugal and industrious in her home. And even more, when she chooses the true-hearted, hard-working American man of modest means over the leisured European aristocrat she stabilizes and perpetuates American values. In short, while it cannot be denied that Hale presents a fully domestic picture of American womanhood in *Northwood* and allocates specifically public concerns to men, it is also true that she politicizes and publicizes the domestic realm within which she situates her women characters.

There is also a second level on which women are implicated in American politics in *Northwood*—the level of discourse rather than story. The narrator of this book is clearly identified as a woman; Hale published the book under her own name. Her constant narrative interpolations alternate with the pronouncements of Squire Romilly and other men in the book, who are in any case her constructions and can speak only the words that she writes for them. Hale is thus writing men, and writing men's political discourse, staking out writing—and reading—as ways by which women could appropriate politics for themselves. Insofar as the public sphere is constituted by print, women are free to enter it. When we consider that the novel, as a genre, was already conventionally perceived as a female domain dominated by love and fashion we may think of *Northwood* as a counterstatement about what the novel—the American novel—and its American women readers might be or become. Their literary activity represents a public extension of the republican mother's home task of constructing the characters and value systems of her sons and embodies the cultural work of the "republican public mother." Thus, the national character as represented in *Northwood*'s admirable Squire Romilly is doubled and shadowed by a female version of the national character expressed as the figure of Hale the woman author, a figure who is equally politically engaged, savvy, and significant as the squire himself—a figure who authorizes the squire and thus in some sense is prior to him.

Hale was always opposed to slavery, but in the 1827 *Northwood* she approached it simply as one among many cultural sectional differences, showing less concern for the institution's disregard of the slave's human rights than for its bad effect on the slaveholder character. She saw in slavery the main explanation for the white Southerners' lack of (New England) moral fiber; the institution freed them from the healthy imperatives of the work ethic. It also puffed up their pride and gave them false—indeed, un-American—notions of class. Insofar as these criticisms implied an antislavery position, however, that position was qualified by a pragmatic sense that gradual emancipation was the only way to avoid secession or violence, either of which would terminate the union. She took refuge in the platitude that, since God had permitted slavery, he would end it in his own good time. She maintained that Africans could never become part of an American republic based in citizen equality because they could never become equal to whites. While believing that Africans probably *were* inferior to white people, she was more certain that white Americans would never *accept* blacks as equals, and so would always prevent blacks from functioning as citizens. Emancipated slaves, therefore, needed a republic of their own. From the first, accordingly, Hale advocated Liberian colonization and, in the Uncle Tom–inspired 1852 revision of *Northwood,* this political position became much more prominent.

Northwood, while only modestly successful, led to Hale's appointment as editor of a newly established Boston-based journal, the *Ladies' Magazine,* which continued until Louis Godey bought and merged the magazine with his *Lady's Book* in 1837. Hale wrote much of the material in the *Ladies' Magazine,* including a series of "American sketches" collected in *Sketches of American Character* (1829) and *Traits of American Life* (1835). These lightly narrativized essays furthered and sophisticated the discursive strategies of *Northwood,* whereby the authorial persona commented without gender embarrassment or disguise on a wide range of public and national topics. As *Sketches* announces in its preface, "it is the *free* expression of that spirit [the spirit of man], which, irradiated by liberty, and instructed by knowledge, is all but divine, that gives to Americans their peculiar characteristics. To exhibit some of these traits, originated by our free institutions, in their manifold and minute effects on the minds, manners, and habits of the citizens of our republic, is the design of these sketches."[8] In *Traits* a piece called "Political Parties" makes an important distinction between partisan politics and other political activity and identifies suprapartisan politics as particularly appropriate for women. "I do not say," the spokeswoman character explains to her two nieces, "that ladies should abstain from all political reading or conversation; that they should take no interest in the character or condition of their country." She continues, with characteristic rationalist aplomb: "I cannot think, in a land so favoured as ours, such indifference and ignorance is excusable in a rational being. But their influence should be expected to allay, not to excite animosities; their concern should be for their whole country—not for a party."[9]

Suprapartisanship in American life has always been a political strategy for assailing the other person's party, but for Hale it represented the essence of republicanism—a recognition that one's own interest should always come second to the interest of the whole. Over time suprapartisanship became her ever more gender-specific response to the dangers of disunion posed by North-South differences. If the men of the North and South could not agree, perhaps women's influence over them could keep the union together. For Hale, then, suprapartisanship was women's proper way of being political in the Unionist cause, not a sign of women's withdrawal from the political issues agitating the polity.

In 1838, a year after she became editor of the *Lady's Book*, Hale serialized her one historical closet drama in its pages. The subject of this five-act Shakespearean tragedy, *Ormond Grosvenor*, is nominally the American Revolution (according to the preamble it was written to "illustrate the spirit of the American Revolution, or the struggle between principles of civil Liberty—then first developing their power in this country—and the prescriptive privileges of aristocratic domination in the old world")[10] but is actually North-South relations. The action takes place in South Carolina and centers on a hero who rejects his English title and fights with the Americans. This story line, couched in blank verse, permits such lofty Enlightenment articulations of American republican ideals as the following:

> We'll raise, on Liberty's broad base,
> A structure of wise government, and show
> In our new world, a glorious spectacle
> Of social order. Freemen, equals all,
> By reason swayed, self-governed, self-improved,

And the electric chain of public good,
Twined round the private happiness of each.[11]

The contrast between England and America tries to establish by implication that North and South are more like each other than either is like the nations of the Old World. The partnership of North and South is also expressed in prose, as a plain soldier from New England explains to his southern counterpart that "this war is permitted by an over-riding wise Providence, not only to make America free, but as all the states must unite to carry it on, we shall become, in a good measure, one people; and this we shall remain forever. All our perils will be shared together, and our glories must be enjoyed. . . . Like brothers, shoulder to shoulder, we will go on through this war, and then like brothers, hand in hand, will we proceed in the march of improvement."[12]

From the time that she became editor of the *Lady's Book,* however, Hale also increasingly focused on women as local agents in history as well as its recorders, commentators, and hero trainers. For example, she serialized much of Elizabeth Ellet's *Women of the American Revolution* before it appeared in book form. She also published many historical tales featuring female heroism.[13] Sensitive to emergent Victorian ideology, she also began to stress the moral efficacy of women's role, shifting from post-Revolutionary, rationalist theories of republican womanhood toward Victorian theories of intuitive womanly spirituality. Women began to occupy the center of her world's stage.

By the 1850s Hale's political work began oscillating—as it dealt with slavery, women's rights, and territorial expansion—between a residual republican rationalism and an essentialist gender theory identifying redemptive Christian spirituality with the feminine and looking to this spirituality for solutions to social ills. Behind the development of this essentialist view one senses not only the pressure of Victorian mores but also a loss of confidence in the power of reason to override sectional interests. Differently stated, Hale began to lose faith in the human nature on which her idea of the nation had been predicated. In attributing gender to traits that earlier she had taken as constitutive of general human nature, she was looking for a way to install in feminine nature a salvific force that she had not previously felt a need for.

After passage of the Fugitive Slave Law seemed to focus all the various disagreements and differences between North and South on the single issue of slavery, and abolitionism became more vocal and socially respectable in the North, Hale stepped up her campaign for colonization. When the women's rights movement—a movement affiliated from the first with abolitionism—got actively under way Hale conceded that it signified a new social awareness among women but deplored its private, selfish focus. For women to organize on their own behalf (or worse still, on behalf of a disunifying political project) seemed to her to be just the wrong thing. As for expansionism, she saw this movement alternately as capable of destroying whatever virtue was left in the American polity or—if women provided spiritual leadership—as destined to spread republican Christianity throughout the globe. These revisions in Hale's cultural practice were energetically expressed in 1852 and 1853. In 1852 she entered the lists against *Uncle Tom's Cabin* with a revision of *Northwood* which pointed up what Hale now claimed were her novel's original antiabolitionist, pro-union sentiments.

> *Northwood* was written when what is now known as "Abolitionism" first began seriously to disturb the harmony between the South and the North. In the retirement of my mountain home, no motives save the search for truth and obedience to duty prompted the sentiments expressed in this work; nor has a wider sphere of observation, nor the long time for examination and reflection changed, materially, the views I had then adopted. These views, based on the conditions of the compact the framers of the Constitution recognized as lawful, and the people of the United States solemnly promised to observe, have been confirmed by a careful study of the word of God, as well as of human history. (*Northwood,* iv)

The new *Northwood* presented an extraordinary millennial vision of American slavery as the seedbed of a Christian Africa that would be produced by emancipated, repatriated blacks. American slavery became a blessed, divinely ordained event—"The mission of American slavery is to Christianize Africa" (*Northwood,* 408). The paragon Squire Romilly was reconstructed as a deep thinker on the slavery question; the last chapter of the 1852 *Northwood* contains extracts from his newly created journal on such topics as "Of Slavery and its Reformers," "What the Bible Says of Slavery," "Is American Slaveholding Sinful?" "How the Slave Is to Be Made Free," and "Of the Bible and the American Constitution" (*Northwood,* 394–399). Sidney Romilly uses his father's journal as a virtual Bible when running his plantation; Hale thus covertly imbues her own written words with the power to unite the nation. To Sidney's wife she allocates a more conventional womanly task (though a task that, in southern political life, was illegal)—educating the slaves for freedom and Liberia. Even as she denies Africans a place in the American polity, Hale affirms European imigration: "Let them come. We have room for all, and food, too; besides, we want their work, and they want our teaching. We shall do each other mutual good" (*Northwood,* 165).

The revised *Northwood* did not expand on the Liberian alternative, so Hale followed it with a second antiabolitionist, pro-colonization work in 1853, *Liberia; or, Mr. Peyton's Experiments.* This book combined fiction, history, and geography to propagandize for Liberia. Hale went so far as to claim that the emigrating former slaves would not only bring Christianity to Africa; they would bring Christianity itself to a higher level of development than it had known among the Anglo-Saxons. How could this be achieved by individuals who were clearly inferior to Anglo-Saxon whites? she asked rhetorically: "Does the dark race, in all its varieties, possess a capacity for understanding and living out the deep laws of the world's ruler, Christianity, as the offspring of the followers of Odin never did and never can, understand and act it?" And she answered:

> If the old Egyptian Sesostris had paused to contemplate the illiterate wanderers of Greece, to whom Cadmus was just striving to make known the letters of Phoenicia, would not Plato and Aristotle have seemed as impossible to him as the existence in Africa of a higher Christianity than has yet been seen seems to us? Would not the present position of the Teutonic race have appeared equally incredible to the founder of the Parthenon, the loungers in the gardens of the Academy?[14]

One sees here a flourishing of historical knowledge typical of many republican women who, as I have argued in "From Enlightenment to Victorian," appropriated history as a sign of their mental equality with men. *Liberia* itself is in part a historical narrative, including a brief general history of Africa as well as a detailed history of the settlement of Liberia along with geographical segments detailing the country's climate and agricultural possibilities. The plot follows several emancipated African Americans as they undergo various humiliating defeats while attempting to live decent lives in the United States and Canada. They blossom out into full humanity only when they emigrate. One character says, "The first moment I stepped my foot on Liberia, I felt like a different man. . . . It is a blessed thing to be able to bring up a family of children where they need not be ashamed of their color, and where their feelings as well as their rights are respected" (*Liberia*, 219). Insofar as there is a main character, it is a black woman named Keziah, a strong-minded heroine whose force of personality and capacity for principled thinking makes her the leader of the group—a black, feminized version of the republican hero, leading her little band of pilgrims to the new New World.

On the penultimate page of *Northwood* in its 1852 version Hale parts with the reader, "in friendship, I hope," and continues:

> Mine is no partizan book, but intended to show *selfishness* her own ugly image, wherever it appears—north or south: and, also, to show how the good may overcome the evil.

> "Constitutions" and "compromises" are the appropriate work of men: women are conservators of moral power, which, eventually, as it is directed, preserves or destroys the work of the warrior, the statesman, and the patriot.

> Let us trust that the pen and not the sword will decide the controversy now going on in our land; and that any part women may take in the former mode will be promotive of peace, and not suggestive of discord. (*Northwood*, 407)

Neither *Northwood* nor *Liberia* were about women. Both were about the United States and included women within the national mission. In both, as in most of her other work, Hale also claimed the domain of print for women and showed, through her own example, how Christian American women could and should enter the public and political spheres. In the ambitious *Woman's Record* of 1853 Hale goes well beyond these gestures, centering on woman's power, arguing for her divine spiritual mission, and recentering history on her image.

Woman's Record is a nine hundred-page historicized compendium of women's biographies, presenting female spirituality as the united motive force of destiny, or history. The book offers itself as a celebration of all the women it describes and claims to describe the lives of all the celebrated women who have ever lived—even Jezebel, whose story "shows the power of female influence."[15] Hale writes as a eulogist, critic, moralist, scholar, polemicist, and disputations theologian. She lists one hundred thirty-seven sources for the *Record* as well as personal interviews and private correspondence, including encyclopedias, histories, biographical dictionaries, individual biographies, memoirs, journals, newspapers, and miscellaneous books about the condition of women in French, Italian, and also English. It means to be a world event as well as to record world events. In Hale's words, "I have sought to make [*Woman's Record*] an assistant in home education; hoping the examples shown and characters portrayed, might have an inspiration and a power in advancing the moral progress of society" (*Record*, 687).

The main part of the book anchors some 1,650 life histories in a four-part historical structure that shows women and Christianity emerging together as the motive force of history. Each biographical sketch situated its subject in a particular historical moment within which her womanly power was constrained or deformed by male dominance. Over time power shifts away from men, and the nature of power itself changes. The implicit lesson for suffragists here is that their project, failing to align itself with spiritual power, remains enthralled by male definitions. Hale argues that women who play the game of history with men's rules must certainly lose and that their loss is the world's loss.[16]

Woman's Record has clear connections to a conventional millennialist-nationalist vision of world history wherein history at the present moment culminates in the United States, which in turn is the vanguard nation in the coming global extension of Christianity and the advent of the millennium. Hale's innovation on this narrative of Manifest Destiny is to introduce *woman* as a term of equal force with *Christian* and *nation*. She had, of course, always stressed the Christian basis of the American republic, but her Christianity had not been gender specific, had in fact been most ably represented by rational republican men. Now in the *Record* she identified the Christian with the feminine and, therefore, declared that women were inherently superior to men. "That the laws Christ enjoined on his followers are preeminently favourable to the development of [woman's] faculties, while they repress or denounce the peculiar characteristics usually called *manly,* is an irrefragable proof that her nature was the best" (*Record,* xli); "The fact that the Saviour of the world, the Son of God, inherited his human nature entirely from his mother, can hardly be too often pressed on the attention of Christians" (*Record,* 65). "Physical strength, earthly honours, riches, worldly wisdom, even the gifts of intellect and the pride of learning, our Saviour put all these down far, far beneath *meekness, mercy, purity, patience, charity, humility;* qualities and graces always considered peculiarly feminine; qualities and graces his blessed mother had displayed and commended" (*Record,* 129).

Women themselves have usually recognized the congruence of Christianity with their own nature, Hale claims. "Many queens and princesses have the glory of converting their husbands to the true faith, and thus securing the success of the Gospel in France, England, Hungary, Spain, Poland, and Russia. In truth, it was the influence of women that changed the worship of the greater part of Europe from Paganism to Christianity" (*Record,* 66). In brief, the Christian message is precisely the superiority of women, whose destined mission is to Christianize the world, and history inevitably progresses toward a world dominated by Christian and Christianizing women. Without Christianity women are underestimated, degraded, enslaved; without women Christianity is misunderstood, devalued, corrupted. When every woman has become a Christian, and every man has recognized woman's superiority, history will come to an end, and the endless era of perpetual peace will arrive.

The *Record*'s four historical eras are: from the creation to the birth of Christ; from A.D. 1 to A.D. 1500; from 1500 to 1850; and from the present forward. The general preface outlines a gender history in support of this scheme. In the pre-Christian era women "had only their natural gifts of a lovelier organization of form, and a purer moral sense, to aid them in the struggle with sin which had taken possesion of the brute strength, and human understanding of men" (*Record,* xl). After Christ "woman had now the aid of the blessed Gospel, which seems given purposely to develop her powers and sanction her influence" (*Record,* xli). Around 1500 the invention of print gave a freedom to woman's mind that matched the earlier emancipation of her soul, so that now men who are philosophers, philanthropists, patriots, and Christians "find in educated women, as the Bible represents her mission, and this Record shows her influence and her works, their best earthly helper, counsellor, encourager, and exemplar" (*Record,* xli).

The United States enters the narrative in the fourth era. "A new element of improvement, now in course of rapid development, is destined to have a wonderful effect on the female mind and character. This element is individual liberty, secured by constitutional laws" (*Record,* xli). The last hundred years, she writes later on, have been "remarkable for the development of genius and talent in a new race of women—the Anglo-Saxon" (*Record,* 152). Later still she singles out the twenty million English Anglo-Saxons who "hold the mastery of mind over Europe and Asia; if we trace out the causes of this superiority, they would centre in that moral influence, which true religion confers on the female sex." And, she continues,

> there is still a more wonderful example of this uplifting power of the educated female mind. It is only seventy-five years since the Anglo-Saxons in the New World became a nation, then numbering about three millions of souls. Now, this people form the Great American Republic, with a population of twenty-three millions; and the destiny of the world will soon be in their keeping! The Bible has been their "Book of books" since the first Puritan exile set his foot on Plymouth Rock. Religion is free; and the soul, which woman always influences where God is worshipped in spirit and truth, is untrammelled by code, or creed, or caste. . . . The result is before the world,—a miracle of national advancement. American mothers train their sons to be Men! (*Record,* 564)

In this rhetoric, as throughout the *Record,* Hale yokes together Enlightenment rationalism and Victorian spiritualism and has it both ways—mind transcends body when she wants woman to be rational; mind is gendered in body when she wants her to be spiritual.

The presentation in the *Record* is didactic, designed to show the direction of the historical flow so that living women can recognize their duties in and to history. The introduction to the second edition proclaims that "on the right influence of women depends the moral improvement of men; and that the condition of the female sex decides the destiny of the nation" (*Record,* vii). Observing that her record shows women in every age and nation attaining eminence without special preparation and in spite of obstacles and discouragement, Hale then advances her Christian argument for female activism: "If the Gospel is the supreme good revealed to the world, and if this Gospel harmonizes best with the feminine nature, and is best exemplified in its purity by the feminine life . . . then surely God has, in applying this Gospel so directly to her nature, offices, and condition, a great work for the sex to do" (*Record,* viii–ix).

Then follows a lengthy theological disputation. "I entreat my readers, *men,* who I hope will read heedfully this preface, to lay aside, if possible, their prejudices of education, the erroneous views imbibed from poetical descriptions and learned commentaries, respecting the Creation and the Fall of Man. Go not to Milton, or the Fathers, but to the Word of God; and let us from it read this important history, the foundation of all true history of the natural character and moral condition of mankind" (*Record,* xxxvi). Hale interprets Genesis to show that Adam alone, and therefore only men, fell. Man—not woman—"was rendered incapable of cultivating by his own unassisted efforts, any good propensity or quality of his nature. Left to himself, his love becomes lust, patriotism, policy, and religion, idolatry. He is naturally selfish in his affections; and *selfishness* is the sin of depravity" (*Record,* xxv–xxxvi). Eve, representative of all women, "was not thus cast down" (*Record,* xxxi). Saint Paul's claim that woman was made for man is true but "not in the sense that this text has heretofore been interpreted." If woman was supposed to help man, she self-evidently had to be superior to him in whatever area she was supposed to provide aid. Since she is not as strong as a man and lacks his "capacity of understanding to grasp the things of earth," she could not "help him in his task of subduing the world"; therefore, she must have been "above him in her intuitive knowledge of heavenly things; and the 'help' he needed from her was for the 'inner man'" (*Record,* xxxvi–xxxvii).

Ceding the physical and material world to men, reserving the higher domain of morality, values, and meaning to women, Hale argues in the preface and again in her biography of Eve—"the crowning work of creation, the first woman, the mother of our race" (*Record,* 38)—that the Fall consisted in the splitting of an original and perfect human unity, symbolized by the couple, into better and worse parts, with the better part (woman) subjected to the worse (man). "While [Adam and Eve] were one, *Adam* was perfect. It was not till this holy union was dissolved by sin that the distinctive natures of the masculine and the feminine were exhibited" (*Record,* 39). Now, if man were inherently superior to woman, there would be nothing wrong with making woman subject to him. Instead, the fine-grained has been made subject to the coarse; brute strength has gained dominion over mental and moral powers. In brief, male domination is itself the Fall of Man. Historical progress toward a Christianized world involves the gradual replacement of this unnatural, or perhaps all-too-natural, condition with a state in which women have everywhere assumed their rightful places as men's spiritual and intellectual guides.

Since she did not imagine that there could be any dispute over whether, in fact, women are weaker than men, Hale turns a potential deficit to her advantage and presents it as a mark of superiority, as mind and spirit are superior to body. In effect, she draws on and endorses a Victorian iconography of embodiment whereby the materially weaker physical body of the woman becomes the sign of less body, hence more spirit. This difference between women and men legitimates—indeed, demands—the presence of women in the public sphere. But women in the public sphere must be women, not imitation men.

> Those who hold the doctrine of sexual equality will be no doubt shocked to hear that I am convinced the difference between the constructive genius of man and woman is the result of an organic difference in the operations of their

minds. That she reasons intuitively, or by inspiration, while he must plod through a regular sequence of logical arguments, is admitted by all writers on mental philosophy; but there is another difference which has not been noticed. Woman never applies her intuitive reasons to mechanical pursuits. It is the world of life, not of things, which she inhabits. Man models the world of matter. These manifestations are precisely such as would result from the differences in the nature of the two sexes, as I have described them in Adam and Eve. (*Record,* xlvi)

Hale's description of women's particular kind of spiritual mentality does not, however, lead her to propose for them a particular female language; her retreat from Enlightenment rationality does not obliterate her commitment to a rational discourse that draws on a human language common to men and women alike. "One of the most subtle devices of the power of darkness to perpetuate sin," Hale observes, "is to keep women in restraint and concealment—hidden, as it were, behind the shadow of the evil world. They may not even express openly their abhorrence of vice—it is unfeminine; and if they seek to promote good, it must be by stealth, as though it were wrong for them to be recognized doing anything which has a high aim." But, she goes on, since the Savior "was constantly bringing forward female examples of faith and love, encouraging the exertions and commending the piety of his female followers" (*Record,* 563), he evidently did not mean for women to keep silent in the face of moral wrong.

To Hale the historical movement toward the restoration of a prelapsarian human wholeness coinciding with and requiring the elevation of women is inevitable. The progress of history is quantitatively demonstrated by the much larger number of modern women's biographies than biographies from ancient times, and the role of literature in that progress is represented by the large number of literary biographies in the modern sections of the *Record.* (Indeed, the book is still a useful source for information about women writers.) But the pace of historical progress is not constant, nor does history march forward without impediment; contemporary women who do not understand the Zeitgeist may make serious mistakes, even to the point of obstructing the inevitable.

Therefore, no matter how much woman is supposed to be a peacemaker and peacekeeper, Hale feels justified in judging the projects of other women. While strongly endorsing Catharine Beecher's campaign for women's education, Elizabeth Blackwell's for women physicians, and Sarah Peters's to open a school of design (that is, a vocational school) for women, Hale disputes positions espoused by George Sand, Lydia Maria Child, Margaret Fuller, Harriet Martineau, Lucretia Mott, and Dorothea Dix. She complains that Child did not follow the example of Christ because "in no case did He lend aid or encouragement to the agitation of political questions"; but a few sentences later she amends this statement, noting that, had Child written on behalf of colonization "as she has poured her heart out in a cause only tending to strife, what blessed memorials of these long years, would now be found to repay her disinterested exertions!" (*Record*, 620). What distresses her most, as we might expect, are expressions of sexual equality and identity. "It is evident that Mrs. Mott places the true dignity of 'woman' in her ability to do 'man's work,' and to become more and more like him. What a degrading idea; as though the worth of porcelain should be estimated by its resemblance to iron! Does she not perceive that, in estimating physical and mental ability above moral excellence, she sacrifices her own sex, who can never excel in those industrial pursuits which belong to life in this world?" (*Record*, 753). Sand's manly attire "makes her a recreant from the moral delicacy of her own sex, without attaining the physical power of the other" (*Record*, 642).

As they marshal evidence, and read the record as providing evidence, against the view of progress proposed by well-meaning but wrongheaded women's rights women, these biographies manifest the antiwoman suffrage political purpose of the *Record*. As part of what today might be called a "cultural feminist project," one that stoutly rejects gender equality and identity, Hale tellingly omits from her supposedly complete record such women as Mary Wollstonecraft, the Grimké sisters, and all the organizers of the Seneca Falls conference except Lucretia Mott.

Still *Woman's Record* praises a wide range of women reformers who spoke out—who had to speak out—in pursuit of their goals. Notwithstanding her omissions, the book brings a female polyvocality into the public arena, instituting along with its talk of "woman" not so much woman's voice but women's voices at the center of contemporary history. It could be hypothesized that Hale's gender revisions served to retheorize women's claim to public discourse from its cultural moment of origin in the immediate post-Revolutionary period into the cultural moment of a later and politically much different period, where, however, the same national and political issue was still at stake—the survival of the republic.

Hale lost her fights to unify and save the union without war, which was, after all, men's typical way of resolving political disagreement. But although the *Lady's Book* adopted (by Hale's and Godey's mutual consent) a policy of ignoring the Civil War, Hale made no secret of her own Unionist sympathies. Even the silence of the *Lady's Book*—leaving aside Louis Godey's purposes here—is comprehensible as a means of preserving a space wherein the imagined community of the republic might continue to exist, a space from which the reconstruction of a union might proceed after the war was over. While Sarah Hale's career, no more than that of any other human being, comprises a seamless rational web, the nationalist and political purposes for which she wrote constitute a discernible motif throughout. She wrote in her autobiographical entry in the *Record* that "the wish to promote the reputation of my own sex, and do something for my own country, were among the earliest mental emotions I can recollect" (*Record*, 687). Her work shows the impress of these political ambitions.

12

The Myth of the Myth of Southern Womanhood

The concept of an "Old" South, imaginable only from the perspective of a "New" one, must represent the imagination of the New as much or more than the reality of the Old. As Lucinda H. Mackethan writes, "the design of images for a popular literature stocked with belles and cavaliers, courtships and duels, mansions and cotton blossoms, and, at the heart of the scene, wistfully reminiscing darkies, had to await the actual demise of the plantation world."[1] In its literary form, where regional images are superimposed on the structures of an Eden, Arcadia, or Camelot, the "Old South" may be virtually all myth and no history.

Recent specialized and revisionary historical studies of the South have increasingly demonstrated this mythic character of the Old South concept. Some such studies imply that the apparently incontrovertible fact on which the myth depends for its aura of validity—the fact that the South is a coherent region with "an identifiable culture that can be sharply differentiated from the rest of the United States"—is actually a nationalist fantasy, which the concept is designed to install in the guise of truth. Some historians now see the South as "at most a minor variation on the American norm," while others maintain that the Southern part of the United States is in reality a disparate collection of localities and settlements, each of which has its own history.[2] Others again focus on social strata within individual settlements and describe historical experience from a plurality of carefully specified and particularized perspectives.[3] These approaches reflect and implement a rejection of the consensus that has dominated study in American literature and history since the 1950s.

But the fact that a myth is a myth—that is, a falsehood—does not mean that it lacks power. And if it has power, then it has real—that is, material—effects. Indeed, many theorists of history propose that nations and nationalities cannot be established without myths that establish group identity; a crucial task of such myths is to supply the new group with a history.[4] And whatever the reality of its heterogeneity, a concept of the South as a homogenous and distinct region of the country has been in existence since at least the early nineteenth century, if not before. This concept acquired new force as slaveholding states drew together to defend their economic system. And it was necessarily redefined again when the system failed.

But to write a phrase like "slaveholding states drew together to defend" is to have begged the question of group identity, for the "states" did nothing; only some *in* the states, speaking *for* the states, articulated concepts of the South. Who is "the South" when "the South" speaks? Richard Gray claims that study of the South's intellectual history of the South is equivalent to the study of the development of Southern myth, because the single project of Southern thinkers has been "writing the South," that is, inventing "a" South to write about.[5] But who are those thinkers? And how are they chosen by the intellectual historian?

Full study of the Southern myth, then, would deal with it structurally, historically, ideologically, and materially, taking into account its producers and their motives, its dissemination, its change over time, its internal coherence, and its effectiveness—that is, the extents to which it compelled the assent of the South's various populations and/or controlled their behavior. My more limited concerns here will be with the gap between standard antebellum and postbellum versions of the myth and with the different approaches to a definition of the South in the writing of some Southern women before the Civil War and again at the end of the nineteenth century, when compared to the work of Southern men. Southern women writers before the Civil War, though fully committed to the notion of the South as a distinct region, were inclined to stress a gender commonalty between Northern and Southern women and, thereby, in some sense, to try to undo the divisive effects of Southern exceptionalist rhetoric. And at least some Southern women writers at the end of the century and after turned against the postbellum Southern myth and attempted to expose it *as* myth in order to move the South and its women beyond its restrictions. In both these endeavors, moreover, in contrast to the male intellectuals whose view was wholly male centered (even in their supposed chivalric celebration of women), the women writers represented the South as it was experienced by (white) women.

Intellectual historians in search of the origins of the Old South have long seen novels as a major source and have identified a genre that they call the "plantation novel." Francis P. Gaines, the first student of the type—and the historian on whom all later research has depended—says that the first plantation novels were John Pendleton Kennedy's 1832 *Swallow Barn* and William Alexander Caruthers's 1836 *The Cavaliers of Virginia*.[6] William R. Taylor, in *Cavalier and Yankee*, adds to this antebellum plantation tradition only Nathaniel Beverly Tucker, included for his 1836 *George Balcombe*.[7] Neither Gaines nor Taylor has much to say about the representation of Southern women in this fiction, perceiving quite rightly it is preoccupied with the patriarch. And despite Taylor's claim that the plantation novel originated in the antebellum era, his description of it demonstrates a rupture between ante- and postbellum fiction, even though he argues for continuity. He describes antebellum plantation literature as "by and large, complex and fluid, especially when contrasted with the saccharine and sentimental stereotype which proved so popular in the eighties and nineties," and adds that, "if these [antebellum] writers have anything to say about the place of the Cavalier gentleman in the nineteenth-century South, it is to call his usefulness into question. His characteristic improvidence, his almost childish impetuosity and irresponsibility, his lack of enterprise and his failure to move with the times—in sum, his inflexibility and inadaptability—spell his doom."[8] In point of fact, however, the ignorance of the antebellum Southern male writers concerning the eventual doom of the Cavalier gentleman was precisely what enabled them to criticize him so freely. For, as Gray points out, in the postbellum plantation novel "aspects of the patriarchal character that had once been construed as faults, or at the very least weaknesses" were transmuted into "positive merit. Rashness, impetuosity, and foolhardiness were now marshaled unhesitantly under the banner of 'courage.'"[9]

Neither Gaines nor Taylor nor any other mainstream analyst of the Southern "mind" are in a position to comment on the severe critique of the patriarch conducted in writings by Southern women both before and after the Civil War—because they have not read such writings. It is unfortunate, therefore, that recent studies of the image of women in plantation fiction rely on them for the antebellum material. Ann Firor Scott in *The Southern Lady* explains that a constellation of ideas about women that were not peculiar to the antebellum South took exceptional root there on account of Southern fiction. But she accepts Taylor's word about the antebellum plantation novel and mentions only Tucker herself.[10] Anne Goodwyn Jones begins her study of Southern women's critique of the ideal of Southern womanhood by announcing that "Southern men have toasted and celebrated Southern womanhood since the South began to think of itself as a region, probably before the American Revolution," but her evidence of such male behavior is from 1920; she similarly bolsters a reference to pre–Civil War sources by describing a Southern fraternity ritual of 1934. "An early challenge to the image as it had developed during the ante-bellum period came during the Civil War," she continues, "when Southern women played an active role."[11] But actually antebellum works by both canonized men and uncanonized women show active Southern women. Jones has taken Taylor as authority for the antebellum tradition.

Kathryn Lee Seidel's study of the Southern belle also follows Taylor; it takes *Swallow Barn* as the first plantation novel and derives the first representation of the Southern belle from it, notwithstanding that the character appears in only a handful of the book's forty-nine chapters. Although Seidel grants that this character, Bel Tracy—an athletic horsewoman and falconer with a bad complexion—does not behave or look like a postbellum fictional ideal, she nevertheless asserts that "antebellum novels had presented the reader with an ideal image of Southern woman," a "paradigm of earthly virtue whose central task was to correct the innately wayward man whose flaws threatened the seat of Victorian bliss, the home," in contrast to "the reality of antebellum life," which was that "even the most privileged woman labored on plantations as manager, nurse, and teacher." [12] But I have not found this particular image either in those male-authored novels where Seidel locates it or in women's antebellum plantation novels, which, on the contrary, were at pains to show women as managers, nurses, and teachers. Actually, there is no contradiction between presenting a woman as a paradigm of earthly virtue *and* showing her as actively laboring in these ways. The contradiction is, rather, between the antebellum representation of an active woman and the postbellum representation of a protected, cherished idol, preserved through male sacrifice for the amenities of gracious living.

The jointly edited 1985 *History of Southern Literature* agrees that *Swallow Barn* is the "fountainhead of plantation literature" and situates it in an antebellum fictional tradition consisting of works by Kennedy, Tucker, Caruthers, and Cooke, all "linked by a thorough-going pride in the South, a concern for political issues, particularly slavery and secession, and a patriotic devotion to Virginia and its cavalier legend." The history dismisses two of the three antebellum Southern women writers it mentions—Southworth and Hentz—as pulp writers and comes up with the faintest of praise for the third, Augusta Evans, who "explored, albeit in unpruned prose, the ambitions and capabilities of women more honestly than most of the nineteenth-century writers could ever do." [13] (By "nineteenth-century writers" here, the context makes clear, the author means *women* writers; it is not imagined that men might have a responsibility to explore women's capabilities.) And finally, Richard Gray, taking William Gilmore Simms as his prototypical author of plantation fiction (*Swallow Barn* is not even in the index), rightly observes that Simms's work, along with that of Caruthers and Tucker and others, exhibits "a willingness to accept the patriarchal model as an adequate explanation of the South—a readiness to believe that there was such a thing as 'the Southerner,' recognizably different from other Americans, and that this difference could be defined almost entirely in terms of the South's feudalism, its commitment to an antique, gentlemanly way of life." In other words, though Gray recognizes the exclusively male focus of this writing, he does not comment on the omission of women. [14] Nor, for that matter, does he comment on their exclusion from his own account, which discusses only Eudora Welty at any length and mentions in passing a total of six other women.

As a corrective to this doubly faulty standard account—faulty in its exclusion of women writers and faulty in its perception of the representations of women in work by men—we should stress again Seidel's finding that the belle of *Swallow Barn* (whether or not *Swallow Barn* is to be granted the status of progenitor) is a minor character constructed without reference to any ideal of Southern womanhood. Even more significant, the plantation mistress in *Swallow Barn* is described in terms that accord better with the findings of such scholars as Scott, Catherine Clinton, and Elizabeth Fox-Genovese about the realities of life for antebellum Southern white women on plantations than with postbellum idealizations. For, according to Kennedy, while the patriarch

> amuses himself with his quiddities, and floats through life upon the current of his humor, his dame . . . takes charge of the household affairs, as one who has a reputation to stake upon her administration. She has made it a perfect science. . . . She rises with the lark, and infuses an early vigor into the whole household. And yet she is a thin woman to look upon, and feeble; with a sallow complexion and a pair of animated black eyes which impart a portion of fire to a countenance otherwise demure from the paths worn across it, in the frequent travel of a low-country ague.[15]

This is virtually all that *Swallow Barn* has to say about the plantation mistress, and the belle, as already noted, gets similarly short shrift. Kennedy, like the other antebellum writers, was simply not interested in women; they did not form part of his myth of the patriarchal South.

There is, however, an antebellum woman-authored, woman-centered writing that shows plantation life much more as it really was, or at least as new research finds it. This represented life might be described as the antithesis of postbellum fantasy, since it is marked by strenuous physical toil and endless managerial responsibility for the matron, along with excessive chaperonage and tedious restraint for her daughter, the Southern belle. More often than not, this labor is performed for, and the restraint imposed by, a man whose devotion to "his" women was considerably less than entire. Not that he pursued other women—on this matter the Southern women were decorously silent; rather, his devotion was to himself. In depicting the Southern planter's hedonistic self-absorption both antebellum male and female fiction writers agree; their representation contrasts to the ideal of Cavalier self-sacrifice which was to emerge after the Civil War had been lost.

In *Woman's Fiction* I featured twelve popular authors of domestic fiction, who, along with Harriet Beecher Stowe, were probably the most widely

read women writers of the antebellum period.[16] Five of these were Southern: Maria McIntosh, E.D.E.N. Southworth, Caroline Lee Hentz, Marion
Harland, and Augusta Evans Wilson. (These were not, it should be clear,
the only antebellum Southern women writers.) To be sure, Hentz was a
Northerner who settled in the South, but McIntosh was a Southerner who
settled in the North—so, if anything, this mobility suggests a fluidity of
sectional boundaries where women are concerned. The five Southerners
may have been the most popular of the group, and they were certainly the
most prolific. Since the South was less settled than the North and by all
accounts had fewer readers, the success of these antebellum Southern women
writers depended on Northern readership, and all of them published in the
North. Thus, from the point of view of economic realities as well as ideology Southern domestic writers had to satisfy Northern expectations; at
the same time, however, the prominence of Southerners in the enterprise
means that domestic fiction was jointly developed by Northern and Southern women writers.

In domestic fictions by Southern women set on plantations the plantation
looks more like the place that revisionary historians have described than a
Golden Age institution. Emphasis falls on the isolation of the plantation and
on the monotony, arduousness, deprivation, lack of privacy, and vulnerability to uninhibited male power experienced by plantation women. Plantation mistresses work hard; planters take their ease. The continual economic
insecurity that prevails is attributed directly to the laziness, profligacy, or
irresponsibility of the planter, along with the exclusion of women from
economic decision making. Such opulence and leisure as there is on the
plantation is enjoyed by the planter and his friends and purchased with
the labor and oppression of the women. In short, the system is run for the
planter's benefit by his wife and his daughters (and to a lesser degree in these
fictions, by his slaves).

This is not to say, however, that in depicting the difficulties and drudg-
eries of Southern life for women the authors represented women—or,
at least, their heroines—as beaten down by them. On the contrary, even
young and "untried" women are towers of strength. The burden of antebellum Southern women's fiction was—just as in the North—that women
were strong and that men needed to submit to their influence, to give them
in reality the power that was assigned to them in rhetoric. The psychological appeal of this fiction, both South and North, was its promise of possible
self-actualization, of personal and social identity for women independent of
men, and its vision of a useful role for women on a national scale.

Southern and Northern women writers varied the regional settings and
particularities of their novels. But they did not present different visions of
women's character, the womanly ideal, or the ideology surrounding and
supporting them. Rather, they showed different circumstances within and

against which women's aims are articulated and realized. In the North such aims involved resistance to the materialism and commercialism of a rapidly industrializing and urbanizing order. The novels attempted to soften the pains of modernization, even while celebrating a middle-class style of life as optimal for women, children, and the nation. Antebellum Northern women writers seldom looked back to the rural conditions of their eighteenth-century grandmothers with much regret over a lost way of life, imperfect though they found the present-day world. Indeed, novels immensely critical of rural life were commonly produced by Northern domestic writers precisely because that life was seen as destructive to women. The up-and-coming nineteenth century in the United States was mainly seen by them as a time of progress and opportunity for their sex. The city is often a space of opportunity—see, for example, *The Lamplighter* (1854) and *Ruth Hall* (1854). Among nineteenth-century innovations viewed favorably by Northern women writers were the suburb and the summer country house, both of which rescued country life from rural practices and imbued it with urban sophistication.

In the work of Southern women, by contrast, the women's ideology was launched within a fundamentally agrarian order and, therefore, attempted to hasten the advent of modernization with its promise of the middle-class style of life in which women could be at once cherished and powerful. Because society in the South was represented as arrested at an earlier stage of historical development than the North, and to the extent that the Southern male was thought to be defending his way of life precisely for its agrarian basis, the woman's ideology is actually more revolutionary there than in the North. Seeing that Northern life seemed to be making a space and finding a function for independent women in its advocacy of a "home" run by women—while Southern life kept home as the very locus of male power—Southern women wrote domestic fiction with a particular rhetorical intensity. (This intensity may derive, as well, from the strong oratorical tradition in Southern letters.) The absence, invisibility, or represented inferiority of women in antebellum Southern men's fiction could well have looked like evidence of Southern men's disregard of woman and thus helped provoke Southern women writers into particularly energetic insistence on female community as well as called out the comparatively greater melodrama with which they plotted their stories of female struggle, escape, and self-empowerment.

The chief plantation situations in women's fiction are that: (1) the plantation is lost through the extravagance, gambling, speculation, or downright criminality of the patriarch; (2) the patriarch attempts to force his daughter (the heroine) into a marriage of convenience either because he is about to lose his plantation or because he is greedy for a larger estate; and (3) the patriarch disappears or is otherwise absent and the burden of maintaining the plantation falls on the heroine. Novels with plenty of plot often used all three motifs, and all occur in the novels of the five Southern women writers mentioned above as well as in works by others like Eliza Dupuy, whose 1857 *The Planter's Daughter* is paradigmatic.

In this novel the widower planter lives beyond his means and loses the plantation; the son will not hold a paying job because such work does not suit his idea of maleness. The three women in the book—the unmarried aunt who has raised the daughters and the two daughters themselves—salvage their own lives by setting up a girls' school. One of these two never marries; the other resists the attempts of a neighbor to seduce and then to rape her. Also in 1857 Marion Harland's *Moss-Side* took as one of three plot lines the story of a woman whose father forbids her to marry the man she loves and requires her to pass the best years of her life at the rundown plantation Moss-Side, where she is his servant. The novels of the immensely popular E.D.E.N. Southworth are replete with patriarchs who are at once tyrannical and fatuous, wives who are broken in spirit, and daughters who must escape if they are to salvage anything of a personal identity. That the daughters eventually return to rescue their mothers and convert or supplant the patriarch is the comedic finale that carries Southworth's conviction about what the South ought to be or become.

Such antebellum Southern women's fiction was like antebellum Northern women's fiction in making the case for the individual woman and for the good results of her influence—if she is allowed to exert it. The Southern female protagonist was not different in character from her Northern counterpart. Both were somewhat romantically inclined and erotically innocent. The extent of the heroine's piety and its significance for the story differed according to author, not region; no American heroine in this fiction was irreligious, but, in general, the more pietistic novels were written by Northerners. Passivity and submissiveness, although heavily stressed traits in the etiquette books that Barbara Welter cites in her important work on the "cult of true womanhood," were seldom attributes of the fictional heroine (although they were often part of the makeup of the heroine's foils).[17] On the contrary, the point of these novels was to feature an ideology of work and "self-dependence" for women. The Southern version of this heroine was usually particularly strong-minded, intrepid, and forceful; unlike her Northern counterpart, she was sometimes allowed to be personally ambitious. (Augusta Evans Wilson's Beulah and Edna Earle, for example, both want to be—and they become—famous writers.)[18] In none of her representations is she manipulative, and seldom is she a coquette. Heroines North and South strive toward the same goals and are judged by the same standards. Individual achievement, a measure of independence, useful work, modest accumulation and economic security, domestic influence, personal happiness—these are the measures of their success.

Antebellum Southern women writers did not restrict their representation to the plantation; there are plenty of poor Southern white women and numbers of yeoman and urban women as well, especially in Southworth's fiction, which also essayed (with indifferent success) some black and mixed-race minor characters. Hentz's popular *Linda* (1850) had an American Indian prominent in its cast of characters. The novels of Augusta Evans Wilson, who emerged as the region's most popular and respected woman writer, featured poor young women who not only had to work but who also glorified in that necessity.

This kind of Southern domestic writing flourished in the years after Stowe's *Uncle Tom's Cabin* appeared in 1852, an event that might be presumed to have called out a certain kind of defensive self-consciousness in Southern women novelists and engender aggressive counterresponse. Though some Southern women did write anti-Tom books (as did Northern women), their strategy was not to show Southern women as exceptional; rather, it was to show the identity of women across regional boundaries. Thus, Maria McIntosh's *Lofty and Lowly* (1862) married a Southern woman to a Northern man, and Hentz's *The Planter's Northern Bride* (1854) showed how easily an admirable and idealistic young Northern woman could fit into Southern life; making her "Southern" woman a "Northerner," she stressed similitude, not difference. Plantation owners, in this favorable representation of the type, were different from Northerners because they were faced with and fulfilled the responsibility of taking care of a huge dependent population. In stressing the dependency of slaves on masters rather than the reverse, to be sure, these pro-slavery novels contributed to the eventual reformulation of antebellum myth in postbellum terms. Yet by making benevolence and charity and other socially responsible emotions the leading features of the Southern system, Hentz for one was presenting the South as dedicated to the same active feminine values that energized other domestic fiction.

There are other responses to the coming crisis besides anti-Tom fiction in Southern women's writing but none that posited a uniquely Southern woman. Dupuy's *Planter's Daughter* seems to imply that if the South goes under to Northerners—for the plantation is eventually lost to a Northern capitalist—it will be on account of the dereliction of its men. And some Southern women, particularly Southworth, produced antislavery novels of their own or—like Northern women—wrote novels of eventual migration to a garden-like West. The difference between Northern and Southern migration novels was that Northerners were escaping city life, Southerners country life; from different perspectives women writers from both regions converged on the West with a common set of images.[19]

At the same time there is no doubt that, in presenting the South as a laggard region caught in a sort of time warp, the Southern women ignored or denied the chattel slavery that made the case different from that in the

North or, for that matter, other rural societies in the European West. Their representations of blacks were to a large extent identical to those of the male writers; either they showed blacks as constitutionally suited for servitude, or they focused on house blacks, whom they presented merely as domestic servants. The drive to align themselves with Northern women and to further a domestic ideology was accompanied by a refusal to dwell on what, to more radical Southern women (e.g., the Grimké sisters), was precisely the important point. Hence their work is intricately traversed by unacknowledged conflicts over race, gender, and nationality.

Whatever the writing strategies that the Southern women deployed unaware, I think there is no doubt that their stress on commonalty of Northern and Southern women was deliberate. Not only, as mentioned, did they need to stress likeness to sell their books to Northern audiences, not only because, as white, middle-class women, they saw their own individual interest served by the domestic ideology involved, but also, I think, because, as adherents of the ideology, they believed that they might do something to mitigate the sectional crisis. Harriet Beecher Stowe was severely criticized by Northern as well as Southern women (for example, Sarah Hale polemicized against *Uncle Tom's Cabin* in the pages of *Godey's Lady's Book*) because she had departed from woman's traditional and vital role as peacemaker. And it is likely that the obvious inability of women's domestic ideology to deter war played some role in turning postbellum women away from it.

In the postbellum era the concept of the Old South emerged as a defensive celebration of the lost cause. Still male-centered, it was also intended to exonerate the patriarch, whose behavior might have been seen equally as causing the war and losing it. In much postbellum plantation writing previously dominated groups—blacks and women—testify to the benefits they had enjoyed under antebellum patriarchal arrangements. In the immediate postbellum years evidence furnished by the stereotyped "darky" was particularly central, but by the turn of the century Southerners (having largely won, perhaps, the battle of Jim Crow) increasingly configured the myth around the image of the white Southern belle. But just as the Old South was created by the lost cause, as was the darky who presumably flourished in those good old times, so was she.

The idea of Southern womanhood distinct from an ideal of womanhood more generally, or American womanhood more generally, enters substantially into American women's writing only at this time. We may summarize the ideological contrast between Southern womanhood in antebellum and postbellum Southern fiction by observing that the postbellum idealization, absorbing women within the structure of a nostalgia for feudal mores, disowns the all-important self-actualizing motives of the antebellum representation and goes beyond denigration to the virtual obliteration of the active woman. Of course, the loss of the war inspired many Southern women, like Grace King of New Orleans, to make common cause with their men by dedicating themselves to the myth of the Old South and to the immolation of Southern women within that myth. And it can be presumed that the ongoing emancipation of women as an inevitable by-product of modernization, the emergence of the so-called New Woman in the South—and also in the North—invited a counterideal of self-abnegating femininity among traditional women as well as men. Their post–Civil War myth of Southern womanhood is not essentialist; it does not claim that Southern women are—or, more precisely, were—inherently different in some way from women elsewhere. On the contrary, it is maintained that they were made different by the system in which (or under which) they lived, their privileged situation in the antebellum South having allowed for the utmost development of womanly nature. As Ann Firor Scott writes, "If talking could make it so, antebellum Southern women of the upper class would have been the most perfect examples of womankind yet seen on earth." [20] This is a claim about nurture, not nature, clearly offered as a defense of imagined antebellum Southern mores. More specifically, it is a defense or celebration of the antebellum Southern male, who instituted and defended these mores and thus created and protected these women. The real point of the myth is that Southern women owe Southern men, who have given so much for them, a reciprocal loyalty and gratitude.

The postbellum woman of the Old South comes in two versions—belle and matron. Functioning within a larger description of Southern life, these types are at the pinnacle, the crown, the apex, of that life. As the highest product of the system, Southern women are to a large extent its justification. The Southern belle is a princess, idle and free; the Southern matron a queen, always busy, to be sure, but busy with gracious ceremony and elegant appearances. The supposed high degree of civilization in the South is specifically attributed to its freedom from drudgery—in a word, to slavery—and consequent freedom for white women to pursue and cultivate the social graces and the arts of life. Southern women, embodiment of these graces, are what the South as a whole has cultivated; they *are* Southern culture. The use of exotic flower imagery for Southern women is more than ornamental. By suggesting that the slave system has existed in order to produce its flower, Southern womanhood, the image makes women dependent on and hence complicit in chattel slavery. Moreover, in his role as the gardener the Southern male comes across as subordinate to his product—and devoted to it. The perfection of the flower vindicates him.

The recorded behavior and privilege of the great planters is masked by the fictional charade of their devotion to the flower of Southern womanhood. Rehabilitation of the image of the antebellum Southern patriarch, therefore, is another important element of this postbellum myth. The myth of Southern womanhood, thus read, is really a myth of Southern manhood.

Southern women after the Civil War certainly contributed novels to the "new" tradition. But romanticized plantation fiction idealizing the earlier South through narcissistic emphasis on women was hardly all that they wrote. As practitioners of regional and "local color" modes, they dealt with elements that had little to do with the plantation, whether it be "in the Tennessee mountains" or in the resort colonies of upper-class New Orleans Creoles. In so doing, they implicitly deconstructed the monolithic vision of the South that was presented in the plantation novels, showing a South variegated by locality and crosscut by differences of class, race, ethnicity, and gender. They rejected a vision of the South which took the highest class for the whole. Overall, they contributed to the democratization of Southern literature while adding an important critical dimension to its treatment of Southern privilege. These contributions have been minimized by the general devaluation of local color as a minor literary form.

Additionally, some Southern women writers themselves identified the myth as a myth and perceived the falseness of its pedigree. Among numerous possible instances, let me single out Ellen Glasgow, whose attack on the myth of Southern women involves both a dismantling of its substance and an exposure of its phony historicism.[21] Glasgow wrote one Civil War novel and no antebellum historical fiction. After some early novels with male protagonists she concentrated on contemporary heroines, whom she showed as doubly caught in an ahistorical destructive sexual drive and a historically specific destructive upbringing, an upbringing that is the product of postbellum nostalgia. Women characters in her fiction are reared according to what is *thought* to be the way in which Southern belles were reared before the war, in order to remain faithful to the ideals of the Old South. But in fact, none of them live on plantations, nor did any of those who have charge of their upbringing. The entire structure of belief is based on fantasy.

An excellent example of Glasgow's critique is to be found in her 1913 *Virginia,* her first novel to feature a woman protagonist.[22] Virginia, a heroine whose name imparts regional significance to her story, lives in Dinwiddie, Virginia, whose population of twenty-one thousand is sustained by railroad-dependent industry, especially tobacco and peanut processing. The story opens in 1884, when Virginia is not yet twenty: She was born, in other words, just when the Civil War ended. Her parents are both town dwellers, as is her influential teacher, Miss Batte. (The reader is encouraged to sound the names Dinwiddie and Batte aloud, in order to catch Glasgow's puns.) Although Miss Batte and Virginia's mother are both frequently alluded to as "ladies" and "gentlewomen" (which they certainly are by standards of behavior but certainly not by birth), Glasgow gives them no prewar history, in effect making them and the values they inculcate come into existence during and after the war. Thus, the prewar world to which they allude so often is the creation of the war and its aftermath, and their affiliation to its imagined traditions is a way of imagining *themselves* as members of a displaced aristocracy. Miss Batte's house, within which she conducts her young ladies' academy, is the visible representation of this fact: Its facade "had borrowed from the face of its mistress the look of cheerful fortitude with which her generation had survived the agony of defeat and the humiliation of reconstruction. After nineteen years, the Academy still bore the scars of war on its battered front" (9–10). Miss Batte and her vocation have been called out by the war and its aftermath.

Later we are told that, "in spite of the fiery splendour of Southern womanhood during the war years, to be feminine, in the eyes of the period, was to be morally passive" (148–149). "The period"—the postbellum period—is turning its back on woman's history, which in any event begins only with the war. Thus, again the "real" antebellum period vanishes, and the Old South emerges as a postbellum fantasy. The point of the story is that Virginia's upbringing is totally unsuitable for the world in which she lives, that she is created as an anachronism—a fact that may charm the observer but is tragic for its victim.

The Old South that the New South is imagining is made possible by the loss of the war, but in Glasgow's shrewd account it is not the lost war that makes it necessary. Its retrospective shape is actually a function of the present in Dinwiddie. For Dinwiddie is not a ruined plantation; it is a thriving industrial town. And that is what the South, in celebrating a mythic Old Order, is seeking to deny. The myth of the antebellum South in Glasgow's *Virginia* is a response not to ruin but to prosperity, a guilty denial of the obvious modernization of the South, which can only mean the "Northernization" of the South. There is no possible economic reason for Miss Batte, nineteen years after the war, to keep her house in disrepair. But there is an ideological reason: to deny the reality of Southern recovery. The myth is a way for the South to conceal its similarity to the North through insistence on its fidelity to an exceptional history.

What Glasgow particularly shows in *Virginia,* moreover, is that, as women transmit and embody this myth in benighted sincerity, men get to enter and enjoy the modern (Northern) world. This demonstration links Glasgow immediately to the demystifying project of the antebellum Southern women and identifies the same target—the unrepentant, self-indulgent, and self-centered male—as these women's nemesis. An interesting intertextual moment showing that Glasgow herself recognized this link occurs early on in *Virginia* through an allusion to E.D.E.N. Southworth. The handsome youth whom Virginia will marry, an aspiring playwright, makes his mark in the household by criticizing the women for reading the "immoral" works of "Mrs. Southworth."[23] As a result of this criticism, her novels disappear from the premises. Southworth's grim depiction of the lives of Southern women, diversified by her range of character and enlivened by heroines of tremendous energy and fortitude, are here recognized for their subversive content. Indeed, Southworth's precedence is seen throughout Glasgow's writing, perhaps nowhere more strongly than in *Barren Ground* (1925), which is considered her most powerful novel. The allusion to Southworth in *Virginia* suggests that the postbellum ideal of Southern womanhood could not take hold unless the works of the women antebellum writers were taken out of the record, and it signals Glasgow's determination to carry the lost tradition forward.

Such determination is also recorded in Katherine Anne Porter's Miranda stories of the 1930s—in "Old Mortality" (1931), where the postbellum fictions of Southern womanhood are critiqued even as their suffocating power is acknowledged, and in "The Old Order" (1937), which presents a view of antebellum women's lives much more in accord with "reality" than with "myth." Even a book so apparently controlled by the myth of the Old Order as Margaret Mitchell's *Gone with the Wind* (1936) undercuts that myth through its representation of not one but two formidable Southern heroines. Scarlett and Melanie—reinscriptions of the belle and matron, respectively, of antebellum women's fiction—demonstrate versions of feminine agency, of womanly power and endurance, and (despite the sundering effect of sexual rivalries) of female community.

It will be seen even from this brief and incomplete review that, when the contributions of women writers toward representing a national or a regional identity are omitted from American literary history, important continuities and contradictions in the history of such representations disappear. The skepticism of Southern white women's views of the South and Southern men's ideas of the South, registered in fiction from the antebellum period into the twentieth century, is lost from view, as is their joining with white Northern women writers in a project of domestic fiction. Whatever the shortcomings of their approach and the limits of their sympathies, they at least recognized the need to prevent Southern men from having the only word.

Part 3

Feminist Writing, Feminist Teaching: Two Polemics

13

The Madwoman
and Her Languages

Why I Don't Do Feminist
Literary Theory

Perhaps the central issue in academic literary feminism right now is theory itself. "Early" academic literary feminism—if one may use this word for an enterprise only launched in the early 1970s—developed along two clear paths: first, a pragmatic, empirical attempt to look at women, in society or in texts, as images in literature, as authors, as readers; second, a visionary attempt to describe women's writing in a reconstructed future, an attempt in which description often merged with exhortation. Theory developed later, mainly in response to what Elaine Showalter has described as an androcentric "critical community increasingly theoretical in its interests and indifferent to women's writing."[1] In other words, feminist theory addresses an audience of prestigious male academics and attempts to win its respect. It succeeds, so far as I can see, only when it ignores or dismisses the earlier paths of feminist literary study as "naive" and grounds its own theories in those currently in vogue with the men who make theory: deconstruction, for example, or Marxism. These grounding theories manifest more than mere indifference to women's writing; they are irretrievably misogynist. As a result of building on misogynist foundations, feminist theorists mainly excoriate their deviating sisters.

Feminism has always been bifurcated by contention between pluralists and legalists. Pluralists anticipate the unexpected, encourage diversity; legalists locate the correct position and marshal women within the ranks. As for recent literary theory, it is deeply legalistic and judgmental. Infractions—the wrong theory, theoretical errors, or insouciant disregard for theoretical implications—are crimes. Pluralists "dance"; theorists "storm" or "march."[2] Literary theories—in striking contrast to scientific theories—are designed to constrain what may allowably be said or discovered. Such totalizing by feminist theorists reproduces *to the letter* the appropriation of women's experience by men, substituting only the appropriation and naming of that experience by a subset of women: themselves.[3] Such structural repetition undermines the feminist project.

It is easier to totalize when one restricts application of theories to texts already sanctioned by the academy. These restrictions, however, elide such difficult matters as the relation of the canon to standards of "literariness,"[4] or of gender to genre. There is nothing natural or universal about "creative writing." Women or men in Western society undertaking to produce what they hope will be viewed as "serious" writing do so in complicated, culturally mediated ways. "Seriousness" as a criterion of literary merit, for one obvious example, implies a profound Victorian patriarchal didacticism and is often used to denigrate the popular women's genres. Still, no matter how our standards change in the future, to name a work as "literary" will always endow it with a degree of artifice which must inevitably traverse and confuse any hypothesized necessary, immutable relation between "women writing" and "writing by women."

Present feminist theory encourages us, as a chief means of expanding the concept of the literary, to study private—hence, presumably, "natural"— writings of women. But even diaries and letters are written according to rules. And such "expansion" could well be understood rather as a contraction of the idea of writing and an iteration of the stereotype of woman as a wholly private, purely expressive being. Such reinscription, indeed incarceration, of women in the private sphere seems to me an ominous countertrend in an era notable for the dramatic entry of women into hitherto all-male preserves of public activity: not to mime men but to save our own lives *from* men. More specific to literature, the trend involves rendering invisible the public forms in which women have long written and continue to write so well. We neglect the writings—as writings—of (for example) Hannah Arendt, Margaret Mead, Suzanne Langer, and Rachel Carson. Indeed, we neglect all "nonimaginative" discourse: feature writing, journalism, scientific works both professional and popular, philosophical essays, legal briefs, advertising. At the root of the neglect, simply, is the desire to maintain "difference," for all current theory requires sexual difference as its ground. The title of a special issue of the androcentric journal *Critical Inquiry,* "Writing and Sexual Difference," made this assumption clear, and it appropriated the feminist label for theories that necessarily assumed differences fully known. Differences abound, but what they are, how they are constituted, what they entail, and whether they must be constant seem to me, above all, questions that a feminist might ask, questions that are now least adequately answered. Today's feminist literary theory makes asking an act of empirical antitheory and hence heresy. It is more concerned to be theoretical than to be feminist. It speaks from the position of the *castrata.*

To accept woman as castrated is to evince a "hegemonic" mindset that recapitulates and hence capitulates to fear, dislike, and contempt of women.

What will concern me in the rest of this essay are some foci of misogyny in present theory. I concentrate on four recurrent motifs, which I name: the madwoman; a female language; the father; the mother.

The Madwoman

The name comes from Sandra M. Gilbert and Susan Gubar's impressive and influential study of nineteenth-century British women writers, *The Madwoman in the Attic*.[5] Their book applies traditional close reading and image study techniques to the texts of already canonized nineteenth-century women writers, in search of a sign of the writers'—presumably shared—biographical situation as writers. It assumes, then, that a sign will be found and finds it in the recurrent figure of the madwoman. Literary achievement for the nineteenth-century woman, they claim, was psychologically costly because it required defiance of the misogynist strictures and structures of Victorian patriarchy. Defiance had to be hidden; suppressed, it smoldered as a pure rage revealed in the furious madwoman who disrupts or ruptures so many women's texts. Gilbert and Gubar derived this theory of the woman writer from Harold Bloom's "anxiety of influence." That theory had created authorship as an exclusively male phenomenon, wherein would-be powerful poet sons struggled to overthrow, while avowing loyalty to, already powerful poet fathers. Possibly, its ulterior motive was to eliminate women from the canon; possibly, the hostile male tradition against which Gilbert and Gubar found their madwomen authors struggling in what they labeled an "anxiety of authorship" was, at least partly, hypostatized in the work they took as their starting point. Possibly, however, Bloom simply expressed traditional misogyny in contemporary terms.

Gilbert and Gubar modified Bloom in one important way. His approach was ahistorical, imposing a quasi-Freudian father and son conflict on literary history as a function of the ineluctable nature of the (male) poet's psyche. The "anxiety of authorship," however, is advanced as a historical concept, a fruitfully accurate description of the state of literature and attitudes toward it in a particular place at a particular time. But though advanced as a historical fact, the anxiety of authorship, except for Emily Dickinson, is demonstrated only by intratextual evidence; thus, *The Madwoman in the Attic* assumes the existence of the historical and literary situation which its textual readings require. Strikingly absent, too, from consideration of the historical moment in the analysis is the appearance among women of a realizable ambition to become professional writers. Traditionally hermeneutic, Gilbert and Gubar concentrate on a hidden message—female anxiety of authorship—while reading past the surface evidence that their studies provide for the arrival of the woman professional author.

The madwoman who names Gilbert and Gubar's book is the nonlingual Bertha Mason from *Jane Eyre*. Gilbert and Gubar read her as "Jane's truest and darkest double . . . the ferocious secret self Jane has been trying to repress" (360). Jane, then—though Gilbert and Gubar do not explicitly say this—must be a vision of woman as she might in the future become, rather than any woman presently existing, since women presently existing contain the madwoman within their psyche. While seeing this figure as Jane's alter ego as well as Brontë's, Gilbert and Gubar find little that is redemptive about her, and, considering the way she is described, this is no wonder. "In the deep shade, at the further end of the room, a figure ran backwards and forwards. What it was, whether beast or human being, one could not, at first sight, tell; it grovelled, seemingly, on all fours; it snatched and growled like some wild animal; but it was covered with clothing, and a quantity of dark, grizzled hair, wild as a mane, hid its head and face." Further on, Jane notes how "the clothed hyena rose up, and stood tall on its hind feet" (chap. 26).

I can't ignore the work Brontë has put into defining Bertha out of humanity. Not a scintilla of recognition of Bertha's likeness to herself disturbs Jane's consciousness or fashions an ironic narrator discourse by which she might be corrected. The creature is wholly hateful, and no wonder: She has *stolen Jane's man*. Jane's rage against Rochester, one might say, is deflected to what a feminist might well see as an innocent victim. The woman rather than the man becomes her adversary; that woman's death is as necessary for Jane's liberation as is Rochester's blinding. How, then, do Gilbert and Gubar "read" a woman's death as a good thing for women? It seems to me that they have been so far convinced by Brontë's rhetoric as not to see Bertha as a woman. "She" is simply the figuration of anger, at once true and false—true to the situation of women in patriarchy but, since patriarchy is a false system, witness to its falseness. Her disappearance will simply mark the passing of a false order, not the passing of a female subject. Gilbert and Gubar are not, to be sure, entirely happy with the novel's denouement, suggesting that "Brontë was unable clearly to envision viable solutions to the problem of patriarchal oppression" (369), but they refer here to the unfortunate damage inflicted on Rochester. They do not doubt that Bertha's elimination from the fiction is a pure good.

A Female Language

Among Charlotte Brontë's outrages on her madwoman is the denial of ability to speak; Bertha will never get to tell her own story (Jean Rhys corrected this in *Wide Sargasso Sea*). But simultaneously influential with Gilbert and Gubar's work, French feminist literary theory appears to accept the figure of the madwoman as redemptive. She is taken to be not what women have regrettably been made by a contemptuous and oppressive culture but what women either essentially are or have fortunately been allowed to remain, in a society that brackets but cannot obliterate the innate disruptive, revolutionary force of the female. Since society is bad, this force is good. The madwoman, articulating "otherness," becomes the subject. But so long silent, what will she say, and how will she say it? A theory of uniquely female language emerges. Descriptions and prescriptions result from a common procedure: Features of the dominant language, masculine because dominant, are identified; opposite features are advanced as appropriate for women.

Christiane Makward, one of the important translators of and commentators on French feminism, describes the female language: "open, nonlinear, unfinished, fluid, exploded, fragmented, polysemic, attempting to speak the body, i.e., the unconscious, involving silence, incorporating the simultaneity of life as opposed to or clearly different from pre-conceived, oriented, masterly or 'didactic' languages."[6] The women usually associated with this idea are Hélène Cixous and Luce Irigaray, both trained as psychoanalysts by Jacques Lacan, their worldview marked with his patriarchism. While they sometimes attempt to write in the style they recommend, both agree that such a language has never existed before. It is not a language that socially marked "women" have used in the past because such socially marked women are not "true" women at all. A student of the nineteenth-century concept of true womanhood experiences an odd sense of time warp: Application of the theory demonstrates, mainly, the absence of "woman" from women's writing. The theory is also applied by certain especially ingenious critics to discover the mandated language in canonical women's texts via deconstruction.[7] Deconstruction, however, is a procedure whose vocabulary, shared by nonfeminists and men, yields identical results no matter whose texts it analyzes.

More often, the theory is an agenda for the way women might or should write in the future; to me it seems a guarantee of continued oppression. The most militant theorists do not use the language they call for; the theory incorporates wholly traditional notions of the feminine. Domna C. Stanton, another sponsor of French feminist theory in this country, writes, "recurring identification of the female in *écriture féminine* with madness, antireason, primitive darkness, mystery" represents a "revalorization of traditional 'feminine' stereotypes."[8] Makward, again, writes that "the theory of femininity is dangerously close to repeating in 'deconstructive' language the traditional assumptions." It is an essentialist definition making women "incapable of speaking as a woman; therefore, the most female course of action is to observe an hour of silence, or to scream. . . . Women are resigning themselves to silence, and to nonspeech. The speech of the other will then swallow them up, will speak *for* them."[9]

Actually, women are not resigning themselves to silence and nonspeech; we cannot afford to, and, as we enter the public arena in increasing numbers, we are not silent, and we do not (publicly) scream. Wishing to speak *to effect,* we use rational sequential discourse, and, evidently, we use it well. Have we, then, chosen to become *men?* Before assenting, consider that this open, nonlinear, exploded, fragmented, polysemic idea of our speech is congruent with the idea of the hopelessly irrational, disorganized, "weaker sex" desired by the masculine Other. The theory leads to a language that is intensely private, politically ineffectual, designed to fail. Women entering public life, whether as Supreme Court justices or organizers of tenants' unions, disprove the theory empirically, and, indeed, would follow it at their peril. They leave "advanced" theorists of women's literature far in the rear, expose their theory as an esoteric luxury. Then, too, along with relegating woman to uselessness, the theory affirms belles-lettres as an elite pastime.

Feminists reacting to this theory maintain that nothing inherently bars us from the use of common speech, denying the argument that the "mother tongue" is really an alien, "father" tongue. In one essay Hélène Cixous announced: "Too bad for [men] if they fall apart upon discovering that women aren't men, or that the mother doesn't have one. But isn't this fear convenient for them? Wouldn't the worst be, isn't the worst, in truth, that women aren't castrated?"[10] Cixous's identification of language with castration derives from the Lacanian reading of Freud's late version of the Oedipus complex, in which the threat of castration becomes the instrument of male socialization. Cixous's suggestion here is quite different from her assertions elsewhere that women really are castrated and hence, having nothing to lose, must remain unreconstructedly asocial.

In their "Sexual Linguistics,"[11] Gilbert and Gubar propose that twentieth-century women's writing has been shaped by our need to contend with the "intensified misogyny with which male writers greeted the entrance of women into the literary marketplace" (a belated greeting, by the way, since women have dominated the market since the mid nineteenth century); this, along with men's anxiety over the loss of their own literary language, Latin, the father tongue (another tardy awareness, since Anglo men have used English as their main literary language since the seventeenth century), forced women into fantasies of "alternative speech." Such fantasies have dominated women's writing since the turn of the century and consist in a subterranean celebration of the real state of affairs, which is that it is women, not men, who have the primary relation to language (the mother tongue). Thus, men and women's writing alike in this century represents sharply differentiated recognitions, however distorted, of the linguistic as well as biological primacy of the mother.

In this intriguing argument it is now men, not women, who experience anxieties of authorship—women, not men, who own the language; nevertheless, Gilbert and Gubar can only see women's writings as compensatory and competitive fantasies. Men are ceded possession of the very language that is the woman's domain, women driven into a defensive posture. I would respond that, if women are "really" primary in the essentialist way that Gilbert and Gubar describe them, then the historical phenomena described could not have happened; that it need not happen (history is always contingent, anyhow, not necessary); and finally, most crucially, that it did not happen so massively that we must identify the form of twentieth-century women's writing with it.

As alternative linguistic fantasists, women are not distinguishable from male modernists (of course, their content is different, but their language is not), and modernism is only one kind of feminine practice in the twentieth century. The idea of an alternative language is as much an apotheosis of the modernist creed as a residue of exclusion from modernism. Emily Dickinson (no longer the cowering recluse of *The Madwoman in the Attic*) appears in "Sexual Linguistics" as the great celebrant of maternal witchcraft, but, while granting that she may be the strongest womanist poet in English, we cannot deny that she has been perceived by many excellent critics as a precursor of modernism in her private, expressive, self-communing verse. Virginia Woolf and Gertrude Stein, other prime instances in the new Gilbert and Gubar argument, are also as modernist as they are feminist. We can view modernism, in short, as the creation as much of women as men writers, a view that the gender-differentiating theory Gilbert and Gubar employ cannot encompass. My point would not be that there are no differences but that, when you start with a theory of difference, you can't see anything but. And when you start with a *misogynist* theory of difference, you are likely to force women into shapes that many may find unnatural or uncongenial. Such women also have voices. If they—we—are drowned out or denied, what has our theory accomplished, except to divide woman from woman?

Another way of viewing modernism is not as something new in our century but as the culmination of entrepreneurial, self-oriented individualism that, in the nineteenth century, was identified by many popular women writers as especially masculine, controlled by selfish and self-aggrandizing commercial motives, involving a will to power, a drive to omnipotence, and the like. Against such values, nineteenth-century women (at least in America) fashioned a "female" ethic—not of private, alternative musings but of domestic responsibility and communal action apart from self. Nineteenth-century popular American women writers, including feminists, were vitally concerned to gain access to the public sphere in order to transform it by their social and domestic idealism; for this goal, none other than the language in use could possibly serve. Therefore, they availed themselves of it; nor did they have any doubt that it was "their" language as much as it was men's. Hence we might identify a linguistic tradition of woman's writing precisely by its reappropriation of the mother tongue, its emergence from privatism with an implicit claim that this powerful language is ours as much as it is men's.

And yet again, Elizabeth Hampsten's excellent study, *Read This Only to Yourself: The Private Writings of Midwestern Women*,[12] shows that nineteenth-century working-class women, unaffected by pretensions to literariness and uninterested in public discourse, wrote letters and diaries in a way opposite to that enjoined by any theories of women's language that have subsequently emerged to locate and, I believe, enforce sexual difference.

The Father

It becomes clear that the theory of women's language is closely tied to a theory of the feminine personality, and, because Freud is the originator of modern psychological theorizing on the feminine, an encounter with Freud might seem unavoidable. Yet we live in an age in which Freud is much questioned. As science, of course, his theories have yet to win respectability. As cure, his methods do no better than chance. As a body of philosophical writings, his works are shot through with inconsistencies and vaguenesses. And from various sources within the profession he founded there are now serious doubts expressed about his integrity. What cannot be doubted, however, is the profound misogyny that underlies his descriptions of and prescriptions for women.

Thus, one would think that he could have been ignored by feminists interested in a theoretical base for their own forays into a theory of women's writing. On the contrary, however, literary feminist theorists have elevated him (and Lacan, his up-to-date surrogate) and in so doing have probably given his ideas new currency and prestige. To my perception (and at the risk of undercutting my own position I have to say it) this attachment to Freud—assuming that it is not simply opportunistic—manifests precisely that masochism that Freud and his followers identified with the female. We are most "daddy's girl" when we seek—as Jane Gallop not long ago expressed it—to seduce him.[13] Our attempt to seduce him, or our compliance with his attempt to seduce us, guarantees his authority. If Freud is right, there is no feminism.

Observing the Lacanian basis of contemporary French feminist theory, Christiane Makward roots "the problem of the feminine" in psychoanalytic theory because "the vast majority of those critics and writers—female or male—which [*sic*] have attempted to rationalize their perception of the different in the relation of women to language have done so on the basis of neo-Freudian postulates."[14] The key phrase here is "perception of the different." The most important questions (to me) for research and analysis—what differences there "really" are, how they are constituted, and what they "signify," not to mention the problematic role of language in the very framing of the questions—are all bypassed by this axiomatic assumption of known, immutable difference. To the extent that any idea of a recuperated future, no matter how modest, is an inalienable part of the concept of "feminism" we have here a program that, despite its claims, looks very much like antifeminism.

The program is not unique to French feminists, with their particular historical relation to Lacan. In England Juliet Mitchell has been a strong exponent of the need to retain Freud in a feminist vision of the female personality, and in this country the more recent work of Nancy Chodorow has had a striking impact on feminist literary criticism.[15] Chodorow argued that the questions "why do women want to be mothers?" and "why do they raise daughters who want to be mothers in turn?" could not be accounted for by any combination of biological marking and upbringing but required an intrapsychic, specifically Freudian explanation. She proposed that girls failed to separate from their mothers because the mothers failed to separate from them with a resulting fluidity of boundary between self and others. In effect, Chodorow answered her questions by adducing the stereotyped notion of the female personality, which, to be sure, she rearticulated in somewhat more timely language; in so doing she gave that stereotype a new efficacy in the construction of a feminine reality. Despite the comments of feminist psychologists that at best Chodorow's was an untested hypothesis, this theory must have satisfied a need among literary feminist critics, for it has inspired numerous readings of women writers based on the assumption of their less organized, more connected and fluid personalities.

It is certainly no secret that the historical Freud was both misogynist and antifeminist. It is demonstrable, too, that the misogynist and antifeminist tendencies in Freud's writings became much more pronounced in his work after World War I, when he broke with many of his followers because of his new emphasis on the castration complex. The post–World War I malaise, exacerbated by the relatively rapid emancipation of women after 1920, manifested itself in his case by defection and dissent of his followers precisely on the question of the feminine; by the virtual disappearance of that kind of female patient who had made his reputation and on whom, therefore, he depended (the hysteric, who did indeed use "body language" as her means of speaking); and by the appearance of women psychoanalysts. One might say that the obedient daughter, who could only speak with and through her body, and who was released into speech by Freud—thus becoming his creation—gave way to or was supplanted by the rebellious daughter, who dared to match him word for word. Her rebellion, of course, was no more than the representation of herself as an equal, rejecting his stewardship, his fatherhood. It is not really surprising that Freud reacted with a marked intensification of his ideas about female inferiority, but he might have done differently.

For example, the Oedipus complex (itself now an ever more problematic concept) shifted attention from the boy's loving attachment to his mother to his fearful relation with his father. The mother was altered from the subject of a compelling heterosexual love to the object of a same-sex rivalry. And the castration complex, introduced to explain how the Oedipus complex came to an end, made it impossible for girls, who cannot be castrated, to become adults.[16] "In the absence of fear of castration the chief motive is lacking which leads boys to surmount the Oedipus complex," Freud wrote in "Femininity" (1933). "Girls remain in it for an indeterminate length of time; they demolish it late and, even so, incompletely. In these circumstances the formation of the super-ego must suffer; it cannot attain the strength and independence which give it its cultural significance, and feminists are not pleased when we point out to them the effects of this factor upon the average feminine character."[17] Freud's gibe at the feminists makes his purpose clear; he catches feminists in the double bind, denying that they are women and asserting that, as women, these feminists cannot be the rational beings they claim to be, capable of original thought. It was part of Freud's intellectual machismo to reserve original thought for the male; that reservation is still powerful in academia.

Freud's late writing—"Some Psychical Consequences of the Anatomical Distinction between the Sexes" (1925), "Female Sexuality" (1931), and "Femininity" (an essay added to the *New Introductory Lectures* in 1933)—greatly exaggerated his never slight attention to the penis. Not having a penis is a *lack*, an objectively real *inferiority*, a castration *in fact*.[18] The little girl on first seeing a little boy's penis is instantly struck with her shame and inferiority, while the boy regards the naked little girl with "horror at the mutilated creature or triumphant contempt for her."[19] Those without the penis can never be initiated into the culture's higher life nor contribute to it. The aims of therapy are different according to the genital apparatus of the patient: Those with a penis are helped to enter the world; those with a vagina are taught to "resign" themselves to marginality. Any woman's attempt to overcome feelings of inferiority vis-à-vis men is interpreted as the wish for a penis which, "unrealizable," is, or can be, the "beginning of a psychosis."[20] Of course, this is all a fantasy, yet claiming that fantasy overrode the real world, Freud advanced this fantastic difference as the legitimizing basis of every sexist stereotype and proscription. This fantasy, or so it seems to me, is too patently useful, too crassly interested, and too culturally sophisticated to qualify as an emanation from the Unconscious.

Lacan too—or, perhaps, Lacan even more. At least Freud knew that his "laws" of human development were mostly broken; his livelihood depended on the broken law. Lacan's laws are unbreakable, and he is hence a far less "forgiving" father than Freud. With Lacan we are always and forever outside. Lacan's deployment of the castration complex as the basis of the model for the symbolic order into which children—boys—are initiated takes one particularly "sexist" element in Freud's rich system (which contained many ungendered insights) and makes it the whole story.

Lacan claimed throughout his career that he had rescued Freud from a dated biologism by reformulating his theory as linguistics, but he resorted to biologism shamelessly when it suited him. Thus, in his 1972 seminar, produced in an ambience not unlike that faced by Freud in the 1920s—the growth of feminism, the arrival of female analysts as competition—he *pronounced* women into silence: "There is no woman but excluded by the nature of things which is the nature of words, and it has to be said that if there is one thing about which women themselves are complaining at the moment, it's well and truly that—it's just that they don't know what they are saying, which is all the difference between them and me."[21] Them and me: The difference (since women are clearly doing just what Lacan's theory says they can't do) is not how women act but what they essentially are and cannot help but be. Lacan's defenders, including Juliet Mitchell and Jacqueline Rose, have claimed that he was attempting, here and elsewhere in his attacks on the French feminists, to counter their return to an overt biologism and a worship of the Eternal Feminine. But I find linguistic essentialism no improvement on the biological. Lacan's ideas of women belong neither to his realms of the real nor the symbolic but to his imaginary. Both Freud and Lacan make haste to correct the fantasies of *others* in order that their own prevail. Not truth, but power, is the issue.

The Mother

In attempting to save Freud for feminism (to save him more generally for today's world) many have turned to the concept of the pre-Oedipal mother and proposed her to balance the Oedipal father in the life history of the child. But it seems to me that the pre-Oedipal mother plays, in such thinking, the role that patriarchs always allot to mothers: She shores up the father. Since the aim is to help out Freud rather than to help out women, such a result may have been inherent in the project.

The very term *pre-Oedipal* suggests the primacy of the Oedipal phase. Why not call the Oedipal phase the "post-Cerean"? Even more bizarre is the coinage "phallic mother," which suggests that the child responds to the pre-Oedipal mother only because she or he believes that the mother has a penis. The pre-Oedipal mother is rudely rejected when the child discovers the mother's appalling "lack," such rejection indicating that the attachment to the mother was based on fantasy, now to be rectified by the Oedipal phase. In a word, the child was never "really" attached to the mother, only fantasized such an attachment; the "real" attachment was always to the father.

The concept also affirms the mother's disappearance as agent and subject from the child's life early on—by age five if development is "normal." And while allowing influence, it limits it to a global, nonverbal or preverbal, endlessly supportive, passively nurturing presence. Here is one source for the idea of the *adult* woman's language as unbounded, polysemous, and the like—a residual memory of our mother in the days before we understood her language, that is, in the days before we had a language of our own. Many feminists celebrate the mother's body fluids as her "language."

Of course, we all know in our rational moments that the mother's influence lasts far beyond the age of five. But even if we were to grant its waning at that age, we surely know that the mother's role in the child's earliest life is not so simple as this pre-Oedipal model makes it out to be. (At least we who have been mothers know.) To take the matter of most concern for literary theory we know that the mother is the language teacher and begins her task before the child is even a year old; normal children in all cultures are thoroughly verbal though not yet fully syntactical by the age of three. And there is—*pace* Lacan—no sudden break, no startling initiation into the order dominated or constructed by language; language from the first is part of the child's relation to the mother. What purpose does the theory of an exclusively nonverbal stage serve? It minimizes the mother.

As the mother's influence on children of both sexes persists long beyond the age of five, so does that influence on a maturing child become yet more complex, albeit increasingly diluted, encompassing many activities that patriarchal rhetoric attributes to the father. Mothers make children into human and social beings through a continuous process in which instruction and nurturance are indistinguishable. No doubt, the social world into which our mothers initiated us, and into which we initiate our sons and daughters, is dominated by men and supported by a rationalizing symbol system, but it differs crucially from the patriarchal social world of Freud and Lacan, in that mothers are demonstrably unlike the mothers of their theories.

Pre-Oedipal, then, is an interested fantasy of the maternal. Its purpose—to contain and confine mothers and hence women within the field of the irrational—is evident; to espouse such a fantasy is to accede to a male appropriation of the mother and her language. Why do feminists do it? Perhaps it is no more than hegemonic fatigue. I offer two other possibilities: First, some women feel the same fear and jealousy of the mother that appears to underlie Freud's writing (this is the thesis of Dorothy Dinnerstein's *The Mermaid and the Minotaur*);[22] second, a theory in which women have had nothing to do with the world is comforting and inspiring. To put this somewhat differently: The Freudian and the feminist agendas may coincide when feminists do not like their mothers or when feminists want to imagine women possessing a revolutionary power that we cannot have if we have been part of the system all along. To say this is not to blame the victim but, rather, to question our ability to carry, after so many centuries of implication, any pure revitalizing force. Our powers are limited, and our agendas for change will have to take internal limitation into account.

These issues are sharply evident in recent feminist literary work on mothers and daughters. It provides testimony, often unwitting and in contradiction to its stated intentions, of the deep-seated hostility of daughters to mothers. (Mothers do not speak of daughters in this discourse.) Adrienne Rich's *Of Woman Born* excoriates the male establishment for forcing the *role* of motherhood on women while denying us the *experience* of it but is strikingly cold when not silent on the writer's own mother. Nor does Rich's poetry speak to her mother, committed to women though it may be.[23] Even at the moment when the daughter-writer or daughter-feminist claims that she is seeking the mother in order to make strengthening contact she reveals that the mother she seeks is not *her* mother but another mother, preferably an imaginary mother. Perhaps feminism has become confused with maturation.

In much criticism it is the pre-Oedipal mother who is looked for, sought not to combat patriarchy but to defend against the real mother. Here, for example, from *The Lost Tradition,* a collection of essays on the mother-daughter relation (all written from the standpoint of daughters): "confronting the Terrible Mother in order to move beyond the entanglements of the mother/daughter relationship . . . claiming her as metaphor for the sources of our own creative powers, women are creating new self-configurations in which the mother is no longer the necessary comfort but the seed of a new being, and in which we are no longer the protected child but the carriers of the new woman whose birth is our own."[24] We have made the mother our child; we are self-mothered; we move beyond the entanglements of our real mother by imprisoning her in metaphor. The Terrible Mother is called on to perform a matricide.

Karen Elias-Button also comments that the mothers portrayed in contemporary fiction by women "seem to have little existence apart from their children and dread their daughters' independence as if it means their own death."[25] If works with such images were written by men, no feminist would hesitate to label them projections: How like a male to imagine that his mother has no life except in him! "The most disturbing villain in recent women's fiction is not the selfish or oppressive male but instead the bad mother."[26] The author may "dispose of" fear of the mother "by rendering the mother so repulsive or ridiculous that the reader must reject her as her fictional daughter does. Another tactic is for the author to kill the mother in the course of the narrative."[27] The matricidal impulse could not be plainer. Moving into the past, we find that today's women writers join a long tradition. The mothers of fictional heroines in the period ending with Jane Austen "are usually bad and living, or good and dead."[28] The women novelists of the period from Fanny Burney to Mrs. Gaskell and George

Eliot create very few positive images of motherhood."[29] Real mothers—of Harriet Martineau, George Eliot, Emily Dickinson, Ellen Glasgow, Edith Wharton, Willa Cather—all are faulted by their daughters for failing them, and these daughters are taken at their word by today's feminist daughter-critic.

Think now for a moment about Jane Eyre and Bertha Mason. Who, after all, might Bertha Mason be—she to whom Rochester is already married? *Jane Eyre* is replete with images of ferocious female power, and Jane turns to Rochester, at first, as to a refuge. That refuge is sullied by the presence in the nest of another woman, who is made repulsive and ridiculous, so that the reader must reject her, and is killed before the narrative is out, so that the daughter can replace her. Even Gilbert and Gubar perform an unconscious matricide when they define a literary tradition, "handed down not from one woman to another but from the stern literary 'fathers' of patriarchy to all their 'inferiorized' female descendents" (*Madwoman*, 50). Evidently, by the time of the Brontës and George Eliot there were literary mothers available; either these nineteenth-century women rejected them as Jane rejected Bertha, or Gilbert and Gubar forgot about them as they were caught up in the challenge of producing a respectable (fathered rather than mothered) feminist literary theory.

A difference more profound for feminism than the male-female difference emerges: the difference between woman and woman. If the speaking woman sees other women as her mother, sees herself but not her mother as a woman, then she can see her mother (other women) only as men or monsters. There is no future for a commonalty of women if we cannot traverse the generations. One sees only here and there signs of something different. Julia Kristeva says that we must challenge "the myth of the archaic mother" in order for women to enter society as participant beings[30]—but her language is aggressive toward the myth, not its patriarchal perpetrators; Dinnerstein writes that one must come to see the "first parent" as "no more and no less than a fellow creature."[31] Dinnerstein seems sentimental here, but her point is crucial. It goes beyond her own Freudian emphasis to imply that the family model of daddy, mommy, and me is inimical to the human future. And since the family triangle, and its inevitable oddly named "romance," is the veritable nurturing ground of patriarchy, it "must" be abandoned before there can be a "true" feminist theory. It has probably never existed in reality; one can wonder what a theory deliberately developed from childhood fantasies describes other than childish fantasies and how such a theory serves feminist intentions. Indeed, whether children see the world as Freudians say they do is something we will never know so long as Freudian scholars are the only ones to ask the question.

I am writing this as a pluralist. Essays in feminist journals are permeated with musts and shoulds,[32] with homily and exhortation and a fractiousness that at most puts "sisterhood" under erasure and at least means that the totalizing assumptions of theory are fictions. In the late 1960s feminism was called "women's liberation." It seemed to promise us that we could, at last, try to be and do what we wanted; it proposed that women could help each other to become what they wanted. Women's liberation didn't suggest we all had to be one thing. To find oneself again a conscript, within a decade, is sad.

14

Matters for Interpretation
Feminism and the Teaching
of Literature

Second-wave feminism has revealed how thoroughly our social arrangements and inner lives are pervaded by culturally constructed and enforced gender distinctions that operate to women's disadvantage. As a social and political movement, feminism has practical goals: to counteract the damage done to women by these invidious distinctions and to dismantle them as soon as possible. Feminism does not—need not—claim that gender inequity is the only thing wrong with the world nor that there are no differences between men and women. Where differences are concerned, however, feminists argue that some differences are effects, not causes, of inequity; others are excuses for inequity, not determinants of it; and all connections between alleged real differences and their representations are tenuous and dominated by the interests of those who make the connections. Finally, even should specific gender differences unproblematically emerge as undisputedly *there,* their meanings are matters for interpretation.

In addressing the injustices that follow from, and depend on, acceptance of gender inequity feminists have developed two different strategies. One is to revalue such traditionally female attributes as compassion, empathy, and nurturance so that those who exercise them will no longer be considered socially inferior to those who do not. Another is to attack the barriers that keep women from direct access to our culture's sources of power, property, and pleasure. To the extent that society as a whole is concerned feminists believe that a society where "female" qualities are appreciated and biological females have access to the full range of human choices available in the culture will be a considerable improvement on the one we live in now.[1]

Though academic literary study might seem to be remote from the field of feminist struggle, in fact, it has been central in second-wave feminist thought and practice. Not least because (like most post-Enlightenment political movements) feminism is partly constructed by and heavily dependent on print culture, feminists who specialize in print artifacts have emerged as experts. In addition, literature comprises an enormous reservoir of gender-focused and gender-determined texts through which feminist concerns may be made visible. And literature, as one of the most widely studied school subjects, gives feminist teachers of literature at least brief access to a huge (although narrow) population.

Since the early 1970s academic literary feminists have vastly expanded the number and range of literary works available for scrutiny in the classroom and developed a variety of complex, compelling, gender-sensitive interpretations of these newly considered works. We have at the same time produced a plethora of striking new readings of familiar works by standard authors. We have, indeed, put in question many of the assumptions on which the concept of the standard, or canonical, author depends, especially ideas of the transcendent male and the universal theme. We have challenged the claim that literary works are valuable to the extent that they transcend history, insisting that no work transcends history, that the very desire to transcend history is a historical phenomenon reflecting changing notions of what transcendence might be. To feminists the concept of the universal theme is a delusion or an interested strategy of those controlling the canon. Feminists have also studied the specific strategies that critics and teachers, as well as writers and their retinues, have deployed to give particular works the status of masterpieces. Such work has both made the previously unexamined masculine bias of traditional literary canons ludicrously evident *and* clarified the principles by which canonical change is accomplished and justified.

Most of us are not antiliterature. But we have insisted that, since literature does not consist of transcendently valuable masterworks, teaching and reading "it" should have other purposes than to develop sentiments of reverence and uncritical appreciation. It's probably a measure of our effectiveness that academic feminism is now automatically identified by secular right-wing critics as a profound danger to traditional humanism. Allan Bloom (*The Closing of the American Mind*), Roger Kimball (*Tenured Radicals*), and Dinesh D'Souza (*Illiberal Education*) are only three of many who attack feminist critical practice for undermining the ideals of objective standards and true achievement. There is no question that certain feminisms are outspokenly antihumanist, as well they might be given the mistreatment and denigration of women under the aegis of a humanist practice. But antihumanist feminisms, I think, too readily equate humanism with its uglier, less generous manifestations. In ceding humanism to ideologues who want to identify it with entrenched privilege they forget that it emerged historically as an expression of belief in human—not necessarily male—possibility. I want to see feminism rather as the logical and (I hope) inevitable expansion of humanistic principles to all individuals such that human value is not a priori diminished by biological sex nor compromised by invidious gender-based teachings.

The word *individuals,* however, points to a concept that some feminists reject. To many multiculturalist or Marxist feminists it is a tainted bourgeois Western idea. Some think that it denies the social, cultural, and historical determinants of identity (an oddly individualistic attack on individualism!); others, that it is a state of being reserved for Western males. However this may be, the discord among even feminist practitioners indicates that women are already much more individual than a binary gender system is capable of recognizing. This is because gender is just one of many social determinants; because it is prescriptive not descriptive; because transmission of prescriptives is never flawless; because many areas of everyday life evade cultural supervision; and because models of the system are products of our own socially constructed perceptions as much as of "the system" itself as it exists objectively, really.

Even those extreme antihumanist social constructionists who deny all human agency (except their own) concede that multiple social forces impinge unevenly on each subject, producing subjects who differ from each other as well as within themselves. It is this very multiplicity that produces uniqueness, and if determined subjects are unique, then they are individual. Narrowing the view to gender determinants alone, we note that, if gender ideals are always only imperfectly transmitted, then anyone's exemplification of her or his assigned gender will only be partial. And since gender norms vary in history and differ according to class, age, ethnicity, nationality, regionality, religion, political orientation—to name only a few influential variables; the trinity of race-class-gender is hopelessly crude—uninstructed attempts to read any particular man or woman (who, in any case, only approximates the ideal) through any presumptively accurate gender code may be far off the mark.

Too, socialization succeeds even less in its attempts to control subjectivity than in controlling experience and shaping behavior. And subjectivity is the (perhaps imaginary) site from which literature in the West has been produced for the last two centuries and what literature is often (whether deludedly or no) defensive about. Subjectivity, conversely, makes a poor tool for recognizing itself as the product of social, political, economic, or historical forces; it is constructed to experience itself not as an effect but as a source, even if that source is multiple and divided. Therefore, although the human sciences—among them the practice of literary criticism—may seek to delegitimize authorial authority (always with the exception of the practitioner's authority), writers tend to insist on it. This means that the fit between any particular writer and the writer's construction by gender is a matter for interpretation, no less if the writer offers her textual self as representative of her gender than if she proudly proclaims that self's individuality.

This complex situation is further complicated by the fact that college literature is an institutionally defined subject implemented in classrooms traversed by numerous general and specific social norms. In most literature classes the main work carried on is producing and indoctrinating students in interpretations of literary works which they would likely not have come up with on their own.[2] Feminist pedagogy in such classrooms has mainly meant featuring specifically feminist interpretations, which, feminists assume, will convince their students, especially their women students, to become feminists themselves. My view is that, if the feminist teacher's interpretations are the content of the course, feminism is not prticularly well served because students are in the same relationship to that teacher as they are to any other teacher. For them the feminist is overridden by the teacher, even experienced as a particularly old-fashioned dictatorial kind of teacher. To put it crudely, insofar as cultural authority is "male," the feminist teacher imposing her views on a class is structurally a man. Resistance to that kind of teacher is often interpreted by the feminist who meets it—wrongly, I think—as resistance to feminism "itself." Yet it is altogether unclear what a specifically feminist pedagogy might consist of, in the literature or any other classroom; most essays on the subject are still at the visionary, hortatory stage—like this one, perhaps.

If some feminists want to take charge in the classroom as feminists and intellectually coerce the students into submission to feminist views, others think it more desirable—more feminist or, at least, more feminine—to democratize the classroom by decentering it.[3] But the feminist teacher's attempts to escape her authority are constrained because every classroom is bound into a larger academic setting and because students themselves often perceive decentering as a disingenuous manipulative strategy. More broadly, teaching in all cultures is necessarily an intervention, a relation of structured inequality through which desired knowledge or skill is transferred from those who have it to those who do not. Unlike some other relations of structured inequality, this one works toward eventual equalization rather than perpetuating difference. But this equalization of power is not to be achieved except by an equalization of knowledge; it has, as its precondition, a mutual recognition of an existing inequality. This is why students often perceive the would-be decenterer either as a teacher who has nothing to teach or—worse still—as a teacher who doesn't want to teach.

If the work of the literature classroom is to produce "original" interpretations, then it would seem that the desired equalization consists of enabling students to become their own interpreters. This goal is antithetical to that of installing the teacher's interpretation, even if it is a feminist interpretation. And if a particular aim of the feminist teacher is to transmit power to *women* students, it is especially important for her to encourage the production of original interpretations from members of that group. If by virtue of her feminism this teacher already "knows" what women are, is prepared to hear women speak only in some supposed communal woman's voice, and—worst of all—imagines that shared gender compels women students to reproduce her own reading (this when there are by now countless published feminist interpretations), then her feminism becomes the obstacle to its own realization.

A few years ago I went to a colloquium on theories of the woman reader. All the speakers agreed that readers read for pleasure; the issues are whether and how women might read various specific works pleasurably. The conundrum for most at this psychoanalytically weighted event rises from the presumption that literary works are structured by male psychological imperatives and convey a male thematics, so that women can find pleasure in them only by assuming the male stance (what feminist film critics in particular call the position of the transvestite) or by accepting and transvaluing a relegation to the position of narcissist-masochist, delighting in being made the object of oppressive, even murderous attention.[4]

Traditional women's texts—that is, texts that have survived the various exclusionary procedures of canon formation—are dismissed at this gathering on the grounds that they can only reflect the dominant value system. Where women are concerned the goal of canonical texts, whether male or female authored, is taken to be producing and maintaining false consciousness. Under the influence of so-called French feminism speakers hope for a future in which an as yet unimaginable woman's writing will emerge, a writing demonstrating that no true women had ever written before or that women themselves had not yet come into being.

Notwithstanding the ahistorical cast of this vision, the speakers at this meeting were attacking the claim of canon defenders that "high art" liberates through its transcendence of history. Indeed, they were proposing that this defense of high art is itself an articulation of false consciousness. But they did not turn to noncanonical literature as an alternative. Given their assumption that female reading pleasure (perhaps *all* female pleasure?) is false consciousness, they had to approach works that real (i.e., nonacademic) women readers read "voluntarily" as even more culturally corrupt than canonical works. And of course, they had to deny and override the testimony of women readers themselves. Thus, a repressed belief in the potentially emancipatory powers of high art influenced the conference after all. A focus on texts typically found in English and American literature courses, and a concern with how properly to read them, revealed that the *women readers* of concern in this colloquium were women *student* readers, who were to be taught how to read properly in order to be remade as new women—that is, as women who would read in the manner of the teacher. The teacher's task is to instruct women readers in the displeasures of the text, emancipating by indoctrinating.

The chief example of a deleterious text at this gathering was D. H. Lawrence's *Lady Chatterley's Lover*, a text, according to one speaker, worse than any Alfred Hitchcock film. The novel transgressed the rules of feminist psychoanalytic theory by denying women both theoretically allowable pleasures—transvestite or masochist. The figure on display is not the protagonist, Connie, but Mellors, a male character. And Connie gets what she wants throughout most of the book as well as at the conclusion: That is, she gets Mellors. The speaker insisted that the book's failure to conform to the psychoanalytic model disqualified it as a serious candidate for female pleasure.

The rhetorical conjunction of the word *serious* with the word *pleasure* invites a detour into the long-standing Western historical association of women with pleasure in a denigrating sense. Opposing female *pleasure* to male *duty* or *virtue* antedates Virgil and continues through Roland Barthes and Jacques Derrida. Where literary interpretation is the issue the binary opposes mindless (female) to thoughtful (male) pleasure, or weak to strong minds. Through interpretation the (normatively male) practitioner is separated from immediate bodily reading pleasure; the pleasure of interpretation—distanced from the body, mediated by thought—is taken to be beyond the capacities of women. One can thus sympathize with a feminist project to rupture the connection between women's pleasure and the activity of reading, even though it does not fully escape the privileging of mental pleasure and in a sense, therefore, reinscribes dualism. If successful, this project could simultaneously rescue women from false consciousness and demonstrate that their analytic abilities are as powerful as men's.

The main issue for me during this presentation, however, was not so much the favoring of one kind of pleasure over another; it seems appropriate for academics to focus on intellect. It was rather the denial that *Lady Chatterley's Lover* could be enjoyed by women *tout court*. For the novel can be and has been experienced as pleasurable by many women. Some of these women were me. I was an inexperienced fifteen-year-old when I read it for the first time, and I found it erotically exciting beyond anything I had previously encountered. Along with several high school friends I pored over its explicit scenes, which seemed to me to combine, in exactly the right proportions, descriptions of the physical and a heady romanticism conveyed in what struck me at the time as wonderful writing. By situating the sexual passages in a love story and describing them in literary language, Lawrence created a safe space for a bookishly inclined teenage female to recognize her own (heterosexual) eroticism.

This adolescent enthusiasm was not gender aberrant for my time, place, class, background—the book circulated among a group of friends, all of whom enjoyed it. As a group, we were perhaps deploying the novel as the site of a homosocial initiation ritual into heterosexuality, whereby our individual pleasures were reified and publicized through this shared object. (We also fell collectively in love with the high school quarterback, certain male movie stars, and so on.) And female enthusiasm for romantically inflected heterosexual representations is not aberrant today, although perhaps few women would select *Lady Chatterley's Lover* as a prime example of it. For, now that videocassette recorders have increased the production of pornographic films for home showing to women and couples (heterosexual and lesbian women and couples alike), it turns out that the repetitious, organ-centered events of traditional male pornography have little appeal for us. Successful woman–centered pornography requires a romantic story line that decouples sex from violence; attends to setting, character development, and human emotions; and puts more "art" into the films. D. H. Lawrence knew to do these things in *Lady Chatterley's Lover*.

Insofar as female–centered pornography takes a Lawrentian form in our culture, it suggests that one common feminist idea about gender difference between women's and men's texts is probably wrong. I refer to the frequently encountered feminist belief that all conventional, or "classical," texts are structurally male—that traditional Aristotelian narrative with its beginning, rising action, middle, climax, ends, and agents who are unified characters is uncongenial to women because we are suited by nature or culture to produce and enjoy open, repetitive, static, or circular structures. The case of gendered pornography suggests oppositely that it is simplistic to associate the nonlinear with women. Indeed, to define Aristotelian structures as male and, therefore, antagonistic to women and then proceed to develop the story of eventual triumph over them through the creation, after struggle, of a truly woman-centered literature is precisely to plot the issue according to Aristotle. Moreover, the idea that male pleasure consists of mastering and consuming the object, female pleasure of oceanic submission to the power of the same object, represents just another paternalistic dualism. The crude division between male and female sexual pleasure reductively assumes that sexual pleasure is the only kind and conveys as well a caricature of diverse human sexualities.

Story, then, is a way of making structure that is available to both genders, and pleasure is multiple both within and across subjects. The feminist attempt to tell me that I did not enjoy *Lady Chatterley's Lover* is, patently, an attempt to instruct me in pleasure, to school my pleasures. Well, my first reading of the book was immensely pleasurable. Why should I have to deny this or apologize for it? If I had been a feminist, or more sexually sophisticated, or less literary, or different in any number of ways from what I was, my first reading would no doubt have differed from what *it* was. But was it, therefore, wrong?

I next read the novel when I was in my early twenties and preparing for Ph.D. preliminary examinations. My aim in this reading was to place the book in Lawrence's development. Comparing it to works like *The Rainbow* and *Women in Love,* I located in it the moment when Lawrence's "realism"—that is, his attention to complexity, specificity, and unpredictability of character along with the social determinants of such character—was giving way to a quasi-fascist populism that (dishonestly) equated intellectuals with the aristocracy. This time, then, I read the novel through the lens of a fairly complicated sense of literary history, interpreting it as incipient right-wing political allegory, thus the beginning (in my judgment) of Lawrence's decline.

This was not pleasure reading, but I took considerable satisfaction in getting the better of an uncongenial text and escaping Lawrence's designs on me. I experienced these designs, however, less in relation to my being a woman than with my being or becoming an intellectual. (I was at least incipiently an intellectual but certainly no aristocrat.) It seemed that, by using Connie's choice of one man over another to validate male worth, Lawrence gave women considerable structural power. In my first reading her choice had appeared to me simply to designate the better man; now it seemed to ratify the better cause.

Still, though diminished, buffered, and intellectualized, the book's earlier sexual power was not entirely obliterated. I was now a graduate student appropriately married to another graduate student; the novel put me in mind of various earlier dalliances with appealing young men who were certainly not destined to be graduate students. If, on first reading, *Lady Chatterley's Lover* had been for me a perfect instance of female heterosexual pornography, it now shaped itself as a perfect female escape fantasy, safely realizing the impossible romance within a narrative that closed before the actual consequences of running away with the wrong man had to be faced.

Here, as in my first reading, the note of safety sounds. In the first instance I was provided with a safe space for erotic fantasy, in the second a safe space for romantic infidelity, when in both cases the real thing would have had extremely destructive consequences. In both cases the book encouraged fantasizing and gave the activity a structure—and I suppose that the fantasy component of literature was part of what the anti-Lawrentian speaker objected to. In a world where we are called to work fantasy activity of *any* sort is potentially destructive: Where id was, shall ego be. The most popular books for women—the ubiquitous romances found at every drugstore and supermarket—are frankly fantasy, supplements rather than guides to life. To the extent that they forestall social or individual change they can be viewed as structurally conservative, regardless of their content. So the speaker resisting *Lady Chatterley's Lover* is perhaps resisting its resistance to change.

I have not read *Lady Chatterley's Lover* a third time. Lawrence's style now seems shrill, clumsy, and repetitious; his pontificating tedious; his social programs dangerous; and his ignorance immense. I rejoice that, as an Americanist, I have no responsibility to teach him. But obligingly (for in this colloquium situation I was positioned as a woman student), I attempted an imaginary sympathetic rereading of the novel. The no-longer-young woman that I now am, veteran of feminism and numerous life events, viewed with interest the spectacle of a male-authored novel with a female protagonist and a secondary male character whose chief attributes are: a desire to commit himself to one woman, the will and ability to attend to that woman's sexual pleasure, and a readiness to display himself as sexual object for her approval. Even his constant lecturing can be seen as part of a sexual display directed toward mentalized women. Even as he decries the intellectual establishment, Lawrence installs true intellectuality in Mellors, so that, when Connie chooses him, she doesn't abandon intellect but recognizes it. Mellors, then, might be a male character who is configured with particular reference to the (intellectual) woman's desire—of course, as that desire is imagined by the male writer. Whether he imagines it correctly or not is to be discovered only by women readers' responses to the novel—by their acceptance or rejection of the fictional representation.

This makes the novel one that reverses the traditional social positions of male and female. One might read it as Utopian fantasy or escapist daydream, as I did the first two times. One might also search for moments in "real life" that reverse the norms of sexual politics, allotting power to the woman and requiring the man to display himself as the object of her possible choice. Such moments are not far to seek in Western culture: They are, collectively, called courtship. *Lady Chatterley's Lover* might be named a comedy of courtship.

And if during courtship the powers of male and female are (temporarily) reversed, it can only be that, in a novel about courtship presented from the woman's point of view, the reader positions are also reversed, which means that the implied reader of this novel is a woman. Then, one hazards, the novel enacts the extratextual courting of a socially specific kind of woman reader by a male author through a male heterosexual display. Lawrence, in short, is wooing women readers as he imagined women readers to be. Pedagogically, I could easily imagine using this perception to initiate classroom discussions in which formalism, feminism, reader response, and historicism might all be brought together.

To return to the speaker's iteration that absolutely no woman could derive any pleasure of any kind from this book, it may now be interpreted as objecting less to the quietistic effect of fantasy than to its positive dangers.

She was urging (imaginary) women to resist the seduction of the text because after seduction comes abandonment and after courtship comes (in the most benign case) laundry and dirty dishes. Precisely because *Lady Chatterley's Lover* did not place women as transvestites or masochists, because it escaped false consciousness by giving women a power over men which, however, they do not really have, the book was deemed particularly dangerous. It was the task of a feminist teacher to uncover the deadly hook beneath the beguiling surface and create, in Judith Fetterley's well-known phrase, resisting readers.

The presumed target of the speaker's crusading urge could only be the ignorant, the innocent. Her stance was, simply, that of Victorian moral realism. This is a common enough pedagogical position, though until recently not deployed against canonical texts; historically, rather, canonical texts have been chosen in some large measure for their ability to counteract the dangerous wiles of popular literature. What is aimed for here is to rupture the blissful uncritical connection between reader and text and to erase the memory of that connection by enforcing a new, unpleasurable, feminist interpretation. Ideally, no woman at all should read *Lady Chatterley's Lover*. Second best, no woman should enjoy it. Saying that no woman could take pleasure from *Lady Chatterley's Lover,* the speaker was instructing her audience in womanhood as much as in D. H. Lawrence.

But wasn't the implied uninstructed reader also a woman? Wasn't I, occupying the student position in this event, actually a plurality of women, producing a plurality of readings, no one either more right or more wrong than any other, each exactly congruent with the moment of my life which called it forth? (And isn't this composite yet another interpretation, exactly right—I hope—for the polemic in which it is embedded?) Finally, didn't the very intensity of the speaker's insistence that no woman could take pleasure from *Lady Chatterley's Lover* betray the intention to make women renounce the unenlightened pleasure they *had* taken from the book? That is, did not her very position call for a prior pleasure as its ground?

Deferring to the speaker's seriousness, I decided not to ask these questions at that time. And so, acquiescing to the force of a presentation informing me of my error in enjoying *Lady Chatterley's Lover,* I became—temporarily, as this essay proves—a silenced woman. And this happens to women students all the time. Silenced, perhaps resisting—but how are we to know?—readers are, after all, institutionally typical. Are they more silenced, or less silenced, in the classroom of a woman teacher? Of a feminist teacher?

Robert Scholes writes that "more than any other critical approach feminism has forced us to see the folly of thinking about reading in terms of a Transcendental subject: the ideal reader reading a text that is the same for all. This does not happen. Readers are constituted differently and different readers perceive different features of the same texts."[5] In my view little is gained by substituting two gendered Transcendental subjects for the one that we had before.

The anti-Lawrentian speaker was trying to shape the members of her audience into identical replicas of a Transcendental woman reader resisting *Lady Chatterley's Lover*. Because gender study in the field of literature pedagogy (indeed, gender study more generally) tends to focus on two gendered Transcendental student readers, variations among readers of the same gender as well as the similarities across gender are obscured, sometimes inadvertently and sometimes as a deliberate artifact of the study's design.[6] For example, in discussing gender differences in student writing, Thomas Fox offers the writing of two students, Ms. M and Mr. H, as exemplary of women's and men's languages, without any evidence that these are in any way typical of the genders on whose behalf they are advanced. It appears that the choice was determined by the correspondence of these students' writings with stylistic traits already given in the gender literature. And in reading the responses of Ms. M and Mr. H to Hawthorne's "The Birthmark," the teacher interprets—that is, chooses selectively from a dense array of signals—these responses to make them yield the particular correspondences he is after. He overlooks the (to me) astonishing fact that both students "identify" with Georgiana, the female character (if that is the right word for this allegorical entity), and stresses instead the different reasons given for this identification, reasons that he interprets as gender distinct.[7]

In her groundbreaking essay "Gender and Reading" Elizabeth A. Flynn describes differences between men and women students writing about short stories, including Ernest Hemingway's "Hills like White Elephants." She argues both that men respond more aggressively, women more cooperatively, to texts and that women make better readers.[8] To analyze her student responses Flynn classifies three kinds of reading, two of which are "bad." One bad kind—unique to the men in her sample—is named "dominant," or "resisting": The reader rejects the alien text "and so remains essentially unchanged by the reading experience." A second kind of bad reading is "submissive," where "the text overpowers the reader and so eliminates the reader's power of discernment." This is how a majority of both men and women in her group read. A third response, the "good" kind, is one in which "reader and text interact with a degree of mutuality"; although not unique to the women, it is exhibited more often by them than by the men (286).

On the basis of these findings she proposes that men tend to be dominant readers and that women tend to be interactive readers, and she explains that this is because women possess "a willingness to listen, a sensitivity to emotional nuance, an ability to empathize with and yet judge" (286). The scheme installs a stereotypical difference that makes women uniformly superior, constrasting aggressive, competing men to sympathetic, cooperating women. That it is always better to be sympathetic than resistant is a judgment; Flynn seems to imagine all stories as distressed clients needing female ministrations. The opponent of *Lady Chatterley's Lover* would not have agreed.

In any event it makes dubious statistical sense, when a majority of all students produce "submissive" readings, to define the genders as fundamentally different. Granted that the "dominant" and "interactive" discourses fall out largely along gender lines, they are not gender norms. One unanalyzed difference, however, which is apparently statistically significant is that the men read in all three ways, the women in only two. This makes the women's responses more uniform. What does this mean? If women really *are* less diverse than men, then the fact has many social determinants, one of which is that women are often held to a more uniform standard—granted less individuality—than men.

In "Gender Bias in Teachers' Written Comments," for instance, Linda Laub Barnes reports that men and women teachers alike tolerate a greater range of writing styles when they grade papers supposedly written by male students.[9] In fact, the "student" papers in this experiment were written by the experimenter according to supposed gender qualities of style and then alternately presented as written by men or women, so that the same paper appeared sometimes as male authored, sometimes female authored. The teachers were, thus, responding not to gendered people but to textual effects as mediated by gendered names. Inventing the men and women whose papers they read, teachers of both genders were scripting the women into uniformity, the men into individualism. Where supposed women's papers were concerned men more than women teachers urged the students to adopt a male voice, a behavior that can be read equally as the male teacher's insensitivity to the woman's voice or the woman teacher's resistance to women students who wrote like men; it's a matter for interpretation.

To return to the (statistically insignificant) contrast between resisting and interactive readers. Flynn's idea of a good interactive reading is one that extracts a "consistent pattern of meaning from among the seemingly incompatible stimuli" present in the work, a meaning that is "finally achieved only when tensions are resolved" (270). In view of the array of multivocalizing interpretive strategies current in criticism today it is evident that the text here is text-according-to-teacher, which raises the possibility that the minority of resisting men were resisting not the text "itself" but the teacher. Gender difference here could be interpreted as men's greater readiness to dispute or challenge the teacher, this teacher, this feminist teacher.

However feminist teachers feel about disputatious men, they ought to be pleased when women challenge their authority qua authority. Yet in practice feminist teachers seem to like authority as well as other teachers. In her cheerful best-seller *You Just Don't Understand* Deborah Tannen makes a three-hundred-plus-page pitch for women as nonhierarchical conversation-alists, while admitting that she much prefers women auditors because they uncritically accept and respect her authority. She *likes* compliant girls.[10] But shows of compliancy and respect for authority can be interpreted as no less hierarchical than demonstrations of competition and resistance, although they probably do signify absence of an expectation of ever having authority oneself. That more women than men produced readings that Flynn ap-proved, then, may be a matter of their greater sensitivity to the teacher's signals coupled with a desire to please her (or not to offend her), rather than any particular sensitivity to literary texts.

The occasional resisting male student could have been resisting the par-ticular interpretation, the demand for interpretation as the classroom ac-tivity, or the teacher. The reading that Flynn interprets as the most resistant of all is, curiously, especially hostile to the *male* character in "Hills like White Elephants." The male student uses two details about the man—his thorough knowledge of abortion procedure and the many hotel labels on his luggage—to surmise that he's an irresponsible playboy. The teacher judges this response "overly judgmental"; a different teacher might praise its sensitivity to textual detail. Indeed, if the underlying structure of classical fiction pits a protagonist against an antagonist, this student might be thought of as reading in just the right interactive way—looking for textual clues about whose side he's to take. A different teacher might concur that the depiction of the male character is highly critical and be pleased that the student recognizes this, even though Hemingway—Mr. Macho him-self—wrote the story. From yet another angle, however, in criticizing the male character this male student may have been trying, girlishly, to please the teacher by writing as he imagined a feminist would want him to write.

What did please this feminist teacher was a woman student's response observing that, "typically, in the end, the male's dominant values have come through. She agrees to have the abortion and says that there is nothing wrong. Unfortunately this relationship will probably end because conflicts are not resolved. To have a meaningful relationship, they must be more open" (281). Imagining that openness would improve this fictional relation-ship rather than terminate it, failing to see that the conflict between the characters *is* resolved in the only way that the represented structure of male dominance allows, supposing that the misfortune is to have the relationship end rather than continue—all of these interpretive gestures rest on a faith in heterosexual companionship and human good intentions that this hard-boiled story is perhaps aiming to undermine. And one could interpret the reading as resistant or rejecting, not interactive, since it substitutes the read-er's sentimentalism for the writer's cynicism.

Consistent with a model of reading as sympathetic cooperation with the story, the teacher classified as resisting all responses that reported difficulty in reading. Since only men wrote that they found "Hills like White Elephants" hard to read, the procedure automatically made women out to be better readers. There are more explanations for women's failure to acknowledge difficulty than that they didn't experience it. They may have decided that mentioning this fact was irrelevant to the assignment as they understood it; they may have elected to conceal it. They may also have found the story easy to read. In the first two cases women are certainly playing the classroom game better than men, perhaps because they have more to lose if they play it badly. If women did find the story easy to read, it could be because they are more practiced readers than men, not because they are especially willing to listen, sensitive to emotional nuance, and the like. The gender question then might be: Why are women more practiced readers than men? The various obvious sociocultural explanations—that men have other things to do than read, that women are housebound and meet little social resistance if they become "English teachers"—remind one of the uneven conditions within which gendered reading is produced.

One male writes of "Hills like White Elephants": "My impression of the story was that it wasn't a story at all. It was just a short conversation between two people. The story consisted of just a couple of pages filled with quotes. . . . [It] just starts right up and doesn't tell anything about who the people are or about what is going on. I had to read through the story a couple of times just to figure out what they were talking about. Nothing was said right out in the open about getting an abortion" (277). To the teacher this student simply rejected the story "because he could not understand it. The text, for him, was 'just a couple of pages filled with quotes'" (277–278). Actually, the student doesn't say that this is what the story *was* but rather what it *consisted of,* and one could maintain that he describes the text correctly. Having approached the story as a construct as well as a transparent medium for conveying meaning, he can see its unconventional brevity and its virtually exclusive reliance on dialogue. Though lacking a technical vocabulary, he notes a repertory of absences: no omniscient narrator, no description of setting, no capsule biographies for the characters, no attribution of dialogue—as well as dialogue that is particularly unrevealing from the point of view of an outsider. In brief, he picks up on many of the technical innovations for which Hemingway gained literary renown. From my perspective he is certainly interactive with the text, and I suspect that he is interacting in a way that Hemingway himself would have appreciated. The point of deploying all these technical experiments would be lost if nobody recognized them.

Among exponents and proponents of the gender-distinct superior female voice no scholar has been more tenacious, influential, and eloquent than psychologist Carol Gilligan, whose work Flynn acknowledged throughout her essay. Gilligan's *In a Different Voice* consolidated the gender differences that she observed into a contrast of male separateness and female connection and used this contrast to distinguish a typically female ethic of care from a male ethic of rights.[11] Women, inseparably connected to others (though the determinants of that connectedness are not analyzed), make moral choices by thinking of other people's needs and desires, men by thinking of abstract rights and justice.

This work has been challenged by a range of feminist social scientists for a variety of reasons. But Gilligan countered initial objections to her impressionistic method by frankly acknowledging that it was interpretive: "Data alone do not tell us anything; they do not speak, but are interpreted by people. I chose to listen . . . to attend . . . to observe. . . . On the basis of these observations and my reading of psychology, I made a series of inferences."[12] Rather than recognizing, however, that, because it was interpretive, her work necessarily constituted as well as described its subject, Gilligan—like an old-style New Critic—offered her expertise as a guarantee of correctness. Seemingly innumerable studies emanating from her Center for the Study of Gender, Education, and Human Development iterate and expand the doctrine of the different voice, which is more and more called both "natural" and "authentic."[13]

Interpretation being what it is, however—a set of multiply determined choices from a dense network of signals—it is easy to work up different readings of even the highly edited texts that Gilligan provides. Take, for example, contrasted segments of interviews with two eleven-year-old children, Jake and Amy. The two-column presentation imposes a questionable parallelism; since the interviewer participates much more forcefully in Amy's case than in Jake's, Amy's responses are evidently much more a collaborative product than his. The boy is left free to represent himself; the girl is guided.

Jake answers the question "what does responsibility mean?": "thinking of others when I do something" because "you have to live with other people," and "if you do something that hurts them all, a lot of people will end up suffering." Amy's much more supervised response is that, "if something looks really fun but you might hurt yourself doing it because you don't really know how to do it and your friends say, 'well, come on, you can do it, don't worry,' if you're really scared to do it, it's your responsibility to yourself that if you think you might hurt yourself, you shouldn't do it" (37).

From these two responses Gilligan develops a paradigm of the separated, noncaring male and the connected, caring female. I grant that Jake posits himself as separate but see his response as falling well within normal senses of the term *caring*—it's a reasonable word for glossing the phrases "thinking of others" and "a lot of people will end up suffering." And though granting that Amy describes a situation of interconnectedness, I propose that she does not so much seem to care for her friends as fear them. Jake says that responsibility means standing up for others, Amy that it means standing up for herself. Which of these is a caring answer? Thus, from this interview material one can produce an interpretation that counters Gilligan's tendentious reading.

Gilligan, expanding her interpretation, comments that the "most striking" difference in the two interviews "is the imagery of violence in the boy's response, depicting a world of dangerous confrontation and explosive connection, where she sees a world of care and protection" (38). It is not difficult, however, to interpret Amy's response as equally violence fraught, since she describes friends as urging her to do something that will very likely hurt her. There is violence in her account—and fear. The violence is what might be done to her. Violence to Jake is what he might do, not suffer. *This* gender distinction—which I readily accept—might be interpreted then as power/powerlessness enforced by physical coercion. Amy is quite right to fear violence; violence is done to women every day. As for Jake: Since men *do* currently have the cultural power to inflict harm, I'm glad that he plans to use his so responsibly.

To put this differently, the rights/care ethic, if it is indeed particular to women in some statistical sense, may obviously be interpreted as a product of male dominance. A 1991 report called *Shortchanging Girls, Shortchanging America,* commissioned by the American Association of University Women, for which Gilligan was a consultant, discovers and—as its title makes clear—deplores an alleged drop in self-esteem in (white) girls between elementary and high school which is significantly larger than the drop in self-esteem in (white) boys during the same years. Perhaps the so-called ethic of care and loss of self-esteem are mutually constituting. Of course, as soon as we begin to describe the ethic of care as interactive with low self-esteem, its attractiveness diminishes considerably.

At the same time the ethic of care is itself enforced by subjecting women who display high self-esteem to all kinds of social pressure, including pressure from other women. During the 1991 hearings concerning Clarence Thomas's appointment to the U.S. Supreme Court Anita Hill was roundly criticized by several female coworkers for aloofness, careerism, professional wilfullness, and other self-regarding traits. Linda Laub Barnes finds women teachers much more fastidious than men teachers about mechanics, form, and general correctness in both men's and women's papers. She hypothesizes that women's insecure academic status drives them to such punctiliousness as a way of "exercising linguistic authority; men are less constrained" (152). Low self-esteem, or feelings of powerlessness, in this instance produces not an ethic of care but of rectitude. To be sure, one might argue that by correcting their students, women teachers demonstrate care, but this is to make "care" mean whatever it is that women do.

The phenomenon of women policing women, indeed, is more often than not simply ignored in discussion of women's caring, communal, intimate discourse. This is strikingly clear in Tannen's *You Just Don't Understand*. Iterating a thesis of women as connected, communal, nonhierarchical, affiliative, and so on, Tannen's book is actually stuffed with examples of girls and women criticizing each other, putting each other down, gossiping malevolently about those who are absent, excluding, and otherwise keeping each other in line—all in the name of nonhierarchical intimacy. (See, e.g., 87, 108, 126, 177, 217–218, 255, 259–261, 293.) "I'm not mad at Deena or anything. I'm not mad at Millicent or Rita. But . . . it's so hard to make plans with all of them at once . . . because Rita gets in fights with Millicent and Deena thinks that Millicent's being a bitcher, and it's so mean" (260).

If this is what girls' and womens' talk is really like, it's understandable that feminists might try to screen it. But this screening simply replicates the policing that attempts to make all women into the same "woman." It is complicit with the system through which women come to lose (or conceal) their self-esteem and learn to adopt (or feel) the placating, self-dismissive, self-sacrificing attitudes of a "true womanhood" that is not far removed from Victorian ideology. I am, thus, not contesting the claim that many—especially contemporary, young, white, American, middle-class—women often speak and write about literature according to gender patterns that can be interpreted along stereotypical lines. I am certainly not arguing that such behavior should be denigrated and silenced. I am proposing, however, that casting women's discourse into gender-distinct patterns is often already an interpretation on which a second overlay of interpretation produces the standard woman.

Too, I suspect that the standard woman appears less often than the proponents of women's differences are prepared to see. Mary Field Belenky and three colleagues reported in *Women's Ways of Knowing* on a study designed to supplement Gilligan by investigating how women attained their own distinctive voice.[14] Transcripts of interviews with one hundred thirty-five college-age women (not all students) were used to construct a five-step process according to which women moved from silence on through "subjective knowledge" finally to reach "connected knowing."

The data supporting this scheme, however, noted only two or three women at the silenced position (22) and "very few" women at the connected position (124). Close to half were at the subjective stage (57), making it a matter of faith or desire that they would eventually become connected knowers. At the subjective stage, however—according to the authors themselves—women didn't think about the consequences of their actions and often disregarded others (77–78); they were impatient, dismissive, belligerent, oppositional, and argumentative; they utilized ploys to "isolate, shout down, denigrate, and undo the other" (84); they were "stubbornly immune to other people's ideas. They saw what they wanted to see, and ignored the rest, listened to the inner voice and turned a deaf ear to other voices" (98). The very same women described themselves to the interviewers as generous and caring, open to anything. Evidently, they knew what women were supposed to be but (not yet) how to be one. Despite data that could be read as total disconfirmation of their assumptions, the authors present their study as evidence of Gilligan's ethic of care.

One afternoon in 1990 I watched part of a "Sally Jessy Raphael" show talking about fraternity rape. The four panelists included two psychologists, a victim of fraternity rape now in her thirties who counseled rape victims, and the lawyer for a recent victim "Susan" who was suing the fraternity. Susan herself sat behind a screen and answered Sally's occasional questions to her in a disguised voice. Sally asks why women submit to such rape. The counselor explains that the situation is life threatening, so the woman is afraid to resist. Sally asks Susan if she was afraid, and Susan answers no—she was too drunk at the time to feel anything. Her answer is not only ignored; it is also overridden by one of the psychologists, who immediately reintroduces the theme of mortal danger.

Later Sally asks why so few women prosecute. The experts explain that women, socialized in families where men are dominant, have no context that would enable them to imagine taking legal action against men. "How about you?" Sally asks Susan. "No," says Susan, "in my family my mother is very dominant." Again her response is ignored. Susan is not the woman she "ought" to be, the pathetic woman victim these experts are looking for. But arguably, the woman she ought to be would not be suing the fraternity that raped her. Susan has actually made the experts' case, because her response to her situation is aberrant. Yet I don't know a feminist who wouldn't want more women to act like Susan and wouldn't do what she could to bring that situation into being. The battered women's shelter is not the literature classroom, but, by analogy, we ought to help our women students depart from stereotype, and we ought to notice when they're already doing so.

How is this to be done? No voluntary disempowerment of the teacher, per se, will be of much use. Yet it should be possible to recognize the individuality of women students as we already recognize that of men, to teach a wide range of works in a variety of ways, to rethink the dominance of interpretive activity in the classroom, to remember that all interpretations (even our own) are contingent and none absolutely correct. If we don't try to do these things, the only voice in the classroom will be the teacher's, and then it makes no difference if her voice is feminist or not.

Notes

Chapter 1: Melodramas of Beset Manhood

1. Marlene Springer, ed., *What Manner of Woman: Essays on English and American Life and Literature* (New York: New York University Press, 1977).

2. See Lyle H. Wright, *American Fiction: A Contribution Towards a Bibliography*, vol. 1, *1774–1850*, 2d ed. (San Marino, Calif.: Huntington Library Press, 1969).

3. Marius Bewley, *The Eccentric Design: Form in the Classic American Novel* (New York: Columbia University Press, 1963), 15, 291.

4. F. O. Matthiessen, *American Renaissance* (New York: Oxford University Press, 1941), ix.

5. Robert E. Spiller et al., eds., *Literary History of the United States* (New York: Macmillan, 1959), xix.

6. Joel Porte, *The Romance in America: Studies in Cooper, Poe, Hawthorne, Melville, and James* (Middletown, Conn.: Wesleyan University Press, 1969), ix (emphasis added).

7. A good essay on this topic is William C. Spengemann's "What Is American Literature?" *Centennial Review* 22 (Spring 1978): 119–138.

8. See Jay B. Hubbell, *Who Are the Major American Authors?* (Durham, N.C.: Duke University Press, 1972).

9. Ibid., 335–336.

10. Richard Poirier, *A World Elsewhere: The Place of Style in American Literature* (New York: Oxford University Press, 1966), 5.

11. Spiller, et al., *Literary History of the United States,* 1211.

12. Lionel Trilling, *The Liberal Imagination* (Garden City, N.Y.: Anchor Books, 1950), 7–9.

13. Leslie Fiedler, *Love and Death in the American Novel* (New York: Criterion Books, 1960), 93.

14. Charles Brockden Brown, *Wieland*, ed. Sydney J. Krause and S. W. Reid (Kent, Ohio: Kent State University Press, 1978), xii.

15. Trilling, *Liberal Imagination,* 206.

16. Richard Chase, *The American Novel and Its Tradition* (Garden City, N.Y.: Anchor Books, 1957), 55, 64.

17. Fiedler, *Love and Death in the American Novel,* 236.

18. Annette Kolodny, *The Lay of the Land: Metaphor as Experience and History in American Life and Letters* (Chapel Hill: University of North Carolina Press, 1975).

19. Chase, *American Novel,* 5.

20. Poirier, *A World Elsewhere,* 3, 5, 9.

21. Donald M. Kartiganer and Malcolm A. Griffith, eds., *Theories of American Literature: The Critical Perspective* (New York: Macmillan, 1962), 4–5.

22. Eric J. Sundquist, *Home as Found: Authority and Genealogy in Nineteenth-Century American Literature* (Baltimore: Johns Hopkins University Press, 1979), xviii–xix.

Chapter 2: Putting Women in Their Place

1. "The Women of Cooper's Leatherstocking Tales," *American Quarterly* 23 (1971): 698–709.

2. Histories of the American historical novel tend to focus on Cooper; see, for ex-

234 *Notes to Pages 21–23*

ample, George Dekker, *The American Historical Novel* (New York: Cambridge University Press, 1987). Michael Davitt Bell, *Hawthorne and the Historical Romance of New England* (Princeton: Princeton University Press, 1970); and Lawrence Buell, *New England Literary Culture: From Revolution through Renaissance* (New York: Cambridge University Press, 1986), focus on New England Puritan novels with relatively little attention to their American Indian content. Louise K. Barnett, *The Ignoble Savage: American Literary Racism, 1790–1890* (Westport, Conn.: Greenwood Press), argues that all American Indian portrayals are racist; Sherry Sullivan, "Indians in American Fiction, 1820–1850: An Ethnohistorical Perspective," *Clio* 15 (1986): 239–257, finds that, of the one in six 1820s works featuring American Indians, 78 percent treat them sympathetically. Sympathy, however, requires sentimentalizing them in Eurocentric terms. See also G. Harrison Orians, *The Cult of the Vanishing American* (Cleveland: n.p., 1934). For the historical context in which Indian stories developed, see Francis Paul Prucha, *American Indian Policy in the Formative Years* (Lincoln: University of Nebraska Press, 1962); Roy Harvey Pearce, *The Savages of America: A Study of the Indian and the Idea of Civilization*, rev. ed. (Baltimore: Johns Hopkins Press, 1965); Robert W. Mardock, *The Reformers and the American Indian* (Columbia: University of Missouri Press, 1971); Wilcomb E. Washburn, *Red Man's Land / White Man's Law: A Study of the Past and Present Status of the American Indian* (New York: Scribner's, 1971); Bernard W. Sheehan, *Seeds of Extinction: Jeffersonian Philanthropy and the American Indian* (Chapel Hill: University of North Carolina Press, 1973); Richard Slotkin, *Regeneration through Violence: The Mythology of the American Frontier, 1600–1860* (Middletown, Conn.: Wesleyan University Press, 1973); Francis Jennings, *The Invasion of America: Indians, Colonialism, and the Cant of Conquest* (Chapel Hill: University of North Carolina Press, 1975); Michael Paul Rogin, *Fathers and Children: Andrew Jackson and the Subjugation of the American Indian* (New York: Knopf, 1975); Robert F. Berkhofer, Jr., *The White Man's Indian: Images of the American Indian from Columbus to the Present* (New York: Knopf, 1978); Richard Drinnon, *Facing West: The Metaphysics of Indian-Hating and Empire-Building* (New York: New American Library, 1980); Reginald Horsman, *Race and Manifest Destiny: The Origins of American Racial Anglo-Saxonism* (Cambridge: Harvard University Press, 1981); Brian W. Dippie, *The Vanishing American: White Attitudes and U.S. Indian Policy* (Middletown, Conn.: Wesleyan University Press, 1982).

3. James Fenimore Cooper, *The Wept of Wish-ton-Wish* (1829; reprint, Columbus, Ohio: Charles E. Merrill, 1970), 149.

4. Some critics argue that women wrote more empathetically about the frontier and American Indians than men, even recognizing a shared oppression under white male patriarchy; I do not find this to be so. See, for example, Annette Kolodny, *The Land before Her: Fantasy and Experience of the American Frontiers, 1630–1860* (Chapel Hill: University of North Carolina Press, 1984); Leland S. Person, Jr., "The American Eve: Miscegenation and a Feminist Frontier Fiction," *American Quarterly* 37 (1985): 668–685; Carolyn Karcher, "Introduction," *Hobomok, by Lydia Maria Child* (New Brunswick, N.J.: Rutgers University Press, 1986); Sandra Zagarell, "Expanding 'America': Lydia Sigourney's *Sketch of Connecticut*, Catharine Sedgwick's *Hope Leslie*," *Tulsa Studies in Women's Literature* 6 (1987): 225–245; Christopher Castiglia, "In Praise of Extra-Vagant Women: *Hope Leslie* and the Captivity Romance," *Legacy* 6 (1989): 3–16.

5. For an analysis of *Yamoyden*, see John P. McWilliams, Jr., *The American Epic: Transforming a Genre, 1770–1860* (New York: Cambridge University Press, 1989), 132–136.

6. *North American Review* 12 (1821): 466–488.

7. Lydia Maria Child, *Hobomok and Other Writings on Indians*, ed. Carolyn Karcher (New Brunswick, N.J.: Rutgers University Press, 1986), 3; hereafter cited parenthetically in the text.

8. Skilled representation of religious dispute helps Child maintain the fiction of a male author while demonstrating her ability to speak "like a man," even as she satirizes male discourse. An oddity of Child's literary career is that her presumed hatred of controversy produced a kind of fascination with it. Details of doctrinal dispute are displayed in *Hobomok* as well as in her three-volume *History of the Progress of Religious Ideas* (1855), which she regarded as her best and most important work.

9. Bell, *Hawthorne and the Historical Romance*, 10.

10. James Fenimore Cooper, *The Last of the Mohicans* (1826; reprint, Albany: State University Press of New York, 1983), 81, 129, 191, 204; hereafter cited parenthetically in the text.

11. There is, of course, considerable discussion throughout Cooper's novels about arms technology; from his perspective firearms do not nullify physical strength, they extend it. No primitivist in this (if in any) regard, he accepts technological superiority as an important attribute of a superior civilization.

12. Catharine Maria Sedgwick, *Hope Leslie; or, Early Times in the Massachusetts*, ed. Mary Kelley (1827; reprint, New Brunswick, N.J.: Rutgers University Press, 1987), 81; hereafter cited parenthetically in the text.

Chapter 3: Nathaniel Hawthorne and His Mother

1. See Hubert H. Hoeltje, "The Writing of *The Scarlet Letter*," *New England Quarterly* 27 (1954): 326–346; and Stephen Nissenbaum, "The Firing of Nathaniel Hawthorne," *Essex Institute Historical Collections* 114 (1978): 57–86.

2. Arlin Turner, *Nathaniel Hawthorne, A Biography* (New York: Oxford University Press, 1980), 208; Julian Hawthorne, *Nathaniel Hawthorne and His Wife* (Boston: Houghton Mifflin, 1884), 1:353–354 (hereafter cited parenthetically).

3. Jean Normand, *Nathaniel Hawthorne: An Approach to an Analysis of Artistic Creation;* tran. Derek Coltman (Cleveland: Case Western Reserve University Press, 1970); and John Franzosa, "'The Custom-House,' *The Scarlet Letter*, and Hawthorne's Separation from Salem," *ESQ* 24 (1978): 5–21, find the biographical significance of the romance to reside in the maternal figure of Hester, as I do. But both subsume this figure into larger, abstract schemes, Jungian and quasi-Freudian respectively, and ignore biographical detail.

4. Mark Van Doren, *Nathaniel Hawthorne* (New York: Sloane, 1949), 9.

5. Norman Holmes Pearson, "Elizabeth Peabody on Hawthorne," *Essex Institute Historical Collections* 94 (1958): 256–276; Randall Stewart, "Recollections of Hawthorne by His Sister Elizabeth," *American Literature* 16 (1945): 316–331; Manning Hawthorne, "Hawthorne's Early Years," *Essex Institute Historical Collections* 74 (1938): 1–21; "Parental and Family Influences on Hawthorne," *Essex Institute Historical Collections* 76 (1940): 1–13; "Nathaniel Hawthorne Prepares for College," *New England Quarterly* 11 (1938): 66–68; "Maria Louise Hawthorne," *Essex Institute Historical Collections* 75 (1939): 103–134; "Nathaniel Hawthorne at Bowdoin," *New England Quarterly* 13 (1940): 246–279; "A Glimpse of Hawthorne's Boyhood, *Essex Institute Historical Collections* 83 (1947): 178–184; Gloria Ehrlich, "Hawthorne and the Mannings," *Studies in the American Renaissance 1980* (Boston: Twayne, 1980), 97–117.

6. Nathaniel Hawthorne, *The Letters, 1813–1843*, ed. Thomas Woodson et al. (Columbus: Ohio State University Press, 1984), 15, 611; hereafter cited parenthetically in the text.

7. Pearson, "Elizabeth Peabody on Hawthorne," 266–268.

8. Ibid., 268.

9. James R. Mellow, *Nathaniel Hawthorne in His Times* (Boston: Houghton Mifflin, 1980), 13.

10. *At Odds: Women and the Family in America from the Revolution to the Present* (New York: Oxford University Press, 1980), 20.

11. Pearson, "Elizabeth Peabody on Hawthorne," 268.

12. Manning Hawthorne, "Nathaniel Hawthorne Prepares for College," 77.

13. Nathaniel Hawthorne, *English Notebooks,* ed. Randall Stewart (New York: Modern Language Association of America, 1941), 23; *French and Italian Notebooks,* ed. Thomas Woodson (Columbus: Ohio State University Press, 1980), 570. Subsequent references to Hawthorne's works citing the Centenary Edition published by the Ohio State University Press will be parenthetically included in the text, noting volume and page number of the edition.

14. *Hawthorne and his Wife,* 1:123–125; Stewart, "Recollections of Hawthorne by His Sister Elizabeth," 323, 327–328.

15. Mellow, *Nathaniel Hawthorne,* 185–186.

16. Turner, *Nathaniel Hawthorne,* 141.

17. Ibid., 142.

18. Louise Hall Tharp, *The Peabody Sisters of Salem* (Boston: Little, Brown, 1950), 185.

Chapter 4: Concepts of the Romance

1. Robert E. Spiller et al., eds., *Literary History of the United States,* rev. ed. (New York: Macmillan, 1953), xix. Nothing has changed.

2. Benjamin T. Spencer's *The Quest for Nationality: An American Literary Campaign* (Syracuse, N.Y.: Syracuse University Press, 1957) remains the best study of this phenomenon; it is telling that it appeared in the decade during which the hegemony of the "romance" was established, for it applies the concern with uniquely American aspects of American literature to historical study.

3. Richard Chase, *The American Novel and its Tradition* (Garden City, N.Y.: Doubleday, 1957).

4. Collected in the 1950 *Liberal Imagination* as part 1 of "Reality in America" and reprinted in Lionel Trilling, *The Liberal Imagination* (New York: Doubleday, 1953), 1–8.

5. Henry Nash Smith, *Virgin Land: The American West as Symbol and Myth* (Cambridge, Mass.: Harvard University Press, 1950); R.W.B. Lewis, *The American Adam: Innocence, Tragedy, and Tradition in the Nineteenth Century* (Chicago: University of Chicago Press, 1955).

6. *The House of the Seven Gables,* vol. 2 of the Centenary Edition of the *Works of Nathaniel Hawthorne* (Columbus: Ohio State University Press, 1965), 1.

7. Chase, *The American Novel and its Tradition,* 20; Leslie Fiedler, *Love and Death in the American Novel,* rev. ed. (New York: Stein and Day, 1966), 145.

8. The material that follows was collected in a study of fiction reviews published mostly between 1840 and 1860 in more than twenty major American magazines. The results of that study, which attempts to establish the actual context of generally accepted ideas within which fiction, and especially the novel, was produced in America during the antebellum period, are described in my *Novels, Readers, and Reviewers: Responses to Fiction in Antebellum America* (Ithaca: Cornell University Press, 1984).

9. Although the novel had become the most popular literary form by 1850—indeed, had achieved that status some decades before then—few critics were willing to abandon all the other genres. And, as Spencer indicates, the debate over literary nationalism focused more on the oration than on any other literary genre and centered least on fiction: "Neither Simms nor his contemporary romancers succeeded in formulating and establishing a markedly indigenous type of fiction, and not until after the Civil War were critics and authors to engage in the long debate over the Great American Novel" (*The Quest for Nationality,* 133, 134).

10. This finding coincides with that of John Paul Pritchard, *Literary Wise Men of Gotham: Criticism in New York, 1915–1860* (Baton Rouge: Louisiana State University Press, 1963), who writes that "all reputable fiction was subsumed under the term novel," that the "novel-romance dichotomy was not consistently observed," that the "term novel embraced the two," and that in discussion "it is rarely possible to discover whether the distinction was active in the writer's mind" (62, 64).

11. Chase, *The American Novel and its Tradition*, 18.

12. *The Marble Faun*, vol. 4 of the Centenary Edition of the *Works of Nathaniel Hawthorne* (Columbus: Ohio State University Press, 1968), 3.

Chapter 5: "Actually, I Felt Sorry for the Lion"

1. This has been the import of two major recent studies: Kenneth S. Lynn, *Hemingway* (New York: Scribners, 1987); and Mark Spilka, *Hemingway's Quarrel with Androgyny* (Lincoln: University of Nebraska Press, 1990).

2. See, for example, Mona G. Rosenman, "Five Hemingway Women," *Claflin College Review* 2, no. 1 (1977): 9–13; Linda Wagner, "Proud and Friendly and Gently," *College Literature* 7 (1980): 239–247; Charles J. Nolan, "Hemingway's Women's Movement," *Hemingway Review* 3, no. 2 (1984): 14–22.

3. Mary Anne Ferguson, ed., *Images of Women in Literature* (1973; reprint, Boston: Houghton, Mifflin, 1985).

4. It could be argued that to respect interpretations by readers who know nothing about Hemingway is to privilege ignorance, but I would counter here that to privilege an (imaginary) construction of the real-life author in this case is to neglect his "art." In today's theoretical climate, where some critics reject the category of "literature" altogether or interpret it as a hegemonic tool of capitalism, it seems important to say that I see literature as a multiply constituted, historically variable, but undeniably material range of categories that significantly influence the production (and, usually, the reception) of written works. Historically specific and diverse formalist approaches seem to me, therefore, appropriate and necessary for understanding the "how" of writing. Much of the gap that has presently opened between academic literary criticism and practicing writers can be traced to critical indifference toward, if not outright suspicion of, authorial craft.

5. For the distinction between voice and focus, see Gérard Genette, *Narrative Discourse: An Essay in Method* (Ithaca: Cornell University Press, 1980); for the idea of fiction as a field that displays multiple and often incompatible voices, see M. M. Bakhtin, *The Dialogic Imagination* (Austin: University of Texas Press, 1981). For the identification of the five foci, or points of view, in "The Short Happy Life of Francis Macomber," see James Nagel, "The Narrative Method of 'The Short Happy Life of Francis Macomber,'" *English Studies* 41 (1973): 18–27.

6. *The Short Stories of Ernest Hemingway: The First Forty-Nine Stories and the Play "The Fifth Column"* (New York: Random House, 1938), 110 (emphasis added) hereafter cited parenthetically in the text.

7. Hemingway and Wilson are quoted in Lynn, *Hemingway*, 432 and 433, respectively. At other points in his life Hemingway said different things about "The Short Happy Life." As always, one takes an author's interpretations skeptically, since they are usually designed as much to protect as to clarify. For an excellent chronicle of Hemingway's orchestration of his public image in the second half of his career, see John Raeburn, *Fame Became of Him: Hemingway as Public Writer* (Bloomington: Indiana University Press, 1984).

8. See John M. Howell and Charles A. Lawler, "From Abercrombie & Fitch to *The First Forty-Nine Stories*: The Text of Hemingway's 'Francis Macomber,'" *Proof* 2 (1972): 213–231—the quote is on p. 224 of that essay. The argument that Margot did not shoot

at her husband, hence did not mean to kill him, was first made by Warren Beck in "The Shorter Happy Life of Mrs. Macomber," *Modern Fiction Studies* 1 (1955): 28–37. The essay was roundly attacked. Reviewing the scholarship in 1968, William White canvassed (and concurred with) the majority who believed that Margot Macomber "meant to kill her husband when she shot at the buffalo" (*American Literary Scholarship: 1968* [Durham: Duke University Press, 1970], 113). White's phrasing here is peculiar, since he repeats the story's wording that Margot shot "at" the buffalo without explaining how shooting at the husband's attacker can be read as meaning to kill the husband. Mark Spilka, the most passionate advocate of Margot as murderer, resolves this dilemma by making Margot kill her husband "unconsciously": "Her conscious impulse to save him has given way to her deeper impulse to destroy him" ("Hemingway and Fauntleroy: An Androgynous Pursuit," *American Novelists Revisited: Essays in Feminist Criticism,* ed. Fritz Fleischmann [Boston: G. K. Hall, 1982], 358). Spilka repeats these words in an expanded version of his argument in *Hemingway's Quarrel with Androgyny* (238). Even while now granting that Wilson is a "used product himself, a sort of passive male hooker" (239), Spilka endorses his earlier reading of Margot. Other exponents of the Beck position, as well as Howell and Lawler, are K. G. Johnston, "In Defense of the Unhappy Margot Macomber," *Hemingway Review* 2, no. 2 (1983): 44–47; and Lynn, *Hemingway.* A different kind of putatively pro-Margot argument, typified by Robert W. Lewis in *Hemingway on Love* (Austin: University of Texas Press, 1965), takes her as a femme fatale constructed by male images of desire.

9. Carlos Baker, *Hemingway: The Writer as Artist,* 3d ed. (Princeton: Princeton University Press, 1963), 187.

10. Ibid., 189–190.

11. Surprisingly, however, Lynn (*Hemingway*) then writes that "Wilson instantly leaps to the conclusion that Margot has deliberately shot Macomber, and he thinks he understands why" (435–436). The end of the story allows no entry into Wilson's thoughts—we know only what he does and says. His words to Margot—"That was a pretty thing to do. . . . He *would* have left you too" (135)—are uttered in a "toneless" (i.e., unreadable) voice, conveying neither sincerity nor the lack of it. I assume we are to think that Wilson knows the killing is accidental; this makes his behavior all the more brutish.

12. Ibid., 434.

13. Mark Spilka has reminded me that Wilson, in asserting that the buffalo is dead, is taking the word of the African gun bearer for this (wrong) fact. This means that the text invites us to see Wilson as ignorant rather than cynical. Since Wilson is translating the gun bearer's words to his auditors, including readers, we are never really to know what the bearer actually said (nor how well Wilson understood him).

14. Howell and Lawler, "From Abercrombie & Fitch," 227. To be sure, the lion had no fear to overcome and in this sense sets an impossible standard for most human beings. Wilson might be exonerated in part by the claim that he stages situations that, no matter how safe in reality, do allow those who believe them dangerous to overcome real fear. The problem, of course, is that the staging leads to real killings.

Chapter 6: Early Histories of American Literature

1. Several of these textbooks are listed in Howard Mumford Jones, *The Theory of American Literature* (Ithaca: Cornell University Press, 1948), 78–118; some are mentioned in passing in Richard Brodhead, *The School of Hawthorne* (New York: Oxford University Press, 1986), 60–63. In his valuable study *American Literature and the Academy* (Philadelphia: University of Pennsylvania Press, 1986), Kermit Vanderbilt describes many of them and pays particular attention to works by Moses Coit Tyler, Charles F. Richardson, and

Barrett Wendell (81–153). None of these scholars, however, takes up the historical narrative presented in these textbooks.

2. Students of historiography across the political spectrum agree that modern history writing is an aspect of the formation of nation-states in the modern era. See, for example, David Levin, *History as Romantic Art: Bancroft, Prescott, Motley, and Parkman* (New York: AMS Press, 1967); George H. Calcott, *History in the United States, 1800–1860: Its Practice and Purpose* (Baltimore: Johns Hopkins Press, 1970); Ernest Gellner, *Nations and Nationalism* (Ithaca: Cornell University Press, 1983); and Eric Hobsbawm and Terence Rangers, eds., *The Invention of Tradition* (Cambridge: Cambridge University Press, 1983). With respect to United States history, see Seymour M. Lipset, *The First New Nation: The United States in Historical and Comparative Perspective* (New York: Basic, 1963); and Lawrence J. Friedman, *Inventors of the Promised Land* (New York: Knopf, 1975). The inescapable narrative, hence fictional, form of history writing has been much theorized; see, for example, Arthur Danto, *Analytical Philosophy of History* (Cambridge: Cambridge University Press, 1965); Louis Mink, "Narrative Form as a Cognitive Instrument," *The Writing of History: Literary Form and Historical Understanding*, ed. Robert Canacy and Henry Kozinki (Madison: University of Wisconsin Press, 1978), 129–158; Hayden White, *Metahistory: The Historical Imagination in Nineteenth-Century Europe* (Baltimore: Johns Hopkins University Press, 1973); *The Content of the Form: Narrative Discourse and Historical Representation* (Baltimore: Johns Hopkins University Press, 1987); Paul Ricoeur, *Time and Narrative*, 3 vols. (Chicago: University of Chicago Press, 1984–88); and Wallace Martin, *Recent Theories of Narrative* (Ithaca: Cornell University Press, 1986). References to the "story" of American literature, with the totalized nation or "we the people" as protagonist, abound in our criticism. Peter Carofiol, among many others, recognizes that to represent "an" American literature it is useful if not necessary to tell a "coherent story" about that literature ("The Constraints of History: Revision and Revolution in American Literary Studies," *College English* 50 [1988]: 605–622).

For the aims of American public schooling, see Horace Mann, *Lectures on Education* (Boston: Ida and Dutton, 1855); Merle Curti, *The Social Ideas of American Educators* (New York: Scribner's, 1935); David B. Tyack, *The One Best System: A History of American Urban Education* (Cambridge: Harvard University Press, 1967); Michael B. Katz, *The Irony of Early School Reform: Educational Innovation in Mid-Nineteenth Century Massachusetts* (Cambridge: Harvard University Press, 1968); Marvin Lazerson, *Origins of the Urban School: Public Education in Massachusetts* (Cambridge: Harvard University Press, 1971); Jonathan Messerli, *Horace Mann: A Biography* (New York: Knopf, 1972); and Stanley K. Schultz, *The Culture Factory: Boston Public Schools, 1789–1860* (New York: Oxford University Press, 1973).

3. Richard Burton, *Literary Leaders of America* (New York: Chautauqua, 1903), v; hereafter cited parenthetically in the text. The other textbooks cited in this study, also cited parenthetically by author's last name, are (in alphabetical order): Katherine Lee Bates, *American Literature* (New York: Macmillan, 1897); Henry A. Beers, *Outline Sketch of American Literature* (New York: Chautauqua, 1887); Walter C. Bronson, *A Short History of American Literature, Designed Primarily for Use in Schools and Colleges* (Boston: D. C. Heath, 1903); Mary Fisher, *A General Survey of American Literature* (Chicago: A. C. McClurg, 1901); Reuben Post Halleck, *History of American Literature* (New York: American Book Company, 1911); Thomas Wentworth Higginson and Henry Walcott Boynton, *A Reader's History of American Literature* (Boston: Houghton, Mifflin, 1903); Brander Matthews, *Introduction to American Literature* (New York: American Book Company, 1897); Henry S. Pancoast, *An Introduction to American Literature* (New York: Henry Holt, 1898); Fred Lewis Pattee, *A History of American Literature, with a View to the Fundamental Principles Underlying its Development: A Textbook for Schools and Colleges* (New York: Silver,

Burdet, 1896); Charles F. Richardson, *American Literature, 1607–1885,* 2 vols. (New York: Putnam's, n.d.); William P. Trent, *A History of American Literature, 1607–1865* (New York: Appleton, 1903); Moses Coit Tyler, *A History of American Literature,* vol. 1: *1607–1676;* vol. 2: *1676–1765* (New York: Putnam's, 1878); Barrett Wendell and Chester Noyes Greenough, *A History of Literature in America* (New York: Scribner's, 1907); George E. Woodberry, *America in Literature* (New York: Harper and Brothers, 1903).

4. This kind of Whig history should not be confused with the progressive, meliorist concept of English Whig history in contrast to Tory history. For the American Whig worldview and its need for history, see Thomas R. Hart, Jr., "George Ticknor's *History of Spanish Literature:* The New England Background," *PMLA* 69 (1954): 76–88; Rush Welter, *The Mind of America, 1820–1860* (New York: Columbia University Press, 1975); Jean V. Matthews, " 'Whig History': New England Whigs and a Usable Past," *New England Quarterly* 51 (1978): 193–208; *Rufus Choate: The Law and Civic Virtue* (Philadelphia: Temple University Press, 1980); Daniel Walker Howe, *The Political Culture of the American Whigs* (Chicago: University of Chicago Press, 1979); Peter Dobkin Hall, *The Organization of American Culture, 1700–1900: Private Institutions, Elites, and the Origins of American Nationality* (New York: New York University Press, 1982); John P. McWilliams, Jr., *Hawthorne, Melville, and the American Character: A Looking-Glass Business* (New York: Cambridge University Press, 1984); and Lawrence Buell, *New England Literary Culture: From Revolution through Renaissance* (New York: Cambridge University Press, 1986).

For the foundation of Whig thought in the federalism that preceded it, see Buell, Hall, Hart, and also William Charvat, *The Origins of American Critical Thought, 1810–1835* (Philadelphia: University of Pennsylvania Press, 1936); Ferris Greenslet, *The Lowells and Their Seven Worlds* (Boston: Houghton Mifflin, 1946); Lewis P. Simpson, ed., *The Federalist Literary Mind* (Baton Rouge: Louisiana State University Press, 1962); *The Man of Letters in New England and the South* (Baton Rouge: Louisiana State University Press, 1973); David Hackett Fischer, *The Revolution of American Conservatism: The Federalist Party in the Era of Jeffersonian Democracy* (New York: Harper and Row, 1965); Paul Goodman, "Ethics and Enterprise: The Values of the Boston Elite, 1800–1860," *American Quarterly* 18 (1966): 437–451; David B. Tyack, *George Ticknor and the Boston Brahmins* (Cambridge: Harvard University Press, 1967); and Ronald Story, *The Forging of an Aristocracy: Harvard and the Boston Upper Class, 1800–1870* (Middletown: Wesleyan University Press, 1980).

The national political history incorporated into late nineteenth-century literary histories draw less on the democrat George Bancroft's celebratory volumes than on two Whig histories: Richard Hildreth's six-volume *History of the United States* (1849–52); and John Gorham Palfrey's *History of New England,* three volumes of which appeared between 1858 and 1864, volume 4 in 1875, and the last, completed by his son, posthumously published in 1889. (The long-lived Palfrey [1796–1881] disseminated his views over many years in the *North American Review,* which he edited from 1835 to 1843). But the story was available as well in dozens of popular school histories written from a Whig perspective, including long-lived textbooks by Charles Goodrich and Emma Willard.

5. On the panic of 1837, see Reginald Charles McGrane, *The Panic of 1837: Some Financial Problems of the Jacksonian Era* (1924; reprint, New York: Russell and Russell, 1965). For the relation between the panic and educational programs, see E.I.F. Williams, *Horace Mann, Educational Statesman* (New York: Macmillan, 1937).

6. The goal of forming character was not limited to primary and secondary schooling. See Louise L. Stevenson, *Scholarly Means to Evangelical Ends: The New Haven Scholars and the Transformation of Higher Learning in America* (Baltimore: Johns Hopkins University Press, 1986), for Yale University; and Hall, *Organization of American Culture,* for Harvard. The difference is that elite schools attempted to form the character of leaders, public

schools those of followers—or, more precisely, those who would choose and then defer to leaders.

7. See Mann, *Lectures,* 34–37; and Curti, *Social Ideas of American Educators,* 143. Messerli, *Horace Mann,* describes Mann's rejection of Elizabeth Peabody's nomination of Nathaniel Hawthorne as a contributor to his school district library series and also his advice to Richard Henry Dana about revising *Two Years before the Mast:* "Many of the scenes and events, which the work describes, would also admit the introduction of moral sentiments, suited to the class of readers for which it is intended" (345). The prime theoretician of surveillance since the Enlightenment is, of course, Michel Foucault; closer to home is David J. Rothman, *The Discovery of the Asylum: Social Order and Disorder in the New Republic* (Boston: Little, Brown, 1971), which, however, does not discuss schools. By recruiting women early on for this expanded teaching system the reformers implicated them (us) in their project from the beginning.

8. For a content analysis of representative nineteenth-century textbooks, see Ruth Miller Elson, *Guardians of Tradition: American Schoolbooks in the Nineteenth Century* (Lincoln: University of Nebraska Press, 1964). Elson discusses the typical representations of the Puritans as the nation's founders (167–169) and observes that most of the early readers—with the exception of McGuffey's—were compiled or written by New Englanders.

9. See Jones, *Theory of American Literature;* and also William Charvat and W. S. Tryon, *The Cost Books of Ticknor and Fields and Their Predecessor, 1832–1858* (New York: Bibliographical Society of America, 1949); William Charvat, *Literary Publishing in America, 1790–1850* (Philadelphia: University of Pennsylvania Press, 1959); W. S. Tryon, *Parnassus Corner: A Life of James T. Fields* (Boston: Houghton Mifflin, 1963); Charvat, *The Profession of Authorship in America* (Columbus: Ohio State University Press, 1968); and, especially, Ellen B. Ballou, *The Building of the House: Houghton Mifflin's Formative Years* (Boston: Houghton Mifflin, 1970), 328–349, 492–516.

10. Horace Scudder, *Literature in School* (Boston: Houghton Mifflin, 1888), 10; hereafter cited parenthetically in the text. Richard Brodhead, whose work first alerted me to Scudder, has written about him as a key figure in the canonization of Hawthorne (*School of Hawthorne,* 59–64). Brodhead focuses on the commodification of New England authors as part of middle-class cultural apparatus; I am looking at the deployment of literature in the more coercive and more conventionally political project of schooling. Not surprisingly, Scudder's general ideas about education meshed with those of bureaucrats like Edwin P. Seaver, secretary of the Massachusetts Board of Education from 1880 to 1904. (For Seaver, see Lazerson, *Origins of the Urban School.*)

11. An advertising circular for 1890 lists forty-two titles in the series, including thirteen by Longfellow and ten by Hawthorne. Authors with more than one pamphlet each were Whittier, Lowell, Holmes, John Burroughs, and Benjamin Franklin; authors with one pamphlet each were Thoreau, Bayard Taylor, Charles Dudley Warner, Emerson, George Washington, and Abraham Lincoln. As capitalist enterprises, publishers like Houghton Mifflin had continually to expand and revise their lists to keep on selling books, so that a destabilizing tendency was at work in the canonizing project from the start. Publishers do not resist canonical change if they can profit from it.

12. It is this exclusionary subtext to which many "canon bashers" of today are responding. Perhaps a majority of turn-of-the-century New England intellectuals believed that Anglo-Saxon behavior could be practiced only by Anglo-Saxons like themselves. Howard Mumford Jones, *Theory of American Literature,* discusses racialism in college English departments and correlates it with the vogue for Anglo-Saxon (79–115).

On New England racialism more generally in this period, see Barbara Miller Solomon, "The Intellectual Background of the Immigration Restriction Movement in New England," *New England Quarterly* 25 (1952): 47–59; Solomon, *Ancestors and Immigrants: A*

Changing New England Tradition (Cambridge: Harvard University Press, 1956); Thomas F. Gossett, *Race: The History of an Idea in America* (Dallas: Southern Methodist University Press, 1963); Stow Persons, *The Decline of American Gentility* (New York: Oxford University Press, 1973); and Joan D. Hedrick, "Harvard Indifference," *New England Quarterly* 49 (1976): 356–372. John Gorham Palfrey fretted in his history that "it has not yet appeared that the Celtic or the African constitution, or that of the aboriginal red man or of strays from one or another despotism of continental Europe or of the heathen East, is competent to struggles and exploits, or to an acute, far-seeing, courageous, and persistent policy, like those by which the later greatness of New England was founded and fashioned by the God-fearing builders of that community" (*History of New England* [Boston: Houghton Mifflin, 1889], 5:ix).

13. Charles A. Goodrich, *History of the United States of America* (Boston: A. K. White, 1828), 73.

14. Shaping literary history to the "great man" format of standard history had, of course, an exclusionary outcome where women's contributions were concerned; so too the focus on a literary culture composed of masculine social networks—Harvard, the Saturday Club, and the like. But the virtual absence of women from the record seems to have been something more or less taken for granted than deliberately aimed at. The two literary histories in my sample written by women show no gender-based tendencies toward counterhistory.

15. The standard account of the formation of academia after the Civil War is Burton J. Bledstein, *The Culture of Professionalism: The Middle Class and the Development of Higher Education in America* (New York: Norton, 1976).

16. For example, the great Jeffersonian Vernon Parrington wrote: "remembering the mingled strains of Melville's ancestry, the critic is tempted to discover in his New England blood the source of his transcendental visions" (*Main Currents in American Thought* [1927; reprint, New York: Harcourt, Brace, 1954], 2:251).

17. In Edward H. Davidson, *Poe: A Critical Study* (Columbus: Ohio State University Press, 1957).

18. A good study of the interconnection of post 1950s mythic and textualist critics is Russell Reising, *The Unusable Past: Theory and the Study of American Literature* (London: Methuen, 1986).

19. For a critique of current historical representations of southern literature, see Michael Kreyling, "Southern Literature: Consensus and Dissensus," *American Literature* 60 (1988): 83–95. At least one early American history text anticipated the revival of the South in literary history, observing that the future of American literature was likely to depend on the South because in that region modern energy, enterprise, and education were balanced by traditionalism and "disinclination to be guided by merely practical aims" and because "the original conservative English stock, which is still dominant, has been more persistent there and less modified by foreign immigration" (Halleck, *History of American Literature*, 291).

20. Annette Kolodny, "The Integrity of Memory: Creating a New Literary History of the United States," *American Literature* 57 (1985): 290–307; Philip Gura, "Turning Our World Upside Down: Reconceiving Early American Literature," *American Literature* 63 (1991): 104–112.

Chapter 7: From Enlightenment to Victorian

1. Emily Noyes Vanderpoel, comp., *Chronicles of a Pioneer School from 1792 to 1833, Being the History of Miss Sarah Pierce and Her Litchfield School* (Cambridge: University Press, 1903), 176–177; hereafter cited in the text as *C*.

2. Scholarship on Enlightenment thought tends to privilege writings by a few men: Locke, Rousseau, Descartes, Paine, Diderot, and so on. I approach the Enlightenment as a widespread cultural moment and movement constructed by thousands of texts, including the women's texts discussed here. See also Londa Schiebinger, *The Mind Has No Sex? Women in The Origins of Modern Science* (Cambridge: Harvard University Press, 1989).

3. For studies on the ideology of republican motherhood, see Linda K. Kerber, *Women of the Republic: Intellect and Ideology in Revolutionary America* (Chapel Hill: University of North Carolina Press, 1980); and Mary Beth Norton, *Liberty's Daughters: The Revolutionary Experience of American Woman, 1750–1800* (Boston: Little, Brown, 1980).

4. Phillis Wheatley's poetry, much of it predating the Revolution, shows occasional traces of republican motivation complicated by dependence on English sponsors; her work, however, is fully devoted to the principles of Enlightenment logocentrism and ungendered mind.

5. Including in some sense its own writing, since the conceptual, lexical, and syntactic structures of textualist-feminist theorizing participate in male-authored discourses—especially Derridean and Lacanian. For an approving exposition of such theory, see Toril Moi, *Sexual/Textual Politics: Feminist Literary Theory* (London and New York: Methuen, 1985); and for a cogent critique, see Rita Felski, *Beyond Feminist Aesthetics: Feminist Literature and Social Change* (Cambridge: Harvard University Press, 1989). Feminist *literary* theory, focused on writing, is only one segment of the larger field of feminist theory.

6. For a bibliographical review of such scholarship, consult Kathleen B. Jones, "Citizenship in a Woman-Friendly Polity," *Signs* 15 (1990): 781–812. Influential examples include Susan Moller Okin, *Women in Western Political Thought* (Princeton: Princeton University Press, 1979); Jean Bethke Elshtain, *Public Man, Private Woman: Women in Social and Political Thought* (Princeton: Princeton University Press, 1981); Hanna Fenichel Pitkin, *Fortune Is a Woman: Gender and Politics in the Thought of Niccolo Machiavelli* (Berkeley: University of California Press, 1984); and Joan B. Landes, *Women and the Public Sphere in the Age of the French Revolution* (Ithaca: Cornell University Press, 1988); as well as the special issue of *Daedalus* 116 (1987) titled "Learning about Women: Gender, Politics, and Power." See also n. 2 above.

7. The useful locution *public sphere* is borrowed from the work of Jurgen Habermas, whose work, however, is not historically specific to the United States. As many commentators have observed, the Habermasian "Enlightenment" is a Utopian alternative to the present day, not a factual account.

8. Hannah Mather Crocker, *Observations on the Real Rights of Women, With Their Appropriate Duties, Agreeable to Scripture, Reason and Common Sense* (Boston: for the author, 1818), 63. Throughout this treatise Crocker hammers at the point that, "although there must be allowed some moral and physical distinction of the sexes agreeably to the order of nature, and the organization of the human frame [i.e., childbearing and strength differential], still the sentiment must predominate, that the powers of mind are equal in the sexes" (5–6).

9. Establishing "female academies," or, as Emma Willard was later to call them, "female seminaries," to educate future republican mothers enlarged women's domain by making female spaces outside the home. This and other uses of various domestic ideologies by women to appropriate or reconstruct public space have been studied by feminist literary scholars and historians of women under the label "domestic feminism." Print was an ally of domestic feminism's push into public space, but it also constituted an imaginary realm in which women could perform invisibly.

10. There are good brief biographies of Warren, Adams, and Logan in Edward T. James, ed., *Notable American Women* (Cambridge: Harvard University Press, 1971). For Warren, the only one of these three authors who has been written about to any extent,

see also Maud Macdonald Hutcheson, "Mercy Warren, 1728–1814," *William and Mary Quarterly* 10 (1953): 378–402; William Raymond Smith, *History as Argument: Three Patriot Historians of the American Revolution* (The Hague: Mouton, 1966); Lawrence J. Friedman, *Inventors of the Promised Land* (New York: Knopf, 1975); Lawrence J. Friedman and Arthur H. Shaffer, "Mercy Otis Warren and the Politics of Historical Nationalism," *New England Quarterly* 48 (1975): 194–215; Arthur H. Shaffer, *The Politics of History: Writing the History of the American Revolution* (Chicago, 1975); Joan Hoff Wilson and Sharon L. Billinger, "Mercy Otis Warren: Playwright, Poet, and Historian of the American Revolution," in J. R. Brink, ed., *Female Scholars: A Tradition of Learned Women before 1800* (Montreal: Eden Press, 1980), 161–182; Lester H. Cohen, "Explaining the Revolution: Ideology and Ethics in Mercy Otis Warren's Historical Theory," *William and Mary Quarterly* 37 (1980): 200–18; *The Revolutionary Historians: Contemporary Narratives of the American Revolution* (Ithaca: Cornell University Press, 1980); "Mercy Otis Warren: The Politics of Language and the Aesthetics of Self," *American Quarterly* 35 (1983): 418–489; "Creating a Usable Future: The Revolutionary Historians," in Jack Greene, ed., *The American Revolution: Its Character and Limits* (New York: New York University Press, 1987), 309–327; Cheryl Z. Oreovicz, "Mercy Warren and 'Freedom's Genius,'" *University of Mississippi Studies in English* 5 (1987): 215–230; Nina Baym, "Mercy Otis Warren's Gendered Melodrama of Revolution," *South Atlantic Quarterly* 90 (1991): 531–554.

11. See E. J. Hobsbawm, *Nations and Nationalism since 1780: Programme, Myth, Reality* (Cambridge: Cambridge University Press, 1990); Benedict Anderson, *Imagined Communities: Reflections on the Origin and Spread of Nationalism* (London: Verso, 1983); Michael Warner, *The Letters of the Republic: Publication and the Public Sphere in Eighteenth-Century America* (Cambridge: Harvard University Press, 1990).

12. For the term *Unitarian evangelicalism,* see Anne C. Rose, *Transcendentalism as a Social Movement, 1830–1850* (New Haven: Yale University Press, 1981).

13. Deborah Norris Logan, *Memoir of Dr. George Logan of Stenton* (Philadelphia: Historical Society of Pennsylvania, 1899), 31.

14. Quoted in Edward Armstrong, preface, *Correspondence between William Penn and James Logan, Secretary of the Province of Pennsylvania, and Others, 1700–1750,* ed. Deborah Norris Logan and Armstrong, 2 vols. (Philadelphia: Pennsylvania Historical Society Memoirs, 1870–72) 1 : viii.

15. Logan, *Correspondence,* 2 : 10n. Here Logan projects an undeveloped alternative to the already-dominant New England Puritan-based origins history.

16. Logan, *Memoir,* 58–59, 72.

17. All too often, however, this work goes unremarked by those who make use of it. The ongoing edition of the Penn correspondence, for one example, prints the letters directly from the manuscripts that Deborah Logan preserved but gives her no credit (presumably because her work is insufficiently scholarly?). For another example; although Eliza Buckminster Lee's 1849 memoir of her Calvinist father and Unitarian brother is a basic document in New England religious and intellectual history, it is read transparently for the record of two men. Nothing is said about the woman's labor of preservation and construction.

18. Mercy Otis Warren, *History of the Rise, Progress and Termination of the American Revolution, Interspersed with Biographical, Political and Moral Observations,* ed. Lester H. Cohen (Indianapolis: Liberty Press, 1989), 1 : xli; hereafter cited parenthetically in the text as *H.*

19. For a full discussion of Warren's representations of women in the *History,* see my "Mercy Otis Warren's Gendered Melodrama of Revolution" (n. 10).

20. Preface to Hannah Adams, *A View of Religions,* 3d ed. (Boston: Manning and Loring, 1801), v. This is a retitled edition of her 1784 *Alphabetical Compendium of the Various Sects.*

21. *A Memoir of Miss Hannah Adams* (Boston: Gray and Bowen, 1832), 10–11. In this memoir Adams describes "the trials which attend literary pursuits" at length but specifically dissociates herself from the assertion that the "penalties and discouragements attending authors in general fall upon woman with double weight." Rather, she says, "I have been too insignificant, and treated with too much candor, fully to realize the above remarks" (*Memoir*, 34, 35). As recipient of an annuity from prominent Federalists, she would have been unwise to complain.

22. Adams, *Memoir*, 14.

23. One important exception to this generalization is Ann Douglas's *The Feminization of American Culture* (New York: Knopf, 1977).

24. On republican millennialism, see James West Davidson, *The Logic of Millennial Thought: Eighteenth-Century New England* (New Haven, Yale University Press, 1977); Nathan O. Hatch: *The Sacred Cause of Liberty: Republican Thought and the Millennium in Revolutionary New England* (New Haven: Yale University Press, 1977); Ruth H. Bloch, *Visionary Republics: Millennial Themes in American Thought, 1756–1800* (New York: Cambridge University Press, 1985).

25. Hannah Adams, *An Abridgment of the History of New England, for the Use of Young Persons* (Boston: Belcher and Armstrong, 1807), 179.

26. A good brief summary of this quarrel is to be found in the Adams entry in *Notable American Women*.

27. This shift is congruent with the shift from the one-sex to two-sex model described by Thomas Laqueur in *Making Sex: Body and Gender from the Greeks to Freud* (Cambridge: Harvard University Press, 1990). For a parallel, more privatistic analysis of Victorian ideology, see Nancy F. Cott's "Passionlessness: An Interpretation of Victorian Sexual Ideology, 1790–1850," *Signs* 4 (1978): 219–236.

28. Among numerous books on middle-class formation, see especially Stuart Blumin, *The Emergence of the Middle Class: Social Experience in the American City, 1760–1900* (Cambridge: Cambridge University Press, 1989). For true women as nonblack, see Hazel V. Carby, *Reconstructing Womanhood: The Emergence of the Afro-American Woman Novelist, 1890–1940* (New Haven, Conn.: Yale University Press, 1987). There has been little notice taken of the attacks on upper-class women in middle-class American Victorianism. It is important to remember, however, that the term *true womanhood* in current discourse denotes merely an abstraction from advice books published in the Jacksonian era; it cannot be identified with any nontextual reality nor retroactively applied even as a rhetorical construct to the earlier period. At best, it is only one of many ways in which women were being rhetorically constituted in the antebellum era within a separate sphere whose content was fluid and contested.

29. On the development of the British novel as a feminized, interiorized form, see Nancy Armstrong, *Desire and Domestic Fiction: A Political History of the Novel* (New York: Oxford University Press, 1987). American domestic fiction was more openly political.

30. On the romanticism of Victorian American intellectual women, see Susan Phinney Conrad, *Perish the Thought: Intellectual Women in Romantic America, 1830–1860* (New York: Oxford University Press, 1976).

31. Sarah J. Hale, *Woman's Record*, 2d ed. (New York: Harper and Brothers, 1855), xlvi. A description of the historical scheme of *Woman's Record* may be found in my "Onward Christian Women: Sarah J. Hale's History of the World," *New England Quarterly* 63 (1990): 249–270. See also the essay on Sarah Hale in this volume.

32. Judith Sargent Murray, *The Gleaner*, vol. 3 (Boston: Thomas and Andrews, 1798), 197–198. Hannah Mather Crocker is the other, and her historical approach is identical to Murray's. (See n. 7.)

33. The Enlightenment concept of ungendered mind retained a stronghold at this time

among some—but not all—of the suffrage women, who may be thought of as precursor in some ways to today's currently out-of-style liberal feminists. The title of Sarah Grimke's 1836 *Letters on the Equality of the Sexes, and the Condition of Women,* makes the case in point with its word *equality.* For an excellent discussion of the perceived threat of woman suffrage to Victorian female political culture, see Paula Baker, "The Domestication of Politics: Women and American Political Society, 1780–1920," *American Historical Review* 89 (1984): 620–646.

34. Michael Davitt Bell's *Hawthorne and the Historical Romance of New England* (Princeton: Princeton University Press, 1970) surveys a subset of these novels focused on Puritan New England. Among other leading topics for antebellum women's historical fiction are the American Revolution, the frontier (i.e., American Indian warfare), and classical Greece and Rome.

Chapter 8: Women and the Republic

1. Linda K. Kerber, in "Separate Spheres, Female Worlds, Woman's Place: The Rhetoric of Women's History," *Journal of American History* 75 (1988): 9–39, describes the concept of separate spheres as a contested rhetorical construct, not an accurate representation of real behavior.

2. On republican motherhood, see Linda K. Kerber, "Daughters of Columbia: Educating Women for the Republic, 1787–1805," *The Hofstadter Aegis: A Memorial,* ed. Stanley Elkins and Eric McKitrick (New York: Knopf, 1974), 36–59; "The Republican Mother: Women and the Enlightenment—An American Perspective," *American Quarterly* 28 (1976): 187–205; *Women of the Republic: Intellect and Ideology in Revolutionary America* (Chapel Hill: University of North Carolina Press, 1980); Mary Beth Norton, *Liberty's Daughters* (Boston: Little, Brown, 1980). For the importance of the idea that mind has no sex in this ideology, see my essay "From Enlightenment to Victorian" in this volume. Kerber makes Judith Sargent Murray the ideology's chief theorizer, but, while claims for gender equality as well as claims for the importance of the study of history abound in Murray's work, it has a universalist, not nationalist, vision of the world family.

3. See Cathy N. Davidson, *Revolution and the Word: The Rise of the Novel in America* (New York: Oxford University Press, 1986). The counsel that young women should substitute history for novel reading is ubiquitous in the early national period.

4. For the change in attitude toward novels after *Waverley,* see my *Novels, Readers, and Reviewers: Responses to Fiction in Antebellum America* (Ithaca: Cornell University Press, 1984).

5. For overviews of the vast and contentious literature on Republican ideology, see Linda K. Kerber, "The Republican Ideology of the Revolutionary Generation," *American Quarterly* 37 (1985): 474–495; Lance Banning, "Jeffersonian Ideology Revisited: Liberal and Classical Ideas in the New American Republic," *William and Mary Quarterly* 43 (1986): 5–19; and Joyce Appleby, "Republicanism in Old and New Contexts," *William and Mary Quarterly* 43 (1986): 20–34. Appleby, in particular, differentiates classical and liberal strains of republican thinking. The most influential works on republicanism have been Bernard Bailyn, *The Ideological Origins of the American Revolution* (Cambridge: Harvard University Press, 1967); Gordon A. Wood, *The Creation of the American Republic, 1776–1787* (Chapel Hill: University of North Carolina Press, 1969); and J.G.A. Pocock, *The Machiavellian Moment: Florentine Political Thought and the Atlantic Republican Tradition* (Princeton: Princeton University Press, 1975).

6. For Willard's life, see William Fowler in *Memoirs of Teachers and Educators,* ed. Henry Barnard (New York: F. C. Brownell, 1861), 125–168; John Lord, *The Life of Emma Willard* (New York: D. Appleton, 1873); anon., *Emma Willard and Her Pupils; or,*

Fifty Years of Troy Female Seminary (New York: by Mrs. Russel Sage, 1898); Alma Lutz, *Emma Willard: Daughter of Democracy* (Boston: Houghton, Mifflin, 1929); Ann Firor Scott, "This New Woman?" *Journal of American History* 65 (1978): 679–703; and *Making the Invisible Woman Visible* (Urbana: University of Illinois Press, 1984), 37–88. See also Thomas Woody, *A History of Women's Education in the United States,* vol. I (New York and Lancaster, Pa.: Science Press, 1929); William L. O'Neill, *Feminism in America: A History,* 2d rev. ed., (New Brunswick, N.J.: Rutgers University Press, 1989), 13; Sara M. Evans, *Born for Liberty: A History of Women in America* (New York: Free Press, 1989), 70–71.

7. Fowler, *Memoirs,* 133.

8. The full title is *An Address to the Public; Particularly to the Members of the Legislature of New-York, Proposing a Plan for Improving Female Education* (Middlebury, Conn.: J. W. Copeland, 1819); hereafter cited parenthetically as *Plan.*

9. David Van Tassell claims that, in the thirty years after American history became a school subject in the 1820s, most Americans got their United States history entirely from textbooks. See his *Recording America's Past: An Interpretation of the Development of Historical Studies in America* (Chicago: University of Chicago Press, 1960), 91; see also George H. Callcott, *History in the United States, 1800–1860: Its Practice and Purpose* (Baltimore: Johns Hopkins Press, 1970), 55–67. Among many American history textbooks Willard's seems to have been the second-best-seller, behind Charles Goodrich's. There were fewer world history textbooks than American history texts since world history was less widely taught. On textbooks and nineteenth-century schooling, see Agnew O. Roorbach, *Development of the Social Studies in American Secondary Education before 1861* (Philadelphia: University of Pennsylvania Press, 1937); John A. Nietze, *Old Textbooks* (Pittsburgh: University of Pittsburgh Press, 1960); Charles Carpenter, *History of American Schoolbooks* (Philadelphia: University of Pennsylvania Press, 1963); and Ruth Miller Elson, *Guardians of Tradition: American Schoolbooks of the Nineteenth Century* (Lincoln: University of Nebraska Press, 1964).

10. Writing in 1874, Catharine E. Beecher said that Willard's institution had educated 13,500 pupils (8,216 after Willard's retirement), including 956 (or less than 6 percent) teachers, of whom 100 had been trained gratis. See her *Educational Reminiscences and Suggestions* (New York: J. B. Ford, 1874), 164. Lord (*Life of Emma Willard,* 217) quotes Willard to the effect that between 1807 and 1838 she herself produced 500 teachers from her total of 5,000 pupils (or 10 percent); Scott (*Making the Invisible Woman Visible,* 67, 71, 75) calculates that in Troy's first fifty years upwards of a thousand of the 12,000 attendees became teachers (or just over 8 percent), with perhaps 250 in this group eventually heading schools or founding schools of their own. Although somewhere between 90 and 95 percent of Troy's students did *not* become teachers, since it was mostly they who memorialized Willard, her project has been misunderstood.

11. Fowler, *Memoirs,* 155. Most discussions of the antebellum women's education movement erroneously conflate Willard's aims with those of Mary Lyon and Catharine Beecher. Lyon and Beecher were indeed chiefly concerned to recruit needy, respectable women (Beecher called them "women of the *medium* working-classes") to Christianize and civilize the growing American proletariat, especially in the western states, and, in Beecher's case, particularly to counter the Roman Catholicism of Irish immigrants (*Educational Reminiscences,* 92–93).

12. Sarah B. Pomeroy, *Goddesses, Whores, Wives, and Slaves: Women in Classical Antiquity* (New York: Schocken, 1975), 38. Notwithstanding its erroneous claim that Spartan allusions are lacking in American discourse, Elizabeth Rawson's *The Spartan Tradition in European Thought* (New York: Oxford University Press, 1969) is a useful introduction to Spartan imagery in the eighteenth and nineteenth centuries. Joan B. Landes, in *Women and the Public Sphere in the Age of the French Revolution* (Ithaca: Cornell University Press,

1988), argues that examples of extravagance and licentiousness among influential French court women undergirded an antiwoman ideology among bourgeois Revolutionary theorists which removed women from the post-Revolutionary public sphere. In the United States the French example was used to bind women to the public sphere.

13. Emma Willard, *Letter, Addressed as a Circular to the Members of the Willard Association* (Troy: Elias Gates, 1838), 12–13.

14. For a summary of Troy's curriculum, see *The Female Student; or, Lectures to Young Ladies,* by Almira Lincoln Phelps (Boston: Carter, Hendee, 1833). Phelps—well worth study in her own right—was Willard's younger sister, her assistant at Troy, and author of the most widely used school botany text before the Civil War. *The Female Student,* reprinted many times, derives from weekly lectures she delivered to the student assembly at Troy in the winter of 1830–31, when Willard was abroad. Phelps was far more pious and less political than her sister; distrustful of narrative, even in its guise as history, she turned to science for religious certainty, exemplifying in a different way from her sister the combination of progressive and retrograde—to speak from a presentist perspective—so frequently met with in these antebellum women.

15. Emma Willard, *Abridgement of the History of the United States; or, Repubic of America* (New York: A. S. Barnes, 1852), vi; hereafter cited parenthetically as *1852.*

16. Phelps's biographer describes Emma and Almira, the two youngest children in the Hart family, listening to tales of Revolutionary heroism and endurance narrated by both parents (Emma Lydia Bolzau, *Almira Hart Lincoln Phelps: Her Life and Work* [Philadelphia: University of Pennsylvania Press, 1938], 7–8). Willard's husband, twenty-eight years her senior, had also been a participant in the Revolution, so that one may imagine her as both parented by and wedded to the Revolutionary moment.

17. Emma Willard, *History of the United States; or, Republic of America,* 4th ed. (New York: White, Gallaher and White, 1831), iii; hereafter cited parenthetically as *1831.*

18. Emma Willard, *History of the United States; or, Republic of America* (New York: A. S. Barnes, 1845), 124.

19. Putting aside the vexed question of what we mean by "identification," I do not mean to suggest that women can identify with female examples or "role models" only. See Barbara Sicherman, "Sense and Sensibility: A Case Study of Women's Reading in Late-Victorian America," *Reading in America: Literature and Social History,* ed. Cathy N. Davidson (Baltimore: Johns Hopkins University Press, 1989), 201–225, for a historical demonstration of the variety of connections that women made to literary characters. The very absence of female representation in narrative histories (as well as in tales of action and adventure) could induce women readers to align themselves with male characters. Such rhetoric of absence is an obvious way to engender female patriots, still widely employed. See, on this topic, Jean Bethke Elshtain, *Women and War* (New York: Basic, 1987); Helen M. Cooper, Adrienne Auslander Munich, and Susan Merrill Squier, eds., *Arms and the Woman: War, Gender, and Literary Representation* (Chapel Hill: University of North Carolina Press, 1989).

20. Kenneth Silverman calls this constellation of violence and family "Whig sentimentalism" in *A Cultural History of the American Revolution* (New York: New York University Press, 1976), 82–87. But he does not comment on the gendering of the images.

21. A content study of antebellum American history textbooks cited by Nietze (*Old Textbooks,* 242), finds that those published between 1797 and 1825 contained an average of 53.8 percent war content; between 1826 and 1845, 49.4 percent; between 1846 and 1865, 40.1 percent. In all editions of Willard's textbooks that I have examined the percentages are higher.

22. But she dropped this passage in later editions. In late editions of the American history Willard praises the American government for acting as guardian to its Indian

wards. The pervasive Christian rhetoric of Willard's textbooks is standard; for the amalgam of republican and Christian principles in American rhetoric, see Ernest Lee Tuveson, *Redeemer Nation: The Idea of America's Millennial Role* (Chicago: University of Chicago Press, 1968); Nathan O. Hatch, *The Sacred Cause of Liberty: Republican Thought and the Millennium in Revolutionary New England* (New Haven: Yale University Press, 1977); Ruth H. Bloch, *Visionary Republic: Millennial Themes in American Thought, 1756–1800* (New York: Cambridge University Press, 1985).

23. Emma Willard, *Last Leaves of American History, Comprising Histories of the Mexican War and California* (New York: Putnam, 1849), 104–105. In *Last Leaves* and in her American history textbooks after 1850 Willard accepts manifest destiny as the territorial expression of a millennial role for the United States. She interprets the Mexican War as a conflict between a Christian (i.e., Protestant) and a non-Christian (i.e., Catholic) nation. Already by 1840 her histories revealed a distinct nativist strain, arguing that foreign despotisms were exporting their human refuse to these shores in order to destroy the American nation. Assuming however that this refuse was here to stay, she argued that the only thing to do with it was educate it.

24. Emma Willard, *Ancient Geography, as Connected with Chronology, and Preparatory to the Study of Ancient History*, 8th ed. (Hartford: Belknap and Hammersley, 1840), 46. Willard wrote almost identically in the *Plan* that "submission and obedience belong to every being in the universe, except the great Master of the whole. Nor is it a degrading peculiarity to our sex, to be under human authority. Whenever one class of human beings, derive from another the benefits of support and protection, they must pay its equivalent, obedience" (15).

25. The supposed sympathy of American antebellum women for American Indians, especially on the grounds of a presumed shared oppression under patriarchy, was much overstated in feminist criticism of the early 1970s. In this regard Willard's histories compare favorably with the woman-centered histories of the American Revolution by Elizabeth Ellet published between 1848 and 1852. These books monumentalize the Revolution and celebrate instances of American female heroism and patriotism as they defended themselves, their families, and their homes against the British, Tories, and Indians in the Revolution and against Indians on the frontier. Ellet's descriptions far outdo Willard in their graphic sensationalism and demonize the Indians in particular.

26. Emma Willard, *Universal History, in Perspective*, 10th ed. (New York: A. S. Barnes, 1850), v.

Chapter 9: The Ann Sisters

1. Charles H. Foster, "Elizabeth Palmer Peabody," in *Notable American Women* (Cambridge: Harvard University Press, 1971), 3:35. The entry overall, however, is succinct and comprehensive. Demeaning and anti-intellectual descriptions of Peabody are ubiquitous in the critical literature; they control even an ostensibly sympathetic biography like Louise Hall Tharp's *The Peabody Sisters of Salem* (Boston: Little, Brown, 1950). Henry James's send-up of Peabody as Miss Birdseye in *The Bostonians* has been much circulated in essays about Peabody and transcendentalism. Such recent serious studies of New England and American Renaissance literature as Lawrence Buell's *New England Literary Culture: From Revolution to Renaissance* (New York: Cambridge University Press, 1986) and Leon Chai's *The Romantic Foundations of the American Renaissance* (Ithaca: Cornell University Press, 1987) refer to her only on their way to discussions of others. For appreciative criticism, see Susan Phinney Conrad, *Perish the Thought: Intellectual Women in Romantic America, 1830–1860* (New York: Oxford University Press, 1976); Philip F. Gura, "Elizabeth Palmer Peabody and the Philosophy of Language," *ESQ* 23 (1977):

154–164; *The Wisdom of Words: Language, Theology, and Literature in the New England Renaissance* (Middletown, Conn.: Wesleyan University Press, 1981); Bruce Ronda, "Elizabeth Palmer Peabody's Views of the Child," *ESQ* 23 (1977): 106–113; Bruce Ronda, ed., *Letters of Elizabeth P. Peabody: American Renaissance Woman* (Middletown, Conn.: Wesleyan University Press, 1984), the introduction to which is currently the best single essay on Peabody; Anne C. Rose, *Transcendentalism as a Social Movement, 1830–1850* (New Haven, Conn.: Yale University Press, 1981); John B. Wilson, "A Transcendental Minority Report," *New England Quarterly* 29 (1956): 147–158: "Elizabeth Peabody and Other Transcendentalists on History and Historians," *Historian* 30 (1967): 72–86. For a review of Peabody scholarship, see Margaret Neussendorfer, "Elizabeth Palmer Peabody," in *The Transcendentalists: A Review of Research and Criticism*, ed. Joel Myerson (New York: Modern Language Association, 1984), 233–241.

2. Rose's term *Unitarian evangelicalism* (*Transcendentalism*, 52) describes very well the fervor with which Peabody held her religious convictions. The view of Unitarianism as a cold and formal religion is, precisely, a Transcendental construction.

3. For Channing's coinage of *egotheism*, see Elizabeth Peabody, *Reminiscences of Rev. Wm. Ellery Channing, D.D.* (Boston: Roberts Brothers, 1880), 365; hereafter cited parenthetically as *Reminiscences*. For the 1859 "Egotheism, the Atheism of To-day," see Peabody's *Last Evening with Allston, and Other Papers* (Boston: D. Lothrop, 1886), 240–252.

4. For discussions of the intrusion of women into the religious domain in nineteenth-century America, Ann Douglas is still unsurpassed, although she describes Peabody only as Channing's devotee (*The Feminization of American Culture* [New York: Knopf, 1977], 21, 102, 190). See also Barbara Welter, "The Feminization of American Religion, 1800–1860," in *Dimity Convictions: The American Woman in the Nineteenth Century* (Athens: Ohio University Press, 1976), 83–102. For Protestant Christianity as empowering northeastern middle-class white women, and for the apparent contradiction between this historical fact and the patriarchal theology and organization of the churches, see Janet Wilson James, ed., *Women in American Religion* (Philadelphia: University of Pennsylvania Press, 1980); and especially the essay by Mary P. Ryan, "A Woman's Awakening: Evangelical Religion and the Families of Utica, New York, 1800–1840," 89–110.

5. Elizabeth Peabody, *First Steps to the Study of History. Being Part First of a Key to History* (Boston: Hilliard, Gray, 1832), 32; hereafter cited parenthetically as *First Steps*.

6. Elizabeth Peabody, *Chronological History of the United States, Arranged with Plates on Bem's Principle* (New York: Sheldon, Blakeman, 1856), 140–141; hereafter cited parenthetically as *United States*.

7. Ruth H. Bloch, *Visionary Republic: Millennial Themes in American Thought, 1756–1800* (New York: Cambridge University Press, 1985), xi. For New England millennialism in the late eighteenth century, see also James West Davidson, *The Logic of Millennial Thought: Eighteenth-Century New England* (New Haven, Conn.: Yale University Press, 1977); and Nathan O. Hatch, *The Sacred Cause of Liberty: Republican Thought and the Millennium in Revolutionary New England* (New Haven, Conn.: Yale University Press, 1977). These books specify and historicize the variants of American millennialism up to the nineteenth century. They agree that the idea of America's particular millennial mission does not begin to develop until the eighteenth century, where it is associated with the millennial thinking of Jonathan Edwards and the annals historiography of Thomas Prince, and they insist that the rhetoric of millennialism did not (perhaps could not) become truly national until the Revolutionary era produced a nation. Davidson also distinguishes late eighteenth- and early nineteenth-century republican millennialism from the secular, expansionist imperial model characteristic of the Jacksonian era and after (260–262). For an impressive argument that the supposed millennial intentions of the first-generation Puritans are an artifact of Colonialist studies since Perry Miller, see Theo-

dore Dwight Bozeman, *To Live Ancient Lives: The Primitivist Dimension in Puritanism* (Chapel Hill: University of North Carolina Press, 1988).

8. These quotations are taken from Elizabeth Peabody's *Key to History, pt. 2: The Hebrews* (Boston: March, Capen and Lyon, 1833), 3 (hereafter cited parenthetically as *The Hebrews*); *The Polish-American System of Chronology; Reproduced, with some Modifications, from General Bem's Franco-Polish Method* (Boston: Putnam, 1851), 117 (hereafter cited parenthetically as *Polish-American*); and *Universal History, Arranged to Illustrated Bem's Charts of Chronology* (New York: Sheldon, 1859), iv–v (hereafter cited parenthetically as *Universal*).

9. Elizabeth Peabody, "My Experience as a Teacher: Principles and Methods of Education," *American Journal of Education* 32 (1882): 737; hereafter cited parenthetically as "My Experience."

10. Elizabeth Peabody, *Sabbath Lessons: or, An Abstract of Sacred History* (Salem: Joshua Cushing, 1810), 8. The importance of Peabody's mother is noted in Ruth M. Baylor's *Elizabeth Palmer Peabody: Kindergarten Pioneer* (Philadelphia: University of Pennsylvania Press, 1965), which concentrates on Peabody as a theorist of the kindergarten. Mary Peabody Mann, Peabody's sister and closest friend, noted that their mother also wrote unpublished dialogue textbooks of astronomy, chemistry, and natural philosophy ("Reminiscences of School Life and Teaching," *American Journal of Education* 32 [1882]: 744).

11. Elizabeth Peabody, *Lectures in the Training Schools for Kindergartners* (Boston: D. C. Heath, 1886), 102–103; hereafter cited parenthetically as *Lectures*.

12. See Linda Kerber, *Women of the Republic: Intellect and Ideology in Revolutionary America* (Chapel Hill: University of North Carolina Press, 1980); and Mary Beth Norton, *Liberty's Daughters: The Revolutionary Experience of American Women, 1750–1800* (Boston: Little, Brown, 1980).

13. At the same time she seemed to realize neither that the arbitrariness and complexity of Bem's color system made it unsuitable as a memory aid, nor that his definitions of what constituted a historical event were profoundly conservative.

14. Gura equates Peabody's and Emerson's views of language as both directed toward interpreting nature. I read Peabody as having no interest in nature and rejecting the ahistoricism, the desire to return to a prehistorical origin, that transcendentalism articulated. Discussions with Barbara Packer have helped me see this difference more clearly. For Peabody's role in purveying texts to Emerson, see Gay Wilson Allen, *Waldo Emerson* (New York: Viking, 1981), 259–260.

15. Elizabeth Peabody, "The Spirit of the Hebrew Scriptures." *Christian Examiner* 16 (1834): 179.

16. Elizabeth Peabody, "The Dorian Measure, with a Modern Application," *Last Evening with Allston, and Other Papers* (Boston: D. Lothrop, 1886), 104; hereafter cited parenthetically as "Dorian." The few critics who have written about this essay assume that *Dorian* means "Greek" and overlook the specificity of its reference to Sparta. Because a rhetoric of Sparta is common in American republican discourse, because Spartan motherhood was particularly recommended as a model for American women and the respect accorded to women in Sparta contrasted to their low status in Athens, and because Athens was generally associated with hedonism rather than self-sacrifice, the distinction is important.

17. Elizabeth Peabody, *Crimes of the House of Austria against Mankind* (New York: G. P. Putnam, 1852), 176; hereafter cited parenthetically as *Crimes*.

18. Peabody found one republican history of Hungary to draw on for contemporary events in *Crimes* as well as for an analysis of the Hungarian constitution. It had been written, interestingly enough, by another New England woman, Mary Lowell Putnam. Originally published as three essays in the *Christian Examiner* in 1850 and 1851, it was

republished in pamphlet form by the *Examiner* in 1851. Mary Putnam, who was James Russell Lowell's oldest sister, appears sporadically in biographies of her brother but has no "history of her own."

19. See Jean Fagan Yellin, *Women and Sisters: The Antislavery Feminists in American Culture* (New Haven, Conn.: Yale University Press, 1989), 154, 160, 214 n. 26.

Chapter 10: Reinventing Lydia Sigourney

1. Sigourney's first book was *Moral Pieces, in Prose and Verse* (Hartford: Sheldon and Goodwin, 1815). Publication was arranged by Daniel Wadsworth of Hartford. The 721 subscribers (listed at the back) are a virtual roll call of conservative first families from Hartford, Farmington, New Haven, New London, Norwich, Middletown, Fairfield, Litchfield, Boston, Salem, Cambridge, Charlestown, Marblehead, and other Connecticut and Massachusetts towns.

2. Lydia Sigourney, *Select Poems* (Philadelphia: E. B. and J. Biddle, 1847), vii.

3. Sigourney's memoir, *Letters of Life* (New York: D. Appleton, 1866 [hereafter cited parenthetically as *Letters*]), lists fifty-six books published in her lifetime, a few of these edited; *Letters* makes the total fifty-seven. She says that uncollected material from almost three hundred different periodicals could produce several additional volumes (366). See also the only biography, Gordon Haight's, *Mrs. Sigourney: The Sweet Singer of Hartford* (New Haven, Conn.: Yale University Press, 1930), 173.

4. For example, Jane Tompkins, in "The Other American Renaissance," *Sensational Designs: The Cultural Work of American Fiction, 1790–1860* (New York: Oxford University Press, 1985), alludes to "Mrs. Sigourney—who epitomizes the sentimental tradition for modern critics" (160). In *Notable American Women*—whose purpose, one thought, was to dismantle stereotypes—Gordon Haight says that "death was always her favorite theme—the death of infants, of consumptive children, of missionaries in Burma and Liberia, of poets and lunatics, of artists and sailors, of college students and deaf-dumb-and-blind girls. Her rhyming of pious truisms made a wide appeal and established a trade that newspaper poets have carried on prosperously" ([Cambridge: Harvard University Press, 1971], 3:289). Students of American literature think that what Griswold did to Poe is a national calamity; for many, still, what biographers have done to women passes for urbanity and even (heaven help us) gallantry.

5. Lydia Sigourney, *Poems* (Boston: S. G. Goodrich, 1827); *Zinzendorff, and Other Poems,* (New York: Leavitt, Lord, 1835); *Pocahontas, and Other Poems* (New York: Harper, 1841).

6. Sarah Hale, *Woman's Record,* 2d ed. (New York: Harper, 1855), 783.

7. "There were plenty of strong souls in the Victorian age whose 'piping took a troubled sound' when they chose to struggle with their doubts rather than drown them out with the cymbals of conformity" (Haight, *Mrs. Sigourney,* 160).

8. Cheryl Walker, *The Nightingale's Burden: Women Poets and American Culture before 1900* (Bloomington: Indiana University Press, 1982). Walker briefly cites three Sigourney poems—two elegies and a poem praising Felicia Hemans—but centers the antebellum women's poetic tradition on Frances Osgood and Elizabeth Oakes Smith.

9. Ann Douglas Wood, "Mrs. Sigourney and the Sensibility of the Inner Space," *New England Quarterly* 45 (1972): 163–187; the cited passage is on 170–171; Richard Brodhead, "Sparing the Rod: Discipline and Fiction in Antebellum America," *Representations* 21 (1988): 67–96; and "Veiled Ladies: Toward a History of Antebellum Entertainment," *American Literary History* 1 (1989): 273–294. Emily Stipes Watts thinks that Sigourney's obituary verse registers but laments women's isolation from public life in

antebellum culture; see *The Poetry of American Women from 1632 to 1945* (Austin: University of Texas Press, 1977), 83–97.

10. The elegies too are public poetry. On republican motherhood, see Linda Kerber, *Women of the Republic: Intellect and Ideology in Revolutionary America* (Chapel Hill: University of North Carolina Press, 1980); and Mary Beth Norton, *Liberty's Daughters: The Revolutionary Experience of American Women* (Boston: Little, Brown, 1980). See also Mary Kelley, *Private Woman, Public Stage: Literary Domesticity in Nineteenth-Century America* (New York: Oxford University Press, 1984).

11. I allude to two well-known essays: Carroll Smith-Rosenberg's "The Female World of Love and Ritual: Relations between Women in Nineteenth-Century America," *Signs* 1 (1975): 1–29; and Barbara Welter's 1966 "Cult of True Womanhood, 1800–1860," reprinted in *Dimity Convictions: The American Woman in the Nineteenth Century* (Athens: Ohio University Press, 1976).

12. Lydia Sigourney, *Letters to Young Ladies* (Hartford: P. Canfield, 1833), 125, 143, 144–145. This discussion draws on a reading of eighteen of Sigourney's books and her descriptive list of all her books in *Letters*, 324–365.

13. Linda Kerber's "Separate Spheres, Female Worlds, Woman's Place: The Rhetoric of Women's History" *Journal of American History* 75 (1988): 9–39, treats the "separate spheres" as a discursive construct rather than an empirical fact and discusses its use and limitations as a tool of cultural analysis.

14. One of Sigourney's first pupils and a lifelong friend, Frances Manwaring Caulkins (whose name has disappeared completely from literary history), wrote two massive local histories of Norwich and New London and became the first (and for a long time the only) woman member of the Massachusetts Historical Society; her work was in part inspired by Sigourney's teaching.

15. For lesson books, see Sigourney's *Evening Readings in History: Comprising Portions of the History of Assyria, Egypt, Tyre, Syria, Persia, and the Sacred Scriptures; with Questions, Arranged for the Use of the Young, and of Family Circles* (Springfield: G. and C. Merriam, 1833)—"written with a desire of aiding a laudable custom, established by some of my particular friends, of devoting an hour in the evening to a course of reading with the younger members of their families, and examinations into their proficiency on the general departments of Education" (v); and *History of Marcus Aurelius, Emperor of Rome* (Hartford: Belknap and Hamersley, 1835)—"this book was commenced as an assistant to parents in domestic education. Its highest ambition is to be in the hand of the mother, who seeks to aid in that most delightful of all departments, the instruction of her little ones" (iii). Haight's bibliography misattributes Lydia Child's 1837 *History of the Condition of Women* to Sigourney.

16. Lydia Sigourney, *Sketch of Connecticut, Forty Years Since* (Hartford, Conn.: Oliver D. Cooke, 1824).

17. Sandra A. Zagarell, "Expanding 'America': Lydia Sigourney's *Sketch of Connecticut*, Catharine Sedgwick's *Hope Leslie*," *Tulsa Studies in Women's Literature* 6 (1987): 225–246. In "Narrative of Community: The Identification of a Genre," *Signs* 13 (1988): 498–527, Zagarell places the *Sketch of Connecticut* in a female genre conformable to the paradigm developed by Carol Gilligan's *In a Different Voice: Psychological Theory and Women's Development* (Cambridge: Harvard University Press, 1982). On the different voice paradigm, see "Matters for Interpretation" in this volume.

18. For succinct descriptions of republican ideologies, see Linda Kerber, "The Republican Ideology of the Revolutionary Generation," *American Quarterly* 37 (1985): 474–495; and Joyce Appleby, "Republicanism in Old and New Contexts," *William and Mary Quarterly* 43 (1986): 20–43. On the religiocentric strain in antebellum New England writing,

see Lawrence Buell, *New England Literary Culture: From Revolution through Renaissance* (New York: Cambridge University Press, 1986).

19. Lydia Sigourney, *Sketches* (Philadelphia: Key and Biddle, 1834).

20. Lydia Sigourney, *Myrtis, with Other Etchings and Sketchings* (New York: Harper and Brothers, 1846), 137–138.

21. Lydia Sigourney, "Traits of the Aborigines of America. A Poem" (Cambridge, Mass.: "from the University Press," 1822). Sigourney says that the poem was written two years before her marriage in 1819 (i.e., in 1817) but that its publication was delayed. Even the 1822 date makes this one of the earlier noncaptivity publications on the American Indian topic. Haight declares that it was Charles Sigourney's idea to annotate the poem and that he wrote the notes as well (*Sweet Singer*, 25; *Notable American Women*, 3:289); Sigourney says only that her husband helped her revise the notes (*Letters*, 327).

22. Lydia Sigourney, "The Western Home," in *The Western Home, and Other Poems* (Philadelphia: Parry and McMillan, 1854); *Lucy Howard's Journal* (New York: Harper and Brothers, 1858).

Chapter 11: Sarah Hale, Political Writer

1. There are no recent biographies of Hale. Ruth E. Finley, *The Lady of Godey's: Sarah Josepha Hale* (Philadelphia: Lippincott, 1932); and Isabelle Webb Entrikin, *Sarah Josepha Hale and Godey's Lady's Book* (Philadelphia: Lancaster, 1946), are the most cited studies. Like virtually everything else written on Hale, they focus on the *Lady's Book* (which they call—what it was not called in its own time—*Godey's*). For scholars who see Hale as Louis Godey's silenced subordinate rather than a power in her own right, see Frank Luther Mott, *History of American Magazines* (Cambridge: Harvard University Press, 1938), 1:580–594; and Cheryl Walker, *The Nightingale's Burden* (Bloomington: Indiana University Press, 1982), 34. Critics who see her as perniciously powerful include Susan Phinney Conrad, *Perish the Thought; Intellectual Women in Romantic America, 1830–1860* (New York, Oxford University Press, 1976); Ann Douglas, *The Feminization of American Culture* (New York: Knopf, 1977); and David Leverenz, *Manhood and the American Renaissance* (Ithaca: Cornell University Press, 1987).

2. Linda K. Kerber's "Separate Spheres, Female Worlds, Woman's Place: The Rhetoric of Women's History," *Journal of American History* 75 (1988): 9–39, is the best exposition of the position that the "spheres" were and are contested discursive formations rather than descriptions of reality. Influential feminist scholarship attacking while reifying the woman's sphere includes Barbara Welter, "The Cult of True Womanhood: 1820–1860," *American Quarterly* 18 (1966): 158–174, reprinted in *Dimity Convictions: The American Woman in the Nineteenth Century* (Athens: Ohio University Press, 1976), 21–41; and Gerda Lerner, "The Lady and the Mill Girl: Changes in the Status of Women in the Age of Jackson," *Mid-Continent American Studies Journal* 10 (1969): 5–15. Revisionary feminist scholarship discerning strength and value in the women's sphere includes Nancy Cott, *The Bonds of Womanhood: "Woman's Sphere" in New England, 1780–1835* (New Haven, Conn.: Yale University Press, 1977); Mary Beth Norton, *Liberty's Daughters: The Revolutionary Experience of American Women, 1750–1800* (Boston: Little, Brown, 1980); Linda K. Kerber, *Women of the Republic: Intellect and Ideology in Revolutionary America* (Chapel Hill: University of North Carolina Press, 1980); Mary Ryan, *Cradle of the Middle Class: The Family in Oneida County, New York, 1790–1895* (New York: Cambridge University Press, 1981); Nancy A. Hewitt, *Women's Activism and Social Change: Rochester, New York, 1822–1872* (Ithaca: Cornell University Press, 1984); Mary Beth Norton, "The Evolution of White Women's Experience in Early America," *American Historical Review* 89 (1984):

593–619; and Paula Baker, "The Domestication of Politics: Women and American Political Society, 1780–1920," *American Historical Review* 89 (1984): 620–647.

3. Barbara Bardes and Suzanne Gossett, *Declarations of Independence: Women and Political Power in Nineteenth-Century American Fiction* (New Brunswick, N.J.: Rutgers University Press, 1990), 22.

4. Nicole Tonkovich Hoffman, "Sarah Josepha Hale," *Legacy* 7 (1990): 51.

5. In citing *Northwood* I use the more accessible revision: *Northwood; or, Life North and South* (New York: H. Long, 1852); when speaking of the 1827 version I use material in the 1852 edition retained from the earlier work. The 1827 subtitle, "A New England Tale," stresses the New England imperialism of Hale's original project. The revised version, and Hale's reasons for revision, are discussed below. Throughout I use the 1852 spelling of the chief characters' family name—Romilly—rather than the 1827 Romelee.

6. Lawrence Buell, *New England Literary Culture: From Revolution through Renaissance* (New York: Cambridge University Press, 1986), 296. See also William R. Taylor, *Cavalier and Yankee: The Old South and American National Character* (New York: George Braziller, 1961), 96–133, for a discussion of Hale's representation of the southern male (the Cavalier) in contrast to the New Englander (the Yankee).

7. Bardes and Gossett, *Declarations of Independence*, 17. They also write that *Northwood* addresses general issues of political culture rather than "the leading controversies of Jacksonian democracy" involving commerce (banks and tariffs), urbanization, territorial expansion, immigration, and the trade-off between individualism and order (19). Many of the issues are in fact coded in Squire Romilly's discourse; and it is not caviling to insist that the issue of the North-South divide implicates many or most of these concerns and constitutes, in its own terms, a political issue of the utmost urgency in antebellum America. Moreover, just as Hale's superficially nonpartisan campaign to make Bunker Hill a national monument was actually deeply implicated in Masonic–anti-Masonic politics (see Paul Goodman, *Towards a Christian Republic: Antimasonry and the Great Transition in New England, 1826–1836* [New York: Oxford University Press, 1988], 98), so numerous apparently bland details of *Northwood* might, upon closer study and further research, disclose political implications. Two suggestive instances occur when Squire Romilly opines on the local highway taxation system in a way that must have had immediate political resonance in its own day and when another character contrasts the grasping, money-grubbing Connecticut character to the truly republican New Hampshire type. A long segment on how to organize and finance public education must have had at least local political resonance. Numerous English-American comparisons along with discussion of how the two countries should relate to each other would certainly have conveyed political meaning to New Englanders in 1827 as well as in 1852.

8. Sarah Hale, *Sketches of American Character* (Boston: Putnam and Hunt, 1829), 8.

9. Sarah Hale, *Traits of American Life* (Philadelphia: Carey and Hart, 1835), 127.

10. Sarah Hale, *Ormond Grosvenor*, in *Godey's Lady's Book* 16 (1838): 33.

11. Ibid., 50.

12. Ibid., 146.

13. See Laura McCall, "'The Reign of Brute Force is Now Over': A Content Analysis of *Godey's Lady's Book*, 1830–1860," *Journal of the Early Republic* 9 (1989): 231–232.

14. Sarah Hale, *Liberia: or, Mr. Peyton's Experiments* (New York: Harper and Brothers, 1853), 185; hereafter cited parenthetically in the text.

15. Sarah Hale, *Woman's Record*, 2d ed. (New York: Harper and Brothers, 1855), 43; hereafter cited parenthetically in the text. The second edition expands the text (and intensifies the antiabolitionist and antiwoman's rights sentiment) without revising its earlier sections.

16. The pages that follow derive from part of an essay on *Woman's Record* called

"Onward Christian Woman: Sarah J. Hale's History of the World" (*New England Quarterly* 63 [1990]: 249–270); in that essay, however, I focus on the *Record*'s playful multivocality and say little about its political intentions.

Chapter 12: The Myth of the Myth of Southern Womanhood

1. Lucinda H. Mackethan, "Plantation Fiction, 1865–1900," in Louis D. Rubin, Jr., and others, *The History of Southern Literature* (Baton Rouge: Louisiana State University Press, 1985), 209.

2. Richard Gray, *Writing the South: Ideas of an American Region* (Cambridge: Cambridge University Press, 1986), xi.

3. See, for example, Orville Vernon Burton, *In My Father's House Are Many Mansions* (Chapel Hill: University of North Carolina Press, 1985).

4. See, for example, Ernest Gellner, *Nations and Nationhood* (Ithaca: Cornell University Press, 1983); Benedict Anderson, *Imagined Communities: Reflections on the Origin and Spread of Nationalism* (London: Verso, 1983); Eric Hobsbawm and Terence Rangers, eds., *The Invention of Tradition* (Cambridge: Cambridge University Press, 1983); and Hobsbawm, *Nations and Nationalism since 1780* (New York: Cambridge University Press, 1990).

5. Gray, *Writing the South,* xii; see also Wilbur J. Cash, *The Mind of the South* (New York: Knopf, 1941); Lewis P. Simpson, *The Man of Letters in New England and the South* (Baton Rouge: Louisiana State University Press, 1973); and *Mind and the American Civil War: A Meditation on Lost Causes* (Baton Rouge: Louisiana State University Press, 1989).

6. Francis Pendleton Gaines, *The Southern Plantation: A Study of the Development and Accuracy of a Tradition* (New York: Columbia University Press, 1924).

7. William R. Taylor, *Cavalier and Yankee: The Old South and American National Character* (New York: Braziller, 1961).

8. Ibid., 148, 154.

9. Gray, *Writing the South,* 91.

10. Ann Firor Scott, *The Southern Lady: From Pedestal to Politics, 1830–1930* (Chicago: University of Chicago Press, 1970).

11. Anne Goodwyn Jones, *Tomorrow Is Another Day: The Woman Writer in the South, 1859–1936* (Baton Rouge: Louisiana State University Press, 1981), 3, 12–13. This treatment of women substantiates Michael Kreyling's complaint that Southern literary critics in effect reinstitute the hegemonic myth that they should be analyzing ("Southern Literature: Consensus and Dissensus," *American Literature* 60 [1988]: 83–95).

12. Kathryn Lee Seidel, *The Southern Belle in the American Novel* (Tampa: University of South Florida Press, 1885), 126.

13. Mackethan, "Plantation Fiction," 93, 102, 211, 226–227.

14. Gray, *Writing the South,* 61–62.

15. John Pendleton Kennedy, *Swallow Barn* (1852; reprint, New York: Hafner, 1962), 39; see also Scott, *Southern Lady;* Catherine Clinton, *The Plantation Mistress: Woman's World in the Old South* (New York: Pantheon, 1982); Elizabeth Fox-Genovese, *Within the Plantation Household: Black and White Women of the Old South* (Chapel Hill: University of North Carolina Press, 1988).

16. Nina Baym, *Woman's Fiction: A Guide to Novels by and about Women in America, 1820–1870* (Ithaca: Cornell University Press, 1978). This is probably not the place to dispute David Reynolds's contention, in *Beneath the American Renaissance* (New York: Knopf, 1988), that women's domestic fiction was not nearly as popular as scholars like me have made it out to be. Reynolds bases his claim on a simple title count of published works and offers no sales, reprinting, or circulation figures. What this method actually

produces—although Reynolds fails to mention it—is the finding that the most popular of all antebellum authors was Timothy Shay Arthur.

17. Barbara Welter, "The Cult of True Womanhood," *Dimity Convictions: The American Woman in the Nineteenth Century* (Athens: Ohio University Press, 1976), 21–41.

18. *St. Elmo*, technically, is a postbellum novel, having been published in 1867. But the regional and female ideologies of its story, which avoids all mention of the Civil War and moves its heroine between South and North in an undated, ahistorical time, read consistently with her antebellum writing. Recognizably postbellum representations of the antebellum South in the sense I am developing here dominate, however, in her novels of the 1870s and after. In this sense she comprises an almost paradigmatic instance of the overwriting of antebellum by postbellum mythology.

19. For a discussion of antebellum fantasies of the frontier in women's writing, see Annette Kolodny, *The Land before Her: Fantasy and Experience of the American Frontiers, 1630–1860* (Chapel Hill: University of North Carolina Press, 1984).

20. Scott, *Southern Lady*, 4.

21. For a general overview of Glasgow's depiction of women characters, see Linda Wagner, *Ellen Glasgow: Beyond Convention* (Austin: University of Texas Press, 1982).

22. Ellen Glasgow, *Virginia* (Garden City: Doubleday, Page, 1913); hereafter cited parenthetically in the text.

23. For the banning of Southworth and other (from our perspective) safe, supposedly "sentimental" writers from turn-of-the-century libraries, see Dee Garrison, "Immoral Fiction in the Late Victorian Library," *American Quarterly* 28 (1976): 71–89.

Chapter 13: The Madwoman and Her Languages

1. Elaine Showalter, "Feminist Criticism in the Wilderness," *Critical Inquiry* 8 (1981): 181. In 1992, theory is not a central feminist issue; it dominates academic feminism.

2. I borrow these terms from Wendy Martin, *An American Triptych: Ann Bradstreet, Emily Dickinson, Adrienne Rich* (Chapel Hill: University of North Carolina Press, 1983), 229. These terms do not apply to theories as such but to styles that appear to override theories.

3. These words were originally written before the appalling account of life in the French Mouvement Libération des Femmes—a feminist ideal for many literary theorists—appeared in *Signs*. See Dorothy Kaufmann-McCall, "Politics of Difference: The Women's Movement in France from May 1968 to Mitterand," *Signs* 9 (1983): 282–293.

4. See Lillian S. Robinson, "Treason Our Text: Feminist Challenges to the Literary Canon," *Tulsa Studies in Women's Literature* 2 (1983): 83–98.

5. Sandra M. Gilbert and Susan Gubar, *The Madwoman in the Attic: The Woman Writer and the Nineteenth-Century Imagination* (New Haven, Conn.: Yale University Press, 1979); hereafter cited parenthetically in the text.

6. Christiane Makward, "To Be or Not to Be . . . a Feminist Speaker," in *The Future of Difference*, eds. Alice Jardine and Hester Eisenstein (Boston: G. K. Hall, 1980), 96.

7. Mary Jacobus, "The Questions of Language: Men or Maxims and *The Mill on the Floss*," *Critical Inquiry* 8 (1981): 222.

8. Domna C. Stanton, "Language and Revolution: The Franco-American Disconnection," in Jardine and Eisenstein, *Future of Difference*, 86.

9. Makward, "To Be or Not to Be," 100.

10. Hélène Cixous, "The Laugh of the Medusa," *Signs* 1 (1976): 885. As Diane Griffin Crowder, an expert on Cixous, has recently observed in a review in *Tulsa Studies*, "Cixous is not a feminist in any sense that the American movement would recognize" (*Tulsa Studies in Women's Literature* 4 [1985]: 149). This being patently the case, the zeal of

American literary feminists to put her at the apex of feminist theory is all the more puzzling.

11. Sandra M. Gilbert and Susan Gubar, "Sexual Linguistics," *New Literary History* 16 (1985): 515–543.

12. Elizabeth Hampsten, *Read This Only to Yourself: The Private Writings of Midwestern Women* (Bloomington: Indiana University Press, 1982).

13. Jane Gallop, *The Daughter's Seduction: Feminism and Psychoanalysis* (Ithaca: Cornell University Press, 1982). A young literary-academic feminist of my acquaintance tells me that most feminists of her generation are feminists precisely because they recognize the abjectness of their attitudes toward men. That recognition has been the starting point for many of us, but a theory that valorizes or prescribes abjectness seems to me to confuse the starting point with the end.

14. Makward, "To Be or Not to Be," 102.

15. Nancy Chodorow, *The Reproduction of Mothering* (Berkeley and Los Angeles: University of California Press, 1976). Another influential book of the same sort is Carol Gilligan, *In a Different Voice* (Cambridge: Harvard University Press, 1982). Both of these works have had more impact on feminist literary studies than in their own social science fields, largely because the evidence on which their arguments are based are, by social science standards, deplorably weak.

16. The real Freudian scandal, however—one to shame a feminist advocate of a meeting of feminism and psychoanalysis—is the substitution of the Oedipus complex for the seduction theory on the grounds that it would be impossible for all those women (and men) to have been telling the truth when they testified to childhood sexual abuse. What we are learning of child abuse these days exposes this uncharacteristic eruption of "common sense" into Freud's discourse as a dreadful hypocrisy. And indeed, the logic of this replacement was always poor—much like saying that it would be impossible for all those cases of tuberculosis to have been caused by the same bacteria.

17. Sigmund Freud, "Femininity," in *Psychoanalysis and Feminism,* ed. Juliet Mitchell (New York: Pantheon, 1974), 88.

18. Sigmund Freud, "Analysis Terminable and Interminable," in *The Collected Writings of Sigmund Freud* (London: Hogarth Press, 1953–74), 5:356.

19. Sigmund Freud, "Some Psychical Consequences of the Anatomical Distinction between the Sexes," in *Psychoanalysis and Feminism,* 191. No empirical evidence is offered; and for Freud there is only "the" distinction. My argument does not deny differences; I stress the plural. I believe that differences are multiple, variable, and largely unresearched and not understood; therefore, any theory based on only one is trivial.

20. Freud, "Analysis Terminable and Interminable," 357.

21. Quoted in Juliet Mitchell and Jacqueline Rose, eds., *Feminine Psychology: Jacques Lacan and the école freudienne* (New York: Norton, 1982), 144.

22. Dorothy Dinnerstein, *The Mermaid and the Minotaur: Sexual Arrangements and Human Malaise* (New York: Harper and Row, 1976).

23. Adrienne Rich, *Of Woman Born* (New York: Norton, 1976).

24. Karen Elias-Button, "The Muse as Medusa," in *The Lost Tradition: Mothers and Daughters in Literature,* ed. Cathy N. Davidson and E. M. Broner (New York: Ungar, 1980), 205.

25. Elias-Button, "Muse as Medusa," 192.

26. Judith Kegan Gardiner, "On Female Identity and Writing by Women," *Critical Inquiry* 8 (1981): 356.

27. Ibid.

28. Janet Todd, *Women's Friendship in Literature* (New York: Columbia University Press, 1980), 2.

29. Susan Peck MacDonald, "Jane Austen and the Tradition of the Absent Mother," in Davidson and Broner, *Lost Tradition,* 58.

30. Julia Kristeva, "Women's Time," *Signs* 7 (1981): 29.

31. Dinnerstein, *Mermaid and the Minotaur,* 164.

32. See Jane Marcus in her attack on pluralism, "Storming the Toolshed," *Signs* 7 (1982): 622–640, especially 626: "she must . . . she must . . . she must." If that *she* is *me,* somebody (once again) is telling me what I *"must"* do to be a true woman, and that somebody is asserting (not incidentally) her own monopoly on truth as she does so. I've been here before.

Chapter 14: Matters for Interpretation

1. I am painfully aware that every word in the two preceding paragraphs closes down issues that are very much a matter of current feminist debate. My approach perceives forms of gender consciousness defining women either as separate-but-equal, or as systemically privileged, as nonfeminist. And I am writing here about American activist feminism, stressing its shared project rather than its divisions. American activist feminism is a reformist rather than revolutionary movement whose anticipated outcome is liberal pluralist rather than Utopian. It depends on coalition among differently thinking feminists and between feminists and other groups. Feminist theory, which has come to control a great deal of academic feminist discourse, is a much more internationalist, esoteric, professionally controlled, and textualist endeavor that articulates and differentiates a wide range of carefully specified positions. Since its endlessly generative principle is the exposure of discursive contradiction, it is far less forgiving of contradiction than a pragmatic materialist feminism can afford to be.

2. Unfortunately, almost no work has been done on what "students" do with literature when they are not students, and such work would be extremely difficult to carry out since most "students" don't read "literature" except as students.

3. For a defense of authoritarian feminist pedagogy, see Dale F. Bauer, "The Other 'F' Word: The Feminist in the Classroom," *College English* 52 (1990): 385–396; and her response to a demurral from Deborah Kennedy, *College English* 53 (1991): 103–104. As is typical in authoritarian regimens, Bauer rejects the distinction between public and private on which the construction and defense of the individual depends, holding that no domain of human practice should escape the teacher's scrutiny. For a good description of would-be nonauthoritarian feminist teaching and its discontents, see Constance Penley, "Teaching in Your Sleep," *Theory in the Classroom,* ed. Cary Nelson (Urbana: University of Illinois Press, 1986), 129–148.

4. As, for example, in the films of Alfred Hitchcock. So far as I know, however, no empirical study has been done to discover how many women actually like Hitchcock films, or, if they do, why. The premises of film theory and feminist film theory have been critically scrutinized by Noel Carroll in *Mystifying Movies: Fads and Fallacies in Contemporary Film Theory* (New York: Columbia University Press, 1988); and "The Image of Women in Film: A Defense of a Paradigm," *Journal of Aesthetics and Art Criticism* 48 (1990): 349–360, respectively.

5. Robert Scholes, "Reading like a Man," in *Men in Feminism,* ed. Alice Jardine and Paul Smith (New York: Methuen, 1987), 206.

6. I know only one study disputing that gender globally affects interpretation—Judith A. Howard's and Carolyn Allen's "The Gendered Context of Reading," *Gender and Society* 4 (1990): 534–552. The essay describes an experiment in which the readers' gender had little effect on interpretation. The authors worked with the conventional expectation that women readers would show more empathy to the characters and situations

in fiction than men. They found that empathy correlated with life experience, not gender: Older students were more empathetic than younger ones, older men more empathetic than younger women. Anne Fausto-Sterling has demonstrated at length that gender studies failing to demonstrate differences (or, conversely, demonstrating no difference) usually don't get publicity. See her *Myths of Gender* (New York: Basic, 1985).

7. See Thomas Fox, *The Social Uses of Writing: Politics and Pedagogy* (Norwood, N.J.: Ablex, 1990), 51–70. The students were writing on the topic "tell which character(s) you most closely identified with and which character(s) you identified with least." Many reasonable interpretive possibilities are foreclosed in this assignment: Students *must* approach the story's agents as "characters," must "identify" with at least one of them, but not with the narrator, and so on. Though the teacher calls his project political and anti-individualist, the self-to-self ideology of "identification" and the imputing of selves to Hawthorne's sketchy figures imply an individualist ideology.

8. Elizabeth A. Flynn, "Gender and Reading," in *Gender and Reading*, ed. Elizabeth A. Flynn and Patrocinio P. Schweickart (Baltimore: Johns Hopkins University Press, 1986), 267–288; hereafter cited parenthetically in the text. Since I work with only part of her examples, I urge the reader to think of "Flynn" as an interpretation, a personage constructed by my text.

9. Linda Laub Barnes, "Gender Bias in Teachers' Written Comments," *Gender in the Classroom: Power and Pedagogy,* ed. Susan L. Gabriel and Isaiah Smithson (Urbana: University of Illinois Press, 1990), 140–159; hereafter cited parenthetically in the text.

10. Deborah Tannen, *You Just Don't Understand: Women and Men in Conversation* (New York: Ballantine, 1991), 128, 169, 254, 256; hereafter cited parenthetically in the text. Tannen exemplifies the sociolinguistic approach to gendered language dubbed "cross cultural" in contrast to the feminist "dominance" model associated with the work of Nancy Henley, Cheris Kramarae, Robin Lakoff, and Dale Spender.

11. Carol Gilligan, *In a Different Voice: Psychological Theory and Women's Development* (Cambridge: Harvard University Press, 1982); hereafter cited parenthetically in the text.

12. Carol Gilligan, "Reply," *Signs* 11 (1986): 328.

13. See, for example, the various papers collected in *Mapping the Moral Domain: A Contribution of Women's Thinking to Psychological Theory and Education,* ed. Carol Gilligan, Janie Victoria Ward, and Jill McLean Taylor (Cambridge: Harvard University Press, 1988). It is significant to the coercive totalizing that I am describing that this school of research claims to display the woman's different voice in its research and scholarship. If you disagree, you're really a man.

14. Mary Belenky et al., *Women's Ways of Knowing: The Development of Self, Voice, and Mind* (New York: Basic, 1986); hereafter cited parenthetically in the text.

Index